Plurals and Events

Current Studies in Linguistics
Samuel Jay Keyser, general editor

Plurals and Events   Barry Schein

The MIT Press
Cambridge, Massachusetts
London, England

This book was set in Times Roman by Asco Trade Typesetting Ltd., Hong Kong, and was printed and bound in the United States of America.

First printing.

Library of Congress Cataloging-in-Publication Data

Schein, Barry.
　Plurals and events / Barry Schein.
　　　p.　cm. — (Current studies in linguistics series ; 23)
　Includes bibliographical references and index.
　ISBN 0-262-19334-5
　1. Grammar, Comparative and general—Number. 2. Grammar, Comparative and general—Quantifiers. 3. Semantics. 4. Language and logic. I. Title. II. Series.
P240.8.S34　1993　　　　　　　　　　　　　　　　　　　　　92-47494
415—dc20　　　　　　　　　　　　　　　　　　　　　　　　　　CIP

For Donca and Aaron

Contents

Acknowledgments

I owe a special debt to Samuel Bayer, Jim Higginbotham, Norbert Hornstein, Peter Lasersohn, Peter Ludlow, Remko Scha, and Ken Wexler, who read through an earlier draft or large stretches of it and provided me with extensive comments. In the last stages of copyediting, Peter Lasersohn discovered a flaw prompting extensive revision, but I am happy to say that the result is a somewhat simpler technical apparatus and a somewhat shorter book. A reading group at MIT, whose members were Irene Heim, Jim Higginbotham, Kathrin Koslicki, Utpal Lahiri, Josep Macia-Fabrega, Friederike Moltmann, Robert Stainton, Zoltán Szabó, and Jason Stanley (acting as corresponding secretary for the group) prepared comments on the first two chapters. I heard again about these chapters from a reading group at UCLA, whose members were Filippo Beghelli, Dorit Ben-Shalom, Manuel Español-Echevarria, Hyunoo Lee, Ivana Lyon, Friederike Moltmann, Seungho Nam, Tim Stowell, Melody Sutton, and Anna Szabolcsi. The present version has also benefited directly from discussions with George Boolos, Richard Larson, Dick Oehrle, Roger Schwarzschild, Anna Szabolcsi, Jaap van der Does, Karina Wilkinson, and Sandro Zucchi, and from the students and auditors in a seminar at USC: Daeho Chung, Petra Hendriks, Elena Herburger, Liliana Sánchez, Pirkko Suihkonen, and Shin Watanabe. This book would have been greatly improved had I heeded all of their recommendations. I hope they will find that their pains have resulted in at least some improvement.

I wish also to thank my editor, Alan Thwaits, for his skill and forebearance in preparing the final manuscript, and Filippo Beghelli for preparing the index and proofreading the final set of page proofs.

Chapter 2 expands section 2 in Higginbotham and Schein 1989.

Plurals and Events

Chapter 1
Introduction

1 "Essential" Plurals

Underlying the semantics of how noun phrases (NPs) combine with predicate phrases is a primitive notion of what it means for a predicate to be true of an *object*. When a NP, such as *John* in (1), refers to an object, the sentence is true just in case the predicate is true of the object referred to, as spelled out in (2) to (5).

(1) John left.

(2) *John* refers to x.

(3) sentence (1) is true $\leftrightarrow$ the predicate *left* is true of x

(4) *left* is true of x $\leftrightarrow$ x left

(5) sentence (1) is true $\leftrightarrow$ x left

Sometimes a NP, like *every boy*, does not refer to an object. In that case, the problem of how to interpret a sentence such as (6) is considered solved when it is reduced to predications of objects. Here the semantics of quantification shows how the meaning of the sentence depends on predication.

(6) Every boy left.

Thus, (6) is true just in case the predicate *left* is true of every object that is a boy, as in (7).

(7) sentence (6) is true $\leftrightarrow$ for every x such that *boy* is true of
     x, *left* is true of x

"Essential" plurals, as George Boolos has called them, do not so readily reduce to predications of objects:[1]

(8) The rocks rained down.

(9) The stars that presently make up the Pleiades galactic
cluster occupy an area that measures 700 cubic light
years.[2]

(10) The elms are clustered in the middle of the forest.

Example (10) does not say of the individual elm that it is clustered in the forest.

The relations in (11) and (12) provide other cases of essentially plural predication.

(11) The movers lifted the piano.

(12) The boys ate the pies.

Suppose all the pies were consumed by each boy eating only a part of each pie. Then (12) is true, but since no individual boy has eaten any one pie, it will not come out true by predicating *eat* of *objects*:

(13) *eat* is true of $\langle x, y \rangle \leftrightarrow x$ eats y

1.1   Plurals as singular terms that refer to plural objects
The fundamental problem of plurals is how to extend reference and predication to sentences containing essential plurals. One answer to the problem, not mine, gives up the naive view of what an object is. The *objectual* view of plurals, as we will call it, proposes that there are plural objects.[3] A NP refers to one of these objects in just the way it refers to a more familiar object:

(14) The elms are clustered.

(15) *the elms* refers to x

(16) sentence (14) is true $\leftrightarrow$ the predicate *clustered* is true of x

(17) *clustered* is true of $x \leftrightarrow x$ is clustered

(18) sentence (14) is true $\leftrightarrow x$ is clustered

The NP *the elms* in (14) refers to the group of elms, and this is simply a different object from any of its constituent elms. It has its own properties, one of which, if (14) is true, is being clustered.

The objectual view makes few demands on the logical form of sentences. As (14) through (18) and the logical form in (19) suggest, predicates have their usual structure, and there continue to be just first-order variables.

(19) clustered$((\iota x)(\text{elms}(x)))$[4]

The only addition is that the universe of discourse has expanded to include plural objects.

1.2 Plurals as predicates in a Davidsonian logical form

The view that I will argue for here sticks to the naive idea about what an object is, at least, in rejecting the idea that plural terms refer to plural objects.[5] Instead, I hold that plural predication requires a different logical form for the predicates of natural language, a logical form that derives from Donald Davidson 1967.[6] All predicates are, first of all, about events. As (20) shows, the relevant notion of event must be broad enough to include states or situations.

(20) The elms are clustered in the forest.

This sentence is about an event of being clustered, and its verb, 'cluster(e)', denotes such events. Given the event, how do we understand that the elms are clustered in the forest, when the NP *the elms* fails to refer to an object that covers forest?

Singular predication will prove sufficient if each argument has a constituent expressing its relation to the denoted event:

(21) INFL(e, x) $\wedge$ cluster(e) $\wedge$ In(e, y)

The relation between *each* elm and the event of being clustered is expressed by 'INFL'.[7] It says of any elm x that it is in the cluster.

In reducing (20), with a plural term, to the singular predications in (21), we could try to assert of each elm that it is in the cluster. But asserting just that is too weak to convey what is expressed by (20). Suppose, for example, that the forest is a square mile densely covered with one tree for every square foot. The trees are all beeches except for two half-dead elms located at a great distance from each other. The trees are clustered, and so are the beeches, but not the two elms. Since, however, each elm is in the cluster of trees, (20) would be true if that were all it expressed.

Clearly, for (20) to be true, we need an event of being clustered whose *only* participants are the elms. Formula (22) expresses such a condition on events without admitting plural objects:

(22) $\forall x$(INFL(e, x) $\leftrightarrow$ Fx) $\wedge$ cluster(e)...

'F' is a predicate letter, and 'Fx' is to be read as 'x Fs' or 'x is an F'. The expression in (22) says that any object x participates in event e if and only if x is an F, which is to say that all and only the Fs are clustered. In the logical form for (20), we take the predicate F to be the NP *the elms*.

A plural term, as Michael Bennett (1972) and George Boolos (1984, 1985a, 1985b) have suggested, is a predicate. It does not refer to a plural object. It denotes individuals, exactly those that we normally think of plurals as denoting. It remains to be seen how the logical form of *the elms* takes up a singular predicate 'elm(y)' and delivers a predicate that takes the place of F in (22), one true of all and only the elms:

(23) $(\imath Y)(\exists y Yy \wedge \forall y(Yy \leftrightarrow \text{elm}(y)))$

The logical form of *the elms* is a second-order definite description. It describes that predicate Y, which is true of all and only those things y that are elms. This description is to be substituted for F in (22):

(24) $\forall x(\text{INFL}(e, x) \leftrightarrow (\imath Y)(\exists y Yy \wedge \forall y(Yy \leftrightarrow \text{elm}(y)))(x))$
      $\wedge \text{cluster}(e) \ldots$

The expression that results denotes an event e only if it is a clustering of the elms, as required.

Without plural objects, the problem of plural predication leads us to posit a more complex logical form. Following Davidson (1967), I see what are elsewhere seen as primitive, polyadic predicates as consisting of a lexical head (a verb or adjective expressing some concept of events) and a family of associated θ-roles, where each θ-role expresses a relation between objects and events. Plural predication is reduced to singular predication of objects and events. A sentence reports the exploits not of a plural object but of an event that has perhaps several objects participating in any one θ-role. In my view, an essential plural corresponds to a predicate introduced into logical form, as F is in (22), to characterize all and only what bears the θ-role to event e.

Since a θ-role is necessary for each instance of plural predication, decomposition must apply to any argument position where a plural might occur. This view thus agrees with Castañeda's (1967) and Parsons's (1990) view that no two NPs ever occupy argument positions in the same primitive relation. Each has its own θ-role:[8]

(25) a. Brutus stabbed Caesar
      b. *$\exists e \, \text{stab}(e, b, c)$
      c. $\exists e(\text{Agent}(e, b) \, \& \, \text{stab}(e) \, \& \, \text{Theme}(e, c))$

2   The Major Features of Logical Form

Why give up a straightforward, objectual view of plurals for a more complex analysis? Perhaps, a subscriber to Davidsonian logical form will relish an escape from plural objects. Suspecting as much, an uncharitable reader will think that the excuse for the new analysis is to serve the parochial needs of someone who, having given in to events, is compelled by ontological scruples to do what he can to hold out against plural objects. If this were so, I would agree that the project holds little interest. But my conclusions rely on no prior commitment to events or to Davidsonian logical form, nor do I even expect you to think that it makes good sense to buy a complex logical form if it purchases a reduced ontology. Chapters 2 through 4 promise to show that the view sketched here is the only game in town in the semantics of plurals. Two independent lines of argument converge on two results: that plural terms are predicates, and that the semantics of plurals require a particularly radical version of Davidsonian decomposition, which I will call *separation*.

I will return to these lines of argument in the course of sketching more of the proposal. The project is not only to address those questions of plural reference and predication raised by such examples as (8) to (12) but also to deliver a semantics that fits the wide variety of contexts in which plurals occur. The argument for separation arises only when one considers how a view of plurals will extend to more complex cases.

2.1 Reduction of plural predication to singular predication

The argument that plural terms are predicates starts with an observation. That speakers know that inferences like (26) to (28) are valid reflects their grasp of a certain relationship between the reference of plural and singular terms.

(26) The elms are clustered in the forest $\vdash$ There exists an elm

(27) Every one of the elms is tall $\vdash$ Every elm is tall

(28) Every elm is tall $\vdash$ Every one of the elms is tall

On the objectual view, knowledge of this relationship amounts to the mastery of some axioms to the effect that *the elms* refers to the plural object that consists of all and only the individual elms. Chapter 2 shows that the axioms sustaining the objectual view run into Russell's paradox, and the ways out of the paradox are shown to be semantically inadequate. In contrast, if there are no plural objects, then there is no need to relate them to singular objects. The predicative view escapes the paradox while validating such inferences as (26) to (28). In this way Russell's paradox comes to decide an important question about logical syntax. Plural terms are predicates.

Now if plurals are themselves predicates, the questions then arise, How do all those predicates in the sentence *The elms are clustered* (*in the forest*) hang together, and how does the speaker understand that the sentence is true just in case things are a certain way with the individual elms. Both questions are answered by reducing plural predication to singular predication of objects and events, as I have done in section 1.2. The plural NP assigned a θ-role is a predicate, F in (29), that denotes all and only those singular objects that bear the relation to the event:

(29) $\forall x(\Theta(e, x) \leftrightarrow Fx)$

If a speaker understands what it is for an object to participate in an event in a certain way, then, according to (30), he will understand that the sentence is true just in case every elm has participated in that way.

(30) $\exists e(\text{cluster}(e) \wedge \forall x(\text{INFL}(e, x) \leftrightarrow \text{the elms}(x)))$

The line of argument from Russell's paradox leads directly to the conclusion that plurals are predicates, which in turn calls for a Davidsonian decomposition.

Chapter 3 provides some empirical evidence to corroborate the predicative view of plurals and Davidsonian decomposition. Note that the logical syntax of NPs is divided if plural terms are predicates. Some NPs, definite and indefinite descriptions such as *the elms* and *some elms*, are second-order expressions, while others—*every elm*, *most elms*, *no elm*—remain first-order. (As it turns out, all definite and indefinite descriptions, whether singular or plural, are second-order.) The first part of chapter 3 supports the second-order syntax. For reasons independent of Russell's paradox, variables have to be sorted into singular and plural anyway, and some syntactic contexts will select one sort and not the other. There are no quantifiers, apart from definite and indefinite descriptions, that appear to range over plural objects. This is certainly contrary to the spirit of the objectual view. If indeed there are plural objects, then surely one should be able to quantify over them just as one quantifies over singular objects. On my view, semantic and syntactic differences coincide in a difference between first- and second-order quantifiers.[9]

The second part of chapter 3 provides evidence for an elementary consequence of decomposition. Note that decomposition expresses the intended relation between the participants only if they are taken to exhaust their θ-roles. This is a general fact, whatever the status of plural reference. The logical form (31) succeeds in saying that **b** eats **p** only if for some e, **b** is the only Agent in e and **p** is e's only Theme. Otherwise, (31) could be true where **b** eats not **p** but something else in e and **p** is eaten by something other than **b**.

(31) $\exists e(\text{Agent}(e, \mathbf{b}) \wedge \text{eat}(e) \wedge \text{Theme}(e, \mathbf{p}))$

The decomposed predicate lacks the means to say that **b** eats **p** within e, although it would be entirely within the resources of a primitive relation 'eat$(e, \mathbf{b}, \mathbf{p})$' to assert that **b** eats **p** in e, whether or not there are other eaters and other things eaten in e. The second part of chapter 3 shows that any theory based on polyadic predicates will nevertheless have to mimic the limited expression of a decomposed predicate. Suppose that **e** is an event of four boys eating four pizzas, and suppose that part of it is an event of boy $\mathbf{b}_1$ and boy $\mathbf{b}_2$ eating pizzas $\mathbf{p}_1$ and $\mathbf{p}_2$. Although those two boys ate those two pizzas within or at **e**, the polyadic predicate must not allow that eat$(\{\mathbf{b}_1, \mathbf{b}_2\}, \{\mathbf{p}_1, \mathbf{p}_2\}, \mathbf{e})$. The event relates only to those pluralities covering the entire event: eat$(\{\mathbf{b}_1, \mathbf{b}_2, \mathbf{b}_3, \mathbf{b}_4\}, \{\mathbf{p}_1, \mathbf{p}_2, \mathbf{p}_3, \mathbf{p}_4\}, \mathbf{e})$. The polyadic predicate behaves as if it had a Davidsonian decomposition.

Still waiting in reserve is an independent, direct argument for a radical version of decomposition, to be introduced in section 2.3 below. The argument for separation will in no way depend on the conclusion that plurals are predicates. Were we to ignore Russell's paradox and stick to the objectual view, the argument for separation will of its own demand reference to events and decomposition into θ-roles.[10]

2.2   First-order quantifiers and a mereology of events

Davidsonian logical form reveals other commitments once it is made to cohere with other aspects of natural-language quantification. It commits us almost immediately to a mereology of events and to the thesis that every first-order quantifier occurs with a quantifier over parts of events. In (32a), according to discussion by Taylor (1985) and Davies (1991) of similar examples, each organ student must have her own event in which she alone holds down the organ key for sixteen measures.

(32)   a.   Unharmoniously, every organ student sustained a note on the Wurlitzer for sixteen measures.
        b.   In slow progression, every organ student struck a note on the Wurlitzer.

(33) $[\exists e : \text{unharmonious}(e)][\text{every } x : Sx][\exists e' : e' \leq e]$
        $(\text{strike}(e') \wedge \forall z(\text{INFL}(e', z) \leftrightarrow z = x)\ldots)$

The sentence would not be true if, for example, one of the students keeps it going for eight measures only to be relieved by another student for the remaining eight. For each to have an event of her own, the first-order quantifier must include within its scope a quantifier over events. The familiar scope reading that relates each student to a note on the Wurlitzer can be obtained in no other way. It is, however, not the individual note that is unharmonious but the ensemble. The students each play only a part in the larger unharmonious action. Similarly, in (32b), *a slow progression* can only describe an ensemble event. The students' solitary events must be related to the larger one as parts to whole. The quantifier over events therefore contains the condition that $e' \leq e$ (e' is part of e).

Chapter 7 discusses the syntax and semantics of first-order quantifiers and the quantifiers over events that occur with them.

2.3 Separation

Davidsonian logical form, which has figured so far in an account of plural reference and predication, finds support independent of an answer to such foundational questions. Certain combinations of plurals and first-order quantifiers yield truth conditions that clamor for Davidsonian logical forms, or at least for a syntactic property that they most naturally instantiate. The crucial combinations reproduce the pattern in (32) to (33) with the adverb replaced by a plural, which applies to an event whose internal structure is further elaborated by the first-order quantifier and its scope. The interpretation combines scope independence between *three video games* and *every quarterback* with the scope dependency of *two new plays*:

(34) a. Three video games taught every quarterback two new plays.
     b. Three hundred quilt patches covered over two workbenches each with two bedspreads.

(35) $\exists e([\exists X : 3(X) \wedge \forall x(Xx \rightarrow Gx)]\forall z(\text{INFL}(e, z) \leftrightarrow Xz) \wedge \text{teach}(e)$
$\wedge [\text{every } y : Qy][\exists e' : e' \leq e](\forall z(\text{TO}(e', z) \leftrightarrow z = y)$
$\wedge [\exists W : 2(W) \wedge \forall w(Ww \rightarrow Pw)]\forall z(\text{OF}(e', z) \leftrightarrow Wz)))$

(36) Three video games were teaching, and *there* every quarterback was taught two new plays.

Three video games have taught the quarterbacks, and each has learned two new plays. The part-whole relation among events ($e' \leq e$) is what connects quantification over quarterbacks and their solitary events to the larger event where three video games are the teachers. Somehow their teaching can be divided up so that every quarterback has a part in which he is taught two new plays. In the particular context shown in (37), one quarterback is taught by only one of the video games without ever having any contact with the other two video games, which are the sole instructors for the remaining quarterback.

(37)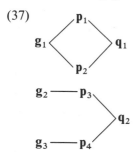

What is interesting about (34a) is that it combines a distributive character-ization of what each was taught with a crucial vagueness about what game taught what quarterback. My view is that such vagueness is the result of cross-reference to events: there was an event of every quarterback being taught two new plays, and *there* three video games were the teachers. To focus on the relevant class of quantifier interactions, I have given an example (34a) with a context (37) that is easily diagrammed. One should not be misled by the fact that the particular context (37) can be de-scribed without events solely in terms of relations among individuals: $\text{teach}(g_1, p_1, q_1)$ & $\text{teach}(g_1, p_2, q_1)$ & $\text{teach}(g_2, p_3, q_2)$ & $\text{teach}(g_3, p_4, q_2)$. The picture can be further complicated by mereological relations among the objects and events involved. So, consider (34b). The tailor has taken 300 quilt patches from his stock to fabricate four bedspreads, which now cover over the workbenches. It cannot be assumed that any of the patches of irregular shape and size was sewn into any one bedspread. The tailor may have divided it among several. It may furthermore be the case that no group of fewer than the 300 quilt patches cover any workbench. All that can be said is that there was an event of two workbenches each being covered over with two bedspreads, and *there* 300 quilt patches made up the covers. The cross-reference to events is essential.

Now as far as the earlier argument for Davidsonian logical form goes, or for that matter as far as any Davidsonian arguments go, it suffices if all decomposition is consigned to the lexicon, as in the meaning postulate in (38), where in any case we expect conceptual analysis to introduce all sorts of new notions.[11]

(38) 'V(e, F, G)' is true

$\quad\quad \leftrightarrow \forall x(\text{Agent}(e, x) \leftrightarrow Fx) \wedge \text{V*e} \wedge \forall x(\text{Theme}(e, x) \leftrightarrow Gx)$

The only novelty on the left-hand side of (38) is the extra place for events, which you are sure to view benignly in the light of tense and aspect, and the fact that plural NPs correspond to predicates F and G.[12] The logical syntax is more or less left untouched, as it is under the objectual view of plurals. Verbs remain atomic, polyadic expressions, however Davidsonian one turns out to be in explicating their truth conditions on the right-hand side. But lexical decomposition, I will argue, is not enough.

The argument for a radical decomposition is an argument that decomposition enters into the logical syntax. Suppose that it can be shown that the logical form for (34) has to be the one in (35), which is roughly paraphrased in (36). That the decomposition is syntactic follows immediately. Note that the INFL θ-role is separated from the others by the intervening quantifier *every quarterback*. The quantifier includes within its scope the TO and OF θ-roles but not the INFL θ-role. Note further that the θ-roles are predicated of distinct events: the INFL θ-role applies to e, and the others are predicated of a part, e'. A decomposition that can be taken to be merely lexical would allow one to substitute the quadratic predicate in (39) for the θ-roles and event property.

(39) 'teach(e, G, y, P)' for
　　　'teach$(e) \wedge \forall x (\text{INFL}(e, x) \leftrightarrow Gx) \wedge \forall x (\text{TO}(e, x) \leftrightarrow x = y)$
　　　$\wedge \forall x (\text{OF}(e, x) \leftrightarrow Px)$'

To do this, *all* the θ-roles and the event property must occur together and relate to the same event. The decomposition is irreducibly syntactic when it scrambles the θ-roles among the sentence's other elements, as with the intrusive quantifier *every quarterback*, or when it applies the θ-roles to distinct events. *Separation* is thus the separation of θ-roles in logical syntax. As it turns out, it is essential in capturing the vagueness about who did what to whom illustrated by the truth of (34) in situations like (37). The NPs must bind argument positions in θ-roles separated from one another. Predication of events holds it all together, but predication of events in a part-whole relation is crucially not predication of the same event.

The burden of chapter 4 is to show that separation is essential. It is straightforward that the truth conditions of sentences like (34) are correctly rendered by separating θ-roles. The effort is in showing that it is the only way. The chapter shows that no formula based on an atomic, polyadic predicate yields the correct truth conditions. Theories that admit an additional place for events, '$V(e, \alpha_i, \ldots, \alpha_j)$', with or without a Davidsonian lexical semantics, fail, along with those that do not have the additional event place, '$V(\alpha_i, \ldots, \alpha_j)$'. Furthermore, the argument is in-different to the treatment of plural predication and reference to plural objects.

The result is robust in another crucial dimension. I assume that any interesting theory will have a quantificational apparatus at least adequate to treat essential plurals, such as those discussed in section 1, and the familiar scope readings that first-order quantifiers give rise to. In arguing against atomic, polyadic predicates, I will *not* hold the theory responsible for some of the more interesting readings surveyed below in section 3. Apart from this minimum, I allow any schema for quantification, includ-ing *n*-ary quantifiers, if it will help. When the argument against primitive polyadicity is that the available logical forms are expressively too weak, we grant great latitude in quantification. When the argument is that ex-pressive power is too strong, then, of course, we assume that primitive polyadicity is burdened with only the minimum quantification theory. Despite the favorable conditions, primitive polyadic predicates prove to be inadequate. The conclusion, then, is the radical one that Davidsonian decomposition occurs in the logical syntax.

2.4   Cross-reference to events

Let us assume the result of chapter 4, that separation is essential for a class of sentences that includes the simple case of (34). Recall that sen-tences in the class combine quantifiers that are scope independent of each other with one or more dependent quantifiers. In (34), *three video games* and *every quarterback* correspond to the independent quantifiers, and *two new plays* is the narrow-scope, dependent quantifier. If the conclusions about radical decomposition are correct, the logical form requires sepa-rated conjuncts, as in (36), and these conjuncts are held together by a cross-reference to events. A reasonable logical form for (34) puts every-thing in the scope of an existential quantifier that binds event variables in both conjuncts, as in (40). It appears that the cross-reference to events is adequately represented as variable binding.

(34)   Three video games taught every quarterback two new plays.

(36)   Three video games were teaching, and *there* every quarterback was taught two new plays.

(40) $\exists e([\exists X : 3(X) \wedge \forall x(Xx \to Gx)] \forall x(\mathrm{INFL}(e, x) \leftrightarrow Xx) \ldots$
       $[\text{every } y : Qy][\exists e' : e' \leq e] \ldots)$

Appearances being misleading, it turns out that even this simple case will require something else to properly relate the three video games' teaching to every quarterback's being taught two new plays. The immediate concern, however, is that the success of variable binding even as a way to approximate the cross-reference is an artifact of the example and its choice of quantifiers, which happen to all be increasing. Variable binding is not a fully general way to cash out the cross-reference to events in all cases of essential separation. It fails in those cases with nonincreasing quantifiers, such as (41) and (43).

(41) No more than three video games taught no more than two quarterbacks (each) two new plays.

(42) Video games taught no more than two quarterbacks (each) two new plays, and *there* no more than three video games taught quarterbacks new plays.

(43) No more than three detectives (each) solved exactly two crimes for no more than five agencies.

(44) No more than three detectives (each) solved exactly two crimes for agencies, and *there* detectives solved crimes for no more than five agencies.

In (41), the decreasing quantifiers, *no more than three video games* and *no more than two quarterbacks* may be understood as cumulative, independent quantifiers, while the remaining quantifier, *two new plays*, has narrow scope. This scope assignment is characteristic of essential separation, but the decreasing quantifiers cannot be allowed to fall within the scope of an existential quantifier that would bind event variables in the separated conjuncts. It would mistake the meaning of (41) if its logical form asserted that there was an event in which no more than three video games taught quarterbacks and no more than two quarterbacks were each taught two new plays:

(45) *$\exists e([(\leq 3)x : Gx][\exists e' : e' \leq e](\text{teach}(e) \wedge \forall z(\text{INFL}(e, z) \leftrightarrow x = z))$
$\wedge [(\leq 2)y : Qy][\exists e' : e' \leq e]\ldots)$

An immediate difficulty is that the assertion is nearly vacuous. There are always events where nothing much happens. But even on the assumption that context raises to salience more interesting events,[13] (45) is still mistaken. For (41) does not assert of a given context that no more than three video games taught quarterbacks new plays. Rather, it asserts that the events of quarterbacks each being taught *two* new plays involved no more than three video games. More video games may have instructed the quarterbacks who were taught only one play.

If we are to maintain the view that essential separation is an effect of referring to events, then the separation of cumulative quantifiers demands a more general theory of pronominal (descriptive) cross-reference to events, one that in effect will provide the reference for *there* in the paraphrases in (42) and (44). In (42) it must refer to whatever events there were of quarterbacks being taught two new plays, and in (44) to whatever events there were of detectives each solving exactly two crimes. Thus the cross-referring term bears two important characteristics. First, it is second-order, because the antecedent clause may describe no events and, as we will see later, because a plurality of events is sometimes described. Second, it must recover some notion that the antecedent clause describes certain events *exactly*. The formal proposal develops an analogy between cross-reference to events and the descriptive anaphors in (46), which refer cumulatively to whatever donkeys any farmer bought.[14]

(46) a. Few farmers bought a donkey, but they were hitched together in a short mule train anyway.

  b. Few farmers bought a donkey, but the donkeys were hitched together in a short mule train anyway.

  c. Few farmers bought donkeys, but they were all hitched together in a short mule train anyway.

As it turns out, the notion of the events exactly described by a clause is what is missing also from those representations where variable binding appears at first sufficient. Ultimately, (40) will be replaced by something along the lines of (47), which can be read as in (48).

(47) $\exists e([\exists X:\ldots]\forall z(\text{INFL}(\text{there}_i, z) \leftrightarrow Xz)\ldots$
   $[_i[\text{every } y : Qy][\exists e' : e' \leq e]\ldots])$

(48) Within some event, every quarterback is taught two new plays, and that was by three video games.

The correctness of the above paraphrases in (42) and (44) is taken up in chapter 9. The cumulative interpretation of (43) is crucially vague about the number of crimes solved for any one agency. Separating *no more than five agencies* and its θ-role from the other arguments in the antecedent clause leaves *exactly two crimes* only within the first conjunct. The logical form for the independent, cumulative quantifiers thus finds an essential asymmetry between their scopes. As will be shown, the intended interpretation would not be represented by any logical form where *no more than two detectives* and *no more than five agencies* have scope over identical formulas:[15]

(49) *No more than two detectives (each) solved exactly two crimes for
     agencies, and (*there*) for no more than five agencies did detectives
     (each) solve exactly two crimes.

All such symmetric logical forms impose a condition on how many crimes
are related to each agency that is absent from the interpretation, which is
vague on this point, as expected from separation.

    Assuming, then, an asymmetric logical form where *exactly two crimes*
does not occur in the second conjunct, the need for cross-reference to
events follows immediately. Contrary to the paraphrase in (50), which
omits *there*, the cumulative interpretation does not entail that no more
than five agencies were the beneficiaries of detectives solving crimes:

(50) No more than two detectives (each) solved exactly two crimes for
     agencies, and for no more than five agencies did detectives solve
     crimes.

It entails only that no more than five agencies were the beneficiaries of
detectives (each) solving *exactly two* crimes. More agencies may have been
benefitted from the detectives solving some other number of crimes. The
paraphrase in (44) is appropriately restricted by *there* referring to just
those events of detectives (each) solving exactly two crimes.

    To summarize my view, an adequate logical language will have four
important features.

1. It will reduce plural predication to singular predication of objects and
events via a Davidsonian decomposition.
2. It will introduce a mereology of events. A Davidsonian logical form
accommodates first-order quantification in natural language by assuming
that every first-order quantifier has within its immediate scope a quantifier
over parts of events.
3. To represent the truth conditions of sentences that combine independent and dependent quantifiers, the θ-roles are separated in the logical
syntax and then held together by reference to events.
4. If reference to events is to hold together *all* cases of essential separation
and to be adequate for all of them, then the logical language will have
descriptive anaphora to refer to events.

The argument for these features rests on motivating the first and third
features, Davidsonian decomposition and separation. As remarked, a
commitment to the other features will follow almost immediately from
these.

In chapter 2 Russell's paradox and the problem of plural reference will compel us to view plurals as second-order expressions, as predicates. If plurals are predicates, then some sort of Davidsonian decomposition, lexical or syntactic, is called for to explain how a sentence hangs together and how the speaker understands that the sentence is true just in case the individual objects are a certain way. The argument for second-order syntax thus leads indirectly to a Davidsonian analysis, to the first feature that any adequate logical language will have. A commitment to at least a lexical decomposition finds some further support from the second part of chapter 3, where on empirical grounds it is shown that polyadic predicates have to mean what decomposition says they should mean: for any given event, any argument exhausts all individuals bearing the relevant θ-role in that event.

As for separation, the third feature of the logical language, a second, independent line of argument leads directly to it, and again, a fortiori, to decomposition, the first feature. Chapter 4 lays out the argument that the decomposition in logical syntax is essential because of the expressive limitations of primitive, polyadic predicates.

Although the predicative view of plurals leads to Davidsonian decomposition, I should point out that decomposition, whether lexical or syntactic, does not by itself preclude an objectual view of plural reference. One might take plural objects to be the values of variables in Davidsonian logical forms. The argument for separation is indifferent to whether or not one helps oneself to them. The argument against the objectual view derives solely from Russell's paradox and chapter 3's empirical considerations showing a need to sort the variables into two types just as second-order logic would do. The argument from Russell's paradox that plurals are predicates and the argument from separation do, however, converge on Davidsonian logical forms.

Having fitted the logical language with four major features, we face the empirical and formal problems presented by the variety of interpretations that plurals and quantifiers give rise to. After summarizing the basic data, I return to an overview of chapters 5 to 12, which develop a semantics for plurality and quantification.

3 Basic Data

The interactions of plurals and quantifiers for both the limiting results of chapters 2 through 4 and the more specific proposals in the rest of this work fall into the following basic cases. First are the elementary cases illustrating essential plurals, which I will tend to call the *sum of plurals* reading:

(51) The rocks rained down.

(52) Some boys ate some pies.

(53) Three movers lifted four pianos.

When several plurals occur, the relation among them is vague. Nothing specifies which boys ate which pies, nothing requires that any one boy ate any one pie, and this makes the plurals essential. Characterisic of this class, quantified expressions are scope-independent. Thus, for the sum-of-plurals reading of (53), there are just three movers and four pianos, and the sentence is true if there is some event at which the three movers lifted and the four pianos were lifted, (and obviously it need not be that the three movers lifted the four pianos all at the same time).

The second class includes the most familiar instances of scope assignment, where the wide-scope NP is fully *distributive*:

(54) Every boy ate two crisps.

(55) Some movers (each) lifted four pianos.

(56) Few movers (each) lifted a piano.

The third class comprises *semidistributive* interpretations, where a first-order quantifier appears to quantify over pluralities:

(57) No more than ten students collaborated on three problems.

(58) Few composers agreed that they should collaborate.

(59) Exactly forty unionists gathered in public squares.

Sentence (57) asserts that no more than ten students are such that any one of them collaborated on three problems with other students. In this example the apparent quantification over pluralities includes within its scope the quantifier *three problems*. In (58) the quantifier over pluralities appears also capable of binding pronouns. That is, those who it is agreed should collaborate are those who agree to it, and the sentence asserts that few composers are party to such agreements. (For a discussion of some of the restrictions on the distribution of [semi]distributive interpretations that have been noted in the literature, see n. 16.)

The fourth class of interpretations I will call *event-dependent*. L. Carlson (1980, 1982) has observed that sentences (60) to (62) have an interpretation of which I will say that a universal quantifier over events is restricted by the verb phrase (VP) and includes within its scope any quantifier in subject position.

(60) Few experts (ever) agree.

(61) Thirty Democrats vote with the President.

(62) No more than ten advanced students (ever) collaborated on three problems.

The event-dependent interpretation of (62) asserts that whenever there is a collaboration on three problems, it involves no more than ten advanced students:

(63) $[\forall e : \text{collaborate}(e)$
$\wedge [\exists Y : 3(Y) \wedge \forall y(Yy \rightarrow Py)] \forall y(\text{on}(e, y) \leftrightarrow Yy)]$
$[(\leq 10)z : Sz][\exists e' : e' \leq e] \forall x(\text{INFL}(e', x) \leftrightarrow x = z)$

(64) "Whenever there is a collaboration on three problems, no more than ten students are involved."

The event-dependent interpretation is not one that admits the alternative paraphrase in (65) (although we have no need to deny that the alternative is yet another reading of the sentence (62)).

(65) a. "For any three problems, no more than ten advanced students collaborated on them."
   b. "Whenever there were three problems, no more than ten advanced students collaborated on them."

Both (64) and (65) agree that the interpretation assigns wide-scope to some sort of generic or universal quantifer. The following context shows that the quantifier is restricted by the VP and quantifies over events, as in (63) and (64). Suppose that the linguistics olympiad is a team sport in which the members of a team collaborate on some assigned problems. The olympiad seats each team at its own table, and the table is given three problems. Suppose further that there is a pool of, say, ten problems from which the three given to any one team are randomly chosen. The olympiad is large enough so that it happens that several teams work on the same three problems. In this context, one can utter (62) intending to convey that at any one table, there were no more than ten advanced students. Only the work at a single table is a collaboration. Students from different tables belong to rival teams and could hardly be thought of as collaborators. Quantifying over the events of collaboration, as in (63) and

(64), represents the intended assertion. In contrast, (65) neglects to raise a quantifier over events of collaboration, and any such quantifier remains within the scope of *no more than ten advanced students*. Thus the formula in the scope of the universal quantifier over problems will have a semi-distributive interpretation. For any three problems, it asserts that no more than ten students were among students that collaborated on them. In this olympiad, every team has three advanced students. The observation is that in this context one can truthfully assert (62) under its event-dependent interpretation, and it comes out true as represented by (63) and (64). But in this olympiad it turns out that the same three problems have been assigned to four teams. It is not true that no more then ten advanced students collaborated on them, since there were twelve advanced students among the four teams. Each of these twelve participates in a collaboration on the three problems:

(66) $\text{Team}_1 — \{\mathbf{p}_1, \mathbf{p}_2, \mathbf{p}_3\}$ $\text{Team}_k — \mathbf{P}_k$
       $\text{Team}_2 — \mathbf{P}_2$ $\text{Team}_{k+1} — \{\mathbf{p}_1, \mathbf{p}_2, \mathbf{p}_3\}$
       $\vdots$ $\text{Team}_{k+2} — \mathbf{P}_{k+2}$
       $\text{Team}_j — \mathbf{P}_j$ $\vdots$
       $\text{Team}_{j+1} — \{\mathbf{p}_1, \mathbf{p}_2, \mathbf{p}_3\}$ $\text{Team}_l — \{\mathbf{p}_1, \mathbf{p}_2, \mathbf{p}_3\}$
       $\text{Team}_{j+2} — \mathbf{P}_{j+2}$
       $\vdots$

The suggested paraphrases in (65), which are false in the context, do not, then, convey the true event-dependent interpretation. The argument shows that the event-dependent interpretation makes *no more then ten students* dependent on a quantifier that quantifies over the individual collaborations. The context and the examples, as they are, do not show that the event quantifier is restricted by the entire VP, including *on three problems*, rather than just the verb *collaborate*. A somewhat more complicated context demonstrates the latter point. Suppose that the olympiad allows a team to choose either three moderate problems or two more difficult ones, and instead of (62), consider the event-dependent interpretation of (67):

(67) Exactly ten advanced students collaborated on three problems.

The event-dependent interpretation is true just in case those teams that chose three problems each involve exactly ten advanced students. Note that neglecting to include *on three problems* in the restriction to the event quantifier, as in (68), falsely entails that every team collaborated on three problems.[17]

(68) "At any collaboration, exactly ten students collaborated on three problems."

The fifth class of interpretations I follow Scha 1981 in calling *cumulative quantification*. It includes all those interpretations where nonincreasing quantifiers, such as *exactly two detectives* and *no more than three crimes*, are independent:

(69) Exactly two detectives solved exactly three crimes.

(70) No more than five detectives solved no more than seven crimes.

As Scha points out, cumulative quantifiers cannot be expressed as a sum of plurals. Sentence (69) is not equivalent to (71).

(71) $[\exists x : 2(x) \land \forall z(z \in x \rightarrow Dz)][\exists y : 3(y) \land \forall z(z \in y \rightarrow Cz)]$
    $\text{solve}(x, y)$

(72) $[\exists x : (\leq 5)x \land \forall z(z \in x \rightarrow Dz)][\exists y : (\leq 7)y \land \forall z(z \in y \rightarrow Cz)]$
    $\text{solve}(x, y)$

Sentence (69) entails that some two detectives solved some three crimes, but unlike (71), it also asserts that no other detectives solved any other crimes. Similarly, (70) asserts that no detectives except perhaps for at most five solved crimes and no crimes except perhaps for at most seven were solved by detectives. But (72) does not impose any upper bound on the numbers of detectives solving crimes.

4 The Plan

As already outlined, chapters 2 to 4 present the foundational arguments that the logical language is characterized by four major features: reduction to singular predication via a Davidsonian logical form, a mereology of events, separation, and cross-reference to events. A semantics for plurality and quantification is developed in the remaining chapters, which address some of the empirical and formal questions raised by the variety of interpretations in which plurals and quantifiers participate. Apart from those considerations related to Russell's paradox, the decision to divide the syntax and semantics of quantifier phrases into first- and second-order is defended on empirical grounds mainly in chapter 3, section 1. Further evidence turns up in chapter 9, section 5, and chapter 10, especially n. 3 (see also Higginbotham and Schein 1989 and Schein 1992), while chapter 7 discusses the more theory-internal reasons for this classification. Chapter 5 presents some background on θ-roles, events, and contexts of events, and chapter 6 introduces the background semantic theory and translation. The meaning of natural language first-order quantifiers and the implicit quantification over parts of events is laid out in chapter 7, which also takes up the relation between second-order quantifiers and quantifying over parts of events. Chapter 8 treats semidistributivity. Here separation has an interesting and unexpected application. It would at first appear that semidistributivity involves implicit quantifiers over groups and, from examples such as (73), that such (second-order) quantifiers may bind pronouns, as in (74).

(73) Few impresarios coauthor what they coproduce.

(74) $[\text{few } x : Ix][\exists X : Xx \wedge \forall x(Xx \rightarrow Ix)][\exists e : \text{coauthor}(e)]$
$\quad (\forall x(\text{INFL}(e, x) \leftrightarrow Xx)$
$\quad \wedge [\exists Y : [\exists e : \text{coproduce}(e)](\forall x(\text{INFL}(e, x) \leftrightarrow Xx)$
$\quad \wedge \forall y(\text{OF}(e, y) \leftrightarrow Yy))]\forall y(\text{OF}(e, y) \leftrightarrow Yy))$

This entails that few are among the groups in which the impresarios are coauthoring and coproducing together. It turns out, however, that if such quantifiers over groups are used to represent semidistributivity, they are subject to certain constraints on their scope. But these constraints conflict with binding pronouns. The quantifiers cannot both bind the pronouns that refer to the implicit groups and respect the constraints on scope. In my account, semidistributivity involves the functor co-, which can modify any θ-role. Its scope is, of course, fixed. There is then no quantifier to bind the pronoun in (73), which becomes instead a descriptive anaphor along the lines suggested by the paraphrase in (75), where the pronoun *they* becomes the definite description *the coauthors in that event*:

(75) Few impresarios are coauthors in an event that is a coauthoring of what the *coauthors in that event* coproduced.

The content of the pronoun is just the subject's θ-role, an independent constituent according to separation.

Chapters 9 to 12 are about cumulative quantification and the semantics of cross-reference to events. Since the claim is that the logical form of cumulative quantification contains a descriptive anaphor that refers to events, I widen the discussion to include some of the problems of descriptive anaphora that appear directly relevant. Among them is the cumulative reference of plural pronouns, as, for example, when *them* in (76) refers to the donkeys that farmers bought.

(76) Every farmer bought a donkey, and they hitched them together in a mule train.

Another is how to distinguish contexts where a pronoun seems not refer to all the objects that meet its descriptive condition, as in (77), from contexts where a pronoun does bear maximal reference, as in (78):

(77) A man came to the office today. He tried to sell me an encyclopedia. (Donnellan 1978)

(78) a. John owns some sheep, and Harry vaccinated them. (Evans 1977)
     b. Few senators voted for JFK, and they were all junior. (Evans 1977)

Both of these problems find their analogues in the cross-reference to events contained in the logical form of cumulative quantifiers. They are discussed in chapter 10.

The basic cases of cumulative quantification discussed in the literature are those where the quantifiers are all of the same type: all nonincreasing. Chapter 11 contains speculations on how to extend my view to cases that appear to mix types:

(79) Two boys ate no more than a dozen pizzas (between them).

The quantifier *no more than a dozen pizzas* accumulates whatever pizzas the two boys ate jointly or severally. I suggest that there is a connection between the interpretation of relative clauses such as *whatever pizzas two boys ate* and the semantics of quantifying into questions.

Chapter 12 is a critique of those proposals that would treat some of the elementary cases of cumulative quantification in terms of *n*-ary quantifiers.

Throughout this work, I assume with many others that the classes of interpretations surveyed in section 3 are formally distinguished and are therefore a source of ambiguity in the logical form of sentences. Appendix I addresses a proposal due to Verkuyl and van der Does (1991) that eliminates the logical forms expressing the sum-of-plurals and fully distributive interpretations and attributes these readings to the vagueness of semidistributive interpretations.

Definitions, rules, my notational conventions, and illustrative examples are collected together in appendix II.

A final caveat. Occasionally, in a paraphrase that is especially faithful to the logical form it glosses or in an informal argument that is meant to indicate how the argument would go in the formal language, I allow myself to impose on grammar and good style. So, for example, the objectual view of plurals holds that the reference of a plural term is to an individual, a plural object, and that there are predicates such as 'elms(x)' that denote these individuals. Speaking for this theory, I allow myself to say, where **a** refers to the elms, that **a** *is* elms. The singular number agreement underlines the fact that the plural object is an individual. My hope is that such things will be more help than bother for the reader trying to follow the argument.

Chapter 2
Plural Reference

1 Plural Reference and Predication

A speaker in understanding a sentence understands how things in the world have to be for that sentence to be true. In giving an account of a speaker's understanding of this connection between sentences and things in the world, we appeal to a notion of predication—that the predicates grasped by speakers are true of objects in the world. A speaker comes to understand that (1) is true if and only if John left, because he knows that *leave* is true of an object just in case it leaves and the name *John* refers to John.

(1) John left.

(2) *John* refers to **a**.

(3) sentence (1) is true $\leftrightarrow$ the predicate *left* is true of **a**

(4) *left* is true of **a** $\leftrightarrow$ **a** left

(5) sentence (1) is true $\leftrightarrow$ **a** left

The problem of plurals is how to extend reference and predication to sentences containing essential plurals. The objectual view makes quick work of it.[1] The universe is expanded to include plural objects alongside the ordinary, singular objects, and plurals simply refer to these. Thus, *the elms* in (6) refers to the group of elms, or something like it, and this object is distinct from any of its constituent elms. It has the property of being clustered, which no single elm does.

(6) The elms are clustered.

(7) *The elms* refers to **a**.

(8) sentence (6) is true $\leftrightarrow$ the predicate *clustered* is true of **a**

(9) the predicate *clustered* is true of **a** ↔ **a** is clustered

(10) sentence (6) is true ↔ **a** is clustered

The primitive notion of predication is extended to plural objects. So to understand a predicate in one's language is to grasp a concept that denotes plural objects, among others, as in (9). In understanding the sentence in (6), a speaker knows that it is true just in case the *one* plural object that *the elms* refers to is clustered in the forest.

2   What Speakers Know about Plurals and Russell's Paradox

Of course, a speaker knows more. He grasps a certain relationship between the plural object and the singular objects that make it up. That understanding is partially reflected in the fact that anyone who knows the language knows the validity of three sorts of inference, exemplified in (11) to (13):

(11) The elms are clustered in the forest ⊢ There exists an elm

(12) Every one of the elms is tall ⊢ Every elm is tall[2]

(13) Every elm is tall ⊢ Every one of the elms is tall

The first inference simply illustrates that any true assertion about a plural object $(\iota x)\Phi$ entails the existence of a singular object that is Φ, and (12) and its converse (13) point out some elementary facts about distributivity. The understanding reflected in these inferences is not very subtle. Any speaker who knows the meaning of plurality knows at least this much.

On the objectual view, to acquire the knowledge of plurals reflected in the above inferences, a speaker must have mastered a family of extralogical axioms in addition to the semantics of predication and quantification. We will spend some time canvassing these axioms. You will see that the apparent innocence of saying that there are things, there are groups of them, and plurals refer to these cannot last if the objectual view is to bring inferences (11) to (13) within the speaker's ken.

Our purpose in this chapter is to give the logical reasons for rejecting the objectual view, namely that the axioms run up against Russell's paradox, and to introduce in its place the foundations for the semantics of a language with second-order terms. Treating plurals as predicates both escapes the paradox and derives inferences (11) through (13) as a matter of logic, without supplement from extralogical axioms. The import of Russell's paradox for plural terms has been laid out in three articles by

George Boolos (1984, 1985a, 1985b), whose discussion I follow. My foundations are just those he presents in "Nominalist Platonism."

To anticipate the argument from Russell's paradox, I mention the crucial fact that leads to the objectual view's undoing. In declaring that plurals refer to objects, the objectual view decides once and for all what the logical form of (12) and (13) must be. Consider the quantifier phrase *every one of the elms*. Since, *the elms* refers to an object, the quantifier's restriction must contain the relation 'is-one-of (x, y)' between the plural object and the objects quantified over. Thus the objectual view must take inferences (12) and (13) to involve sentences (14) and (15).

(14) [every x : is-one-of(x, the elms)] tall(x)

(15) [every x : elm(x)] tall(x)

It is committed to the view that distributivity is relational. The form of (13), for example, is to infer that every singular object that is-one-of the plural object $(\iota x)\Phi$ is F if every singular object that is Φ is F. The inference depends on what the speaker knows about the relation *is-one-of*.

Observe now that a speaker is not prepared to accept (12) unless he already recognizes that the inference in (16) is valid:

(16) There exists an elm $\vdash$ The elms exist

For if (16) were not known, (12) would have to be rejected, since there might very well be an elm that is short but no plural object for *the elms* to refer to. The logical form of (16) is also decided if it is to license an inference between the logical forms (14) and (15). It has to be an axiom about the relation *is-one-of*, equivalent to (17).

(17) $\exists x$ elm(x) $\vdash$ $\exists y \forall x$ (is-one-of(x, y) $\leftrightarrow$ elm(x))

(Formula (17) unpacks the definite description *the elms*.) Yet (17) has the form of a comprehension axiom. So, to account for distributivity, the objectual view is committed to a comprehension schema and all the risks from Russell's paradox that it entails. No theory with reference to plural objects, however circumscribed and unambitious in its coverage, escapes these risks if it at least pretends to account for the elementary facts about distributivity. But this is, of course, where any theory of plurals begins.

3   A Semantics for the Objectual View

I would like to show in some concrete fashion the knowledge necessary to support inferences (11) through (13). So I choose to analyze the subject in (18) in a particular way. The conclusion to be reached, that the inferences need axioms, is, however, independent of this choice.[3]

(18) The elms are clustered.

(19) cluster$((\iota x)(\text{elms}(x)))$

Let us assume that *the elms* is a referring expression occupying an argument position, as in (20) and (21):

(20) $\ulcorner(\iota x)\Phi(x)\urcorner$ refers to **a** $\leftrightarrow \ldots$ **a** $\ldots$

(21) $\ulcorner F(\iota x)\Phi(x)\urcorner$ is true $\leftrightarrow \exists y(\ulcorner(\iota x)\Phi(x)\urcorner$ refers to $y \wedge \ulcorner F\urcorner$ is true of $y)$[4]

Assume further that *the elms* is a description, in the sense that its logical form will contain a predicate true of the object referred to. Thus,

(22) $\ulcorner(\iota x)\Phi(x)\urcorner$ refers to **a** $\rightarrow \Phi(\mathbf{a})$.[5]

Reference to that unique, plural object, the elms, is composed in some way from the objects that the predicate is true of. Since we have assumed that it will also be true of the plural object itself, the predicate 'elms(x)' must be a plural predicate, just like 'cluster(x)':

(23) 'cluster(x)' is true of **a** $\leftrightarrow$ **a** is clustered

(24) 'elms(x)' is true of **a** $\leftrightarrow$ **a** is elms

I defer for the moment exactly how to relate the plural predicate to a singular predicate 'elm(x)' except to note that any elm or any group of things each of which is an elm is sure to correspond to an object that 'elms(x)' is true of. Given this predicate, our immediate concern is to secure reference to the unique object *the elms*:[6]

(25) '$(\iota x)(\text{elms}(x))$' refers to **a** $\leftrightarrow \forall y(\text{elms}(y) \leftrightarrow y \leq \mathbf{a})$

(26) $\ulcorner(\iota x)\Phi(x)\urcorner$ refers to **a** $\leftrightarrow \forall y(\Phi(y) \leftrightarrow y \leq \mathbf{a})$[7]

The reference of *the elms* is to some object a such that everything that is elms is part of it. So all elms are part of it. The converse, that any part of a is elms, is also necessary, to keep out the beeches. Certainly, under a naive understanding of the part-whole relation $\leq$, there can only be one object a that meets the description. For uniqueness it suffices that the relation be reflexive and antisymmetric:[8]

(27) $x \leq x$ (reflexive)

(28) $(x \leq y \wedge y \leq x) \rightarrow x = y$ (antisymmetric)

So that the reference of *the elms* accords with intuition, I assume that the relation is also transitive:

(29) $(x \leq y \wedge y \leq z) \rightarrow x \leq z$ (transitive)

If, for example, plural objects were sets, assuming transitivity would identify the relation as *is a subset of* ($\subseteq$). If we excluded the empty set from
the range of y in (25), *the elms* would refer to the set **a** whose subsets in-
cluded all the sets of elms and sets of nothing else: $\forall y(\text{elms}(y) \leftrightarrow y \leq \mathbf{a})$.
This is just the set of all elms, as desired.[9]

The schema in (26) applies also to a singular definite description, such
as *the elm*. Referring successfully to a unique object requires a predicate,
'elm(x)', that denotes only singular objects:

(30) '$(\iota x)(\text{elm}(x))$' refers to **a** $\leftrightarrow \forall y(\text{elm}(y) \leftrightarrow y \leq a)$

So if **a** is an elm that all elms are part of, it is the unique elm.

3.1   Axioms relating singular and plural predicates

Seeing that singular and plural descriptions contain different predicates,
'elm(x)' and 'elms(x)', we consider now how to relate them. The question
takes a specific form: how to relate 'elm(x)' and 'elms(x)' so that the
inference in (31) is supported.

(31) The elms are clustered in the forest $\vdash$ there exists an elm

In general, what must a speaker know, knowing that any true assertion
of a plural object entails the existence of a singular object?

On our current assumptions, the speaker knows the theory in (32) to
(36), which he brings to bear on the logical forms in (37) for the sentences
in (31):

(32) $\ulcorner F(\iota x)\Phi(x)\urcorner$ is true $\leftrightarrow \exists y(\ulcorner(\iota x)\Phi(x)\urcorner$ refers to $y \wedge \ulcorner F\urcorner$ is true of $y)$

(33) $\ulcorner(\iota x)\Phi(x)\urcorner$ refers to **a** $\leftrightarrow \forall y(\Phi(y) \leftrightarrow y \leq \mathbf{a})$

(34) 'cluster(x)' is true of **a** $\leftrightarrow$ **a** is clustered

(35) 'elms(x)' is true of **a** $\leftrightarrow$ **a** is elms

(36) 'elm(x)' is true of **a** $\leftrightarrow$ **a** is an elm

(37) cluster$((\iota x)(\text{elms}(x))) \vdash \exists x\, \text{elm}(x)$

Understanding the predicates in (35) and (36), this speaker is prepared,
under appropriate conditions, to recognize that a singular object, a tree,
is both an elm and elms. But knowing the truth of the premise in (31) does
not prepare him to accept the conclusion. He infers the existence of a
plural object that is elms but not the existence of an elm. That is, (38) is
the closest the theory comes to (37):

(38) cluster$((\iota x)(\mathrm{elms}(x))) \vdash \exists x\,\mathrm{elms}(x)$

The theory must be supplemented in some way to support the inference in (39), which together with (38) will yield (37).

(39) $\exists x\,\mathrm{elms}(x) \vdash \exists x\,\mathrm{elm}(x)$

To this end I introduce a predicate, 'At(x)' (read "x is atomic"), that denotes all and only singular objects:

(40) At$(x) \leftrightarrow_{\mathrm{df}} \forall y(y \leq x \rightarrow y = x)$

'Elm(x)' and 'elms(x)' are then related by condition (41):

(41) $\mathrm{elms}(x) \leftrightarrow \exists y(\mathrm{At}(y) \wedge y \leq x) \wedge \forall y((\mathrm{At}(y) \wedge y \leq x) \rightarrow \mathrm{elm}(y))$[10]

Knowing (41), the speaker draws the inference in (39): if there is an object that is elms, then, by (41), there must be a singular object, and it must be an elm. Putting this together with the theory in (32) to (36) licenses the inference in (31).

The knowledge of a condition like (41) presumably arises from a derivational relationship between singular and plural predicates. More concretely, I will assume that the plural morpheme is an operator taking predicates of singular objects into predicates of plural objects:

(42) $\mathrm{N}+\mathrm{s}(x) \leftrightarrow_{\mathrm{df}} \exists y(\mathrm{At}(y) \wedge y \leq x)$
$\wedge \forall y((\mathrm{At}(y) \wedge y \leq x) \rightarrow \mathrm{N}(y))$[11]

We will see better how the inference in (31) guides formulating the relation between 'elm(x)' and 'elms(x)' if we consider briefly an alternative. We might have taken the plural predicate to be basic and defined an operator to derive singular predicates:

(43) $\mathrm{N_{pl}}+\varnothing(x) \leftrightarrow_{\mathrm{df}} \mathrm{At}(x) \wedge \mathrm{N_{pl}}(x)$[12]

(44) $\mathrm{elm}(x) \leftrightarrow_{\mathrm{df}} \mathrm{At}(x) \wedge \mathrm{elms}(x)$

Knowing (44) cannot take the place of (41). A speaker knowing (44) instead cannot infer from the existence of a plural object that is elms that there is an elm. He does not know that such a plural object has singular objects as parts, and if there are parts, he does not know that any is an elm. Clearly, speakers knowing the validity of inferences like (31) must know more, something along the lines of (41).

The theory now revised to include (42) is also adequate to support the converse of (39), i.e., that the existence of a singular object entails the existence of a corresponding plural object:

(45) $\exists x \, \text{elm}(x) \vdash \exists x \, \text{elms}(x)$

(46) There exists an elm $\vdash$ There exist one or more elms

If **a** is an elm, then it is also elms, according to (41). The reflexivity of the part-whole relation guarantees this.[13]

3.2 Comprehension principles

To have a proper regard for the scope of this theory, we should canvass some of its limitations. In general, it will not sustain inferences that one might attribute to the knowledge that for any elms, there is a plural object, those elms, that they are part of.

One example it fails with is minimally different from (46). It will not support the inference that if there is an elm **a** and an elm **b**, there is the pair of them:

(47) There is an elm, **a**, and there is an elm, **b** $\vdash$ the elms, **a** and **b**, exist

(48) $\exists x \exists y (\text{elm}(x) \wedge \text{elm}(y)) \vdash \exists z (x \leq z \wedge y \leq z \wedge \text{elms}(z))$

For any elm, there is a plural object elms, but given any two objects each of which is an elm, nothing in the theory guarantees that there is a plural object of which they are both part. The defect is remedied with an axiom that puts a condition on the part-whole relation. Informally, it states that for any two objects, there is a plural object that includes them *and nothing else*. The exclusion, (41) will verify, is necessary to license the inference of (47) that a plural object including elm a and elm b is itself elms:

(49) $\forall x \forall y \exists z (x \leq z \wedge y \leq z \wedge \forall u(u\mathbf{O}z \leftrightarrow (u\mathbf{O}x \vee u\mathbf{O}y)))$ (join)

(50) $x\mathbf{O}y \leftrightarrow_{\text{df}} \exists z(z \leq x \wedge z \leq y)$ (overlap)[14]

The momentary interest of the join axiom is that its statement does not use the singular and plural predicates 'elm(x)' and 'elms(x)'. Although the inference in (47) relates their extensions, it does not go beyond (41) in requiring axioms that use the predicates. But this is not a general remark about those inferences that one would accept knowing that for any elms, there is the plural object those elms. An important exception is (51):

(51) There exists an elm $\vdash$ The elms exist

(52) $\exists x \, \text{elm}(x) \vdash \exists y \, y = (\iota x)(\text{elms}(x))$

For any fixed enumeration of elms, the join axiom will guarantee the existence of a plural object that includes them.[15] But nothing in the theory passes from the existence of an elm to the existence of an object that comprehends all elms and only elms.[16]

This proves to be a crucial gap. Without a theory adequate to (51), we have no account of the speaker's competence to draw the most obvious inferences, those illustrating distributivity:

(53) Every one of the elms is tall $\vdash$ Every elm is tall

Recall that the objectual view introduces 'is-one-of(x, y)' to relate the object the elms to the objects quantified over in *every one of the elms*. The form of (53) is then (54):

(54) [Every x : is-one-of$(x,$ the elms)]tall(x)
       $\vdash$ [Every x : elm(x)]tall(x)

Without (51), a speaker is in no position to accept (54). He supposes that there may be a short elm and that there may be no object for *the elms* to refer to. With the elms nonexistent, everything that bears a relation to them is indeed tall. The premise is true, vacuously, but the conclusion is plainly false.[17]

We arrive now at the brink of paradox. If the objectual view is to explain what speakers know about plurals, reflected in inferences such as (53), it must articulate an axiom that will guarantee the existence of the plural object the elms if at least one elm exists. Mastery of the theory and axiom explains the knowledge of (53). We thus have the following axiom schema, which is commonly called a principle of *comprehension*. Its instances substitute singular predicates for N, certain choices of which give rise to Russell's paradox.[18]

(55) $\exists x N(x) \rightarrow \exists z\, z = (\imath x)(N + s(x))$ (comprehension)

(56) $\exists x\, \text{elm}(x) \rightarrow \exists z\, z = (\imath x)(\text{elms}(x))$[19]

We first reduce (55) to the standard form in which comprehension is usually stated, relying on the relevant clauses of the theory in (57) to (59):

(57) $\ulcorner F(\imath x)\Phi(x)\urcorner$ is true $\leftrightarrow \exists y(\ulcorner (\imath x)\Phi(x)\urcorner$ refers to $y \wedge \ulcorner F\urcorner$ is true of $y)$

(58) $\ulcorner (\imath x)\Phi(x)\urcorner$ refers to $\mathbf{a} \leftrightarrow \forall x(\Phi(x) \leftrightarrow x \leq \mathbf{a})$

(59) $N + s(x) \leftrightarrow_{\text{df}} \exists y(At(y) \wedge y \leq x) \wedge \forall y((At(y) \wedge y \leq x) \rightarrow N(y))$

Eliminating the definite description by (57) and (58), (55) becomes

(60) $\exists x N(x) \rightarrow \exists y \forall x(N + s(x) \leftrightarrow x \leq y)$.

Applying (59) to eliminate the plural operator, we then derive (61):

(61) $\exists x N(x) \rightarrow \exists y \forall x (\forall z ((At(z) \land z \leq x) \rightarrow N(z)) \leftrightarrow x \leq y)$

The consequent of (61) states that there is an object whose every part is such that any of its *singular* parts is an N, and that everything whose singular parts are each an N is part of that object. The transitivity of the part-whole relation reduces (61) to (62):[20]

(62) $\exists x N(x) \rightarrow \exists y \forall x ((At(x) \land x \leq y) \leftrightarrow N(x))$ (comprehension)

Formula (62) is a comprehension schema in a more familiar form.[21] For any predicate 'N', it (conditionally) asserts the existence of an object y that collects together in some sense the objects that 'N' denotes.

Comprehension is conditional on the existence of something N. This is necessary to avoid a contradiction that becomes apparent if we instantiate 'N' as the predicate *thing not identical to itself*:

(63) $\ldots \exists y \forall x ((At(x) \land x \leq y) \leftrightarrow \neg x = x)$

The clause asserts that there is some object a that includes all and only things not identical to themselves. Since there are none of these, one might at first take the clause to assert the existence of an empty class, which is no contradiction. Recall, however, the definition of 'At(x)':

(64) $At(x) \leftrightarrow_{df} \forall y (y \leq x \rightarrow y = x)$

If **a** is empty, then At(**a**). Since **a** meets the condition that At(**a**) and $\mathbf{a} \leq \mathbf{a}$, (63) requires that $\neg \mathbf{a} = \mathbf{a}$. Thus this clause, if unqualified, asserts the existence of something not identical to itself. This contradiction is avoided in (62). It withholds asserting the existence of the plural object unless the predicate denotes. Note that this is consistent with the meaning of the plural definite description *the things not identical to themselves*, which simply fails to refer.

3.3 Paradox

The paradox of the objectual view is this: there is no way to both give a true semantics for plural terms and avoid contradiction. The Russell predicate derives a contradiction from the comprehension axiom, but unlike the tame example just discussed, the plural description formed from the Russell predicate refers. Efforts to avoid contradiction lose reference, as we will see in section 3.4.

If comprehension has the form in (65), the Russell predicate to be substituted for Φ is ' $\neg R(x,x)$ '.

(65) $\ldots \exists y \forall x (R(x,y) \leftrightarrow \Phi(x))$

(66) $\exists x N(x) \rightarrow \exists y \forall x((At(x) \wedge x \leq y) \leftrightarrow N(x))$ (comprehension)

Given the comprehension principle in (66), (67) is the Russell predicate, which is equivalent to (68), by reflexivity:

(67) $\neg(At(x) \wedge x \leq x)$

(68) $\neg At(x)$

Note that (68) is true of nonatoms, that is, plural objects. These exist, and so the relevant instance of (66) entails (69), from which contradiction follows immediately in (70):

(69) $\exists y \forall x((At(x) \wedge x \leq y) \leftrightarrow \neg At(x))$

(70) $\exists y(At(y) \leftrightarrow \neg At(y))$

In the mereological setting, the Russell predicate is variously expressed by *nonatom*, *plural object*, or *thing that nothing is a proper part of*, and the comprehension principle will fail when it tries to fix the reference of such definite descriptions as *the nonatoms*, *the plural objects*, or *the things that nothing is a proper part of*. In a treatment of plurals that more closely mirrors set theory, the comprehension principle determines reference by a membership condition, as in (71), where the Russell predicate is, of course, $\neg x \in x$.

(71) $\ldots \exists y \forall x(x \in y \leftrightarrow N(x))$

The contradiction is then elicited by substituting for 'N' a complex phrase such as *sets that do not contain themselves*, or *things that do not contain themselves*. The relative clause expresses something equivalent to the Russell predicate. The head noun denotes plural objects, either because plural objects are identified with sets or because the head noun, e.g., *things*, denotes everything there is, including plural objects. The objectual view requires a comprehension principle to secure the reference of plural terms. Whatever relation is used in the comprehension principle to do the work of '$At(x) \wedge x \leq y$' or '$x \in y$' comes back to haunt the objectual view of plural reference. The plural terms formed from the Russell predicates refer, but the comprehension principle leads to a contradiction. Boolos (1984, 1985a, 1985b) has put the problem sharply in examples similar to the following two:

(72) If there is a set that does not contain itself, then there are sets among which is every set that does not contain itself.

(73) If there is a set that does not contain itself, then there is a set a member of which is every set that does not contain itself.

The first example is a truism, but the second is false. Yet the objectual view does not tell them apart. It would, if it could, assign the same reference to the plural term in (72) and the singular term in (73).

Boolos's examples translate for the mereologist as (74) and (75).

(74) If there is a plural object, then there are the plural objects.

(75) If there is a plural object, then there is the plural object that every plural object is an atomic part of.

Statement (74) is obviously true, but no believer in plural objects can believe (75). Yet the objectual view cannot tell apart the plural term in (74) and the singular term in (75).

3.4 Ways out[22]

Restrictions on the comprehension principle can save the objectual theory from paradox without, however, saving it from empirical inadequacy. The plural definite descriptions projected from Russell predicates, for example, *the plural objects* or *the sets that do not contain themselves*, are misinterpreted or not interpreted at all, as are the definite descriptions *the objects* or *the sets*, which include in their reference the things denoted by the Russell predicates. Thus, even a restricted version of comprehension will fail to validate (72) or (74), and it will fail to distinguish the reference of the plural term from the corresponding singular term in (73) or (75).

Suppose first that the comprehension principle were qualified to allow for referential failure:

(76) $\exists y \; y = (\iota x)(N + s(x)) \to (66)$

Then the existence of an object that is the plural objects is not asserted unless the plural term *the plural objects* refers.

With comprehension so qualified, the theory only avoids contradiction to fail at an account of distributivity. With the potential for referential failure, the theory will not license what every speaker knows, the validity of inference (77):

(77) Every one of the elms is tall $\vdash$ Every elm is tall

The weakened comprehension principle no longer guarantees for an elm the existence of the elms. We want a less global restriction on comprehension. It should validate inferences about distributivity such as (77), while watching out for the Russell predicate. So consider (78):

(78) $\exists x(N(x) \wedge At(x)) \to \exists y \forall x((At(x) \wedge x \le y) \leftrightarrow (N(x) \wedge At(x)))$

Without contradiction, (78) validates the inference in (77). If there is an elm that is not tall, then, by restricted comprehension, there is a (plural) object whose atomic parts are all and only the individual elms, from which it follows that not every one of the elms is tall, as (77) requires. Now, substituting the Russell predicate for 'N' gives (79), which is simply true, given the false antecedent clause:

(79) $\exists x(\neg At(x) \wedge At(x)) \rightarrow \exists y \forall x((At(x) \wedge x \leq y)$
$\leftrightarrow (\neg At(x) \wedge At(x)))$[23]

Although it delivers the correct interpretation of *the elms* and the like, the theory is silent on the reference of *the nonatoms*, *the plural objects*, or *the things that nothing is a proper part of*, since the conditional in (78) effectively excludes descriptions based on the Russell predicate.

Notice that paradox can be avoided without the conditional in (78). No contradiction is derived from the comprehension principle in (80). Instead of leaving the descriptions based on the Russell predicate uninterpreted, (80) will just get them wrong.

(80) $\exists y \forall x((At(x) \wedge x \leq y) \leftrightarrow (N(x) \wedge At(x)))$

Substituting the Russell predicate for 'N' gives (81), which has the consequence shown in (82) that any part of **a**, the alleged referent for *the nonatoms* or *the plural objects*, is itself not atomic, which is to say that it too has proper parts.

(81) $\exists y \forall x((At(x) \wedge x \leq y) \leftrightarrow (\neg At(x) \wedge At(x)))$

(82) a. $\forall x((At(x) \wedge x \leq \mathbf{a}) \leftrightarrow (\neg At(x) \wedge At(x)))$
     b. $\forall x(x \leq \mathbf{a} \rightarrow \neg At(x))$
     c. $\forall x(x \leq \mathbf{a} \rightarrow \exists y(\neg y = x \wedge y \leq x))$

The unconditional form of restricted comprehension in (80) is thus committed to the existence of an atomless object, any part of which has proper parts. Even if one could decide which such object is the intended referent, it would not fit *the nonatoms* or *the plural objects*. Note, first of all, that the referent of *the elms* is surely among the objects to which *the nonatoms* or *the plural objects* is intended to refer. It is, however, no part of **a**, since the referent of *the elms* itself has the elms as atomic parts. More generally, **a** is not a fitting referent for count-noun phrases such as *the nonatoms* or *the plural objects*, since the objects over which one expects to distribute their reference do not exist in **a**. Were these terms to refer to **a**, any sentence of the form in (83) would be (vacuously) true, and any sentence of the form in (84) would turn out to be false.

(83) a. Every one of the nonatoms is *F*.
      b. Every one of the plural objects is *F*.
      c. [every $x : \text{At}(x) \wedge x \leq \mathbf{a}]Fx$

(84) a. Some of the nonatoms are *F*.
      b. Some of the plural objects are *F*.
      c. [some $x : \text{At}(x) \wedge x \leq \mathbf{a}]Fx$

The objectual view relies on extralogical axioms, comprehension, in particular, to secure the reference of plural terms. Restricting comprehension will avoid paradox, as we have just seen, but it still fails the semantics of certain plural terms.

In a more familiar set-theoretic setting, Russell's paradox is resolved using proper classes.[24] The same limitation on the objectual view is found there.

Suppose that there is a domain of individuals, singular objects in the ordinary sense. Crucially, there is also a disjoint domain of proper classes $\mathscr{C}$, or the like, into which the plural terms will now refer. Their reference is determined by the following restricted comprehension principle:[25]

(85) $\exists x \text{N}(x) \rightarrow \exists y \forall x (x \in y \leftrightarrow (\text{N}(x) \wedge \neg \mathscr{C}x))$
      (restricted comprehension)

The elms refers to that proper class whose members are all and only the individual elms, and this is sufficient for distributivity in (77). Substituting for 'N' the Russell predicate *things that are not members of themselves* leads only to the conclusion that the comprehending class is not itself an individual. Its members are just those individuals that are not members of themselves:

(86) $\exists y \forall x (x \in y \leftrightarrow \neg x \in x \wedge \neg \mathscr{C}x)$

The interest of the theory is that it assigns a plausible interpretation to *the things that are not members of themselves*, the plural term based on the Russell predicate, but it remains a limitation on this way out that an NP such as *the proper classes* ends up referring to the empty class even though the theory supposes that there are many proper classes. According to the theory, the NP refers to that class containing all and only the individuals that are proper classes. It is not a contradiction, just wrong. Similarly, the NP *the things that there are* ends up referring to the individual objects that there are. It does not include in its reference the proper classes. There is this populous domain that the theorist has explicit knowledge of but no expression to refer to its inhabitants, and he cannot use *the things that there are* to refer to whatever he believes there is. This is a straightforward linguistic failure, which will be overcome when plurals are treated as predicates.

The argument against the objectual view of plural reference, whether it is reference to a proper class or to a sum or to whatever, is that it falls into Russell's paradox or it falls short. If it avoids Russell's paradox, then it will misinterpret expressions like *the plural objects, the nonatoms, the things that are not atomic parts of themselves, the proper classes, the things that there are*. It will fail to validate elementary inferences about distributivity that govern our usage of these terms, such as those in (87):

(87) a. If there is a plural object, then there are the plural objects.
     b. If every one of the plural objects has mass, then every plural object has mass.

Moreover, if such plural terms do not refer or *the plural objects* refers to something with no atomic parts or *the proper classes* to the null proper class, then such a theory will also end up judging statements that are analytically false as valid:

(88) a. If there is a plural object, then every one of the plural objects is not a plural object.
     b. If there is a proper class, then every one of the proper classes is not a proper class.

Talk about the plural objects or the proper classes is no different from talk about the elms. A practical theorist committed to the objectual view of plurals might be unimpressed that the theory fails to interpret certain pathological plural terms. Why not just ignore all of this semantical vocabulary: *nonatoms, plural objects, proper classes*, and even *things that there are*? Use it in the metalanguage, and don't worry about the larger fragment that would include it in the object language. Enjoining this practice is the fact that natural language seems to be extensible. If one believes that there are things of a certain sort, one can always recruit a singular noun to denote them, such as *plural object* or *proper class*. Speakers do not care whether they are talking about elms or plural objects. This is certainly the way things appear, and it is the (impossible) burden of the practical theorist to explain it away if his semantics is not going to do it justice. As Boolos points out, the strength of second-order logic and its nominalistic interpretation, which the next section introduces, is that it allows us to refer to and to quantify over whatever we think there is. Also to its credit is that it secures the reference of all plural terms without recourse to any particular metaphysics or extralogical axioms.[26] (Note 26 discusses ways out that appeal to an infinite hierarchy of terms, [*proper*] *class$_i$*.) Once we leave the mereologists behind, we will need events and Davidsonian logical form to hold the sentence together and to say how things are with the ordinary things talked about. Once we have events and Davidsonian logical form, we will see that there is no need for the plural objects, and if we are going to make sense of all plural NPs, including, for example, *the plural objects*, then we had better not have an objectual theory of plurals at all.

4   Second-Order Logic and the Semantics of Plural Terms

Boolos validates the inferences (89) through (91) and the like by taking plural NPs to be predicates.

(89) If there is a proper class, then there are the proper classes.

(90) If there is a thing that there is, then there are the things that there are.

(91) If there is a proper class that does not contain itself, then there are the proper classes that do not contain themselves.

He does so by keeping the nominalism while discarding the grammar. Plural NPs are taken to be predicates. In his nominalistic semantics, the semantic value of a predicate is nothing like a class or its extension. Its values are anything it is true of. The predicate *mortal* denotes Socrates and it also denotes other philosophers as well. So it goes for *the elms*, which is now taken to be a predicate. It does not denote an object that comprehends all elms. Rather, it denotes each elm. On this view, the NP *the proper classes that do not contain themselves* denotes each proper class that does not contain itself, which is what we want. Since we do not ask the plural NP to refer to a comprehending object, we needn't worry about what would happen if such an object were in the domain of quantification. In this way Boolos renders such NPs as *the proper classes* intelligible. If plurals are indeed predicates, then the terms of a sentence such as (92) all turn out to be predicates. I then put them in a Davidsonian logical form: (93). Events are the glue that holds it all together, and they are relied on to explain the connection between the sentence and how things have to be with the individual elms in the world.

(92) The elms are clustered.

(93) $\exists e(\text{cluster}(e) \land \forall x(\text{Theme}(e, x) \leftrightarrow \text{the elms}(x)))$

4.1 Syntax

Second-order comprehension is a *logical* truth:[27]

(94) $\exists X \, \forall x(Xx \leftrightarrow \mathrm{N}'x)$

From the logically trivial '$\forall x(\mathrm{F}x \leftrightarrow \mathrm{F}x)$', '$\exists X \, \forall x(Xx \leftrightarrow \mathrm{F}x)$' follows by second-order existential generalization, and (94) then follows *via* substitution of a formula for a predicate letter.[28]

As Boolos (1985b) relates, second-order logic includes a rule of inference that allows the "substitution of a formula for a relation letter in an already demonstrated formula, ..., on a par with substitution of a formula for a propositional variable or relettering of a variable." "It is well known that in the presence of the other standard rules of logic, the substitution rule and the comprehension schema are deductively equivalent; given either, one can derive the other." The above derives it in one direction. Boolos also gives the proof deriving the substitution rule from the comprehension schema.

Consider now second-order comprehension in a form logically equivalent to (94):

(95) $\exists x \mathrm{N}'(x) \rightarrow \exists X(\exists x Xx \wedge \forall x(Xx \leftrightarrow \mathrm{N}'(x)))$

Boolos proposes that plurals should have second-order logical forms because (95) schematizes an *obvious* truth about the plural noun phrase *some things* (and the plural pronoun *them*):[29]

(96) If there is an N', then there are some things such that every one of them is an N' and every N' is one of them.

True to second-order comprehension, any predicate of the language can replace 'N'', including Russell predicates:

(97) If there is a thing that is not a member of itself, then there are some things such that every thing that is not a member of itself is one of them and every one of them is a thing that is not a member of itself.

Given that the comprehension schema is deductively equivalent to second-order logic, we can argue from the obvious truth of instances of (96) to the general conclusion that second-order logic is the logic of the plural *some things*. Inferences provable from its logical form will be sound in the natural language, and inferences in the natural language that seem to depend only on the meaning of *some things* ought to be logically valid. If we accept, then, that *some things* has a second-order logical form, we can have no doubt that the logical form of 'some $N+s$' ought to be '$[\exists X : \exists x Xx \land \forall x(Xx \to Nx)]$' and the logical form of 'the $N+s$', '$(\iota X)(\exists x Xx \land \forall x(Xx \leftrightarrow Nx))$'. Thus second-order logic is the logic for all plurals. Frequent appeals to intuition will ultimately vindicate this conclusion. In one instance Boolos (1985b) points out that speakers accept existential generalization on plural definite descriptions, which is logically valid in its second-order schematization, as required:

(98) If the rocks rained down, then there are some things that rained down.

(99) rain-down$((\iota X)(\exists x Xx \land \forall x(Xx \leftrightarrow \text{rock}(x))))$
    $\to [\exists X : \exists x Xx]$ rain-down(X)

The assignment of a logical form to *some things* and the asserted fit between logical rules and accepted inferences is, of course, an empirical conjecture. Boolos's remarks show that we can assert the logical form of *some things* to be '$[\exists X : \exists x Xx]$' with the same confidence that we assert the logical form of *something* to be '$\exists x$'.

Let us revisit now those inferences that tested the objectual view. Recall that a speaker will fail to draw the inference in (101) unless he knows (100), for which the objectual view must stipulate comprehension.

(100) There is an elm $\vdash$ There exist the elms

(101) Every one of the elms is tall $\vdash$ Every elm is tall

In a second-order setting the inference in (100) follows without stipulation, since it is an instance of (95), which is logically equivalent to second-order comprehension (94). Second-order logic is thus sufficient for the inference in (101) if the logical form for *every one of the elms* predicates *the elms* of the objects quantified over, as in (102):[30]

(102) [Every $x : (\iota X)(\exists x Xx \land \forall x(Xx \leftrightarrow \text{elm}(x)))(x)]$ tall(x)
    $\vdash$ [Every $x : \text{elm}(x)]$ tall(x)

In comparing the objectual and predicative views, the question I have sought to answer is what must a speaker know about plurals, knowing the validity of certain inferences in which they occur. The answer, according to the predicative view, is that a speaker must know that plurals have a certain logical syntax from which the inferences will follow as a matter of logic (with the possible qualification mentioned in n. 30). A speaker will accept the inferences without thinking that there exist objects comprehending predicates.

4.2   Semantics

First in chapter 1 and again in the preceding section I claimed that plurals
are second-order expressions. For example, the logical form of *some elms*
is the one in (94):

(94) $[\exists X : \exists x Xx \land \forall x(Xx \rightarrow \text{elm}(x))]$

As a claim about meaning, this is sensible only if it is presented with
an interpretation, one that can be judged to fit, or not, our understanding
of plural terms, specifically, our understanding of their reference. In a
systematic semantics this question about reference takes the particular
form of how to fill in the right-hand side of a biconditional such as (103):

(103) σ satisfies $\ulcorner[\exists X : \text{F}]\,\text{G}\urcorner \leftrightarrow \ldots$

To answer, we must know what are the values of second-order variables.

In urging my claim about the logical form of plurals, I have relied
on the standard interpretation of the logical connectives and first-order
quantifiers, and I will continue to do so. But I have also relied on what I
will now call the *naive interpretation* of second-order variables and quantifiers.[31] Second-order (104) is *naively* interpreted as a description of the
predicate that denotes something and is true of everything that is an elm
and nothing else.

(104) $(\iota X)(\exists x Xx \land \forall x(Xx \leftrightarrow \text{elm}(x)))$

Since there is an elm, the description fits the predicate *elm*. In this respect,
the naive interpretation is correct: the term in (104) is a predicate, and it
is true of exactly those things that *elm* is true of. We will see, however, that
it is wrong to quantify over predicates to get this result.

We have been misled to think that the naive interpretation, in quantifying over predicates, escapes the paradox that surrounds the objectual
view of the plural term *the things that are not members of themselves*. It is
easy to be misled: (105) is interpreted as a description of that predicate
that denotes something and is true of everything that is not a member of
itself and nothing else.

(105) $(\iota X)(\exists x Xx \land \forall x(Xx \leftrightarrow \neg x \in x))$

It appears innocuously to describe the predicate *is not a member of itself*.

More generally, the naive interpretation makes the second-order comprehension schema sound true. Certainly, any formula that one might
substitute for 'N(x)' in (106) determines a monadic predicate:

(106) $\exists X \forall x(Xx \leftrightarrow \text{N}(x))$

If we substitute for 'N' the predicate *thing that is not a member of itself*, we assert, again innocuously, the existence of a predicate identical to *is not a member of itself*:

(107) $\exists X \forall x (Xx \leftrightarrow \neg x \in x)$

There is no contradiction, and there are in fact some things that the predicate denotes.

To expose the lurking paradox, reconsider how first- and second-order variables are being interpreted when the logical form of *the elms* is interpreted naively as in (108). The paraphrase is in (109): .

(108) $(\imath X)(\exists x Xx \wedge \forall x (Xx \leftrightarrow elm(x)))$

(109) There is *a predicate* such that *it* is true of *everything* that is an elm and nothing else.[32]

Note first that the naive interpretation is committed to the existence of things other than elms, namely predicates. Since we are elsewhere committed to them, I will not indulge the worry that introspection about the meaning of *the elms* does not reveal a commitment to the existence of predicates. Instead, my concern is the form that (109) allegedly takes. The standard interpretation of the first-order variables is that they range over everything there is and that they occur wherever singular predication does. But then the logical form that (109) paraphrases ought to be an *objectual* quantification over predicates and ought to contain some relation between predicates and elms:

(110) $[\exists y : Py] \forall x (of(x, y) \leftrightarrow elm(x))$

Put another way, whether or not (109) is a fair interpretation of the second-order (108), it is also an interpretation of the first-order (110). In general, any naive interpretation is also an interpretation of a first-order sentence similar in form to (110).

This, however, is not the form of a schema that will always yield truths, as substituting the Russell predicate shows:

(111) $[\exists y : Py] \forall x (of(x, y) \leftrightarrow \neg of(x, x))$

Formula (111) leads immediately to the contradiction that for some predicate p, $of(p, p) \leftrightarrow \neg of(p, p)$. If the naive interpretation is the correct one for the second-order sentences, we are left in a quandary. The same interpretation serves both schemas (112) and (113), a logically valid second-order schema and the paradoxical first-order comprehension principle:

(112) $\exists Y \forall x (Yx \leftrightarrow N(x))$

(113) $[\exists y : Py]\ \forall x(\text{of}(x, y) \leftrightarrow N(x))$

The way out is to recall that the naive interpretation *sounds* true in all its instances, including (107), with a Russellian predicate. It must be that we hear the quantifier *everything* in (114) restricted to exclude predicates:

(114) There is a *predicate* such that *it* is true of *everything* that is an N and nothing else.

(115) $[\exists y : Py][\forall x : \neg Px](\text{of}(x, y) \leftrightarrow N(x))$

There are first-order logical forms that render naive quantification over predicates, but they fall under schema (115). Presumably, (115) embodies a true fact about our conception of predicates, but it is not a *logical* truth. It has, in fact, a form identical to the restricted comprehension schema (85) of the objectual view.

Suppose that one were still to insist on the naive interpretation that second-order quantifiers disguise quantifying over objects of a particular sort. One is then claiming that (116) and (117) mean the same thing.

(116) $[\exists y : Py][\forall x : \neg Px](\text{of}(x, y) \leftrightarrow N(x))$

(117) $\exists Y \qquad \forall x \qquad (Yx \qquad \leftrightarrow N(x))$

But this can be only if a first-order quantifier occurring in a second-order logical form, '$\forall x$' in (117), does not range over all the objects there are. The universe of discourse must be restricted a priori to exclude predicates, which in effect turns into nonsense such singular descriptions and quantifiers as *the predicate*, '$(\iota x)(Px)$', and *every predicate*, '$[\forall x : Px]$'.

Burdened with second-order plural terms, we must look again for an interpretation of second-order quantifiers and variables. All instances of second-order comprehension should be true without any restrictions on the universe of discourse, and the interpretation should not neglect the fact that predication of *any* object is a first-order notion.

Boolos (1984, 1985a, 1985b) suggests that we use plurals, which after all we do understand, to convey the interpretation of their second-order logical forms. The suggestion is the familiar one that we use the language being interpreted to state its semantics. Thus the semantics of the singular 'some N' and the plural 'some N+s' are to be stated in parallel fashion, in the spirit of (118) and (119) respectively:

(118) $\ulcorner$[some v : N]F$\urcorner$ is true $\leftrightarrow$ something that $\ulcorner$N$\urcorner$ is true of $\ulcorner$F$\urcorner$ is true of

(119) $\ulcorner$[some V : N+s]F$\urcorner$ is true $\leftrightarrow$ some things that $\ulcorner$N+s$\urcorner$ is true of $\ulcorner$F$\urcorner$ is true of

In a truth definition adequate to the syntax of quantifiers and variables, the semantic relation *is true of* is formalized as a relation of satisfaction by an assignment of objects to variables. In a strictly first-order language, the assignment is a sequence of objects, a function that assigns to each variable a unique object. The standard clause for 'some N' is the following:

(120) Φ is true $\leftrightarrow$ $\exists s(s$ is a sequence $\wedge$ s satisfies Φ)

(121) s satisfies $\ulcorner$[some $v : $N] F$\urcorner$ $\leftrightarrow$ $\exists x \exists t$(sequence(t) $\wedge$ $t(v) = x$
$\qquad \wedge$ $\forall u((u$ is a variable $\wedge$ $u \neq v) \rightarrow s(u) = t(u))$
$\qquad \wedge$ t satisfies $\ulcorner$N$\urcorner$ $\wedge$ t satisfies $\ulcorner$F$\urcorner$)

In the second-order language, we cannot simply extend this notion of a sequence to the second-order variables. There is no unique object that can serve as *the* value of a second-order variable or as the reference of a predicate. Boolos proposes that a second-order variable be assigned many objects, in the way a predicate can be thought of as denoting each of the objects it is true of. In the clauses that follow, the assignment relation is given as a predicate S denoting pairs $\langle v, x \rangle$ of variable and object. This allows us to use the plural *some pairs* to quantify over assignments. Thus the clause for 'some N + s' reads as in (122):

(122) The pairs S, assigning values to variables, satisfy
$\qquad \ulcorner$[Some $V : $N + s]F$\urcorner$ iff some things are such that some pairs T
$\qquad$ assign them to the variable V, T and S assign the same values to
$\qquad$ other variables, and the pairs T satisfy $\ulcorner$N$\urcorner$ and $\ulcorner$F$\urcorner$.

Clauses like (122) meet all our desiderata. First, predication of a singular object in interpretation does coincide with the occurrence of a first-order variable in logical form. Second, to indulge a latent worry, second-order quantification does not assert the existence of anything beyond what we are already committed to. Third, all instances of second-order comprehension are true, and the universe of discourse is whatever there is.

Here then, is the definition of truth for a sample of the relevant operators:

(123) Φ is true $\leftrightarrow$ $\exists S(S$ are assignment pairs $\wedge$ S satisfy Φ)

(124) S satisfy $\ulcorner$F($v_1, \ldots, v_n$)$\urcorner$
$\qquad \leftrightarrow$ $\exists x_1 \ldots \exists x_n(S(\langle v_1, x_1 \rangle) \wedge \ldots \wedge S(\langle v_n, x_n \rangle) \wedge F(x_1, \ldots, x_n))$

(125) S satisfy $\ulcorner$V$v\urcorner$ $\leftrightarrow$ $\exists x(S(\langle v, x \rangle) \wedge S(\langle V, x \rangle))$

(126) S satisfy $\ulcorner \neg$F$\urcorner$ $\leftrightarrow$ $\neg S$ satisfy $\ulcorner$F$\urcorner$

(127) S satisfy $\ulcorner$F $\wedge$ G$\urcorner$ $\leftrightarrow$ S satisfy $\ulcorner$F$\urcorner$ $\wedge$ S satisfy $\ulcorner$G$\urcorner$

(128) S satisfy $\ulcorner$[some v : N]F$\urcorner$

    $\leftrightarrow$ [some thing x][some pairs T]$(\forall y(T(\langle v, y\rangle) \leftrightarrow y = x)$

      $\wedge\ \forall u((u$ is a (first- or second-order) variable $\wedge\ u \neq v)$

      $\rightarrow \forall x(T(\langle u, x\rangle) \leftrightarrow S(\langle u, x\rangle)))$

      $\wedge\ T$ satisfy $\ulcorner$N$\urcorner \wedge\ T$ satisfy $\ulcorner$F$\urcorner$)

(129) S satisfy $\ulcorner$[some V : N+s]F$\urcorner$

    $\leftrightarrow$ [some things X][some pairs T]$(\forall y(T(\langle V, y\rangle) \leftrightarrow Xy)$

      $\wedge\ \forall u((u$ is a (first- or second-order) variable $\wedge\ u \neq V)$

      $\rightarrow \forall x(T(\langle u, x\rangle) \leftrightarrow S(\langle u, x\rangle)))$

      $\wedge\ T$ satisfy $\ulcorner$N$\urcorner \wedge\ T$ satisfy $\ulcorner$F$\urcorner$)[33]

The difference between plural 'the N+s' and singular terms such as 'the set of the N+s', 'the group of the N+s', or 'the plural object the atomic parts of which are the N+s' that distinguishes the valid inferences of (72) and (74) from those that are invalid in (73) and (75) is just the difference between singular and plural reference.

(72) If there is a set that does not contain itself, then there are sets among which is every set that does not contain itself.

(73) If there is a set that does not contain itself, then there is a set a member of which is every set that does not contain itself.

(74) If there is a plural object, then there are the plural objects.

(75) If there is a plural object, then there is the plural object an atomic part of which is every plural object.

There is no one object that answers the singular description in (73) or (75), but in (72) or (74) there are many objects that answer the description embedded in the plural term, and each of these is just one of the semantic values for that term. Since plural terms do not refer to a comprehending object, there is no need for a principle of comprehension and no threat from Russell's paradox. Whatever the choice of N, if there is an N (and another N), then 'the N+s' is meaningful and refers, which reflects a systematic fact about our use of plurals.

How is it that speakers who understand a sentence with plurals come to know that things have to be a certain way in the world among the first-order objects? When Burge and Link observed that the truth conditions for a sentence like (130) could not be reduced to predications about the familiar objects at hand, the individual elms, they looked for a new concrete particular to anchor predication.

(130) The elms are clustered in the forest.

They thought they found it in aggregates or mereological sums: *the elms* refers to something discernible in the world, of which the individual elms are a part, and speakers grasp concepts such as *clustered* that apply directly to it. A theory mediates between parts and whole, so that one infers that something happens to the individual elms, just as one infers from *Carl runs down the field* that something happens to Carl's legs. This happy theory founders on Russell's paradox. *The elms* turns out not to denote a plural object. It is a predicate denoting many individual objects. The question of plural reference then arises again: How does one grasp the sentence's import for how things are in the world? How does one make sense of essential plurals without plural objects? The mereologists were right to look for new concrete particulars. The ones they should have been looking for are *events*. Sentence (130) gets its grip on the world because the speaker understands that it is true only if there is an event of being clustered in the forest such that each first-order object that *the elms* denotes, that is, each elm, participates in that event, as in (131).

(131) $\exists e(\text{cluster}(e) \land \forall x(\text{Theme}(e, x) \leftrightarrow \text{the-elms}(x)))$

Chapter 3
Polyadicity and Plural Reference

In the account of plurals, Davidsonian decomposition into θ-roles and events plays an active role in the logical syntax: the constituents of the decomposition can be separated from one another, they sometimes apply to overlapping but distinct events, and the cross-reference to events that holds it all together itself has the structure of pronouns. All of this differs markedly from the well-behaved syntax of primitive polyadicity, according to which a verb is simply polyadic and atomic in logical form: $V(e, \alpha_1, \ldots, \alpha_n)$. It always occurs with a full valence of argument positions and expresses a relation of its NP arguments to the same event e. The usual view of a sentence composed of an $(n + 1)$-place relation $V(e, \alpha_1, \ldots, \alpha_n)$ and n NPs is that the n NP argument positions of the verb are always occupied or directly bound by the n NPs. The next chapter on essential separation is a single-minded attack on primitive polyadicity. In this chapter I show two other respects in which any empirically adequate account of plurals will come to resemble mine. First, for reasons independent of Russell's paradox, variables have to be sorted into singular and plural anyway, so quantifiers are classified according to the sort of variable they bind.[1] Second, any predicate that expresses a relation between an event and some pluralities is true only of those pluralities that exhaust all of the participants of the event. A predicate '$V(X, \ldots, e)$' is true of a plurality X and event e only if the plurality is all the participants that bear the relevant θ-role to e. It seems that the lexical analysis of polyadic predicates is Davidsonian, that is, unable to express any relation between objects that does not derive from their participation in the same event:

(1) '$V(e, X_1, \ldots, X_n)$' is true
  $\leftrightarrow V(e) \wedge \forall x(\Theta_1(e, x) \leftrightarrow X_1 x) \wedge \ldots \wedge \forall x(\Theta_n(e, x) \leftrightarrow X_n x)$

In the next chapter, to show that the fault lies with primitive polyadicity, I will assume that the objections raised here to some versions of polyadic logical form have been accommodated in some way.

1   Variables Must Be Sorted into Singular (First-Order) and Plural (Second-Order)

The objectual view of plural reference, that plurals refer to plural objects, seems to demand the least from logical form. As in chapter 2, section 3, simply expand the universe to include plural objects, allow that lexical predicates denote them and that plural terms refer to them:

(2) 'cluster(x)' is true of $\mathbf{a}$ $\leftrightarrow$ $\mathbf{a}$ is clustered

(3) 'elms(x)' is true of $\mathbf{a}$ $\leftrightarrow$ $\mathbf{a}$ is clustered

(4) '$(\iota x)(\mathrm{elms}(x))$' refers to $\mathbf{a}$ $\leftrightarrow$ $\forall y(\mathrm{elms}(y) \leftrightarrow y \leq \mathbf{a})$

Some predicates, such as 'clever(x)', may reduce plural predication to a property of singular objects. Others, such as 'cluster(x)', crucially, will not. This view may also recognize that sentences such as (5) are systematically ambiguous.

(5) The boys lifted four pianos.

A distributive operator D would then be introduced so that the derived predicate denotes an object only if its constituent singular objects meet some condition:[2]

(6) '$Dx[\exists y : 4(y) \wedge \mathrm{pianos}(y)]\mathrm{lift}(x, y)$' is true of $\mathbf{a}$
    $\leftrightarrow$ $\forall z((\mathrm{At}(z) \wedge z \leq \mathbf{a}) \rightarrow$ '$[\exists y : 4(y) \wedge \mathrm{pianos}(y)]\mathrm{lift}(x, y)$'
    is true of z)

(7) $\mathrm{At}(x) \leftrightarrow_{\mathrm{df}} \forall z(z \leq x \rightarrow z = x)$[3]

On this view, the lexical content of quantifiers will also have to be adjusted if they are to express a relation, as in (8), between predicates that denote objects in the enlarged domain.

(8) $[Qx : Ax]Bx$

(9) Few elms are immortal.

(10) Few elms are clustered in the forest.

So long as there were no plural objects, our understanding of the quantifier Q was that it says something about the number of objects that 'A' is true of and the number of objects that 'B' is true of. Sentence (9) was said to be true just in case the objects that both *elm* and *immortal* are true of are few. The quantifiers simply "count" whatever objects the variables range over, that is, whatever objects the predicates are true of. With the variables ranging over plural objects as well, the relationship between quantifier and the predicates it applies to cannot be so simple. The objects that are (groups of) elms and clusters in the forest are not the objects that (10) asserts to be few. The quantifier needs to be supplemented with a notion of atomic parts. It is the atomic parts of the clusters of elms that are said to be few. It should count against this view that such operations on the parts of the denoted objects ar not fully general. Why can't one say, *Much cakes were gathered on the table*? Nevertheless, (11) appears to be adequate for both the semidistributive interpretation of (10) and for those interpretations like (9) where the matrix predicate incidentally imposes a distributive condition on the objects it denotes.[4]

(11) σ satisfies $\ulcorner[\text{few } v_i : \Phi]\Psi\urcorner$
$\leftrightarrow [\text{few } x : \text{At}(x) \land \exists y \exists \sigma_0(\sigma_0 \approx_{v_i} \sigma \land x \leq y \land \sigma_0(v_i) = y$
$\land \sigma_0 \text{ satisfies } \Phi)]$
$\exists y \exists \sigma_0(\sigma_0 \approx_{v_i} \sigma \land x \leq y \land \sigma_0(v_i) = y \land \sigma_0 \text{ satisfies } \Phi$
$\land \sigma_0 \text{ satisfies } \Psi)$

(Here '$\sigma_0 \approx_{v_i} \sigma$' abbreviates '$\forall j(j \neq i \rightarrow \sigma_0(v_i) = \sigma(v_i))$'.) There appears to be no need for a syntax that distinguishes singular and plural variables and quantifiers that choose between them. The unsorted variables of (8) is the general pattern. Such talk as there is about the properties of atomic individuals is left to the lexical semantics.[5] This view claims to take on plurals, at least the core cases of the sum-of-plurals and semidistributive interpretations, without any serious consequences for logical form.

The failure to distinguish singular and plural variables turns out, however, to stand in the way of a fully general account of semidistributivity. When a semidistributive quantifier includes within its scope an increasing quantifier, as in (12), (11) derives an adequate interpretation equivalent to (13), namely, that few composers participate in collaborations on four operas.

(12) a. Few composers collaborated on four operas.
  b. $[\text{few } x : \text{composers}(x)][\exists y : 4(y) \land \text{operas}(y)] \text{ collaborate}(x, y)$

(13) $[\text{few } x : \text{At}(x) \land Cx][\exists z : x \leq z \land Cz][\exists y : 4(y) \land Oy]$
  $\text{collaborate}(z, y)$

But when its scope includes a nonincreasing quantifier, the semidistributive quantifier is misinterpreted. Compare (14) and (15):

(14) Few composers collaborated with some other composers on no
       more than four operas.

(15) Few composers collaborated on no more than four operas.

Sentence (14) has an interpretation that (15) lacks. This is the interpretation where *some other composers* includes within its scope *no more than
four operas*:

(16) [few $x : Cx$][$\exists z : \neg x = z \land Cz$][$(\leq 4)y : Oy$] collaborate$(x, y, z)$

The interpretation is falsified under trivial conditions. Suppose that there
are many composers and, say, exactly one composer never collaborated
with any other composer. Then (16) is false simply because every one of
many composers collaborated with that one composer on no more than
four operas. In chapter 8, I will be concerned with how to avoid assigning
this interpretation to (15). Observe here that this interpretation, under the
scope assignment in (17), is the only one available according to (11).

(17) [few $x : $ composers(x)][$(\leq 4)y : $ operas(y)] collaborate(x, y)

The interpretation that (11) derives is equivalent to (18), which is the
trivially false one.

(18) *[few $x : $ At$(x) \land Cx$][$\exists z : x \leq z \land Cz$][$(\leq 4)y : Oy$]
       collaborate(z, y)

    Consider next what is required to express the intended interpretation
of (15). A composer is counterevidence to the claim that there are few
only if no more than four operas were among the collaborations he took
part in:

(19) [few $x : $ At$(x) \land Cx$][$(\leq 4)y : Oy$][$\exists z : x \leq z \land Cz$]
       collaborate(z, y)

The semidistributive interpretation of (15) is equivalent to (19): few are
the individual composers who each collaborated on no more than four
operas with others. Suppose that Rogers and Hart were the authors of
three operas and Rogers and Hammerstein the authors of three more, and
suppose that neither Hart nor Hammerstein worked on anything else.
Having collaborated with others on six operas, Rogers is no counterexample to (15), but there had better not be many like Hart or Hammerstein.

    It is crucial that the variable 'x' in (19) be restricted to atomic individ-
uals. The correct interpretation is not simply a matter of reversing the
relative scope of *no more than four operas* and an implicit quantifier over
groups. The logical form (20), which omits the restriction to atomic individuals, is trivially false too.

(20) *[few $x : Cx$]$(_\Psi[(\leq 4)y : Oy][\exists z : x \leq z \wedge Cz]$ collaborate$(z, y))$

Those groups that pair a composer with the composer who collaborates with no one are values for 'x' that satisfy Ψ in (20), and every composer is found among these groups.

Given the reference to plural objects and the basic account of such sentences as *The composers collaborated*, it is not open to this view to imagine that a basic predicate like 'composers(x)' denotes only singular objects. If the analysis of (15) is to avoid the absurd interpretations in (18) and (20), it must be that the quantifier *few* selects predicates that denote only singular objects:

(21) [few $x : At(x) \wedge \Phi]\Psi[x]$

This is as much as to say that variables are sorted into singular and plural and quantifiers into which sort of variable they select. *Four composers* allows a variable that ranges over plural and singular objects: '$[\exists X : 4(X) \wedge$ composers$(X)]$'. But few composers selects a variable restricted to singular objects: '[few $x :$ composers$(x)]$'.

Avoiding the absurd interpretations does not yet yield semidistributivity. Since *few* selects a singular predicate, the semidistributive interpretation must be conveyed as a property of singular objects, '$\Psi[x]$' in (21). The underlying predicate 'collaborate(x)' will not denote singular composers on its own. It is left to a semidistributive operator to derive an appropriate predicate ad hoc, as in chapter 8.

The account of semidistributivity with unsorted variables errs when the scope of the semidistributed quantifier includes a nonincreasing quantifier. Sentence (15) is an example where the narrow scope quantifier is decreasing. A more intuitive characterization of the problem becomes available if we make explicit the relation to events. The absurd interpretations are all those where the formula closed by the semidistributive quantifier expresses a property of plural objects that describes its action across several events. The unacceptable *'[$Qy : N'$]$\exists e$ $V(x, y, e)$' would say of a plurality x that it was related to Q many N's across several events. In the context of a semidistributive interpretation, a plural object can be described only by its actions within a single event. The effect singles out nonincreasing quantifiers '[$Qy : N'$]' simply because an increasing quantifier is understood to apply to a single event:

$[\exists y : n(y) \wedge N(y)]\exists e$ $V(x, y, e)$,

or equivalently,

$\exists e[\exists y : n(y) \wedge N(y)]$ $V(x, y, e)$.

There is no similar constraint on expressing properties of singular objects, as we will see below; hence the two sorts of variables. Note that the constraint violates the spirit of the plural-objects view. If indeed there are plural objects, then surely they are just like singular objects in having properties that persist across events. Why should these be inexpressible in the natural language?

On my view, first- and second-order quantifiers have a different syntax, but this disappoints only the expectation that the syntax should be the same for all NPs. The picture that emerges from sorting the variables is then the following, suppressing for the moment the decomposition of the predicate. In general, both first- and second-order quantifiers may close off whatever formulas present appropriate free variables. In particular, both sorts of quantifiers may apply to properties that describe action across several events, as in (22) and (23). The relevant interpretation of (23a) is its most salient, entailing that the same four congressmen met at every session.

(22) a. Few congressmen attended every session.
      b. [few $x : Cx$][every $y : Sy$]$\exists e$ attend(x, y, e)

(23) a. Four congressmen met every session.
      b. [$\exists X : \forall x(Xx \rightarrow Cx)$][every $y : Sy$]$\exists e$ meet(X, y, e)

An illicit interpretation would combine a property about the action of a plurality across events with semidistributivity. But in the proper analysis of (24a), the first-order quantifier *few congressmen* binds only a singular variable and cannot combine directly with a collective predicate, *meet every session*.

(24) a. Few congressmen met every session.
      b. *[few $x : Cx$][$\exists X : Xx$][every $y : Sy$]$\exists e$ meet(X, y, e)

It requires the intervention of an operator to turn the collective predicate into a predicate of singular objects. As we have already seen in the discussion surrounding (16), the semidistributive operator, defined in chapter 8, must not quantify over pluralities in the manner of (24b). The illicit interpretation is thereby excluded. This account is possible because the quantifier *few congressmen* and the like are not taken to quantify indifferently over both singular and plural objects. The variables are sorted.

To show that the relevant semidistributive interpretations are indeed illicit, consider now an example where the narrow scope quantifier is nonincreasing and nondecreasing:

(25) Few senators (ever) cosponsored (in some session or other) exactly ten amendments.

For the context depicted in (26), let S be a caucus of more than a few senators, and let $S_1, \ldots, S_n$ be the nonempty proper subsets of S that are not singletons (in order to be *cosponsors*). Figure (26) depicts a sequence of senatorial sessions in which exactly one amendment is cosponsored, and no amendment is sponsored more than once. The sponsors of the amendment in consecutive sessions are as follows:

(26) $S_1, \ldots, S_n$, S, $S_1, \ldots, S_n$, S, $S_1, \ldots, S_n$, S, $S_1, \ldots, S_n$, S,
$\quad S_1, \ldots, S_n$, S, $S_1, \ldots, S_n$, S, $S_1, \ldots, S_n$, S, $S_1, \ldots, S_n$, S,
$\quad S_1, \ldots, S_n$, S, $S_1, \ldots, S_n$, S

The events of this context are the senatorial sessions. Caucus S has sponsored exactly ten amendments distributed across ten distinct sessions. Note that every senator in caucus S has been a cosponsor in the course of (26) of more than ten amendments. Besides his participation in caucus S, every senator has also been a member of some of the subcaucuses sponsoring amendments.

The semidistributive interpretations of (25) are true in the context. If we understand *exactly ten amendments* to apply to the individual session, as in (27), then (25) is true because in no session are exactly ten amendments sponsored.

(27) $[\text{few } x : At(x) \land Sx] \exists e [10!y : Ay][\exists z : x \le z \land Sz]$
$\quad \text{cosponsor}(e, z, y)$

If *exactly ten amendments* applies to each career, as in (28), then it is true because the individual senator has cosponsored more than ten amendments.

(28) $[\text{few } x : At(x) \land Sx][10!y : Ay] \exists e [\exists z : x \le z \land Sz]$
$\quad \text{cosponsor}(e, z, y)$

Failing to restrict the variable 'x' in (28) to atomic individuals, as in (29), or exporting the quantifier over plural objects so that its scope is a formula expressing a property of plural objects that holds across events yields an interpretation that is false in the context. Recall that the interpretation that (11) derives is equivalent to (30):

(29) $[\text{few } x : Sx][10!y : Ay] \exists e [\exists z : x \le z \land Sz] \text{ cosponsor}(e, z, y)$

(30) $[\text{few } x : At(x) \land Sx][\exists z : x \le z \land Sz][10!y : Ay] \exists e \text{ cosponsor}(e, z, y)$

Caucus **S** is a plural object that has cosponsored exactly ten amendments across its legislative history, and they are more than a few senators. But no acceptable interpretation of the sentence is false in this context.[6] While it is coherent to track the individual senator's career, (28), it is not so for a plural object.

A similar example in a somewhat different setting will provide a context where the acceptable semidistributive interpretations are both false but the intepretation derived from (11) would be true.

(31) Fewer than eleven senators (ever) cosponsored (in some session or other) exactly ten amendments.

(32) **S—A$_1$, U$_1$—c$_1$, ..., U$_6$—c$_6$, S—A$_2$,
      U$_7$—c$_7$, ..., U$_{11}$—c$_{11}$, S—A$_3$**

S is now a caucus of eleven senators, and **U** is a group of eleven senators disjoint from **S**. **U$_1$**, ..., **U$_{11}$** are the eleven proper subsets of **U** that are missing one member. **A$_1$**, **A$_2$**, and **A$_3$** are disjoint sets of exactly ten amendments each, and **c$_1$**, ..., **c$_{11}$** are eleven individual amendments distinct from each other and from those in **A$_1$**, **A$_2$**, and **A$_3$**. The events are again senatorial sessions. Caucus **S** has sponsored thirty amendments distributed across three sessions. The senators in **U** have each cosponsored exactly ten amendments throughout their careers. Every senator of **U** was absent at the cosponsoring of one of the eleven amendments **c$_1$**, ..., **c$_{11}$** but present for the other ten, and he was a cosponsor of no other amendments.

The semidistributive interpretations properly restricted to atomic individuals are all false in the context.

The eleven senators of **S** have each cosponsored at at least one session exactly ten amendments, which falsifies (33), and the eleven senators of **U** have each cosponsored during their careers exactly ten amendments, which falsifies (34).

(33) $[(<11)x : At(x) \land Sx]\exists e[10!y : Ay][\exists z : x \leq z \land Sz]$
     $cosponsor(e, z, y)$

(34) $[(<11)x : At(x) \land Sx][10!y : Ay]\exists e[\exists z : x \leq z \land Sz]$
     $cosponsor(e, z, y)$

The interpretation derived from (11), equivalent to (35), is, however, true in this context.

(35) $[(<11)x : At(x) \land Sx][\exists z : x \leq z \land Sz][10!y : Ay]\exists e$
     $cosponsor(e, z, y)$

The plural objects $U_1, \ldots, U_{11}$ have each cosponsored only one amendment throughout their legislative history, and S has cosponsored thirty. Thus there are no counterexamples to the claim that there are fewer than eleven senators among the pluralities cosponsoring exactly ten. Note that the interpretation comes out true if we assume, as in section 2 below, that 'cosponsor(e, z, y)' requires z to be all the cosponsors at e. Otherwise, the eleven senators of U, who were each among the cosponsors of exactly ten amendments, would be falsifying instances.

2   Exhaustive Reference to an Event's Participants

It will be shown, for sentences (36) and (37) that 'marbles(x) fall(e) into slots(y)' cannot be true of a group of marbles and a group of slots if these are not all the marbles and slots involved in e.

(36) Fewer than fifteen marbles (ever) fall into exactly ten slots.

(37) Exactly ten marbles (ever) fall into exactly ten slots.

The particular context concerns the operations of something like a *pachinko* machine, a turn on which releases a random number of marbles. The marbles then fall into an array of columns held in wooden slots. The machine has 15 slots, but on each turn marbles may fall into all or just some of them. Marbles are not recycled in this machine. After being dropped, they are shunted off. In this context, the events are turns on the machine. We compare two sequences of events. The sequence in (38) contains an event in which 25 marbles fall into 10 slots. In all other turns in this sequence, marbles fall into fewer than 10 slots. In the sequence in (39), one turn results in 28 marbles falling into 13 slots. On a later turn, 10 marbles fall into 10 slots. Again, on all the other turns, marbles fall into fewer than 10 slots.

(38) $\ldots, [|\ 2\ |\ 3\ |\ 2\ |\ 3\ |\ 2\ |\ 3\ |\ 2\ |\ 3\ |\ 2\ |\ 3\ |], \ldots$
$1\ \ \ 2\ \ \ 3\ \ \ 4\ \ \ 5\ \ \ 6\ \ \ 7\ \ \ 8\ \ \ 9\ \ 10$

(39) $\ldots, [|\ 2\ |\ 3\ |\ 2\ |\ 3\ |\ 2\ |\ 3\ |\ 2\ |\ 3\ |\ 2\ |\ 3\ |\ 1\ |\ 1\ |\ 1\ |], \ldots$
$1\ \ \ 2\ \ \ 3\ \ \ 4\ \ \ 5\ \ \ 6\ \ \ 7\ \ \ 8\ \ \ 9\ \ 10\ 11\ 12\ 13$

(40) $\ldots, [|\ 1\ |\ 1\ |\ 1\ |\ 1\ |\ 1\ |\ 1\ |\ 1\ |\ 1\ |\ 1\ |\ 1\ |], \ldots$
$1\ \ \ 2\ \ \ 3\ \ \ 4\ \ \ 5\ \ \ 6\ \ \ 7\ \ \ 8\ \ \ 9\ \ 10$

We now consider whether (38) or the sequence (39) to (40) falsifies (36) and (37) when these are asserted about the operations of the *pachinko* machine. Both sentences are in fact falsified by (38), whether interpreted as event-dependent, as in (41), or semidistributively, as in (42):[7]

(41) a. $[\forall e : [10!y : \text{slots}(y)][\exists x : \text{marbles}(x)]\text{fall}(e, x, y)]$
$[(< 15)x : \text{marbles}(x)][\exists y : \text{slots}(y)]\text{fall}(e, x, y)$

   b. $[\forall e : [10!y : \text{slots}(y)][\exists x : \text{marbles}(x)]\text{fall}(e, x, y)]$
$[10!x : \text{marbles}(x)][\exists y : \text{slots}(y)]\text{fall}(e, x, y)$

(42) a. $[(< 15)x : \text{marbles}(x)][10!y : \text{slots}(y)]\exists e\ \text{fall}(e, x, y)$
$[(< 15)x : \text{marbles}(x)]\exists e[10!y : \text{slots}(y)]\text{fall}(e, x, y)$

   b. $[10!x : \text{marbles}(x)][10!y : \text{slots}(y)]\exists e\ \text{fall}(e, x, y)$
$[10!x : \text{marbles}(x)]\exists e[10!y : \text{slots}(y)]\text{fall}(e, x, y)$

The turn depicted in (38) is an event of marbles falling into exactly 10 slots. It is a relevant event, and the 25 marbles falsify the interpretations.

In contrast, the sequence (39) to (40) does not falsify either the event-dependent or the semidistributive interpretations. Turn (39) is irrelevant. It is not an event of marbles falling into exactly 10 slots, since its marbles fell into 13 slots. The only event in (40) of marbles falling into exactly 10 slots involves exactly 10 marbles. Thus the event-dependent and semi-distributive interpretations of sentences (36) and (37) are true in (39), (40) and in the context that combines the events of (39) and (40). The polyadic logical forms representing these interpretations will, however, not come out true in any context that includes (39), unless it is *false* that the 25 marbles in the first 10 slots m_{1-10} fall into exactly 10 slots, s_{1-10}, at turn e_i in (39):

(43) $\text{marbles}(m_{1-10})\text{fall}(e_i)$ into $\text{slots}(s_{1-10})$

Turn e_i of (39) is an event of marbles falling into 13 slots and should therefore be irrelevant to the truth of the event-dependent and semidis-tributive interpretations. This outcome requires the predicate to be true only of those marbles and slots that are all the participants in the event. Statement (43) is therefore false, while the truth about turn e_i in (39) is that m_{1-13}, the 28 marbles in all 13 slots, fell into s_{1-13}, the 13 slots:

(44) $\text{marbles}(m_{1-13})\text{fall}(e_i)$ into $\text{slots}(s_{1-13})$

The truth conditions of the predicate are those of a Davidsonian analysis, which does not convey any finer-grained relation than participation in the same event:[8]

(45) '$\text{fall}(e, x, y)$' is true
$\leftrightarrow \text{fall}(e) \wedge \forall z(\text{Theme}(e, z) \leftrightarrow z = x) \wedge \forall z(\text{into}(e, z) \leftrightarrow z = y)$

Chapter 4

Essential Separation

An atomic, polyadic predicate does not have separable expressions for the θ-roles or event concept. Wherever it occurs, it appears with its full valence of arguments: '$V(e, x_1, \ldots, x_n)$' or '$V(x_1, \ldots, x_n)$'. It is, however, essential to the meaning of (1) that the θ-role bound into by the subject not occur within the scope of the other quantifiers, as in (2), and that the action of the three video games be related mereologically to what happened to the individual quarterbacks.

(1) Three video games taught every quarterback two new plays.

(2) $\exists e([\exists X : 3(X) \wedge \forall x(Xx \rightarrow Gx)]\forall x(\text{INFL}(e, x) \leftrightarrow Xx)$
$\wedge [\text{every } y : Qy][\exists e' : e' \leq e](\text{teach}(e') \wedge \forall z(\text{TO}(e', z) \leftrightarrow z = y)$
$\wedge [\exists Z : 2(Z) \wedge \forall z(Zz \rightarrow Pz)]\forall z(\text{OF}(e', z) \leftrightarrow Zz)))$

No equivalent expression can be found where, as in (3), the quantifiers all bind into an atomic, polyadic relation. This limitation includes n-ary quantification which finds novel ways to compose the quantifiers closing the polyadic predicate.

(3) $[\exists X : 3(X) \wedge \forall x(Xx \rightarrow Gx)][\text{every } y : Qy]$
$[\exists Z : 2(Z) \wedge \forall z(Zz \rightarrow Pz)]$
$\exists e \text{ teach}(X, y, Z, e)$

Thus (1) is an instance of essential separation.

The problem for polyadic logical form centers on finding a meaning for such predicates as '$\text{teach}(X, y, Z, e)$' in (3) that relate individual objects to plural objects. The search is constrained not only by the truth conditions of (1) but also by the familiar truth conditions of distributivity. Note that, from the point of view of polyadic logical form, the difference between (1) and (4) is only a matter of scope.

(4) a. Every quarterback was taught two new plays by three video games.

    b. [every $y : Qy$][$\exists Z : 2(Z) \wedge \forall z(Zz \rightarrow Pz)$]
       [$\exists X : 3(X) \wedge \forall x(Xx \rightarrow Gx)$]$\exists e$ teach(X, y, Z, e)]

(5) a. Each video game taught every quarterback two new plays.
    b. [each $x : Gx$][every $y : Qy$][$\exists Z : 2(Z) \wedge \forall z(Zz \rightarrow Pz)$]
        $\exists e$ teach(x, y, Z, e)

In (4) the quantifier over individual objects includes within its scope all the
NPs related to plural objects, as (4b) shows. In (1), however, one quantifier has escaped, setting the pattern for all cases of essential separation.[1]
There is no way to fix a meaning for predicates relating individual and
plural objects that is adequate for both ordinary distributive interpretations and cases of separation.

   Characterizing the problem as finding a meaning for 'teach(X, y, Z, e)'
in (3) and similar expressions is meant to be fully general. First, it does not
presuppose the conclusion of chapter 3 that variables must be sorted into
singular and plural. The notation is used here just as a convenience. It
could just as well be assumed that the variables are unsorted and range
over a domain that includes plural objects. When a lowercase variable is
used, it indicates only that the predicate happens to express a condition on
individual objects. Second, the argument will show that there is no *relation in extension* to which the quantifiers apply to yield the meaning of
essential separation. The notation 'teach(X, y, Z, e)' stands for an expression of arbitrary complexity that may express the relevant relation. It may
be a formula with free variables 'X', 'y', 'Z', 'e', or it may be a complex
predicate derived via many operators. I do not mean to exclude any way
in which the relation might be expressed within polyadic logical form, but
I will speak without loss of generality, as if the emergent truth conditions
were obtained directly from 'teach(X, y, Z, e)':

(6) 'teach(X, y, Z, e)' is true of $\langle \mathbf{A}, \mathbf{b}, \mathbf{C}, \mathbf{e} \rangle$ $\leftrightarrow$ ...

To cite an example, there is a question discussed in the literature of how
best to represent the collective use of inherently distributive predicates,
as in (7):[2]

(7) The children are tall.

One possibility is that the logical form contains a tacit distributive operator meaning *each* that mediates between the reference to a plural object
and a predicate typed for singular objects:[3]

(8) [$\iota X : \forall x(Xx \leftrightarrow Cx)$][$\forall x : x$ is-one-of X] Tx

Another possibility relies on the meaning postulate in (9), so that the logical form itself shows a direct predication of the plural object:

(9) a. $[\iota X : \forall x(Xx \leftrightarrow Cx)] \, T(X)$

   b. 'T(X)' is true of **A** $\leftrightarrow \forall x(x$ is-one-of **A** $\rightarrow$ tall$(x))$

When we turn to the question of whether polyadic logical form can in principle express the meaning of (7), there are two cases we might consider. I will use (10) as a schema to cover those logical forms with a quantificational prefix consisting of the definite description and a distributive operator (tacit or overt), and some continuation.

(10) $[\iota X : \forall x(Xx \leftrightarrow Cx)][\forall x : x$ is-one-of $X]$ tall(x)

Because of the structure of the prefix, what is called for is something that expresses a property of singular objects. As attested by the truth conditions reported in (11), there is an appropriate property, so schema (10) is adequate to express (7).

(11) 'tall(x)' is true of **a** $\leftrightarrow$ **a** is tall

Note that (8) falls under (10) but (9) does not, since (9) lacks the required quantificational prefix.

   The wider class of cases is characterized by (12).

(12) $[\iota X : \forall x(Xx \leftrightarrow Cx)]$ tall(X)

I use (12) to cover those logical forms that begin with the definite description and continue with some expression of a property of plural objects. The schema is adequate to represent the meaning of (7) because there are continuations that convey the truth conditions reported in (13).

(13) 'tall(X)' is true of **A** $\leftrightarrow \forall x(x$ is-one-of **A** $\rightarrow x$ is tall)

The schema (12) and the truth conditions (13) abstract away from the form of the continuation. As expected, the logical form and meaning postulate in (9) fall under (12) and (13). The logical form (9a) is parsed into a definite description and continuation, as (12) requires, and the continuation, interpreted according to (9b), has the truth conditions necessary to be an instance of (13). It is important, however, to keep in mind that the logical form in (8) also falls under (12) and (13). Here the continuation following the definite description is the complex formula '$[\forall x : x$ is-one-of $X]$ Tx', which expresses a property of plural objects with exactly the truth conditions (13). Schema (12) is adequate to express (7) in virtue of the property whose truth conditions are those in (13). Either (8) or (9) makes explicit a continuation that bears this out.

Since the charge is that polyadic logical form does not have the resources to express essential separation, it is important to lend it as much rope as it needs. Therefore polyadic logical form is allowed to make any stipulation of truth conditions on the right-hand side of (6) that it sees fit, whether or not it is obvious how to represent those conditions in a reasonable way.

To be adequate for distributivity, a polyadic predicate must express a true relation to the individual objects denoted. That is, 'teach(X, y, Z, e)' is true of $\langle A, b, C, e \rangle$ only if A teaches b C. As it turns out, the fact that distributivity forces any predicate relating plural objects to individual objects to express a true relation is sufficient to put the cases of essential separation beyond the reach of polyadic logical form.[4] In noting this relation among the participants, I leave open the exact relation to the event. Chapter 3, section 2, concluded that the plural objects denoted ought to be all of the objects participating in the event, but the argument concerned predicates relating only plural objects: groups of marbles falling into groups of slots. I allow, if it would help polyadic logical form, that things may be different when plural objects are related to individual objects. The possibilities are shown in (14) through (17), all of which meet the distributivity requirement that a true relation be expressed.

(14) 'teach(X, y, Z, e)' is true of $\langle A, b, C, e \rangle \leftrightarrow A$ teaches b C at e

(15) 'teach(X, y, Z, e)' is true of $\langle A, b, C, e \rangle \leftrightarrow A$ teaches b C at e
    $\& \, \forall X \forall Y \forall Z (X$ teaches $Y Z$ at $e \rightarrow X = A \, \& \, Z = C)$

(16) 'teach(X, y, Z, e)' is true of $\langle A, b, C, e \rangle$
    $\leftrightarrow \forall X \forall Z (X$ teaches b Z at $e \leftrightarrow X = A \, \& \, Z = C)$

(17) 'teach(X, y, Z, e)' is true of $\langle A, b, C, e \rangle$
    $\leftrightarrow \forall X \forall Y \forall Z (X$ teaches $Y Z$ at $e \leftrightarrow X = A \, \& \, Y = b \, \& \, Z = C)$

The truth conditions in (14) abandon exhaustivity altogether when an individual object is involved. Thus it is enough that A, b, and C are among the participants in e, and whatever else happens there, A teaches b C. The truth conditions in (15) assert that the plural objects exhaust all the participants bearing their θ-roles, but (15) allows that the event contains others like b. Note that exhaustivity is not sufficient to guarantee that A teaches b C. It may be true, for example, that only one among A teaches b only one thing among C. The others among A and C are given over to teaching pupils other than b. In (16), exhaustivity is relativized to the individual object. A is everything teaching b, and C is everything taught b. In (17), exhaustivity is absolute. **A**, **b**, and **C** are the only participants in the event. Exhaustivity in (16) and (17) entails that **A** teaches **b** **C**. We are indifferent to how the relation to events is structured, except for the constraint imposed by distributivity. Compare (18), which misinterprets (4) because it does not entail that **A** teaches **b** **C**:

(18) 'teach(X, y, Z, e)' is true of $\langle \mathbf{A}, \mathbf{b}, \mathbf{C}, \mathbf{e} \rangle$
    $\leftrightarrow \exists X \exists Z (X$ teaches **b** Z *at* **e**)
      & $\forall X \forall Y \forall Z (X$ teaches $Y Z$ at **e** $\rightarrow X = \mathbf{A} \ \& \ Z = \mathbf{C})$

The distributive interpretation of (4) is false in (19). One quarterback is taught only one play by two video games, and the other quarterback only one play by one video game.

(19)

The point of distributivity is to insist that each quarterback on his own is related to two new plays and three video games, which is obviously not the case in (19). But the logical form in (4) comes out true if the predicate is interpreted according to (18), which is true of $\langle \{\mathbf{g}_1, \mathbf{g}_2, \mathbf{g}_3\}, \mathbf{q}_1, \{\mathbf{p}_1, \mathbf{p}_2\}, \mathbf{e} \rangle$ and $\langle \{\mathbf{g}_1, \mathbf{g}_2, \mathbf{g}_3\}, \mathbf{q}_2, \{\mathbf{p}_1, \mathbf{p}_2\}, \mathbf{e} \rangle$. The three video games did not teach the two new plays to quarterback $\mathbf{q}_1$, but they all participated in the same event where only those games and plays are involved, and this is all that (18) requires.

It remains to be shown now that any meaning for the predicate adequate for distributivity in that it expresses a true relation fails cases of essential separation.

1   Crucial Truth Conditions for Cases of Essential Separation

1.1   A context where cases of essential separation are true

First observe that the relevant interpretations of sentences (20) to (22) are true in the contexts depicted in (23) and described below. Appearing with the sentences are logical forms that make essential use of separation. The interpretations they represent are true in (23), as required.

(20) a. Three agents sold (the) two buildings (each) to exactly two
       investors.

b. $\exists e([\exists X : 3(X) \wedge \forall x(Xx \rightarrow Ax)]\forall x(\text{INFL}(e, x) \leftrightarrow Xx)$
$\wedge [\imath Y : 2(Y) \wedge \forall y(Yy \rightarrow By)][\forall y : Yy][\exists e' : e' \leq e]$
$(\text{sell}(e') \wedge \forall z(\text{TO}(e', z) \leftrightarrow z = y)$
$\wedge [2!z : Iz][\exists e'' : e'' \leq e']\forall x(\text{OF}(e'', x) \leftrightarrow z = x)))$

(21) a. Three letters of recommendation from influential figures earned the two new graduates (each) two offers.

b. $\exists e(\exists X : 3(X) \wedge \forall x(Xx \rightarrow Lx)]\forall x(\text{INFL}(e, x) \leftrightarrow Xx)$
$\wedge [\imath Y : 2(Y) \wedge \forall y(Yy \rightarrow Gy)][\forall y : Yy][\exists e' : e' \leq e]$
$(\text{earn}(e') \wedge \forall z(\text{TO}(e', z) \leftrightarrow z = y)$
$\wedge [\exists Z : 2(Z) \wedge \forall z(Zz \rightarrow Oz)]\forall z(\text{OF}(e', z) \leftrightarrow Zz)))$

(22) a. Three automatic tellers gave (the) two new members (each) exactly two passwords.

b. $\exists e([\exists X : 3(X) \wedge \forall x(Xx \rightarrow Ax)]\forall x(\text{INFL}(e, x) \leftrightarrow Xx)$
$\wedge [\imath Y : 2(Y) \wedge \forall y(Yy \rightarrow My)][\forall y : Yy][\exists e' : e' \leq e]$
$(\text{give}(e') \wedge \forall z(\text{TO}(e', z) \leftrightarrow z = y)$
$\wedge [2!z : Pz][\exists e'' : e'' \leq e']\forall x(\text{OF}(e'', x) \leftrightarrow z = x)))$

(23)   (20)   (21)   (22)

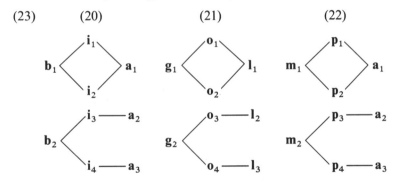

For each of the sentences, it will be helpful to imagine circumstances that make the relative assignment of scope between the plural NPs in the VP especially meaningful. Suppose for (20) that the sale of a building to two or more investors creates the conditions under which a deed can be contested. The relevant intepretation of (20) then reports that (the) two buildings were sold with that risk and three agents were the involved sellers. For (21), suppose that a new graduate's situation is measured by his ability to play one job offer off against another. Naturally, success begins at two offers and improves with the chances for more elaborate ploys as the number of offers increases. The relevant interpretation of (21) reports that three letters of recommendation were responsible for bringing the two new graduates to the minimal level of success. For example (22), suppose that new members in any of several Christmas clubs at any of several banks are enrolled by assigning to each new member exactly two passwords of his own. The assignment of a password is made by computer and received at one of many automatic tellers. At one location, which (22) is about, there are many automatic tellers ejecting passwords for any of the different Christmas clubs. A new member enters the location, approaches one of the tellers, selects the Christmas club of his choice and requests one password. As a security precaution, to request another password he must repeat the process. The relevant interpretation of (22) reports that three automatic tellers were used when (the) two new members enrolled in Christmas clubs.

Each diagram in (23) shows two distinct individuals in its leftmost column each related to two distinct individuals. For (22), these are two new members: m_1, who is given passwords p_1 and p_2, and m_2, who is given passwords p_3 and p_4. Similarly in the figure for (20), there are (the) two buildings b_1 and b_2, and b_1 is sold to the two investors i_1 and i_2, while b_2 is sold to the two investors i_3 and i_4. For (21), (23) shows one new graduate g_1 winning job offers o_1 and o_2 and the other graduate g_2 winning offers o_3 and o_4.

Each of the diagrams in (23) also shows that three individuals bring about the state of affairs described above. The diagram for (22) shows that new member m_1 was given the passwords to his Christmas club by just one automatic teller, a_1, while new member m_2 was given one of his passwords by automatic teller a_2 and the other password by another teller, a_3. The participation of the three individuals is distributed in the same way in all of the diagrams. Thus one agent, a_1, is solely responsible for building b_1, which is sold to exactly two investors, whereas agent a_2 sells building b_2 to one investor, and agent a_3 sells it again to another investor. Similarly, one letter of recommendation l_1 earns the first graduate g_1 his two offers, but the second graduate g_2 wins his two offers each from a different recommendation.

The relevant interpretations of sentences in (20) to (22) and the logical forms that appear with them are true in the contexts of (23). The diagram for (22) in (23) shows an event in which (the) two new members are each given exactly two passwords, and its givers are three automatic tellers. For (20), (23) depicts an event in which (the) two buildings are each sold to exactly two investors, and its sellers are three agents. Finally, the diagram for (21) shows an event in which the two graduates each earned exactly two offers, and its earners are three letters of recommendation.

What is important about these contexts is just this: the event depicted in the third diagram of (23) is an event e such that

(24) $[\imath Y : 2(Y) \land \forall y(Yy \rightarrow My)][\forall y : Yy][\exists e' : e' \leq \mathbf{e}]$
$(\text{give}(e') \land \forall z(\text{TO}(e', z) \leftrightarrow z = y)$
$\land [2!z : Pz][\exists e'' : e'' \leq e']\forall x(\text{OF}(e'', x) \leftrightarrow z = x)).$

But, we will see, (23) fails to verify the counterpart to (24) in polyadic logical form, however we might choose a value for 'X' or construe the polyadic predicate:

(25) a. $[\imath Y : 2(Y) \land \forall y(Yy \rightarrow My)][\forall y : Yy][2!z : Pz]\exists e \text{ give}(X, y, z, e)$
b. $[\imath Y : 2(Y) \land \forall y(Yy \rightarrow My)][\forall y : Yy][2!z : Pz]$
$[\exists Z : Zz \land \forall z(Zz \rightarrow Pz)]\exists e \text{ give}(X, y, z, e)^5$

A further observation, which will prove important in section 4, is illustrated by (26) and the context in (27). Let us suppose that the automatic tellers print each password on two slips of paper, for security reasons. Sentence (26) simply adds to (22) the remark that each password is given on two slips, and the context in (27) bears out the truth of (26) by elaborating what happens in the diagram for (22) in (23).

(26) a. Three automatic tellers gave (the) two new members (each) exactly two passwords (each) on two slips of paper.
b. $\exists e([\exists X : 3(X) \land \forall x(Xx \rightarrow Ax)]\forall x(\text{INFL}(e, x) \leftrightarrow Xx)$
$\land [\imath Y : 2(Y) \land \forall y(Yy \rightarrow My)][\forall y : Yy][\exists e' : e' \leq e]$
$(\text{give}(e') \land \forall z(\text{TO}(e', z) \leftrightarrow z = y)$
$\land [2!z : Pz][\exists e'' : e'' \leq e'](\forall x(\text{OF}(e'', x) \leftrightarrow z = x)$
$\land [\exists W : 2(W) \land \forall w(Ww \rightarrow Sw)]\forall w(\text{on}(e'', w) \leftrightarrow Ww))))$

(27)

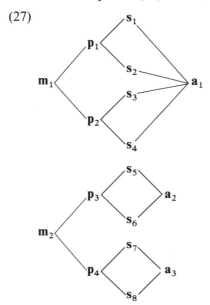

In an event of giving by three automatic tellers, each of the two new members is given exactly two passwords each on two slips of paper. Sentence (26) illustrates the fact that by multiplying the internal-scope relations of the sentence in this way, we do not obtain an interpretation that requires any change in the distribution of automatic tellers to new members and passwords. In (27), a_1 is still the giver of m_1's passwords, and m_2 gets one password from a_2 and the other from a_3, just as in the diagram for (22) in (23).

1.2   A context where cases of essential separation are false

We now turn to the second important fact about sentences (20) to (22). The interpretations under discussion are all false in the contexts depicted in (28).[6]

(28)   (20)   (21)   (22)

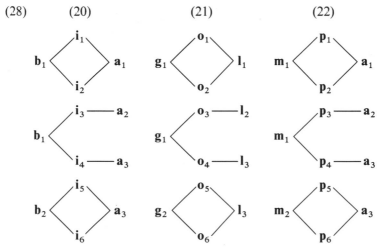

The diagrams in (28) are to be understood in the same way as those in (23). Note that none of them shows two individuals each being related to exactly two individuals. The diagram for (22) shows two new members m_1 and m_2, only one of which, m_2, is given exactly two passwords. New member m_1 is given four passwords. Similarly, the diagram for (20) fails to show two buildings each being sold to exactly two investors. The diagram contains only two buildings, one of which, b_1, is sold to four investors. In the diagram for (21), graduate g_1 garners four offers, and so only one graduate, g_2, earns exactly two offers.

On the assumption that what is shown for (22) in (28) is a single event, there does not exist in that context an event in which (the) two new members are each given exactly two passwords, and so (22) is false. The other

sentences are false for the same reason when what is shown for each of
them is a single event. There is no event in which (the) two individuals are
each related to exactly two other individuals. In the single event shown,
one of them is related to four.

Now observe that one can obtain contexts in which these sentences are
true by dividing what happened in (28) into several events, as in (29), for
example:

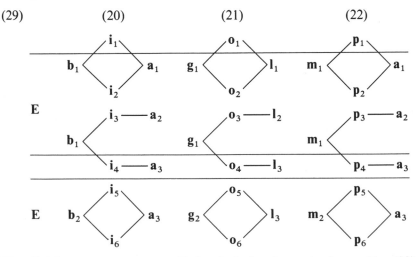

The division creates one event **E** that includes the parts shown. For (22),
it is member $\mathbf{m}_2$'s being given passwords $\mathbf{p}_5$ and $\mathbf{p}_6$ and member $\mathbf{m}_1$'s being
given passwords $\mathbf{p}_2$ and $\mathbf{p}_3$. The relevant interpretation of (22) is true of
E. It is an event of the two new member's each being given exactly two
passwords, and its givers are three automatic tellers.

I would like to eliminate this distraction and find sentences that, interpreted in the way characteristic of essential separation, are unambiguously false in any context containing what happens in (29). My point will
be to contrast the sentences with polyadic logical forms that are unambiguously true in (29) and therefore incorrect representations of this interpretation. Relevant sentences are easy enough to come by. We attain the
desired effect by attaching a frame adverbial, as in (30) to (32), and spec-
ifying that only all of what happens in (29) fits the time frame:

(30) In exactly 24 hours, three agents sold (the) two buildings (each) to
     exactly two investors.

(31) In exactly 24 hours, three letters of recommendation from
     influential figures earned the two new graduates (each) two offers.

(32) In exactly 24 hours, three automatic tellers gave (the) two new
      members (each) (exactly) two passwords.

Alternatively, one might add a descriptive condition, as in (33):

(33) Three automatic tellers gave (the) two new members (each) two
      passwords that began with the same letter.

Event **E** in (29) will fail to verify (33) if, for example, $\{p_1, p_2\}$, $\{p_3, p_4\}$,
and $\{p_5, p_6\}$ are the only pairs of passwords that begin with the same
letter. This particular state of affairs turns out not to falsify the relevant
polyadic logical forms. Yet (33) is false in this context absolutely. There is
no event that would make it true. Consider, for example, **E′** in (34). The
two new members are each being given two passwords that begin with the
same letter, but the givers are not three automatic tellers.

(34)

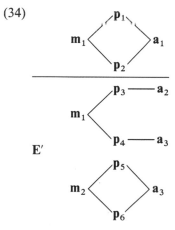

To use (30) to (32) or (33) in an objection to polyadic logical form
would show only that it is led astray when it encounters either such
higher-order expressions as *same*, which hold mysteries of their own, or
adverbial modifiers, which, one may be prepared to concede, involve
events in some crucial way. Since my point is that polyadic logical form
misconstrues plural and singular predication and that the interactions of
singular and plural NPs on their own require reference to events and
separation, I will use examples based on simple scope relations. In (35) the
scope assignment of *a pink slip of paper* has the same effect on truth
conditions as the description added to (33), but within the fragment of
language we are holding polyadic logical form responsible for.

(35) a. Three automatic tellers gave (the) two new members (each)
          (exactly) two passwords on a pink slip of paper.

b. $\exists e([\exists X : 3(X) \wedge \forall x(Xx \rightarrow Ax)]\forall x(\text{INFL}(e, x) \leftrightarrow Xx)$
$\wedge\ [\imath Y : 2(Y) \wedge \forall y(Yy \rightarrow My)][\forall y : Yy][\exists e' : e' \leq e]$
$(\text{give}(e') \wedge \forall z(\text{TO}(e', z) \leftrightarrow z = y)$
$\wedge\ [\exists W : 1(W) \wedge \forall w(Ww \rightarrow Sw)]\forall w(\text{on}(e', w) \leftrightarrow Ww)$
$\wedge\ [2!z : Pz][\exists e'' : e'' \leq e']\forall x(\text{OF}(e'', x) \leftrightarrow z = x)))^7$

The context in (36) is one where (35), so understood, is false absolutely. Any event either fails to have the right number of automatic tellers, new members, or passwords or fails to meet the condition that one slip of paper bears both passwords.

(36)

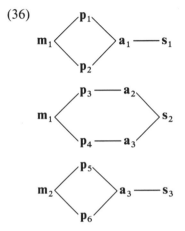

In summary, the sentences we have considered in this section are all false in (28) if the context makes it a single event.[8] And some sentences, such as (35), are false in any domain of events derived from what happened in (28). It is obvious that the logical forms in (20) to (22) and (35) are false where required. Thus they are correct with respect to the two facts observed, namely, that the sentences they represent are true in (23) and false here in (28), with the qualifications noted.

2   Approximating Essential Separation with Polyadic Logical Forms

Having introduced in section 1 some truth conditions for cases of essential separation, let us now consider how polyadic logical form attempts to represent them. For convenience, I will develop just one of the examples for which I have constructed the situations in (23), (28), and (29):

(22) Three automatic tellers gave (the) two new members (each) exactly
      two passwords.

(23)

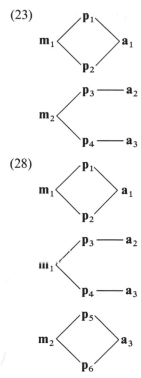

(28)

The relevant interpretation of (22) requires that (the) two new members each be related to exactly two passwords. Thus *(the) two new members* must bind a variable over individual objects and include *exactly two passwords* within its scope. I allow *exactly two passwords* to bind either a variable over individual objects or a variable over sets. As for *three automatic tellers*, the interpretation is about just three automatic tellers, and so *three automatic tellers* cannot be within the scope of the distributive *(the) two new members*. I allow *three automatic tellers* to be distributive, semi-distributive, or undistributed, and I will consider several ways in which its intepretation can interact with that of *(the) two new members*, including the formation of a binary quantifier. (The semicolon in (37) indicates that the scope interaction between *three automatic tellers* and *[the] two new members* is left open.) In short, any possible logical form will conform to (37).

(37) $[\exists X_1 : 3(X_1) \land \forall x(X_1 x \to \mathrm{ATM}(x))]$;
      $[\imath Y : 2(Y) \land \forall y(Yy \to \mathrm{member}(y))][\forall y : Yy][2!z_2 : \mathrm{password}(z_2)] \ldots$
      $\mathrm{give}(\alpha_1, y, \alpha_2, e)$

The location of the event quantifier is also left open. A formula with a free variable over individual objects, y, and a free variable over plural objects or over individuals is closed by the distributive (*the*) *two new members* and *three automatic tellers*.

Recall that the polyadic atomic predicates must express true relations if they are to be adequate for distributivity. Schema (37) stands for logical forms that contain any one of four atomic predicates, which impose at least the following conditions:

(38) 'give(x, y, z, e)' is true of $\langle \mathbf{a}, \mathbf{m}, \mathbf{p}, \mathbf{e} \rangle$ only if $\mathbf{a}$ gives $\mathbf{m}$ $\mathbf{p}$ at $\mathbf{e}$

(39) 'give(x, y, Z, e)' is true of $\langle \mathbf{a}, \mathbf{m}, \mathbf{P}, \mathbf{e} \rangle$ only if $\mathbf{a}$ gives $\mathbf{m}$ $\mathbf{P}$ at $\mathbf{e}$

(40) 'give(X, y, z, e)' is true of $\langle \mathbf{A}, \mathbf{m}, \mathbf{p}, \mathbf{e} \rangle$ only if $\mathbf{A}$ gives $\mathbf{m}$ $\mathbf{p}$ at $\mathbf{e}$

(41) 'give(X, y, Z, e)' is true of $\langle \mathbf{A}, \mathbf{m}, \mathbf{P}, \mathbf{e} \rangle$ only if $\mathbf{A}$ gives $\mathbf{m}$ $\mathbf{P}$ at $\mathbf{e}$

We will now see that logical forms conforming to (37) fail to represent the intended intepretation of (22) and similar interpretations of other sentences. Logical forms conforming to (37) are divided into two cases, discussed separately in section 3 and section 4. In the first case, logical forms without a binary quantifier are shown to represent interpretations that are false in context (23). The second case includes logical forms conforming to (37) in which *three automatic tellers* and (*the*) *two new members* form a binary quantifier. In section 4, we will see that, with the qualifications noted, those logical forms made true in (23) through the use of a binary quantifier are also true in (28) and thus do not agree with the target interpretations, which are false in (28), as we saw in section 1.2.

3   Failure with Unary, Restricted Quantifiers

With only standard quantifiers, the possible logical forms include all choices for the types of variables found in positions α_1 and α_2 in (42).

(42) $[\exists X_1 : 3(X_1) \wedge \forall x(X_1 x \rightarrow \mathrm{ATM}(x))]$
$[\imath Y : 2(Y) \wedge \forall y(Yy \rightarrow \mathrm{member}(y))][\forall y : Yy][2! z_2 : \mathrm{password}(z)] \ldots$
give$(\alpha_1, y, \alpha_2, e)$

I discuss the most interesting choice where they are both variables over plural objects. This allows the relation of who gave what to whom to be as vague as possible, and therefore more likely to yield a logical form that is true in (23). Schema (43) stands for all the logical forms that would be derived by fixing a position for the existential event quantifier:

(43) $[\exists X : 3(X) \wedge \forall x(Xx \rightarrow \text{ATM}(x))]$
$[\iota Y : 2(Y) \wedge \forall y(Yy \rightarrow \text{member}(y))][\forall y : Yy][2!z : \text{password}(z)]$
$[\exists Z : Zz \wedge \forall z(Zz \rightarrow Pz)] \text{ give}(X, y, Z, e)$

As in (38) through (41), the atomic predicate 'give(X, y, Z, e)' is true of automatic tellers **A**, new member **m**, and passwords **P** only if **A** give **m P**. The atomic predicate expresses a true relation between the plural objects and the individual objects, whatever else it may say about events. The polyadic logical form, the absence of n-ary quantifiers, and the expression of a true relation are together sufficient to make the resulting interpretation false in context (23), contrary to the intended interpretation of (22), which is true in (23).

I now show that no group of automatic tellers in (23) and no part of the event or events in (23) satisfy formula (44):

(44) $[\iota Y : 2(Y) \wedge \vee y(Yy \rightarrow \text{member}(y))][\forall y : Yy][2!z : \text{password}(z)]$
$[\exists Z : Zz \wedge \forall z(Zz \rightarrow Pz)] \text{ give}(X, y, Z, e)$

Consider those pairs of a set of automatic tellers and an *individual* new member that satisfy formula (45) for any subevent:

(45) $[2!z : \text{password}(z)][\exists Z : Zz \wedge \forall z(Zz \rightarrow Pz)] \text{ give}(X, y, Z, e)$

We need to ask for each of the new members in (23) which automatic tellers gave him two passwords. There are only two pairs satisfying the formula: $\langle \{a_1\}, m_1 \rangle$ and $\langle \{a_2, a_3\}, m_2 \rangle$. The first automatic teller gave the first new member his two passwords. The second new member was given one of his passwords by the second automatic teller and the other password by the third teller. Thus two automatic tellers gave that new member his two passwords.

Among the pairs that fail to satisfy (45), I should mention in particular $\langle \{a_1, a_2, a_3\}, m_1 \rangle$ and $\langle \{a_1, a_2, a_3\}, m_2 \rangle$. Note that the second and third automatic tellers had nothing to do with giving the first new member passwords, and the first automatic teller had nothing to do with the second new member. Hence the atomic predicate expressing a true relation is not true of $\{a_1, a_2, a_3\}$ and m_1 for any passwords P (and subevents), and it is not true of $\{a_1, a_2, a_3\}$ and m_2 for any passwords P. (The point does not deny the variety of collective interpretations that *Automatic tellers give new members passwords* may be used to express. For discussion, see n. 9.)

As we have just seen, the only pairs in (23) satisfying (45) are $\langle \{a_1\}, m_1 \rangle$ and $\langle \{a_1, a_3\}, m_2 \rangle$. Obviously, no group of automatic tellers pairs with two new members to satisfy (45). Group $\{\mathbf{a}_1\}$ appears in a pair with only one new member $\mathbf{m}_1$, and group $\{\mathbf{a}_2, \mathbf{a}_3\}$ is also paired with only one new member $\mathbf{m}_2$. Thus there is no group of automatic tellers that satisfies formula (44), from which it follows that (43) is false in (23).[10]

As remarked earlier, (43) is the most interesting instance of (42). Other logical forms are obtained by letting 'α_1' or 'α_2' be a variable over individual objects. It should be clear that this will eliminate from the extension of the atomic predicate those quadruples of automatic tellers, new members, passwords, and events that contain groups of automatic tellers or groups of passwords. Since what falsifies (43) is that there are not enough automatic tellers related to more than one new member, these other logical forms will remain false when the extension of the predicate is further reduced.

Sentence (22) has an interpretation that is true in context (23) (and the context that includes both context (23) and the context for (22) in (vi) from n. 5). Any polyadic logical form for this interpretation will conform to (37). This section considered the logical forms that do not contain n-ary quantifiers, those conforming to (42). We have seen that none of these correctly represents the intended interpretation of (22). Their failure is that they are true only if the three automatic tellers each belong to some group or another that gives two passwords to *each* of the two new members. In (23) no set is related to the individual new members in this way. Note, however, that (23) is an event in which the two new members are each given exactly two passwords and the givers in that event are three automatic tellers. This is sufficient to make the relevant interpretation of (22) true and to make a representation that makes use of separation true.

4   Failure with n-ary Quantifiers

The second case of logical forms conforming to (37) includes those in which the outermost quantifiers form a binary quantifier.[11]

(46) $[\exists X_1 : 3(X_1) \wedge \forall x(X_1 x \rightarrow \mathrm{ATM}(x))]$

$[2!z_2 : \mathrm{password}(z_2)] \ldots$
$\mathrm{give}(\alpha_1, y, \alpha_2, e)^{12}$

$[\imath Y : 2(Y) \wedge \forall y(Yy \rightarrow \mathrm{member}(y))]$

Since other choices for α_1 and α_2 in fact lead to interpretations false in (23), I need to discuss only that instance of (46) where both α_1 and α_2 are variables over sets:

(47) $[\exists X : 3(X) \wedge \forall x(Xx \rightarrow \text{ATM}(x))]$

$[\imath Y : 2(Y) \wedge \forall y(Yy \rightarrow \text{member}(y))]$ $[2!z : \text{password}(z)]$
$[\exists Z : Zz \wedge \forall z(Zz \rightarrow Pz)]$
$\text{give}(X, y, Z, e)$

As in the preceding section, I will at first suppress quantification over events and consider any interpretation for the binary quantifier that includes at least the truth conditions in (48):

(48) $\ulcorner[\exists X : \Phi[X]] \times [\imath Y : \Psi[Y]]\Gamma[X, y]\urcorner$ is true only if
$\quad [\exists A : \ulcorner\Phi[X]\urcorner$ is true of $A][\imath M : \ulcorner\Psi[Y]\urcorner$ is true of $M]$
$\quad\quad ([\forall a : Aa][\exists A' : A'a \wedge \forall a(A'a \rightarrow Aa)][\exists m : Mm]$
$\quad\quad\quad \ulcorner\Gamma[X, y]\urcorner$ is true of $\langle A', m \rangle$
$\quad\quad \& [\forall m : Mm][\exists A' : \exists aA'a \wedge \forall a(A'a \rightarrow Aa)]$
$\quad\quad\quad \ulcorner\Gamma[X, y]\urcorner$ is true of $\langle A', m \rangle)$

Note that (48) allows the binary quantifier to divide its reference among several groups of automatic tellers.[13] The binary quantifier in (48) allows the polyadic logical form to escape the difficulty undermining the logical forms of the preceding section. Formula (47) interpreted according to (48) will not require there to be a set of automatic tellers that gives both new members their passwords. It is allowed that various sets contribute to this state of affairs, if they together are three automatic tellers. The binary quantifier also appears to represent the part of the relevant interpretation of (22) that says that the two new members are each given exactly two passwords. The quantifier *exactly two passwords* has narrow scope in (47), and the variable 'y' bound by the binary quantifier is still a variable over individual objects. First observe that, as required for (22), (47) interpreted according to (48) is indeed true in (23). The formula within the scope of the binary quantifier in (47) is formula (45).

(45) $[2!z : \text{password}(z)][\exists Z : Zz \wedge \forall z(Zz \rightarrow Pz)] \text{give}(X, y, Z, e)$

Recall that two pairs were found to satisfy (45): $\langle\{\mathbf{a}_1\}, \mathbf{m}_1\rangle$ and $\langle\{\mathbf{a}_2, \mathbf{a}_3\}, \mathbf{m}_2\rangle$. These now suffice to satisfy the truth conditions of the binary quantifier. Three automatic tellers are divided between the pairs, and so are the two new members. Thus logical form (47) is true in (23).

Next observe that the binary quantifiers that weaken the truth conditions so that (47) is true in (23) weaken them too much. Unlike the acceptable interpretation of (35), the polyadic logical form in (49) is true in (36).

(35) a. Three automatic tellers gave (the) two new members (each) (exactly) two passwords on a pink slip of paper.

b. $\exists e([\exists X : 3(X) \wedge \forall x(Xx \rightarrow Ax)]\forall x(\text{INFL}(e, x) \leftrightarrow Xx)$
$\wedge [\iota Y : 2(Y) \wedge \forall y(Yy \rightarrow My)][\forall y : Yy][\exists e' : e' \leq e]$
$(\text{give}(e') \wedge \forall z(\text{TO}(e', z) \leftrightarrow z = y)$
$\wedge [\exists W : 1(W) \wedge \forall w(Ww \rightarrow Sw)]\forall w(\text{on}(e', w) \leftrightarrow Ww)$
$\wedge [2!z : Pz][\exists e'' : e'' \leq e']\forall x(\text{OF}(e'', x) \leftrightarrow z = x)))$

(49) $[\exists X : 3(X) \wedge \forall x(Xx \rightarrow \text{ATM}(x))]$

$[\exists w : Sw][2!z : P(z)]$
$[\exists Z : Zz \wedge \forall z(Zz \rightarrow Pz)]$
$\text{give}(X, y, Z, w, e)$

$[\iota Y : 2(Y) \wedge \forall y(Yy \rightarrow \text{member}(y))]$

(36)

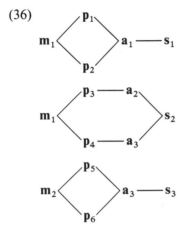

Recall from section 1.2 that (35) is false in (36), no matter how that diagram is partitioned into events. If what happens in (36) is taken to be a single event of three automatic tellers giving new members' passwords, the interpretation is false because that event fails to be one of two members' each being given exactly two passwords. One of the new members, m_1, is given four passwords. Any subevent will either fail to have the right number of participants or fail the condition that a new member receive his passwords on a single slip of paper.

In the logical form in (49), the quantifier, '$[2!z : \text{password}(z)]$', within the scope of the binary quantifier is *not* simply a measure of what each new member is given. The binary quantifier quantifies over pairs that satisfy formula (50), which is true of a set of automatic tellers and an individual new member just in case that set gave that new member exactly two passwords.

(50) $[\exists w : Sw][2!z : \text{password}(z)][\exists Z : Zz \wedge \forall z(Zz \rightarrow Pz)]$
$\text{give}(X, y, Z, w, e)$

The interpretation represented by (49) allows a new member to receive two passwords from *each* set of automatic tellers. Note in particular that (50) is satisfied by the pairs in (51):

(51) $\langle\{a_1\}, m_1\rangle, \langle\{a_2, a_3\}, m_1\rangle, \langle\{a_3\}, m_2\rangle$

Although new member m_1 is given four passwords, he is given exactly two by the first automatic teller on a single slip of paper and exactly two by the first and second automatic tellers, on a single slip of paper. (So that automatic tellers may plausibly share a single slip of paper, imagine that this variety prints passwords on slips of paper that identify the user, which he must provide as a security precaution. The user can reuse a slip of paper if he so chooses.) Since the union of the sets of automatic tellers in (51) is three automatic tellers and the new members are the two new members, the interpretation represented by (49) is thus true in (36).

What has been shown so far is that an intepretation derived from binary quantification and an atomic predicate expressing a true relation between plural objects and individual objects, (49), has truth conditions weak enough for the interpretation to be true in (23) and analogous contexts, but they are also so weak that (49) is true in (36).

Having suppressed consideration of the event place, we have surveyed only those truth conditions that flow from the predicate's expression of a true relation: that automatic tellers X give new member y passwords Z. Since the current objection to a polyadic logical form is that its truth conditions are too weak, we should now consider whether the suppressed relation to events will yield conditions that render the interpretation false in (36), as required, while remaining true in (23).

In pursuing such an interpretation, there are two places from which we might hope to refine the truth conditions of the logical form: what the atomic predicate has to say about the event and the disposition of the quantifier over events. We will find that none of the possibilities allow (47), (49), and similar logical forms to always represent an appropriate interpretation, one that is true in contexts like (23) and false in contexts like (36).

In (14) to (17) I enumerated the possible relations to events open to polyadic predicates. Recall that chapter 3 showed only that relations involving only plural objects must exhaust the participants of the events. Where the predicate expresses a relation to individual objects, we are free to consider the following:

(52) 'give(X, y, Z, w, e)' is true of $\langle \mathbf{A}, \mathbf{m}, \mathbf{P}, \mathbf{s}, \mathbf{e} \rangle$
$\leftrightarrow$ **A** give **m P** on **s** at **e**

(53) 'give(X, y, Z, w, e)' is true of $\langle \mathbf{A}, \mathbf{m}, \mathbf{P}, \mathbf{s}, \mathbf{e} \rangle$
$\leftrightarrow$ **A** give **m P** on **s** at **e**
$\& \; \forall X \forall Y \forall Z \forall W (X$ give $Y Z$ on W at **e** $\rightarrow X = \mathbf{A} \; \& \; Z = \mathbf{P})$

(54) 'give(X, y, Z, w, e)' is true of $\langle \mathbf{A}, \mathbf{m}, \mathbf{P}, \mathbf{s}, \mathbf{e} \rangle$
$\leftrightarrow \forall X \forall Y \forall Z \forall W (X$ give $Y Z$ on W at **e** $\leftrightarrow \mathbf{X} = \mathbf{A} \; \& \; \mathbf{Y} = \mathbf{m} \; \&$
$Z = \mathbf{P} \; \& \; W = \mathbf{s})$

(55) 'give(X, y, Z, w, e)' is true of $\langle \mathbf{A}, \mathbf{m}, \mathbf{P}, \mathbf{s}, \mathbf{e} \rangle$
$\leftrightarrow \forall X \forall Z (X$ give **m** Z on **s** at **e** $\leftrightarrow X = \mathbf{A} \; \& \; Z = \mathbf{P})$

Clause (52) imposes no condition of exhaustivity. Since it adds nothing new, the relation's holding at **e** having been implicit all along, we need not consider (52) any further. Clause (53) requires that plural objects be exhaustive but allows that the event may contain other individual objects bearing the same θ-roles. Clause (54) asserts exhaustivity for all participants, and (55) relativizes exhaustivity to the individual objects. The event contains no others bearing the relation to the given individual objects, but other participants may be related to other individual objects.

These alternatives for the atomic predicate interact with the alternative positions of the event quantifier. There are three cases to consider: placement within the scope of the binary quantifier, (56), placement outside the scope of the binary quantifier, (57), and for the cognoscenti of branching quantifiers, placement within an n-ary quantifier, as in (58), which shows the only one of its kind that may be of any use.

(56) $[\exists X : 3(X) \wedge \forall x(Xx \rightarrow Ax)]$

$\quad (\exists e)[\exists w : Sw][2!z : Pz](\exists e)$
$\quad [\exists Z : Zz \wedge \forall z(Zz \rightarrow Pz)]$
$[\imath Y : 2(Y) \wedge \forall y(Yy \rightarrow My)] \quad$ give(X, y, Z, w, e)

(57) $[\exists X : 3(X) \wedge \forall x(Xx \rightarrow Ax)]$

$\exists e$
$\quad\quad\quad\quad\quad\quad\quad\quad [\exists w : Sw][2!z : Pz]$
$\quad\quad\quad\quad\quad\quad\quad\quad [\exists Z : Zz \wedge \forall z(Zz \rightarrow Pz)]$
$[\imath Y : 2(Y) \wedge \forall y(Yy \rightarrow My)] \quad$ give(X, y, Z, w, e)

(58) $[\exists X : 3(X) \wedge \forall x(Xx \rightarrow Ax)]$

$\quad\quad\quad\quad\quad\quad\quad\quad [\exists w : Sw][2!z : Pz]$
$\quad\quad\quad\quad\quad\quad\quad\quad [\exists Z : Zz \wedge \forall z(Zz \rightarrow Pz)]$
$[\imath Y : 2(Y) \wedge \forall y(Yy \rightarrow My)]\exists e \quad$ give(X, y, Z, w, e)

Since this last alternative will require us to reconsider the meaning of the branching quantifier, I discuss it only after the first two cases are disposed of.

For the first case, (56), where the event quantifier may appear in any position within the scope of the binary quantifier, consider the three events in (36) corresponding to a new member's being given two passwords on a slip of paper:

(36)

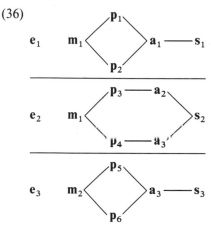

The predicate 'give(X, y, Z, w, e)' is true of $\langle\{a_1\}, m_1, \{p_1, p_2\}, s_1, e_1\rangle$, however exhaustivity applies, since the quintuple satisfies absolute exhaustivity, (54). It is similarly true of $\langle\{a_2, a_3\}, m_1, \{p_3, p_4\}, s_2, e_2\rangle$ and of $\langle\{a_3\}, m_2, \{p_5, p_6\}, s_3, e_3\rangle$. These quintuples will, however, verify that the pairs in (51) satisfy the formulas covered by (59).

(51) $\langle\{a_1\}, m_1\rangle, \langle\{a_2, a_3\}, m_1\rangle, \langle\{a_3\}, m_2\rangle$

(59) $(\exists e)[\exists w : Sw][2!z : \text{password}(z)](\exists e)[\exists Z : Zz \wedge \forall z(Zz \rightarrow Pz)]$
give(X, y, Z, w, e)

But satisfaction by these pairs is sufficient to make the binary quantification true, as we have seen earlier. Thus the polyadic logical forms that fall under this first case fail to represent an interpretation that is appropriately false in context (36).

The second case, (57), places the event quantifier outside the scope of the binary quantifier. This scope eliminates absolute exhaustivity, (54), from the start. There cannot be an event where each of two new members is given passwords and is the only one given passwords, as absolute exhaustivity would require. Such an interpretation would be false in (36), as desired, but it would also be false in (60), where the binary quantification is supposed to yield a truth. (Compare (60) with the diagram for (22) in (23).)

(60)

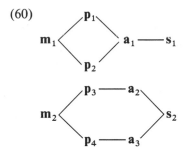

Unrelativized exhaustivity for plural objects, (53), will also lead to an interpretation that is mistakenly false in (60). Any event that includes two new members' each being given two passwords coincides with the entire context, but as we saw in section 3, the three automatic tellers that exhaust this event, $\{a_1, a_2, a_3\}$, do not give passwords to *each* of the new members.

This leaves to the logical forms assigning outside scope to the event quantifier the possibility of interpreting the atomic predicate with an exhaustivity condition relativized to the individual objects, (55). Let everything in (36) be the one event e:

(36)

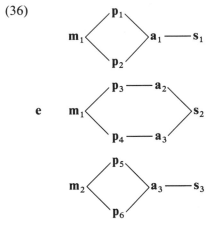

The predicate interpreted according to (55) is true of $\langle\{a_1\}, m_1, \{p_1, p_2\}, s_1, e\rangle$, $\langle\{a_2, a_3\}, m_1, \{p_3, p_4\}, s_2, e\rangle$, and $\langle\{a_3\}, m_2, \{p_5, p_6\}, s_3, e\rangle$. In each quintuple the automatic tellers are all those in the event that relate the new member to the slip of paper. The passwords in each quintuple are similarly exhaustive. As above, these quintuples will verify the binary quantification, and logical form (57) turns out to be true in (36), where sentence (35) says it ought to be false. There are not three automatic tellers that give two passwords on a slip of paper to each of two new members.

It is interesting to note that the binary quantifier combined with a wide-scope event quantifier and relativized exhaustivity does succeed in representing the intended interpretation of the shorter sentence (22).

(22) Three automatic tellers gave (the) two new members (each) exactly two passwords.

The binary quantifier allows it to be said that there are three automatic tellers and the two new members, without saying of any one group of tellers that it gives each of the new members his passwords. The wide-scope event quantifier requires one event to encompass the two members' each being given two passwords. But the binary quantifier divides the tellers among the groups that act within the event to give the members their passwords. The interpretation is then true in (23), as expected.

(23)

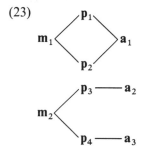

If the context includes only the event that covers all of (28), exhaustivity relativized to the individual objects requires that the passwords related to m_1 are all four given to that member in (28).

(28)

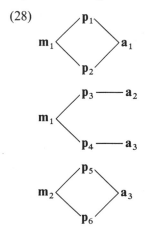

The interpretation then agrees with (22), which is false when (28) is thought of as containing just the one event (see section 1.2). Successful interpretation is, however, the exception. An atomic predicate with more than one variable over individual objects leads to the mistaken interpretation of (35) where exhaustivity is relativized to a pair of a new member and a slip of paper.[14]

The last case for n-ary quantifiers and polyadic logical forms incorporates the existential event quantifier into the n-ary quantifier, as in (58).

(58) $[\exists X : 3(X) \wedge \forall x(Xx \to Ax)]$

$$[\exists w : Sw][2!z : Pz]$$
$$[\exists Z : Zz \wedge \forall z(Zz \to Pz)]$$
$[\iota Y : 2(Y) \wedge \forall y(Yy \to My)]\exists e$ $\qquad \mathrm{give}(X, y, Z, w, e)$

The point of such a structure is to indicate that the existential quantifier is dependent on the distributive the *two new members* but the values assigned to the event variable do not depend on the semidistributive *three automatic tellers*.[15] The intended n-ary quantifier would have the truth conditions in (61), where f is a function from individual objects, such as new members, to events. Since f is a function, it chooses a unique event for each object.

(61) $\ulcorner[\exists X : \Phi[X]] \times ([\iota Y : \Psi[Y]]\exists e)\Gamma[X, y, e]\urcorner$ is true
$\quad \leftrightarrow \exists f[\exists A : \ulcorner\Phi[X]\urcorner$ is true of $A][\iota M : \ulcorner\Psi[Y]\urcorner$ is true of $M]$
$\quad ([\forall a : Aa][\exists A' : A'a \wedge \forall a(A'a \to Aa)][\exists m : Mm]$
$\qquad \ulcorner\Gamma[X, y, e]\urcorner$ is true of $\langle A', m, f(m)\rangle$
$\quad \& [\forall m : Mm][\exists A' : \exists aA'a \wedge \forall a(A'a \to Aa)]$
$\qquad \ulcorner\Gamma[X, y, e]\urcorner$ is true of $\langle A', m, f(m)\rangle)$

Like the first case where the existential quantifier is within the scope of the binary quantifier, we can always choose events corresponding to an individual new member's being given two passwords. In context (36), the predicate will be true of $\langle\{a_1\}, m_1, \{p_1, p_2\}, s_1, e_1\rangle$, $\langle\{a_2, a_3\}, m_1, \{p_3, p_4\}, s_2, e_2\rangle$, and $\langle\{a_3\}, m_2, \{p_5, p_6\}, s_3, e_3\rangle$ to any standard of exhaustivity.

(36)

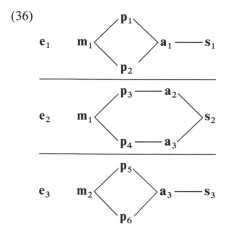

It follows that the triples $\langle\{a_1\}, m_1, e_1\rangle$, $\langle\{a_2, a_3\}, m_1, e_2\rangle$, and $\langle\{a_3\},$ $m_2, c_3\rangle$, satisfy the scope of the branching quantifier. The n-ary quantifier in (61) now imposes the condition that only one event is to be chosen for each new member. Choosing only one will not give the three automatic tellers. The one event that covers all of what happened to m_1 is not a giving of exactly two passwords. Formula (58) is therefore false in (36), as required. It is also obviously true in (60), since there we can choose for each new member a unique event of being given two passwords and three automatic tellers are the givers among those events. Thus (58) appears to render the target interpretation in a polyadic logical form.

Recall from section 1.1 the important characteristic of the target interpretations illustrated by (26).

(26) a. Three automatic tellers gave (the) two new members (each) exactly two passwords (each) on two slips of paper.

    b. $\exists e([\exists X : 3(X) \wedge \forall x(Xx \to Ax)]\forall x(\text{INFL}(e, x) \leftrightarrow Xx)$
$\wedge [\imath Y : 2(Y) \wedge \forall y(Yy \to My)][\forall y : Yy][\exists e' : e' \leq e]$
$(\text{give}(e') \wedge \forall z(\text{TO}(e', z) \leftrightarrow z = y)$
$\wedge [2!z : Pz][\exists e'' : e'' \leq e'](\forall x(\text{OF}(e'', x) \leftrightarrow z = x)$
$\wedge [\exists W : 2(W) \wedge \forall w(Ww \to Sw)]\forall w(\text{on}(e'', w) \leftrightarrow Ww))))$

Elaborating the internal scope relations by adding that the passwords given new members were each on two slips of paper does not require any change in the distribution of automatic tellers to new members and passwords. Context (27) is an event of the two new members each being given exactly two passwords each on two slips of paper, and the givers in that event are three automatic tellers.

(27)

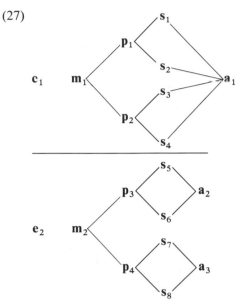

Since a_1 is the giver of m_1's passwords and m_2 gets one password from a_2 and the other from a_3, one discerns in (27) the crucial pattern from section 1.1 of contexts where cases of essential separation are true. The polyadic logical form in (62) is, however, false in (27).

(62) $[\exists X : 3(X) \wedge \forall x(Xx \to Ax)]$

$[\imath Y : 2(Y) \wedge \forall y(Yy \to My)]\exists e$

$[2!z : Pz]$
$[\exists W : 2(W) \wedge \forall w(Ww \to Sw)]$
$\text{give}(X, y, Z, w, e)$

The n-ary quantifier requires that one event be chosen for member m_2. It must be the one event of m_2 being given two passwords each on two slips of paper. If there are to be three automatic tellers between the event chosen for m_1 and the one chosen for m_2, then the event for m_2 had better be related to $\{a_2, a_3\}$. The question, then, is whether $\langle\{a_2, a_3\}, m_2, e_2\rangle$ satisfies the formula in the scope of the n-ary quantifier. It does so only if the atomic predicate is true of $\langle\{a_2, a_3\}, m_2, p_3, \{s_5, s_6\}, e_2\rangle$ and of $\langle\{a_2, a_3\}, m_2, p_4, \{s_7, s_8\}, e_2\rangle$. But the predicate is false of these quintuples, since the two automatic tellers did not both give the individual password p_3 and they did not both give password p_4. The logical form falters on the requirement that the atomic predicate express a true relation among the participants (which, it will be recalled, is necessary for distributivity).

The earlier success of the *n*-ary quantifier incorporating the event quantifier is thus exceptional. It breaks down when the internal scope relations are multiplied. Like the polyadic logical forms without *n*-ary quantifiers (section 3), the derived interpretations are in general false where they should be true.

The fault with polyadic logical form is its syntax, simply the fact that the θ-role bound by *three automatic tellers* does not separate. Suppose that as a last effort to maintain polyadic logical form, one adopted all the other features of Davidsonian logical form. In particular, predicates are fully decomposed into an event concept and constituent θ-roles. For an analysis of (63) to be adequate to express distributivity, exhaustivity must be absolute, as in (64).

(63) Three automatic tellers gave the two new members each two passwords.

(64) 'give(X, y, Z, e)' is true of $\langle \mathbf{A, m, P}, e \rangle$
$\leftrightarrow \forall z(\text{INFL}(\mathbf{e}, z) \leftrightarrow \mathbf{A}z) \wedge \text{give}(\mathbf{e}) \wedge \forall z(\text{TO}(\mathbf{e}, z) \leftrightarrow z = \mathbf{m})$
$\wedge \forall z(\text{OF}(\mathbf{e}, z) \leftrightarrow \mathbf{P}z)$

Each member must have an event where he alone is given passwords if (63) is to entail that he is given two. Davidsonian decomposition simply falls under one of the alternative analyses of the predicate discussed with reference to (54) above. Since exhaustivity is absolute, there must be an existential event quantifier within the scope of all quantifiers binding individual variables. It would be contradictory to say of the same event that each of two members is given passwords there and each is the only one. The logical form is therefore (65), which is equivalent to (66).

(65) $\exists e([\exists X : 3(X) \wedge \forall x(Xx \rightarrow Ax)][\imath Y : 2(Y) \wedge \forall y(Yy \rightarrow My)]$
$[\forall y : Yy][\exists Z : 2(Z) \wedge \forall z(Zz \rightarrow Pz)][\exists e' : e' \leq e] \text{give}(X, y, Z, e'))$

(66) $\exists e([\exists X : 3(X) \wedge \forall x(Xx \rightarrow Ax)][\imath Y : 2(Y) \wedge \forall y(Yy \rightarrow My)]$
$[\forall y : Yy][\exists Z : 2(Z) \wedge \forall z(Zz \rightarrow Pz)][\exists e' : e' \leq e]$
$(\mathbf{\forall x(\text{INFL}(e', x) \leftrightarrow Xx)} \wedge \text{give}(e') \wedge \forall z(\text{TO}(e', z) \leftrightarrow z = y)$
$\wedge \forall z(\text{OF}(e', z) \leftrightarrow Zz)))$

But (66) differs from our (67) only in the placement of the θ-role for *three automatic tellers* (boldfaced).

(67) $\exists e([\exists X : 3(X) \wedge \forall x(Xx \rightarrow Ax)](\mathbf{\forall x(\text{INFL}(e, x) \leftrightarrow Xx)})$
$\wedge [\imath Y : 2(Y) \wedge \forall y(Yy \rightarrow My)][\forall y : Yy][\exists Z : 2(Z) \wedge \forall z(Zz \rightarrow Pz)]$
$[\exists e' : e' \leq e](\text{give}(e') \wedge \forall z(\text{TO}(e', z) \leftrightarrow z = y)$
$\wedge \forall z(\text{OF}(e', z) \leftrightarrow Zz)))$

The reader is invited to review the argument against polyadic logical form with or without n-ary quantifiers, assuming fully decomposed predicates and a mereology of events (which is otiose in (65) and (66)).[16] The constraint that θ-roles are not separated is sufficient to undermine polyadic logical form. We need to be able to characterize an event in the way in which e is described by the last three lines of (67), indifferent to who its INFLers are or what their number is.

Chapter 5

Theta-Roles, Events, and Contexts of Events

Events are individuals in the world. An event is not as solid as a table, but it is as concrete as, say, a baseball game. We talk about events, individuate them, and refer to them directly, as in *That was a fine baseball game*. What is said about events reveals that they can have a complex structure. The predicate 'baseball-game(x)' denotes individuals that contain, according to the rules of the game, opposing teams and players in prescribed roles executing various actions. The roles and actions taken to constitute an event of this kind are a matter of definition, or in this case, invention, and the concept of a baseball game may be so precisely articulated that some of its constituent roles and actions do not exist outside the game. However ad hoc they are, one knows that whatever is a baseball game has these roles and actions fulfilled. Consider (1):

(1) It was a fine baseball game. The home team in that game was some kids from Nanuet, and the visitors in that game were from Bay Ridge.

Because of our knowledge of baseball, we know that the kids from Nanuet and Bay Ridge were pitching, batting, fielding, and idling on the bench. We also know, because the anaphoric *that game* refers to the *same* baseball game, that the Nanuet kids played *against* the Bay Ridge kids. Note that (1) does not contain a dyadic predicate that directly expresses this relation between the two teams. Rather, the knowledge of this relation between them is conveyed indirectly through what we know about the event in which they all participated. Their relation to each other is inferred from a direct relation, the θ-role, that each kid bears to the same game:

(2) Some kids from Nanuet played against some kids from Bay Ridge.

(3) $\exists e([\exists X : \exists x Xx \land \forall x(Xx \rightarrow Nx)]\forall x(\text{INFL}(e, x) \leftrightarrow Xx) \land \text{play}(e)$
$\land [\exists Y : \exists y Yy \land \forall y(Yy \rightarrow By)]\forall y(\text{against}(e, y) \leftrightarrow Yy))$

Note that decomposition is a general method for unpacking any poly-adic relation. The existence of appropriate θ-roles does *not* depend on the success of a claim that there is a small class of thematic relations—such as Agent, Theme, Experiencer—that cross-classify all the arguments to all verbs and that tend to stand in some regular correspondence to syntactic argument positions.[1] If the language had just the three verbs—*eat, enjoy,* and *surround*—there would be scant evidence of thematic relations, but it would not change the evidence, see section 1 below, that the underlying structure consists of an event concept and θ-roles. (For further discussion of thematic relations and θ-roles, see n. 2.)

(4) a. eater(e, x) ∧ eat(e) ∧ eaten(e, y)
    b. enjoyer(e, x) ∧ enjoy(e) ∧ enjoyed(e, y)
    c. surrounder(e, x) ∧ surround(e) ∧ surrounded(e, y)

The account of plurals does however impose a constraint on the content of θ-roles. To reduce plural predication to singular predication, as in (5), the θ-role must be true of each and every participant.

(5) $\forall x(\Theta(e, x) \leftrightarrow Fx)$

Thus, the conditions for bearing any given θ-role in an event are in themselves fairly weak.

One cook or another slices the vegetables or stirs the pot or sharpens knives or prepares the sauce. To do any of these things or to be responsible for any other essential step in the process is to bear the subject θ-role in (6).

(6) The five children cooked the meal.

(7) $\exists e([\iota X : 5(X) \wedge \forall x(Xx \leftrightarrow Cx)]\forall x(\text{INFL}(e, x) \leftrightarrow Xx) \wedge \text{cook}(e)\ldots)$

If the five children only salted water, it is possible that they would still be cooks in some event, as far as the θ-role is concerned. Each child acts in a way that could be part of an event of cooking. It is left to the event concept 'cook(e)' to assert that their salting water did not add up to a meal, and therefore that the sentence is false. Now suppose that there was a proper event of cooking by twenty children to which the five children referred to contributed only the salted water. There is an event of cooking, and the five children were cooks in that event, but (6) is still false, because the five children were not all the cooks.[3] In general, any theory of plural predication is subject to two constraints: it must allow that the objects denoted by a plural argument do different things, and it must require that they do everything there is to do. Other theories may accomplish this with a different, more assertive view of θ-roles. A theory that puts together Davidsonian logical form with plural objects[4] could say that object x is an agent of an event of cooking only if x slices and dices, stirs and fries—a conjunctive condition. On this view, *none* of the twenty children is an agent of an event of cooking, but the plural object corresponding to all of them is. The group of five children salting water is not a cook either. The objection to plural objects turns out, however, to exclude this way of construing θ-roles.

The proposal that the underlying structure of predicates consists of an event concept and θ-roles is given its most sustained and convincing defense by Parsons (1990). He shows that it explains the semantics of several different constructions and their interactions, among which are causatives, inchoatives, nominalizations, temporal adverbials, and some problems in tense and aspect. The following section reviews only those aspects of his argument directly relevant to the semantics of plurals. It centers on the problem of "variable polyadicity," which first led Davidson to propose his logical form.

My discussion of variable polyadicity will say something about the conception of events that Davidsonian logical form is committed to. More is said in section 2, on event identity. As first remarked in chapter 1, if first-order quantifiers are to fit in with Davidsonian logical form, they must include within their scope a quantifier over parts of events. Sections 3 and 4 discuss the question of quantifying over parts of events and the nature of contexts of events.

1   Variable Polyadicity

Davidson is interested in a solution to Kenny's (1963) problem of "variable polyadicity":

(a) Jones buttered the toast in the bathroom with a knife at midnight.

... Most philosophers today would, as a start, analyze this sentence as containing a five-place predicate with the argument places filled in the obvious ways with singular terms or bound variables. If we go on to analyze "Jones buttered the toast" as containing a two-place predicate, "Jones buttered the toast in the bathroom" as containing a three-place predicate, and so forth, we obliterate the logical relation between these sentences, namely that (a) entails the others. Or, to put the objection another way, the original sentences contain a common syntactic element ("buttered") which we intuitively recognize as relevant to the meaning relations of the sentences. But the proposed analyses show no such common syntactic element. (1967, 236)

Davidson proposes that "there is, of course, no variable polyadicity. The problem is solved in the natural way, by introducing events as entities about which an indefinite number of things can be said" (p. 242). The logical relation of (a) to the other sentences is made plain if the predicate is decomposed as in (8):

(8) $\exists e(\text{butter}(e) \wedge \text{INFL}(e,j) \wedge \text{OF}(e,t) \wedge \text{in}(e,b)$
    $\wedge \text{ with}(e,k) \wedge \text{at}(e,m))$[5]

By first-order logic alone, (8) entails the logical form for *John buttered the toast in the bathroom*:

(9) $\exists e(\text{butter}(e) \wedge \text{INFL}(e,j) \wedge \text{OF}(e,t) \wedge \text{in}(e,b))$

Since I lean on θ-roles to reduce plural predication to singular predication, as in (10), my view of plurals is committed to decomposition wherever plurals may occur.

(10) $\forall x(\Theta(e,x) \leftrightarrow \text{F}x)$

As in (11), predication of events must embrace all kinds of situations or states.

(11) a. The blue triangles are similar to the red triangles.
    b. $\exists e(\text{similar}(e) \wedge [\imath X : \forall x(Xx \leftrightarrow (Bx \wedge Tx))]\forall x(\text{INFL}(e,x) \leftrightarrow Xx)$
       $\wedge [\imath Y : \forall y(Yy \leftrightarrow (Ry \wedge Ty))]\forall y(\text{to}(e,y) \leftrightarrow Yy))$

It is therefore consonant with this view that the problem of variable polyadicity is itself a common feature of all verbs, not just those that describe actions, as Davidson points out (1967, 243–244). Parsons (1990) is careful to show that the arguments for an event analysis apply as well to states. It is also important for us that the underlying events and decomposition into θ-roles simply is the analysis of predication. So I will review Parsons's arguments that predication is never polyadic: *'V(e,x,y)'. Unlike Davidson's original proposal but with a refinement suggested by Castañeda (1967), there is no difference in logical form between arguments, such as subject and object, and the objects of prepositional phrases and adverbial modifiers. Every argument has its own θ-role, which is an independent conjunct. To the extent that Parsons's arguments do not carry us all the way to this conclusion, we can let the semantics of plurals decide the question. There is no good reason that a predicate should ever be primitively polyadic.

That there is some kind of decomposition is demanded simply by the fact that some modifiers, locatives in particular, can be iterated indefinitely, as in (12).

(12) They met in a strange country in a park in a cabin ... (Parsons 1990, 288, n. 8)[6]

Quite apart from considerations about entailments, we cannot tolerate an infinite number of primitive relations. It will at first appear, however, that we can have both entailments and a finite lexicon without a decomposition whose constituents are predicates of events. Thus if '$M^2(x, y)$' is a relation between (groups of) meeters and locations, then (13), a logical form for (12) that does not appeal to events, will entail all of the shorter sentences except perhaps for *They met*.

(13) $M^2(x, s) \wedge M^2(x, p) \wedge M^2(x, c)$

This last entailment goes through if the logical form for *They met* asserts that they met somewhere, as in (14).

(14) *They met* $= \exists y M^2(x, y)$

Otherwise, it suffices to have a meaning postulate, as in in (15), relating the dyadic and monadic forms of *to meet*.

(15) $M^2(x, y) \rightarrow M^1(x)$

What shows that events are the entities about which an indefinite number of things are said, as Parsons makes clear, is that the conjunction of (16) and (17) does *not* entail (18):

(16) Brutus stabbed Caesar in the back.

(17) Brutus stabbed Caesar in the thigh.

(18) Brutus stabbed Caesar in the back in the thigh.

In simultaneous gestures, Brutus stabbed Caesar in the back of the chest and in the front of the thigh. Both (16) and (17) are true, but (18) is false. The analysis with underlying events allows that the stabbing in the back is not the same event as the stabbing in the thigh:

(19) $\exists e(\text{stab}(e) \wedge \text{INFL}(e, B) \wedge \text{OF}(e, C) \wedge \text{in}(e, b))$

(20) $\exists e(\text{stab}(e) \wedge \text{INFL}(e, B) \wedge \text{OF}(e, C) \wedge \text{in}(e, t))$

(21) $\exists e(\text{stab}(e) \wedge \text{INFL}(e, B) \wedge \text{OF}(e, C) \wedge \text{in}(e, b) \wedge \text{in}(e, t))$

The conjunction of (19) and (20) does not entail (21). In contrast, the conjunction of (22) and (23) does entail (24). The analysis without events therefore misinterprets (16) through (18).

(22) $\text{stab}(B, C, b)$

(23) $\text{stab}(B, C, t)$

(24) $\text{stab}(B, C, b) \wedge \text{stab}(B, C, t)$

The problem of variable polyadicity occurs in just the same way in sentences about states. The crucial evidence in favor of underlying events is again that the entailments go in one direction and not the other:

(25) The board is grooved with sharp furrows along its edge. (Parsons, 1990, p. 191)
(26) The board is grooved with sharp furrows.
(27) The board is grooved along its edge.

The board is in a state of having grooves with sharp furrows, and it is in a state of having grooves along its edge. But since the sharp furrows are across the corner and the grooves along its edge are blunt, there is no state of the board's being grooved with sharp furrows along its edge.

(28) IBM is in Paris in a hilly area. (Parsons, 1990, p. 195)
(29) IBM is in Paris.
(30) IBM is in a hilly area.

(31) Peanuts taste good with ice cream in Sichuan sauce.
(32) Peanuts taste good with ice cream.
(33) Peanuts taste good in Sichuan sauce.

(34) The table {fits/was useful} in the kitchen in a closet.
(35) The table {fits/was useful} in the kitchen.
(36) The table {fits/was useful} in a closet.

(37) Pat has freckles on the front below the neck.
(38) Pat has freckles on the front.
(39) Pat has freckles below the neck.

These considerations do not yet bring us all the way to the proposed account of variable polyadicity. Unbounded iteration must be analyzed as conjunction, and events must underly the semantics. Furthermore, sentences about states are also analyzed in this way. But no argument has yet shown that a predicate cannot have a finite number of polyadic variants. The logical form of Davidson's sentence, (40), could just be (41), where only the iterative prepositional phrases are independent conjuncts:

(40) John buttered the toast with a knife at midnight in the bathroom.

(41) $\exists e(\text{butter}(e, j, t, k) \wedge \text{at}(e, m) \wedge \text{in}(e, b))$

The suggestion concedes a place for events but attempts to formally distinguish Davidsonian modifiers from the arguments proper. It leaves untouched, however, the problem of variable polyadicity among the arguments. Why should *John buttered the toast with a knife* entail that John buttered the toast? Parsons points out that one of the answers suggested above fails to be a general solution. One might derive the entailment by attributing to *John buttered the toast* a logical form asserting that John buttered the toast *with something*. One supposes that a lexical item does not have variants. Its adicity is fixed, and when some of its arguments do not appear overtly, they are implicitly bound by an existential quantifier. This suggestion is plausible only if the implicit arguments are obligatory. There are, however, examples where the arguments are semantically optional:

(42) John wrote the note to Mary.

(43) a. John wrote the note.
    b. $*\exists e\exists x(W_1(e, j, n, x)$
    c. $\exists e W_2(e, j, n)$

(44) John threatened Mary with a knife.

(45) a. John threatened Mary.
    b. $*\exists e\exists x(T_1(e, j, m, x)$
    c. $\exists e T_2(e, j, m)$

(46) Brutus stabbed Caesar.

(47) a. Brutus stabbed
    b. $*\exists e\exists x S_1(e, b, x)$
    c. $\exists e S_2(e, b)$

Notes need not be written to anyone, threats are not always made with an instrument, and stabbings sometimes miss. The logical forms for (43a), (45a), and (47a) should not entail that some things fulfill these roles.

   If implicit arguments are not the answer, the sentences related by inference contain formally unrelated predicates. Meaning postulates must bear out the inference. Thus the inference from (42) to (43a) requires the postulate that $\forall e\forall x\forall y\forall z(W_1(e, x, y, z) \rightarrow W_2(e, x, y))$. Five postulates are necessary just to support the inferences among the sentences in (48):

(48) a. John wrote a note to Mary with a quill.
    b. John wrote a note to Mary.
    c. John wrote a note with a quill.
    d. John wrote a note.

On this view, every lexical item comes with a family of meaning postulates that spell out the inferential relations among its variants, which vary with respect to the optional but noniterative θ-roles. At this point it is unclear what one had hoped to gain by pursuing primitive polyadicity for the noniterative θ-roles. Surely it is not that one ends up with separate accounts for the inferences in (49) and (50), the first being a logical entailment and the second requiring meaning postulates.

(49) John wrote a note on the back of an envelope $\vdash$ John wrote a note

(50) John wrote a note to Mary $\vdash$ John wrote a note

Someone determined to find polyadicity somewhere can retreat to one more position. Overburdened by the meaning postulates, one could concede to Davidson and Parsons the analysis of variable polyadicity wherever it occurs among semantically optional items. This leaves behind the safe ground of arguments that are semantically obligatory.

(51)   Brutus touched Caesar.

(52) *Brutus touched.

(53)   Caesar was touched.

(54) $\exists e \exists x (\text{touch}(e, x, c))$

If Caesar was touched, then necessarily something touched him. It is safe to assign (53) the logical form in (54), which licenses the inference from (51) without meaning postulates. This view in effect replaces (55) with (56) whenever Θ_i is obligatory.

(55) $V(e) \wedge \ldots \Theta_i(e, x_i) \ldots$

(56) $V(e, x_i) \ldots$

The verb then expresses a primitive polyadic relation between the event and the obligatory arguments. This view might hold some attraction, since it formally recognizes the difference between optional and obligatory arguments.[7] But if this were such a compelling consideration, it would also compel a distinction in logical form for the obligatory manner adverbial in (57).

(57) John worded the letter *(carefully).

(58) John wrote the letter (carefully).

It is doubtful, however, that anyone would endorse on these grounds alone any such difference between the manner adverbials in (57) and (58).

Further reason to suspect the formal distinction between obligatory and optional arguments is that it would obstruct a univocal treatment of thematic relations. At least it will not be apparent in logical form that the theme is the argument that bears a thematic relation with a certain content. The obligatory theme in (59) will have a rather different logical form from the optional theme in (61).

(59) Brutus touched Caesar.
(60) $\exists e(\text{touch}(e, b, c))$

(61) Brutus stabbed Caesar
(62) $\exists e(\text{stab}(e, b) \wedge \text{OF}(e, c))$

There may, of course, be a theory of thematic relations that would find that the logical form in (60) attributes to its third argument a property that is the same as one attributed to the prepositional object in (62) and in virtue of this property both arguments are classfied as themes. There is no a priori reason that logical form should be transparent to thematic relations, as in (63) to (64).

(63) $\exists e(\text{touch}(e) \wedge \text{Agent}(e, b) \wedge \text{Theme}(e, c))$

(64) $\exists e(\text{stab}(e) \wedge \text{Agent}(e, b) \wedge \text{Theme}(e, c))$

Because it effaces the distinction between obligatory and optional arguments, a logical form with transparent thematic relations will itself have to be supplemented by some extralogical theory of why the theme is obligatory in (63). The fact is that logical form cannot transparently represent both thematic relations and the distinction between obligatory and optional arguments.

There is nothing to keep us from assuming that every argument position corresponds to an independent conjunct, and the semantics of plurals gives us two reasons for doing so. First, as remarked above, the account of plural reference and plural predication in chapter 2 demands it, and second, a Davidsonian logical form is necessary for the syntax of those interpretations that demonstrate essential separation, as we have seen in chapter 4.[8]

Beyond these considerations, Parsons (1990, 97–99) offers an ingenious argument that every θ-role is an independent conjunct, even if it is semantically obligatory. Assuming that stabbings require agents and instruments, one can nevertheless give a noncontradictory report of a dream about an impossible situation:

(65) In a dream last night, I was stabbed, although in fact nobody had stabbed me, and I wasn't stabbed with anything.

The dreamer feels the jabs, and the wounds open, but he sees neither the assailant nor the weapon, although he is in a position to do so. If the θ-roles are all independent, there is this noncontradictory report:

(66) $\exists e(\text{stab}(e) \wedge \text{Theme}(e, \text{I}) \wedge \neg\exists x\, \text{Agent}(e, x) \wedge \neg\exists y\, \text{With}(e, y))$

Otherwise, the report lapses into contradiction:

(67) $\exists e(\exists x\, \text{stab}(e, x, \text{I}) \wedge \neg\exists x\, \text{stab}(e, x, \text{I}))$

Parsons worries that the apparent coherence of (65) may have an alternative pragmatic account. The speaker's assertion is literally contradictory, as in (67), but since he is assumed to be rational, he succeeds in communicating that something took place similar to a stabbing.

It seems, however, that coherent reports of this kind reveal enough structure to allay this worry. In (68), *I was stabbed* can communicate that I was stabbed, but not by anyone.

(68) a. In a dream last night, I was stabbed, but it wasn't a real stabbing.
   b. Wounds didn't hurt, open, or bleed.
   c. The assailant and the weapon were invisible.
   d. *The assailant missed. (I wasn't touched.)
   e. The assailant missed, but I got cut anyway.

It cannot, however, communicate that someone stabbed at me but I was not struck. If the literal assertion is that I was stabbed by someone, why should there be such an asymmetry? It contradicts the assertion that I was stabbed in my dream last night if there were none of the *effects* of a stabbing, (68d), but it is no contradiction to deny the agent, as in (68e). If, however, an agent is made explicit, as in (69a), it then becomes contradictory to deny it, (69e).

(69) a. In a dream last night, someone stabbed me, but it wasn't a real stabbing.
   b. Wounds didn't hurt, open, or bleed.
   c. The assailant and the weapon were invisible.
   d. *The assailant missed. (I wasn't touched.)
   e. *The assailant missed, but I got cut anyway.

2 Event Identity

The theory of plurals fortunately does not contribute much to the problems of event identity. Its commitments are just those already inherent in Davidsonian logical form, which Parsons discusses extensively.[9] To show it at its worst, I cite two examples where the ontological commitments are the most likely to raise suspicion. The first of them I owe to James Higginbotham (class lecture, MIT, 1988).

Suppose that Jim drank exactly one beer in exacty one hour. Then both (70) and (71) are true, and so is (72).

(70) Jim drank a beer in nothing less than an hour.

(71) Jim drank beer for an hour.

(72) Jim's drinking of a beer in nothing less than an hour was his drinking of beer for an hour.

One could hardly hope to find a more convincing example of the same event being given alternative descriptions. But if the same event verifies the Davidsonian logical forms in (73) and (74), then that event will also verify the logical form in (75) for the sentence (76).

(73) $\exists e(\text{drink}(e) \wedge \text{Agent}(e, j) \wedge \text{Theme}(e, a \text{ beer})$
$\wedge \text{ in}(e, \textit{nothing less than an hour}))$

(74) $\exists e(\text{drink}(e) \wedge \text{Agent}(e, j) \wedge \text{Theme}(e, \textit{beer}) \wedge \text{for}(e, \textit{an hour}))$

(75) $\exists e(\text{drink}(e) \wedge \text{Agent}(e, j) \wedge \text{Theme}(e, \textit{beer})$
$\wedge \text{ in}(e, \textit{nothing less than an hour}))$

(76) Jim drank beer in nothing less than an hour.

That is, if (72) is a true identity statement, then the conjunction of (70), (71), and (72) should entail (76) according to their Davidsonian logical forms. Sentence (76) is, of course, false. The Davidsonian logical forms are thus committed to the claim that an event that lasts for an hour cannot be the same as one that takes place in an hour. That is, the process of drinking beer for an hour is not the same as the perfective event of drinking beer in an hour. Furthermore, since one does judge (72) to be true, it must be that its predicate asserts not identity but something less demanding, like spatiotemporal coincidence.[10]

The second example concerns symmetric predicates, among which I first consider those that are nonreflexive. The sentences within (77) and (78) are analytically equivalent, but the logical-form proposal is committed to the view that identical events do not verify the equivalent sentences.

(77) a. The Carnegie Deli sits opposite Carnegie Hall.
b. Carnegie Hall sits opposite the Carnegie Deli.

(78) a. Avery Fisher Hall is different from Alice Tully Hall.
b. Alice Tully Hall is different from Avery Fisher Hall.

For if the Carnegie Deli's sitting opposite Carnegie Hall were the same event as Carnegie Hall's sitting opposite the Carnegie Deli, then one could infer from (79) that the Carnegie Deli sits opposite the Carnegie Deli, (81).

(79) a. $\exists e(\text{sits}(e) \wedge \text{Theme}(e, \text{CD}) \wedge \text{opposite}(e, \text{CH}))$
  b. $\exists e(\text{sits}(e) \wedge \text{Theme}(e, \text{CH}) \wedge \text{opposite}(e, \text{CD}))$

(80) a. $\exists e(\text{different}(e) \wedge \text{Theme}(e, \text{AF}) \wedge \text{from}(e, \text{AT}))$
  b. $\exists e(\text{different}(e) \wedge \text{Theme}(e, \text{AT}) \wedge \text{from}(e, \text{AF}))$

(81) a. $\exists e(\text{sits}(e) \wedge \text{Theme}(e, \text{CD}) \wedge \text{opposite}(e, \text{CD}))$
  b. The Carnegie Deli sits opposite the Carnegie Deli.

(82) a. $\exists e(\text{different}(e) \wedge \text{Theme}(e, \text{AF}) \wedge \text{from}(e, \text{AF}))$
  b. Avery Fisher Hall is different from Avery Fisher Hall.

Treating Carnegie Hall's sitting opposite the Carnegie Deli as a distinct event from the Carnegie Deli's sitting opposite Carnegie Hall does not spoil the symmetry of these predicates. What makes a predicate symmetrical is that it satisfies (83), rather than (84):

(83) $\forall x \forall y (\exists e(Ve \wedge \Theta_1(e, x) \wedge \Theta_2(e, y)) \leftrightarrow \exists e(Ve \wedge \Theta_1(e, y) \wedge \Theta_2(e, x)))$

(84) $\forall e \forall x \forall y ((Ve \wedge \Theta_1(e, x) \wedge \Theta_2(e, y)) \leftrightarrow (Ve \wedge \Theta_1(e, y) \wedge \Theta_2(e, x)))$

Certain versions of Davidsonian logical form, mine among them, will force the events to be distinguished just to avoid contradiction in the analysis of any symmetrical predicate, reflexive or not. To secure for (85) the implication that Robin hit Sandy, these versions require that the object (or objects) denoted by any NP be all the bearers of a given θ-role.

(85) a. Robin hit Sandy.
  b. $\exists e(\text{hit}(e) \wedge \forall x(\Theta_1(e, x) \leftrightarrow x = \text{r}) \wedge \forall x(\Theta_2(e, x) \leftrightarrow x = \text{s}))$

If Robin is the sole hitter, then he, rather than some other hitter sharing the event, will have hit Sandy. If θ-roles are related to their NPs in this way, then (86) is understood to say that Robin is the sole resembler in some event, and (87) to say that Robin is the sole meeter.

(86) a. Robin resembles Sandy.
  b. $\exists e(\text{resemble}(e) \wedge \forall x(\Theta_1(e, x) \leftrightarrow x = \text{r})$
    $\wedge \forall x(\Theta_2(e, x) \leftrightarrow x = \text{s}))$

(87) a. Robin met Sandy.
  b. $\exists e(\text{meet}(e) \wedge \forall x(\Theta_1(e, s) \leftrightarrow x = \text{r}) \wedge \forall x(\Theta_2(e, x) \leftrightarrow x = \text{s}))$

Sentence (86) is then necessarily false, unless Robin's resembling Sandy is not the same event as Sandy's resembling Robin and the content of Θ_1, being a resembler, is not the same as the content of Θ_2, being resembled. For theories with plural objects, alternative versions of Davidsonian logical form might not stipulate that the NP denotes all objects bearing the θ-role. To be certain that (85) entails that Robin hit Sandy, meaning postulates for 'hit(e)' would say that anything that is a hitter in an event hits everything that is hit in the event. Any two θ-roles would have to be similarly related. It would then follow from (85) that Robin hit Sandy, even if the event contains other hitters and things hit. On this account, plural objects are essential to recover the sum-of-plurals interpretation. *The girls hit the boys* should not imply that every one of the girls hit every one of the boys. It will not if the only agent in the event is the plural object corresponding to the girls and the group of boys is the only theme. Then, indeed, every hitter hits everything hit, as the meaning postulate requires, without every girl's hitting every boy. If all this is done to avoid exclusive reference to the bearers of a θ-role, then we manage to avoid committing ourselves to distinct events in the case of *reflexive* symmetric predicates. In the event of Sandy's resembling Robin, Sandy need not be the only resembler. Identifying Sandy's resembling of Robin and Robin's resembling of Sandy leads only to the conclusion that Sandy resembles Sandy and Robin resembles Robin. Of course, a nonreflexive symmetric predicate will still have to split events to avoid the false entailments discussed above.

Someone favoring a particular metaphysical thesis about what events are may be skeptical of the nonidentities that symmetric predicates lead to. Everyone, however, must doubt that any coherent notion of events could emerge from a theory that forced Sandy's being dissimilar to Robin and Robin's being dissimilar to Sandy to be nonidentical events but allowed Sandy's being similar to Robin and Robin's being similar to Sandy to be the same. It is perhaps a virtue that the version of Davidsonian logical form without plural objects rules out this possibility. If it is required that the object or objects denoted by an NP be all the bearers of a given θ-role, then every symmetric predicate leads to the finer-grained ontology.

To the skeptic of fine-grained events, there is the further frustration of independent evidence from Peter Ludlow (1987) that symmetric predicates split events. Significantly, his argument does not depend on Davidsonian logical form, which is dispensed with below. Symmetric predicates present a problem, attributed to Hans Kamp and Jan van Eijck (see Heim 1990, 147, n. 6), for construing definite descriptions and unbound pronouns as Russellian definite descriptions. On the face of it, the singular definite descriptions in (88) should simply fail to refer, since there is no unique resembler and no unique resembled.

(88) If someone resembles someone else, the resembler envies the resembled.

This failure of reference also stands in the way of construing the pronouns in (89) as singular, definite descriptions.

(89) If someone resembles someone else, he envies him.

Formula (90) gives the logical form for (88) and (89).

(90) $[\forall e : \exists x \exists y \text{ resemble}(e, x, y)][\exists e' : R(e, e')][\iota x : \exists y \text{ resemble}(e, x, y)]$
$[\iota y : \exists x \text{ resemble}(e, x, y)] \text{ envy}(e', x, y)$

The problem is not unique to singular descriptions. In (91) and (92) it surfaces not as a failure of reference but as the expectation that *the meeters* refers maximally to everyone present, and similarly for *the met*.

(91) If some people meet some other people for the first time, the meeters each introduce themselves to all of those met.

(92) If some people meet some other people for the first time, they each introduce themselves to all of them.

(93) $[\forall e : \exists X \exists Y \text{ meet}(e, X, Y)][\exists e' : R(e, e')][\iota X : \exists Y \text{ meet}(e, X, Y)]$
$[\iota Y : \exists X \text{ meet}(e, X, Y)][\forall x : Xx][\forall y : Yy] \text{ introduce}(e', x, x, y)$

It is plain from the meaning of the sentence, however, that this is not so, since it is not implied that anyone introduced himself to a member of his own party.

I leave it to Ludlow and the others cited in chapter 10 to argue that definite descriptions and unbound pronouns should be analyzed as Russellian definite descriptions. If they are to be so analyzed, then Kamp's and van Eijck's problem is solved, as Ludlow suggests, by relativizing the definite description to events and by supposing that x's resembling y is not the same event as y's resembling x, as in (90). If the events responding to symmetric predicates are fine-grained, then in any one of them the resemblers are not the resembled, and the meeters are not the met. The definite descriptions and the pronouns in the above sentences all end up with their intended reference.

The two examples, Higginbotham's example involving aspect and the example of symmetric predicates, have shown that Davidsonian logical form is committed to a finer-grained ontology than one might have expected at first, especially if one holds Davidson's view that events are individuated by their causal relations. Parsons (1990, 155–159) surveys a number of other cases where the theory forces events to be distinguished and also cases where the theory forces identity.[11]

3   Mereology and Contexts of Events

Sentence (94) reports that the ensemble event was unharmonious and not any one student's note.

(94) Unharmoniously, every organ student sustained a note on the
       Wurlitzer for sixteen measures.

But to assert that each student sustained his own note while attributing disharmony to the collective performance requires quantification over the parts of the larger event, as shown in (95).

(95) $[\exists e : \text{unharmonious}(e)][\text{every } x : Sx][\exists e' : e' \leq e]$
       $(\text{strike}(e') \wedge \forall z(\text{INFL}(e', z) \leftrightarrow z = r)) \dots$

As remarked in chapter 1, first-order quantifiers are always followed by a quantifier over parts of events. I assume that there are enough parts and overlapping events to go around. Suppose that two boys eat two pizzas, each eating half of each pizza. For reasons to be given in chapter 6, we would like to know that there is the event of the two boys eating two pizzas, the two events corresponding to what the individual boys did, each of which is an eating of two half-pizzas, and the two events corresponding to what happened to the pizzas. Each of these events has both boys as participants. So that these five events can be found, I will assume that the space of events is at least as fine-grained as the regions of space and time that events occupy:

(96) If A is any nonnull spatiotemporal region filled by events, there
       exists an event e such that the region filled by e is A.[12]

(This is not to assume that any concept of, for instance, pizza-eating events is so fine-grained, or that it is closed under any of the mereological relations discussed below. See n. 13.) The intended part-whole relation for events and the relation of overlap for events follows closely the natural interpretation of these relations for regions of space and time, and they form a mereology, satisfying the standard axioms in (97):[14]

(97) a. $x\mathbf{O}x$ (read 'x overlaps x')
       b. $x\mathbf{O}y \leftrightarrow y\mathbf{O}x$
       c. $x \leq y \leftrightarrow \forall z(z\mathbf{O}x \rightarrow z\mathbf{O}y)$
       d. $x = y \leftrightarrow (x \leq y \wedge y \leq x)$

   e. $x\mathbf{O}y \leftrightarrow \exists z\forall u(u\mathbf{O}z \leftrightarrow (u\mathbf{O}x \wedge u\mathbf{O}y))$ (meet)

   f. $\forall x\forall y\exists z\forall u(u\mathbf{O}z \leftrightarrow (u\mathbf{O}x \vee u\mathbf{O}y))$ (fusion)

The axioms in (96) and (97) are a fair characterization of those events that occupy space and time, which is as far as they go. What about such abstract events as those in (98)?

(98) Converging on zero, every natural number n is assigned $1/n$.

(99) $[\exists e : \text{converge-on-0}(e)][\text{every } x : Nx][\exists e' : e' \leq e]$
    $(\forall z(\text{INFL}(e',z) \leftrightarrow z = x) \wedge \text{assign}(e') \wedge \forall z(\text{OF}(e',z) \leftrightarrow z = 1/x))$

There is the state of every natural number being assigned (by some function) its inverse, and this state is convergent on 0. We can only assume that the primitive notion of events and parts provides for each natural number the state of being assigned its inverse.[15]

The underlying space of events, as the fusion axiom (97f) makes clear, imposes no condition of spatial or temporal contiguity on what is to count as an individual event. The same activity in the world—whether it is, for example, the moves performed by a moving company in one year or a day's labor of one of its crews—may be truthfully described as an individual event, as a loading of 250 trucks, in one context and as a plurality of events, as loadings of 250 trucks, in another context. To reject spatiotemporal conditions in the underlying metaphysics does not prevent a particular predicate from imposing such a condition on the individuals it denotes. Thus the moves performed by a moving company in one year are unlikely to be an individual event for the predicate 'x is a simultaneous loading of trucks'. The year's business may, however, cover several events that this predicate does denote.

As anyone briefly acquainted with the literature on mereology will know, objects are really no different from events in failing to impose an underlying condition on contiguity. Reichenbach (1947) and Goodman (1956) point out that a discourse may take anything in the world to correspond to its individuals, to be the values of its variables. Reichenbach's example is a house full of furniture. The individuals it contains are arms and legs to a joiner, but to a mover it contains one individual. The joiner's discourse is constructed from predicates, like 'x is joined to y', that denote arms and legs. But the mover's predicate 'x weighs a half ton over net allowance' denotes one scattered individual, the contents of the house. Thus the same stuff in the world, the furniture in the house, is one individual under one description and many individuals under another. What is to be taken as an individual is left to the predicates or to other aspects of the discourse. The underlying scheme of things does not fix physical boundaries.

4   Contexts of Events

To investigate the semantic connection between sentences and events, I ask speakers to judge sentences true or false in given contexts. A context of events is just the relevant events. Much of the evidence of the following chapters comes from the evaluation of sentences in contexts of events that are understood or perceived not to be closed under recombinations of their parts. In such a context, it is not the case that if two events belong to it so does the event that combines them. The existence of such contexts does not reflect a metaphysical thesis. Nonclosure does not, for example, invalidate the fusion axiom, (97f). Rather, contexts, like predicates, vary in what they take to be the relevant individuals. It happens, as we will see below, that a particular event concept like 'x is a loading of one or more trucks' is itself closed under fusion but the context of events is not. In this respect, quantifying over events is again no different from quantifying over objects. This is an important point, since talk about events should be no more obscure than talk about objects. In this connection, I show that the distinction between contexts that are closed under recombinations of their parts and those that are not is one that distinguishes domains of possible and actual individuals, whether objects or events.

4.1   Possible and actual individuals

Recall from chapter 1 that sentences such as those in (100) have event-dependent interpretations that quantify over a domain of individual events, the events in a given context. In the logical form in (101), context appears as a restricting predicate, '$C(e)$'.

(100) a. Few truckers load(ed) up one or more trucks.
       b. Only a few truckers load(ed) up one or more trucks.
       c. No more than twenty truckers load(ed) up one or more trucks.
       d. (Exactly) twenty truckers load(ed) up one or more trucks.

(101) $[\forall e : Ce \land \text{load}(e) \land [\exists Y : (\geq 1)(Y) \land \forall y(Yy \to \text{truck}(y))]$
       $\quad \forall y(\text{OF}(e, y) \leftrightarrow Yy)]$
       $\quad [Qx : \text{trucker}(x)][\exists e' : e' \leq e]\forall z(\text{INFL}(e', z) \leftrightarrow z = x)$

The relevant events are those in the context denoted by the predicate 'load-up-one-or-more-trucks(e)'. What is the extension of this predicate for a given piece of the world, such as the one depicted in (102) and described below, and what in this piece of the world must correspond to an individual event in the context assumed?

(102)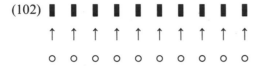

Each block in (102) is a distinct truck, and the circle linked to it is its cargo. Suppose that several truckers loaded up each truck. Each loading of one truck with its cargo is an atomic event for the predicate *load up one or more trucks*. What are the individual events that (102) contributes to the domain quantified over in (100) and (101)? Any fusion of the atomic events is a loading up of one or more trucks. Is it necessary for the domain of events given by a context to include all combinations of the atomic events? Suppose that contexts were always so comprehensive. Then the event-dependent interpretation of sentence (100d), for example, is true just in case any combination of the atomic events in (102) involves 20 truckers. This is possible only if each atomic event involves the same 20 truckers. But the event-dependent interpretation of (100d) does not in general entail that the same twenty truckers participated in every event. In reflecting on that interpretation, one presumably does not asssume that the context of events includes all combinations of atomic events.

The question of what combinations of atoms correspond to individuals in the assumed context concerns not only events but also objects. In general, a context that is closed under combinations of atoms is a context of *possible* individuals. A context of *actual* individuals is not closed under all combinations. I first show how quantifiers over objects sometimes have contexts of possible individuals and sometimes contexts of actual individuals. It will then be shown that the contexts of events quantified over are similarly divided between possible and actual individuals.

Montague (1974a, 1974b) has pointed to (103) and Hazen (1976) to (104) as examples of quantifying over possibilia:

(103) There was a man whom no one remembers. (Montague 1974a, 1974b)

(104) All the buildings the zoning board has prevented from being built would have been monstrous. (Hazen 1976)

In general, possible objects may have possible, nonactual parts. To pursue the analogy to the individual events of (102), I consider the special case of quantifying over possible objects that are all made from actual, existing atoms. This is done by constructing an appropriate context for Hazen's (104).

Suppose for simplicity that buildings are constructed modularly from whole rooms. Also assume that the zoning board's ruling, alluded to in (104), was against some existing defective construction units, a particular warehouse full of modular rooms. Just like the atomic events of (102), these rooms are atomic objects. The individual buildings prevented by the zoning board correspond to combinations of the atoms.[16] In this situation, (104) would be false if there is *any* combination of rooms from that warehouse (in any arrangement) that would not be monstrous. Thus the domain for the quantifier *all the buildings the zoning board has prevented from being built* must be closed under combinations of the atoms.

To evaluate (105), let us now consider a situation in which, contrary to the zoning board's ruling, buildings have been constructed out of the defective rooms in that warehouse.

(105) All the illegal buildings are six stories tall.

It is certain that not every combination of rooms corresponds to one of the constructed buildings. Otherwise, the same room would have to appear in different locations. Sentence (105) has an interpretation that is true if every one of the constructed buildings is 6 stories tall. The context for the quantifier *all the illegal buildings* thus includes only the constructed buildings. Note that if the context included all combinations of rooms, (105) could not have a true interpretation, for some combinations of rooms are surely not six stories tall. In this context the individuals are actual; the combinations of atoms quantified over are the existing individuals.

Another example comparing possible and actual individuals is (106), said while standing before a tree densely covered with leaves:

(106) All the bunches of leaves larger than three are allergenic.

In this example, the individuals quantified over are bunches of leaves, and the atoms are leaves on the tree. The truth of (106) depends on every combination of leaves, any one of which falsifies (106) if it contains more than three leaves and fails to be allergenic. Among the possible bunches in the domain of the quantifier are those that could not exist at the same time if the leaves on the tree were actually segregated. Incompatible bunches require at least one leaf to be in different locations at the same time.

Compare now a context for (107) in which the fallen leaves of the allergenic tree have been raked up into several bunches scattered on the lawn:

(107) All the bunches of leaves (on the lawn) are allergenic.

On the assumption that (106) still characterizes the allergen, (107) is true if each of the bunches one sees on the lawn contains more than three leaves. The sentence is not falsified by the one-, two-, or three-leafed bunches that can be created from the actual bunches lying there. The domain of the quantifier *all the bunches of leaves* (*on the lawn*) is thus not closed under combinations of the atoms. Note that the domain of actual bunches is essentially a partition of the atoms on the lawn, since no leaf is in two places at once. A domain of actual individuals observed at a given moment will never attribute to its atoms more than one location. This property always holds even of stuff in constant flux, like the bits of glass, the atoms, constantly regrouping in a kaleidoscope to form new clusters, the individuals.

There are two different approaches to quantifying over possibles and actuals that it may be helpful to consider. Montague (1974a, 1974b) proposes that the predicate 'E(x)', which attributes existence, picks out the actual individuals from a larger domain that includes all possible individuals. Thus, quantifier expressions such as *all the illegal buildings* and *all the bunches of leaves* (*on the lawn*) are ambiguous between the two interpretations in (108) and (109). Interpretation (108) contains quantifiers over possible individuals, and (109) contains quantifiers over actual individuals:

(108) a. $[\forall x : \text{illegal-building}(x)]$ (possibles)
       b. $[\forall x : \text{bunch-of-leaves-on-the-lawn}(x)]$ (possibles)

(109) a. $[\forall x : \text{illegal-building}(x) \wedge \text{E}(x)]$ (actuals)
       b. $[\forall x : \text{bunch-of-leaves-on-the-lawn}(x) \wedge \text{E}(x)]$ (actuals)

When the quantifier in (105), *all the illegal buildings*, is interpreted as in (109a) its domain includes just the constructed buildings, since only these exist. Similarly, when the quantifier in (107) is interpreted according to (109b), it quantifies only over the bunches on the lawn, since the other bunches one might form from these same leaves do not exist.

An alternative approach, more in line with Hazen's (1976) discussion of modal logic, relies on the property that at any moment, a domain of actual individuals attributes to its atoms only one location. Define a *reification* to be any domain of individuals that has this property. It will more or less partition the atoms.[17] For examples (104) and (105), any way in which one could actually assemble all the rooms from the warehouse into buildings is a reification. For examples (106) and (107), each reification is a different way of actually segregating the leaves of the tree into bunches. On this approach, quantifying over possible individuals involves a modal operator; quantifiers not within the scope of the modal operator have a domain of actual individuals. Thus *All the illegal buildings are monstrous* and *All the bunches of leaves are allergenic* are ambiguous between the interpretations in (110) and (111). The modal operator R means "in any reification."

(110) a. R[$\forall x$: illegal-building(x)] is-monstrous(x)   (possibles)
       b. R[$\forall x$: bunch-of-leaves(x)] is-allergenic(x)   (possibles)

(111) a. [$\forall x$: illegal-building(x)] is-monstrous(x)   (actuals)
       b. [$\forall x$: bunch-of-leaves(x)] is-allergenic(x)   (actuals)

There is always an implicit modal operator whenever a sentence is understood to be about possible individuals. The interpretations of (110) are paraphrased, *In any way there could be illegal buildings, all of them are monstrous*, and *In any way there could be bunches of leaves, all of them are allergenic*.

We return now to events. Whatever the method of quantifying over possible and actual individuals, events are like other individuals. Quantification over events also distinguishes between the possible and the actual. I now construct appropriate contexts first illustrating a domain of possible events.

Suppose that stalls for an abattoir are manufactured so that each holds one hog at a time. This one-on-one relationship between stalls and hogs has for a consequence the event-dependent interpretations of the sentences in (112):

(112) a. One hog {can fit/fits} into one stall at a time.
       b. One stall {can be/is} filled up with one hog at a time.

       c. Two hogs (can) fit into two stalls at the same time.
       d. Two stalls {can be/are} filled up with two hogs at the same time.

       e. *n* hogs (can) fit into *n* stalls at the same time.
       f. *n* stalls {can be/are} filled up with *n* hogs at the same time.

The event-dependent interpretation is paraphrased by (113):

(113) a. Whenever there is a fitting of hogs into n stalls at the same
           time, n hogs fit into them.
       b. Whenever there is a filling up of stalls by n hogs at the same
           time, n stalls are filled up with them.

For any given herd of hogs and available stalls, a sentence in (112) could
be falsified by any conceivable combination of the hogs and stalls. Thus
(112f) is falsified if one can find any n among the given stalls that can be
filled up with other than n hogs.

   In the preceding example, the possible events quantified over do not
combine already existing atomic events. They are only what can possibly
be done to any combination of possible participants among the given hogs
and stalls. We can, however, find a context of already existing atomic
events whose combinations make up all the possible events. Suppose that
hogs have in fact been slaughtered in stalls. We can consider as an atomic
event the period before slaughter when a single stall was filled up with
however many hogs it accommodated. These atomic events exist, since
hogs have been slaughtered in stalls. Recall the event-dependent interpretations of (112), which follow from the one-on-one relationship between
stalls and hogs. These interpretations are meant to be general laws that
hold in arbitrary situations. What in the situation in which hogs have been
slaughtered would disconfirm these interpretations? This interpretation of
(112f) would be falsified if *any* combination of n atomic events among the
existing ones defined above took place at the same time and involved
other than n hogs. Thus the domain of possible events includes recombinations of the atoms.

   To compare a domain of actual events, assume that one is speaking of
the operations of a particular abattoir that follows a particular schedule,
slaughtering hogs in a series of sessions. The actual events can be understood to correspond to the sessions, so the event-dependent interpretation
of (114) is true if at each session 25 hogs fit into stalls:

(114) a. Twenty-five hogs fit into stalls.
       b. Whenever there is a fitting of hogs into stalls, 25 hogs fit into
           them.

Note that this interpretation is not falsified by finding a session in which
some proper subset of the stalls used did not hold 25 hogs. Every event in
the domain must include all the stalls used in some session and all the hogs
held in that session. Although proper parts of these events would also
satisfy the predicate 'fit-into-stalls(e)', they are not individuals in the understood sequence of events.[18] Thus in some contexts there can be a

domain of individual events that is not closed under combinations of its atoms.

As I remarked earlier, what is crucial when we ask speakers to judge the truth of a sentence is that a sentence can be interpreted with respect to a particular context of individual events that excludes alternative combinations of their parts. Events, as we have seen, are no different from other individuals in allowing this and in allowing quantification over all possible events.

The contexts of events used in the examples are contextually specified proper subsets of the events that could be obtained from alternative combinations of their parts. It is sufficient for us that the contexts specified in these examples are judged acceptable, but as part of a larger interest in events, one could ask whether any proper subset of the possible events can be specified as a context of actual events. All of the contexts in the examples have the property, mentioned above, that identifies reifications among domains of individuals. No atomic events, no event stuff, is assigned more than one location. It may be a general constraint on how one thinks about actual events that every accessible context is a reification.

If one can define reifications of events, quantifying over actual and possible events is open to both of the treatments seen earlier for quantifying over actual and possible objects. Thus the event-dependent interpretations of (114), which quantify over actual and possible events, may be interpreted as either (115) or (116).

(115) a. $[\forall e : \text{fit}(e) \land \text{into}(e, \text{stalls})]\, \text{INFL}(e, 25\ \text{hogs})$ (possibles)
     b. $[\forall e : \text{fit}(e) \land \text{E}e \land \text{into}(e, \text{stalls})]\, \text{INFL}(e, 25\ \text{hogs})$ (actuals)

(116) a. $\text{R}[\forall e : \text{fit}(e) \land \text{into}(e, \text{stalls})]\, \text{INFL}(e, 25\ \text{hogs})$ (possibles)
     b. $[\forall e : \text{fit}(e) \land \text{into}(e, \text{stalls})]\, \text{INFL}(e, 25\ \text{hogs})$ (actuals)

4.2   Contexts of events and inferences about cumulativity

No speaker judges the event-dependent interpretation of (117) to entail that the same 20 truckers loaded up each and every truck (if any were loaded).

(117) a. Twenty truckers loaded up one or more trucks.
     b. Whenever there was a loading up of one or more trucks, 20 truckers were involved.

The explanation has been that the event quantifier is restricted to the events of a context and the events of a context are not normally closed under recombinations of their parts:

(118) $[\forall e : Ce \land \text{load}(e) \land [\exists Y : (\geq 1)(Y) \land \forall y(Yy \rightarrow \text{truck}(y))]$
$\qquad \forall y(\text{OF}(e, y) \leftrightarrow Yy)]$
$\qquad [Qx : \text{trucker}(x)][\exists e' : e' \leq e]\forall z(\text{INFL}(e', z) \leftrightarrow z = x)$

If this is true, it would appear to invalidate the inference in (119), which speakers do not hesitate to accept, assuming that these 10 truckers and those 10 truckers are disjoint groups.

(119) These 10 truckers loaded up one or more trucks.
Those 10 truckers loaded up one or more trucks.

The 20 truckers loaded up one or more trucks.

If the existential event quantifier is taken to be restricted to some context of events, there is no reason to expect that the context containing an event of these 10 truckers loading trucks and an event of those 10 truckers loading trucks will also contain the fusion of these two events.

(120) $[\exists e : Ce](\text{load}(e) \land \text{INFL}(e, \text{these 10 truckers})$
$\qquad \land \text{OF}(e, \text{one or more trucks}))$
$[\exists e : Ce](\text{load}(e) \land \text{INFL}(e, \text{those 10 truckers})$
$\qquad \land \text{OF}(e, \text{one or more trucks}))$

$[\exists e : Ce](\text{load}(e) \land \text{INFL}(e, \text{the 20 truckers})$
$\qquad \land \text{OF}(e, \text{one or more trucks}))$

What, then, accounts for the intuitive validity of (119)? The sum-of-plurals interpretation seems to demand that the events are closed under recombinations of their parts, in order to shore up the inference, but the event-dependent interpretation in (117) rejects this. The interpretations are reconciled if the logical form for the sum of plurals is revised so that the existential event quantifier is itself a plural, a second-order expression. If there are some loadings whose agents were these 10 truckers and there were some loadings whose agents were those 10 truckers, then, of course, there are some loadings whose agents were the 20 truckers.

(121) $[\exists E : \forall e(Ee \rightarrow Ce)](\forall e(Ee \rightarrow \text{load}(e))$
$\qquad \land$ the loaders in E were these 10 truckers
$\qquad \land$ loaded in E were one or more trucks)
$[\exists E : \forall e(Ee \rightarrow Ce)](\forall e(Ee \rightarrow \text{load}(e))$
$\qquad \land$ the loaders in E were those 10 truckers
$\qquad \land$ loaded in E were one or more trucks)

$[\exists E : \forall e(Ee \rightarrow Ce)](\forall e(Ee \rightarrow \text{load}(e))$
$\qquad \land$ the loaders in E were the 20 truckers
$\qquad \land$ loaded in E were one or more trucks)

The events verifying the conclusion are just those verifying the premises. The inference is valid without appeal to a new event derived by fusing those verifying the premises (for an alternative, see n. 19). Chapter 6 provides independent evidence that the existential event quantifier is second-order. Later chapters will also spell out the logical forms sketched in (121).

Chapter 6
A Semantics for Plurality and Quantification

An adequate logical language will have the four features introduced in chapter 1. First, it will reduce plural predication to singular predication of objects and events via a Davidsonian logical form. Second, it will introduce a mereology of events. Davidsonian logical form accommodates first-order quantification in natural language by assuming that every first-order quantifier has within its immediate scope a quantifier over parts of events. Third, to represent the truth conditions of sentences that combine independent and dependent quantifiers, it will separate θ-roles in logical form, which are held together by reference to events. Finally, if reference to events is to hold together *all* cases of essential separation and to be adequate for all of them, then, as its fourth feature, the logical language will have descriptive anaphora to refer to events. The argument for these features rests on motivating the first and the third, Davidsonian logical form and separation. As I remarked in chapter 1, a commitment to the other features will follow almost immediately from these. Chapter 2 showed how the foundational question of plural reference bears upon logical form. And chapter 4 laid out the argument that a Davidsonian logical form and separation are essential.

In chapters 6 to 12, I take up the empirical and formal questions that arise once the logical language is fitted with these four major features. The important problems of semidistributivity, cumulative quantification, and cumulative reference I treat in chapters 8 to 10.

The empirical problems are taken up in the context of a formal semantics for plurality and quantification. The formal investigation addresses two questions: how to extend a definition of truth and satisfaction to accommodate plural reference, and how to regiment translation from natural language into logical form, the structure that enters into an inductive definition of truth. It is the burden of translation to assign to a sentence of natural language all and only those logical forms that express its meanings, and these are typically a small subset of what could be composed from the quantifiers, operators, terms, and predicates that have been used to translate it into the logical language. Given a logical language that is rich enough to accommodate the crucial features, translation from natural language will have to be strictly regimented.

The rules provided settle the question about whether there is a rule-governed translation to go along with the claims about how logical form ought to turn out. Yet I do insist that the four major features of logical form be held apart from the details of logical form that I propose and certainly apart from the techniques of translation. An example will illustrate the grounds for such a distinction and why my claims are presented abstractly as features of any adequate logical language. Consider (1) on its cumulative interpretation and the English sentence (2).

(1) No more than two detectives found solutions to no more than five crimes.

(2) No more than two detectives found solutions to crimes, and that was to no more than five crimes.

I champion the claim that these sentences from natural language have the same logical form and that this logical form adheres closely to the structure of (2). We know that the second conjunct in (2) consists (at least) of a pronoun, a quantifier, and a θ-role, and any speaker of English will recognize that this structure supports a fairly complex interpretation, some details of which we turn to shortly. It is just a fact about English that these complex interpretations are accessible to structures, like the second conjunct of (2), that present on the surface little more than pronoun, quantifier, and θ-role. I claim that the logical form of (1) deploys the same elements to the same effect. A modest transformation of (1) puts it into a form where it and (2) will face the same problems of interpretation and end up with the same meaning: extrapose the prepositional phrase (PP) 'to(e, no more than five crimes)' and introduce an anaphoric pronoun to bind the exposed event variable:

(3) [no more than two detectives found solutions]$_i$,
     and that$_i$ ([[$(\leq 5)y : Cy]_j$ to(e_i, t_j))

By merely projecting the natural language onto a fragment of itself (regimentation in the classic sense), such a move does not address any problems latent in the fragment, among which is the analysis of the pronouns in the second conjuncts of (2) and (3). My proposal assumes that an empirical argument can be made that is not entirely dependent on having in hand a theory of anaphora. An argument for a tacit pronoun would point to successful paraphrase (which can be judged because it is an idiom that belongs to the natural language), to the failure of other methods to achieve the same, and to other incidental properties that might betray the presence of a pronoun. The result is the reduction of one problem, cumulative quantification, to other unsolved or controversial problems, such as pronominal anaphora. If only we understood the latter, we would have a complete analysis of cumulative quantification.

I go beyond immediate claims for synonymy and identical structure to document a semantic connection to things and events in the world. After all, I want to persuade you that reference to events and predication of events is what discriminates among the truth conditions of sentences with plurals, and so some definition of truth is called for.[1] To deliver it, I must adopt some view of pronominal anaphora and prejudge any other questions implicated in the interpretation (2). Since cross-reference to events is central to the proposal, I extensively discuss issues surrounding pronominal anaphora (see especially chapter 10). Other things are decided more arbitrarily, just to present a definition that fixes reference in the appropriate way. Note that the cumulative interpretation of (1) requires a long-distance extraction out of a NP. The PP 'to(x, no more than five crimes)' is the complement to the noun *solutions* rather than to the matrix verb *find*. It is not obvious how to relate the extraposed PP to the antecedent clause. The target logical form is the same as that of (2), whatever that is. To reflect on the latter's meaning, it is obvious that *to no more than five crimes* applies not to detectives' findings of solutions but to solutions. We understand that no more than five crimes are among those to which detectives found solutions. Thus the structure consisting of a copula and prepositional phrase in (2) is elliptical for something along the lines of (4) and (5), which reconstruct much of the antecedent conjunct:[2]

(1) No more than two detectives found solutions to no more than five crimes.

(2) No more than two detectives found solutions to crimes, and that was to no more than five crimes.

(4) No more than two detectives found solutions to crimes, and that$_i$ was such that to no more than five crimes did detectives find solutions.

(5) No more than two detectives found solutions to crimes, and
$$[\exists E : \forall e(Ee \leftrightarrow \text{that}_i(e))][(\leq 5)y : Cy][\exists X : \forall x(Xx \rightarrow Dx)][\exists e : Ee]$$
$$(\forall z(\text{INFL}(e, z) \leftrightarrow Xz) \wedge \text{find}(e)$$
$$\wedge [\exists W : \forall w(Ww \rightarrow (Sw \wedge \forall z(\text{to}(w, z) \leftrightarrow z = y)))]$$
$$\forall z(\text{OF}(e, z) \leftrightarrow Wz))$$

Again, it is a fact of English that the second conjunct of (2) supports such an interpretation, which I rely on in proposing the identical structure for (1). My claim is that (1) is the same as (2), ellipsis and all. To derive truth conditions, we cannot let an ellipsis stand in logical form, but I have nothing insightful to say about reconstructing the ellipsis. In fact, although it remains my belief that (1) attains its interpretation by first becoming (2), I say nothing at all about the ellipsis in (2), shortchanging the relation between (1) and (2). The problem of the ellipsis is beyond the scope of this work, and so, to push through a semantics for cumulative quantifiers, a translation for them alone is given. I hope that the details and the ad hoc and provisional stipulations necessary to specify a logical form for which one can fix a definition of truth do not obscure my general claims for the four major features of the logical language.

This chapter sketches some aspects of translation, and section 2 presents the basic assumptions about truth and satisfaction that inform the rest of the semantics. The rules of syntax and the clauses of the truth definition that appear in chapters 6 to 12 are gathered together in appendix II.

1   Translation: LF to Logical Form

In a syntactic structure prior to interpretation, we have simply identified θ-roles (Chomsky 1981) and Davidsonian roles for event participants. To adopt a notation that is more transparent from the point of view of syntax, I let prepositions stand for θ-roles. I assume that syntactic structures have a form similar to (8) before they are translated into logical form:

(6) Every agent sold most buildings to few investors.

(7) $[_S \text{INFL}(e, \text{every agent})$
     $[_{VP} \text{sell}(e) \text{ OF}(e, \text{most buildings}) \text{ to}(e, \text{few investors})]]$

(8) $[_S \text{INFL}(e, \text{NP}_1)[_{VP} \text{V}(e) \text{P}_2(e, \text{NP}_2) \ldots \text{P}_n(e, \text{NP}_n)]]$

Linguistic theory has developed logical form principally with a view toward its role in an account of how a sentence of natural language comes to be ambiguous in virtue of structure.[3] Designated elements that belong to the logical form of a sentence, operators and variables, are expected to result in alternative acceptable interpretations when assigned different scope or different binding. Scope assignment and binding are, however, subject to principles of grammar that constrain movement and binding. On this view, logical form embraces those aspects of interpretation that fall under very general grammatical principles. Consonant with this view, I assume that something like quantifier raising (QR) (May 1977) applies to (8) and the like to derive structures that indicate relative scope. Principles of grammar constrain the derived structures in the usual way with the usual effect on interpretation:[4]

(9)   [every agent]$_i$ [most buildings]$_j$[few investors]$_k$
      [$_S$ INFL(e, t_i) sell(e) OF(e, t_j) to(e, t_k)]

(10) [$Q_i x : N'$]$_i$ INFL(e, t_i)[$Q_j y : N'$]$_j$ V(e) OF(e, t_j)

(11) [$Q_j y : N'$]$_j$[$Q_i x : N'$]$_i$ INFL(e, t_i) V(e) OF(e, t_j)

The structures derived by QR, which I will call *LFs* following common usage, are not those that enter into a definition of truth and satisfaction. The logical forms proper are to be derived from LFs by further rules of translation.[5] I now note some constraints on translation.

Once quantifiers over events are admitted into logical form, it does not turn out that they can just appear anywhere with equally felicitous results. The logical language includes three types of quantifiers over events, an existential quantifier, a universal quantifier, and a second-order definite description. The distribution of the first two is restricted. A clause contains no more than one token of either of them. It is as if these quantifiers were confined to an aspectual system that plucks from the world some events with respect to which the rest of the sentence is evaluated. Once they are chosen, all subsequent reference to events is by definite description, and the rest of the sentence is understood to be a complete and exact description of those events. Chapter 7 will demonstrate this constraint, which is relevant to the interaction of plural reference and quantification over parts of events. Broadly, the point of the constraint is to exclude logical forms whose truth conditions would incorrectly characterize the participation in an event of those referred to by a plural.

A further syntactic constraint applies to the distribution of the universal quantifier over events. In chapter 1, section 3, the universal quantifier was found to be restricted by VP to yield the event-dependent interpretation of (12) ((62) in chapter 1):

(12) No more than 10 students collaborated on three problems.

(13) [$\forall e : collaborate(e)$ *on three problems*][$(\leq 10)x : Sx$][$\exists e' : e' \leq e$]
      $\forall z($INFL$(e', z) \leftrightarrow z = x)$

The VP-restricted quantifier must retain matrix scope:

(14) *[$Qx : N'$][$\forall e : VP$][$\exists e' : e' \leq e$]$\forall z($INFL$(e', z) \leftrightarrow z = x)$

(15) *[QN′]$_i$ [∀e : [$_{VP}$ ... t_i ...][Qx : N′][∃e' : $e' \leq e$]∀z(INFL(e', z)

  ↔ $z = x$)

On certain assumptions, the restriction is not entirely surprising. If the construction were derived by VP-preposing at LF, it could be opaque to further extraction, analogous to VP-preposing in the surface syntax.[6]

The discussion that follows in section 1.1 will give us some reason to believe that the minimal domain for QR adjunction includes the verb, or, more generally, the event concept, when the predicate is a nonverbal projection.[7] Specifically excluded is a movement that terminates in a position short of the main predicate, as in (16):[8]

(16) * ... [$_{VP}$ V[$_{PP}$ NP$_i$[$_{PP}$ P t_i]]]

Finally, I will assume that QR is obligatory for first-order quantifiers.[9] If QR applies optionally to a second-order quantifier, the exposed trace may eventually be bound by an intervening distributive operator, as in (17).

(17) [∃V : Φ]$_i$[... Θ(e, t_i) ...]

  ⇒ [∃V : Φ][... [∀v : Vv] ... ∀x(Θ(e, x) ↔ $x = v$) ...]

(18) Two boys (*each*) ate a pizza.

A second-order quantifier left *in situ* at LF obtains a nondistributive interpretation in logical form:

(19) [... Θ(e, [∃V : Φ]) ...] ⇒ [... [∃V : Φ]∀x(Θ(e, x) ↔ Vx) ...]

1.1 Negative events

No interpretation of (20) expresses the vacuous claim in (21), that there is some event where nothing arrived, or the contradictory one in (22) or its equivalent with a restricted event quantifier in (23), that there was an arriving where nothing arrived:

(20) Nothing arrived.

(21) ∃e[no x : thing(x)](∀z(INFL(e, z) ↔ $z = x$) ∧ arrive(e))

(22) ∃e(arrive(e) ∧ [no x : thing(x)]∀z(INFL(e, z) ↔ $z = x$))

(23) [∃e : arrive(e)][no x : thing(x)]∀z(INFL(e, z) ↔ $z = x$)

Interpretations in which a decreasing quantifier falls within the scope of an existential quantifier over events are not entirely felicitous. The problem is hardly peculiar to Davidsonian logical forms. Admitting any place for events or for points or intervals of time invites it:

(24) $\exists t[\text{no } x : \text{thing}(x)] \text{ arrive}(x, t)$

I do not resolve the problem here, but I assume no one would conclude that predicates have no place for either times or events.

The problem is not one to be addressed by a formal constraint barring decreasing quantifiers from falling within the scope of existential event quantifiers. This scope relation seems necessary if we are going to make room for such apparent talk of negative events, as a felicitous use of (25) would illustrate:

(25) Once, no one knows when exactly, nothing arrived.

The appositive makes plain that specific reference to a time or event is not intended. Sentence (25) expresses a general proposition and so requires an existential quantifier over events or times, as in (26):

(26) $[\exists t : Ct][\text{no } x : \text{thing}(x)] \text{ arrive}(x, t)$

Formula (26) in its scope relations is identical to (24), but (25) is not vacuously true. Presumably the difference lies in a contextual restriction. It must not be trivial that nothing arrived at one of the events or times C. I have nothing to say about the content of C. Perhaps (25) should be considered in the broader context of sentences that appear to talk about causing or perceiving so-called negative events:[10]

(27) It made no one stir.

(28) John saw no one stir.

(29) Gracefully, no one stirred.

In any case, it would be difficult to deny, however the idiom of negative events is ultimately treated, that an existential event quantifier includes within its scope a decreasing quantifier in the logical form of (25). This would suggest that logical forms (21) and (24) represent interpretations that are literally vacuously true.[11]

Although the vacuous interpretations have logical forms that differ slightly from those of acceptable interpretations, such as (25), the same cannot be said for the contradictory interpretations (22) and (23):

(22) $\exists e(\text{arrive}(e) \land [\text{no } x : \text{thing}(x)]\forall z(\text{INFL}(e, z) \leftrightarrow z = x))$

(23) $[\exists e : \text{arrive}(e)][\text{no } x : \text{thing}(x)]\forall z(\text{INFL}(e, z) \leftrightarrow z = x)$

The verb ought not to end up in a position outside the scope of the decreasing quantifier.[12] For this reason I assume that the minimal domain for QR includes the verb. The quantifier is raised to VP or higher.[13]

1.2   The typology of NPs and of quantifiers over events

The claim is that to quantify over objects is to quantify concurrently over
events and their parts. Among the various ways to do this, it would not be
unexpected if the logical form of first-order quantification contained both
quantifiers over events and mereological predicates. A rule to this effect
might be one that applies to structures of the form in (30) to insert a
quantifier over events:

(30) $[QN']_i \Phi \rightarrow [QN']_i [\exists e : e \leq e'] \Phi$

This would be one way to fix the meaning of first-order quantification.
The appeal to parts of events, the proper translation of first-order quantifiers, and the clauses interpreting assigned logical forms are the subject of
chapter 7. If a clause is to contain no more than one existential quantifier
over events, as noted above, then (30) is not the form in which first-order
quantifiers quantify over parts of events. Rather, it will turn out that every
first-order quantifier is followed by a (second-order) definite description
of events. I should point out that, however the first-order quantifiers of
natural language are finally translated, it will look rather different from
the translation of second-order quantifiers. Quantifying over parts of
events fits only our understanding of the first-order quantifiers. The division of natural-language NPs between first- and second-order quantifiers
is thus echoed in the rules that translate these NPs.[14] Each rule specifies
exactly how the quantifiers of its class relate to quantifying over events.
(On the classification into first- and second-order quantifiers, see chapter
2; chapter 3, section 1; chapter 9, section 5; chapter 7; Higginbotham and
Schein 1989; and Schein 1992).

In this classification, *all* descriptions, definite and indefinite, plural and
singular, can be taken to be second-order quantifiers. The singular descriptions need not quantify over parts of events. Thus singular and plural
can be reduced to a difference of cardinal adjective:[15]

(31) a. the elm $[\exists X : 1(X) \wedge \forall x(Xx \leftrightarrow \text{elm}(x))]$
     b. the elms $[\exists X : (> 1)(X) \wedge \forall x(Xx \leftrightarrow \text{elm}(x))]$
     c. an elm $[\exists X : 1(X) \wedge \forall x(Xx \rightarrow \text{elm}(x))]$
     d. some elms $[\exists X : (> 1)(X) \wedge \forall x(Xx \rightarrow \text{elm}(x))]$

The typology of event quantifiers includes second-order definite descriptions as descriptive anaphors cross-referring to events in the logical
form of cumulative quantification. There is also reason to believe that
indefinite reference to events is second-order as well, at least sometimes.

A standard sum-of-plurals interpretation requires indefinite, plural reference to events when it contains a collective predicate of some sort.

(32) Twenty composers collaborated on seven shows.

Sentence (32) could report one large project, but more likely in the cut-throat, impecunious business of Broadway is that some 20 composers joined in rival productions, amounting in all to 7 shows. Plural reference to events will represent an interpretation that is true in the circumstances. Thus, according to (33), some collaborations were such that their collaborators were 20 composers, and their production amounted to 7 shows:

(33) $\exists E([\exists X : 20(X) \land \forall x(Xx \to Cx)]$
$([\forall x : Xx][\exists e : Ee]\text{INFL}(e, x) \land [\forall e : Ee][\forall x : \text{INFL}(e, x)]Xx)$
$\land \forall e(Ee \to \text{collaborate}(e))$
$\land [\exists Y : 7(Y) \land \forall y(Yy \to Sy)]([\forall y : Yy][\exists e : Ee] \text{ on}(c, y)$
$\land [\forall e : Ee][\forall y : \text{on}(e, y)] Yy))$

It is doubtful that a singular quantifier over events would yield a truth in the given situation:

(34) $\exists e([\exists X : 20(X) \land \forall x(Xx \to Cx)]\forall x(\text{INFL}(e, x) \leftrightarrow Xx)$
$\land \text{collaborate}(e)$
$\land [\exists Y : 7(Y) \land \forall y(Yy \to Sy)]\forall y(\text{on}(e, y) \leftrightarrow Yy))$

It is doubtful that the event that is the mereological sum of mutually hostile collaborations is itself a collaboration, as (34) would require. Formula (34) fits only the intepretation of (32) asserting one big project.

I will assume that event quantifiers are like their nominal counterparts. Definite and indefinite descriptions are all underlyingly second-order, whether singular or plural, and so '$[\exists e : \Phi]$' is replaced everywhere with '$[\exists E : 1(E) \land \forall e(Ee \to \Phi)]$'.

2   Truth, Satisfaction, and Second-Order "Modalized" Quantification over Events and Their Parts

Translation must assign to a sentence all and only those logical forms that express its meanings. Systematic translation would seem to slip beyond reach when one surveys the range of formulas used to express quantification over event parts or the new combinations made possible by separation. For example, examining the pair of (35) and (36), one might get the idea that translation allows one to freely introduce several existential quantifiers binding distinct event variables.

(35) Gracefully, every football player pushed the pram up the hill.

(36) $[\exists e : \text{graceful}(e)][\text{every } x : Fx][\exists e' : e' \leq e$
$\wedge \text{push}(e')]\forall z(\text{INFL}(e', z) \leftrightarrow z = x)\dots$

But if this were so, one of the meanings of (37) ought to be that John did something, something else perhaps was done to the toast, and perhaps a third thing happened in the kitchen:

(37) John buttered the toast in the kitchen.

(38) $\exists e \exists e' \exists e'' \exists e'''$ (Agent$(e, \text{John}) \wedge$ buttered(e')
$\wedge$ Patient$(e'', \text{the toast}) \wedge \text{In}(e''', \text{the kitchen}))$

(39) $\exists e$ Agent$(e, \text{John}) \wedge \exists e$ buttered(e)
$\wedge \exists e$ Patient$(e, \text{the toast}) \wedge \exists e \text{ In}(e, \text{the kitchen})$

The rules of translation must somehow exclude assigning to (37) either (38) or (39) as an interpretation.

To address impossible interpretations such as (38) and (39), we will in some way have to fix the distribution of quantifiers over events and the mereological predicates they bind into. As it is, the only acceptable pattern is the one shown in (40), where the domain of any embedded quantifier is restricted to the parts of an event selected in evaluating the immediately superior quantifier:

(40) $[\exists e_0 : \Phi]\dots[\exists e_1 : e_1 \leq e_0]\dots[\exists e_2 : e_2 \leq e_1]\dots[\exists e_3 : e_3 \leq e_2]\dots$

The pattern in (40) recalls the interpretation of tense operators in (41). In evaluating each Past operator, it is understood that its domain of times are those that precede the time introduced by the superior tense operator, if there is one.

(41) PPPΦ

(42) σ satisfies $\ulcorner P\Phi \urcorner$
$\leftrightarrow [\exists t : t \leq \sigma(`t_r')]\exists \sigma_0(\sigma_0(`t_r') = t \wedge \sigma_0 \approx_{`t_r'} \sigma \wedge \sigma_0 \text{ satisfies } \Phi)$

(Here '$\sigma_0 \approx_{`t_r'} \sigma$' abbreviates '$\forall u(u \neq `t_r' \rightarrow \sigma_0(u) = \sigma(u))$'.) What is characteristic of tense logic or modal logic is that quantification over times or possible worlds and the relation that restricts it is "modalized," that is, concealed in the semantic clauses.[16] According to (42), every occurrence of 'P' in a logical form pushes back the implicit reference time t_r.

One way to sidestep the problem presented by (38) and (39) and by any logical form that deviates from (40) is to simply remove from logical forms the mereological predicate $e_i \leq e_j$ and the free use of distinct event variables. Rather than contrive a syntactic constraint to enforce the pattern in (40), let modalizing quantification over events fix the interpretation once and for all. The logical form for (35) will then be more like (43):

(43) $[\exists e : \text{graceful}(e)][\text{every } x : Fx][\exists e : \text{push}(e)]$
$\quad \forall z(\text{INFL}(e, z) \leftrightarrow z = x)\ldots$

There is only an appearance of vacuous quantification in (43). Just like the Past operators in (41), each event quantifier will have its effect on the interpretation. The semantic clauses will guarantee that the pushing event is part of a graceful event.

In some further cases (e.g., the clauses for $\ulcorner \Theta[e, v]\urcorner$, $\ulcorner \Theta[e, V]\urcorner$, $\ulcorner [Qe : \Phi]\Psi\urcorner$, and $\ulcorner [\hat{E} : \Phi]\Psi\urcorner$), I "modalize" in order to unclutter logical form and smooth the translation from syntactic structure. For example, the logical form in (43) is further reduced along the lines of (44). The assertion of uniqueness is then confined to the clause interpreting θ-role constituents. (The notation '$\text{INFL}[e, z]$' in (44) and throughout adapts the convention that uses the brackets in '$\Phi[v_1, \ldots, v_n]$' to list the variables free in an arbitrarily complex Φ rather than to indicate predication of n arguments. The brackets in '$\text{INFL}[e, z]$' and the like signal that the expression receives a complex interpretation, relating events and objects, that is only spelled out in the semantic clauses. Thus, the interpretation of '$\text{INFL}[e, z]$', which is based on the simple relation represented by '$\text{INFL}(e, z)$', is not to be confused with it.)

(44) $[\exists e : \text{graceful}(e)][\text{every } x : Fx][\exists e : \text{push}(e)]\text{INFL}[e, z]\ldots$

What is left after modalization can be taken to represent a certain empirical claim: logical form, the language of the left-hand side, contains the constituents whose permutations by scope assignment and binding give rise to ambiguity. The language of the right-hand side explicates reference, but its syntax does not enter into a calculus for deriving multiple interpretations.

Besides modalizing quantification over events, we will find that quantification over events is also second-order. This conclusion arises in part from the approach to cumulative quantification, which in effect paraphrases (45) as (46):

(45) No more than two detectives solved no more than three crimes.

(46) No more than two detectives solved crimes, and *there* no more than three crimes were solved.

How are we to accomplish the cross-reference indicated by *there*? It cannot be to an event e, since there will be none if no detectives solved any crimes, a situation in which (45) is nevertheless true. The reference must be to whatever events there are in which detectives solve crimes. The second conjunct of (46) asserts that among these, there are no more than three crimes solved. In short, the logical form of *there* in (46) is a second-order definite description of events.[17] Recall that the existential event quantifier in the logical form for the sum-of-plurals interpretation must also be second-order to allow the 20 composers and 7 shows in (32) to be distributed among rival collaborations:

(32) Twenty composers collaborated on seven shows.

In the semantics, I will treat all reference to events and their parts by assigning values to a family of second-order variables $\mathfrak{C}_i$, $0 \leq i$. The definition of truth and satisfaction treats these parameters in a special way. A sentence is said to be true with respect to a context of events just in case the sentence is satisfied by values assigned to the variables in an initial setting that assigns every event in that context to every parameter $\mathfrak{C}_i$, $0 \leq i$. For (47) and (48), recall from the end of chapter 2 that the satisfaction clauses are stated in second-order logic, so that Σ is a plural term (with the number agreement as shown). It denotes pairs $\langle \alpha_i, \mathbf{a} \rangle$, each of which assigns an object $\mathbf{a}$ to a variable α_i. If a given variable is itself second-order, then it may be assigned many values: $\Sigma(\langle 'X', \mathbf{a} \rangle)$ and $\Sigma(\langle 'X', \mathbf{b} \rangle)$, for example. (The quotation and quasi-quotation marks enclosing variables will be henceforth suppressed.)

(47) a sentence Φ is true in a context of events C_0
      $\leftrightarrow \exists \Sigma(\Sigma$ are pairs assigning objects to variables
      $\wedge \ \forall e \forall i (C_0 e \leftrightarrow \Sigma(\langle \mathfrak{C}_i, e \rangle)) \wedge \Sigma$ satisfy $\Phi)$

(48) a sentence Φ is true
      $\leftrightarrow \exists \Sigma(\Sigma$ are pairs assigning objects to variables
      $\wedge \ \forall e \forall i \Sigma(\langle \mathfrak{C}_i, e \rangle) \wedge \Sigma$ satisfy $\Phi)$

A sentence is true *simpliciter* when it is true with respect to whatever events there are.

The distinguished variables $\mathfrak{C}_i$ do not themselves appear in logical form; rather, they occur only in the semantic clauses. For any sentence, where e_i is the event variable appearing with the verb, θ-roles, and modifiers, the quantification over events and their parts affects the values assigned to $\mathfrak{C}_i$. Similarly, a second-order quantifier over such events as '$[\exists E_i : \mathrm{V}(e_i)]$' affects the values assigned to $\mathfrak{C}_i$. The variables e_i and E_i are not themselves assigned values. They are purely syntactic, indicating, for example, that the quantifier is a second-order quantifier over events or, in the case of e, marking an argument position in a predicate denoting events. The $\mathbb{C}_i$ are parameters that restrict all quantification over events, and all quantification over events is reflected in the reassignment of values to these parameters.

To illustrate the assignment of values to the parameters, consider a possible interpretation for a second-order quantifier over events:

(49) Σ satisfy $\ulcorner [\exists E_i : \Phi] \Psi \urcorner$

$\leftrightarrow [\exists E : \exists \Sigma_0 (\forall e(\Sigma_0(\langle \mathbb{C}_i, e \rangle) \leftrightarrow Ee) \wedge \Sigma_0 \approx_{\mathbb{C}_i} \Sigma \wedge \Sigma_0 \text{ satisfy } \Phi]$
$\exists \Sigma_0 (\forall e(\Sigma_0(\langle \mathbb{C}_i, e \rangle) \leftrightarrow Ee) \wedge \Sigma_0 \approx_{\mathbb{C}_i} \Sigma \wedge \Sigma_0 \text{ satisfy } \Psi^{18}$

So far there is nothing remarkable except that the affected values are assigned to the parameter $\mathbb{C}_i$. But if the parameters $\mathbb{C}_i$, $i \geq 0$, mediate all reference to events, then the clauses for primitive concepts, '$V(e)$' and '$\Theta(e, \alpha)$', will have to be adjusted as well so that they are understood to put conditions on the events assigned to these parameters. Thus the interpretation of the quantifier '$[\exists E_i : V(e_i)]$' would invoke (49) and the clause in (50). (See section 2.2 for further discussion of (50).)

(50) Σ satisfy $\ulcorner V[e_i] \urcorner \leftrightarrow \exists e \Sigma(\langle \mathbb{C}_i, e \rangle) \wedge \forall e(\Sigma(\langle \mathbb{C}_i, e \rangle) \rightarrow Ve)$

Note that the variable e_i in the restriction on the quantifier is considered bound by the determiner $\exists E_i$ with like index, the uppercase indicating only that it is second-order. The adjusted clauses must provide for the plurality of events that the parameter denotes. Clause (50) requires that there be some event or events assigned to $\mathbb{C}_i$ and that all of them are V-ings. The θ-roles are similarly construed as expressing a relation between an object or objects and a plurality of events. The provisional clauses in (51) and (52) also take the step mentioned earlier toward reducing the clutter in logical forms.

(51) Σ satisfy $\ulcorner \Theta[e_i, V] \urcorner$
$\leftrightarrow [\forall z : \Sigma(\langle V, z \rangle)][\exists e : \Sigma(\langle \mathbb{C}_i, e \rangle)]\Theta(e, z)$
$\wedge [\forall e : \Sigma(\langle \mathbb{C}_i, e \rangle)][\exists z : \Sigma(\langle V, z \rangle)]\Theta(e, z)$
$\wedge [\forall e : \Sigma(\langle \mathbb{C}_i, e \rangle)][\forall z : \Theta(e, z)]\Sigma(\langle V, z \rangle)$

(52) Σ satisfy $\ulcorner \Theta[e_i, v] \urcorner$
$\leftrightarrow [\forall z : \Sigma(\langle v, z \rangle)][\exists e : \Sigma(\langle \mathbb{C}_i, e \rangle)]\Theta(e, z)$
$\wedge [\forall e : \Sigma(\langle \mathbb{C}_i, e \rangle)][\exists z : \Sigma(\langle v, z \rangle)]\Theta(e, z)$
$\wedge [\forall e : \Sigma(\langle \mathbb{C}_i, e \rangle)][\forall z : \Theta(e, z)]\Sigma(\langle v, z \rangle)$

The condition spelling out the exhaustive role of the events' participants now appears only on the right-hand side. On the left-hand side in logical form we have left only the constituent whose movements figure in the

derivation of alternative interpretations of a sentence. Logical forms like
(54) can now take the place of those in (53).

(53) a. [every $x : Fx$][$\exists E_i : V(e_i)$]$\forall z$(INFL$(e_i, z) \leftrightarrow z = x$)...
     b. [$\exists E_i : V(e)$]([$\exists X : n(X) \wedge \forall x(Xx \rightarrow Fx)$]$\forall x$(INFL$(e_i, x) \leftrightarrow Xx$)...

(54) a. [every $x : Fx$][$\exists E_i : V[e_i]$]INFL$[e_i, x]$...
     b. [$\exists E_i : V[e_i]$]([$\exists X : n(X) \wedge \forall x(Xx \rightarrow Fx)$] INFL$[e_i, X]$...

Clauses (51) and (52) require that the objects that Θ in the event or events
assigned to $\mathfrak{C}_i$ be exactly those assigned to the variable V or v, respectively. In the case of a first-order variable, v, it is left to the clauses interpreting the first-order quantifiers to guarantee that only one object is
assigned to it.[19] (Clauses (51) and (52) do not present the clauses interpreting θ-roles in their final form. Once parts of events are taken into
account, they will have to be reformulated as a condition on the events
that completely overlap the events assigned to $\mathfrak{C}_i$. See section 2.1 below.)

To return now to quantification over parts of events implicit in first-
order quantification, recall that the logical form for (35) uses only one
alphabetic variant of the event variable.

(35) Gracefully, every football player pushed the pram up the hill.

It conceals the part-whole relation between the graceful event and the
individual pushings, to be explicated by the semantic clauses. Clause (49)
does not yet derive the intended interpretation of (35) from a logical form
like (55):

(55) [$\exists E_i : \text{graceful}(e_i)$][every $x : Fx$][$\exists E_i : \text{push}(e_i)$] INFL$[e_i, x]$...

If (55) is interpreted according to (49), the adverb occurs vacuously in
(55), which expresses no connection between the graceful event or events
and the pushings. I revise the semantics so that the interpretation of (55)
will give the right result. As a first step, the quantification is restricted to
those events already assigned to the parameter $\mathfrak{C}_i$:

(56) Σ satisfy $\ulcorner[\exists E_i : \Phi]\Psi\urcorner$
     $\leftrightarrow$ [$\exists E : \forall e(Ee \rightarrow \Sigma(\langle \mathfrak{C}_i, e \rangle)) \wedge \exists \Sigma_0(\forall e(\Sigma_0(\langle \mathfrak{C}_i, e \rangle) \leftrightarrow Ee)$
     $\wedge \Sigma_0 \approx_{\mathfrak{C}_i} \Sigma \wedge \Sigma_0$ satisfy $\Phi)$]
     $\exists \Sigma_0(\forall e(\Sigma_0(\langle \mathfrak{C}_i, e \rangle) \leftrightarrow Ee) \wedge \Sigma_0 \approx_{\mathfrak{C}_i} \Sigma \wedge \Sigma_0$ satisfy Ψ[20]

When evaluating '[$\exists E_i : \text{push}(e_i)$]' in (55), we must find the pushings
among those events that the evaluation of '[$\exists E_i : \text{graceful}(e_i)$]' has assigned to $\mathfrak{C}_i$. These are, if any, a single graceful event. Clause (56) estab-
lishes a connection between this event and the pushings, but more has to
be said if it is to be a part-whole relation.

The mereological predicates and quantification over parts of events that have been removed from logical form appear in the semantic clauses interpreting various operators (and relations). These clauses make use of the following abbreviation:

(57) '$E_i \simeq E_j$' (read "E_i completely overlaps E_j") for
$\quad$ '$\forall e(\exists e'(e\mathbf{O}e' \wedge E_i e') \leftrightarrow \exists e'(e\mathbf{O}e' \wedge E_j e'))$'[21]

The events E_i completely overlap the events E_j just in case any event overlapping an E_i event also overlaps an E_j event, and conversely, any event overlapping an E_j event overlaps an E_i event. In effect, E_i and E_j cover the same area in event space, although they may divide it up differently into its constituent events. The one graceful event of every football player pushing his pram up the hill completely overlaps the many individual pushings.

Substituting '$\Sigma_k(\mathfrak{C}_l)$' for either predicate letter, I will also use the abbreviation in (57) to relate overlapping events to the events assigned a parameter:

(58) '$E_i \simeq \Sigma_k(\mathfrak{C}_l)$' for
$\quad$ '$\forall e(\exists e'(e\mathbf{O}e' \wedge E_i e') \leftrightarrow \exists e'(e\mathbf{O}e' \wedge \Sigma_k(\langle \mathfrak{C}_l, e'\rangle)))$'

Thus, the events E_i are said to completely overlap the events assigned by Σ_k to $\mathfrak{C}_l$.

To obtain the intended interpretation of (35) from the logical form in (55), we could modify (56), incorporating a mereological condition into the interpretation of the existential event quantifier, as in (59):

(59) Σ satisfy $\ulcorner[\exists E_i : \Phi]\Psi\urcorner$
$\quad \leftrightarrow [\exists E : \exists E'(E' \simeq \Sigma(\mathfrak{C}_i) \wedge \forall e(Ee \rightarrow E'e))$
$\quad\quad \wedge \exists \Sigma_0(\forall e(\Sigma_0(\langle \mathfrak{C}_i, e\rangle) \leftrightarrow Ee) \wedge \Sigma_0 \approx_{\mathfrak{C}_i} \Sigma \wedge \Sigma_0 \text{ satisfy } \Phi)]$
$\quad \exists \Sigma_0(\forall e(\Sigma_0(\langle \mathfrak{C}_i, e\rangle) \leftrightarrow Ee) \wedge \Sigma_0 \approx_{\mathfrak{C}_i} \Sigma \wedge \Sigma_0 \text{ satisfy } \Psi)$

According to (59), the existential quantifier selects from whatever events fall within an area that completely overlaps the events assigned to $\mathfrak{C}_i$. Suppose now that sentence (35) is true. There are then some Σ assigning a graceful event to the parameter $\mathfrak{C}_i$ as its unique value, and Σ satisfy (60) according to the usual interpretation for a universal quantifier stated in (61).

(60) $[\text{every } x : Fx][\exists E_i : \text{push}[e_i]]\text{INFL}[e_i, x]\ldots$

(61) Σ satisfy $\ulcorner[\text{every } v_i : \Phi]\Psi\urcorner$
$\quad \leftrightarrow [\text{every } x : \exists \Sigma_0(\forall y(\Sigma_0(\langle v_i, y\rangle) \leftrightarrow y = x)$
$\quad\quad \wedge \Sigma_0 \approx_{v_i} \Sigma \wedge \Sigma_0 \text{ satisfy } \Phi)]$
$\quad \exists \Sigma_0(\forall y(\Sigma_0(\langle v_i, y\rangle) \leftrightarrow y = x) \wedge \Sigma_0 \approx_{v_i} \Sigma \wedge \Sigma_0 \text{ satisfy } \Psi)$

For every football player, '$[\exists E_i : \text{push}[e_i]]$' is evaluated according to (59). There must be some events that completely overlap the graceful event assigned by Σ. Consider, in particular, all the parts of the graceful event. The existential quantifier allows a selection to be made from among these. Since they are all the parts of the graceful event, a football player is sure to find his own contribution. Thus, interpreting (55) according to (59) and (61) delivers for sentence (35) the correct part-whole relation between the graceful event and the many individual pushings.

(35) Gracefully, every football player pushed the pram up the hill.

(55) $[\exists E_i : \text{graceful}[e_i]][\text{every } x : Fx][\exists E_i : \text{push}[e_i]]\text{INFL}[e_i, x]\ldots$

(36) $[\exists e : \text{graceful}(e)]][\text{every } x : Fx][\exists e' : e' \leq e \wedge \text{push}(e')]$
$\forall z(\text{INFL}(e', z) \leftrightarrow z = x)\ldots$

With clause (50) interpreting the verb and the clauses in (51) and (52) for θ-roles, the result is that (55) is equivalent to the more familiar (36). This serves to illustrate how the modalized logical forms are interpreted, removing the mereological relations and the use of distinct event variables to the semantic clauses. As remarked earlier, the quantifier over parts of events that accompanies every first-order quantifier turns out not to be the existential quantifier shown in (55) or (36). Chapter 7 replaces it with a second-order definite description. Nevertheless, the new operator incorporates a mereological condition in just the way (59) does. Whether or not a quantifier incorporates such a condition (the existential event quantifier will in fact be allowed its more usual nonmereological sense), every event quantifier proceeds by assigning values to a parameter $\mathfrak{C}_i$, which then restricts the domain of the next event quantifier.

2.1   Event mereology and the interpretation of θ-roles

It is, of course, an empirical problem to discover where the truth conditions of sentences depend on mereological relations among events. Beyond the quantification over parts of events that goes along with quantifying over objects, we can find mereological effects in the sum-of-plurals interpretation. The analysis of these effects incorporates a mereological condition into the schema interpreting θ-roles.

Recall from section 1.2 that a sum-of-plurals interpretation based on a collective predicate reveals that the existential event quantifier is second-order. The relevant interpretation of (32) reports that some 20 composers joined in rival productions of some 7 shows.

(32) Twenty composers collaborated on seven shows.

There is no single collaboration in which all 20 composers and all 7 shows participated. Plural reference to events straightforwardly represents an interpretation that is true in the circumstances. Thus, according to (33), some collaborations had collaborators amounting to 20 composers and production amounting to 7 shows:

(33) $\exists E_i([\exists X : 20(X) \wedge \forall x(Xx \rightarrow Cx)]\text{INFL}[e_i, X] \wedge \text{collaborate}[e_i]$
$\wedge [\exists Y : 7(Y) \wedge \forall y(Yy \rightarrow Sy)] \text{ on}[e_i, Y])$

A singular quantifier over events will not yield a truth in the given situation:

(34) $[\exists E_i : 1(E)]([\exists X : 20(X) \wedge \forall x(Xx \rightarrow Cx)]\text{INFL}[e_i, X]$
$\wedge \text{collaborate}[e_i] \wedge [\exists Y : 7(Y) \wedge \forall y(Yy \rightarrow Sy)] \text{ on}[e_i, Y])$

The mereological sum of mutually hostile collaborations is not itself a collaboration, as (34) would require. Formula (34) fits only the interpretation of (32) asserting one big project.

Similar sentences requiring plural reference to events show truth conditions that depend on properties of the parts of the events. Suppose that Ninja turtles belong to fraternal orders and that the communal sense of 'share' is intended in (62), so that turtles swapping food at an order's table are sharing with each other but not with turtles in another order seated at another table.

(62) Seventeen turtles shared twenty-three pizzas.

Sentence (62) can report that 17 turtles and 23 pizzas are distributed among several such sharings among brother turtles. Thus, the quantification over events is second-order, as in (63).

(63) $\exists E_i([\exists X : 17(X) \wedge \forall x(Xx \rightarrow Tx)]\text{INFL}[e_i, X] \wedge \text{share}[e_i]$
$\wedge [\exists Y : 23(Y) \wedge \forall y(Yy \rightarrow Py)]\text{OF}[e_i, Y])$

Various collectivizing adverbials will similarly require a second-order event quantifier so that the sentences (64) through (66) come out true in the imagined circumstances.

(64) Seventeen turtles together ate twenty-three pizzas.

(65) Seventeen turtles ate, with each other, twenty-three pizzas.

(66) Seventeen turtles ate, every turtle breaking pizza with every other, twenty-three pizzas.

(67) $\exists E_i([\exists X : 17(X) \wedge \forall x(Xx \rightarrow Tx)]\text{INFL}[e_i, X] \wedge \text{eat}[e_i]$
$\wedge Adverbial[e_i] \wedge [\exists Y : 23(Y) \wedge \forall y(Yy \rightarrow Py)]\text{OF}[e_i, Y])$

Interpretations of (64) through (66) allow that the 17 turtles and 23 pizzas might be scattered among several fraternal suppers that only individually meet the adverbial condition that every turtle in the event breaks pizza with every other. The sentences come out true in the circumstances only if the initial quantifier over events in (67) is second-order.

To put off any question of their communing with other orders, assume that the turtles who sit down together do not know when turtles are supping elsewhere, but suppose that the fraternal orders share a common kitchen that serves pizza by the slice any number at a time. As it happens, not one of the 23 pizzas is eaten at the table of any one of the fraternal orders. Every pizza has been sliced and the slices served at more than one table. This turn of events does not affect the truth of sentences (62) and (64) through (66). They do not require that any one pizza be consumed wholly at just one of the tables. Its consumption may overlap the suppers at several tables. The logical forms (63) and (67) turn out, however, to be false if we leave the θ-roles to be interpreted, as had been suggested earlier, by clauses (51) and (52).

(51) Σ satisfy $\ulcorner\Theta[e_i, V]\urcorner \leftrightarrow [\forall z : \Sigma(\langle V, z \rangle)][\exists e : \Sigma(\langle \mathfrak{C}_i, e \rangle)]\Theta(e, z)$
$\quad \wedge [\forall e : \Sigma(\langle \mathfrak{C}_i, e \rangle)][\exists z : \Sigma(\langle V, z \rangle)]\Theta(e, z)$
$\quad \wedge [\forall e : \Sigma(\langle \mathfrak{C}_i, e \rangle)][\forall z : \Theta(e, z)]\Sigma(\langle V, z \rangle)$

(52) Σ satisfy $\ulcorner\Theta[e_i, v]\urcorner \leftrightarrow [\forall z : \Sigma(\langle v, z \rangle)][\exists e : \Sigma(\langle \mathfrak{C}_i, e \rangle)]\Theta(e, z)$
$\quad \wedge [\forall e : \Sigma(\langle \mathfrak{C}_i, e \rangle)][\exists z : \Sigma(\langle v, z \rangle)]\Theta(e, z)$
$\quad \wedge [\forall e : \Sigma(\langle \mathfrak{C}_i, e \rangle)][\forall z : \Theta(e, z)]\Sigma(\langle v, z \rangle)$

In evaluating (63) and (67), the events assigned to $\mathfrak{C}_i$ must be the individual suppers so that they may be truthfully described as sharings and as events in which every turtle breaks pizza with every other turtle. This is just the consideration requiring the second-order event quantifier. Evaluating the final conjuncts in (63) and (67) according to (51) then requires every pizza to bear the relation 'OF(e, z)' to at least one of the suppers assigned to $\mathfrak{C}_i$, which is to say that every pizza is eaten at one of the tables. This does not fit the imagined circumstances, and the logical forms are mistakenly false there. To divide a pizza among several tables, it will not do to suppose that 'OF(e, z)' means only that at e, z is eaten *from* rather than eaten up. Were that its meaning, the sentences (62) and (64) through (66) would end up implying only that the 17 turtles ate from the 23 pies and not that they ate them, contrary to fact. As simple a sentence as *Leonardo ate the pizza* ($\dots \forall z(\text{OF}(e, z) \leftrightarrow z = \mathbf{p})$), would likewise be true if Leonardo ate from the pizza without eating it up. To let a pizza's consumption overlap several suppers, modify the schema for θ-roles incorporating a mereological relation as in (68) and (69).

(68) Σ satisfy $\ulcorner\Theta[e_i, V]\urcorner \leftrightarrow \exists E(E \simeq \Sigma(\mathbb{C}_i)$
$\land [\forall z : \Sigma(\langle V, z\rangle)][\exists e : Ee]\Theta(e, z)$
$\land [\forall e : Ee][\exists z : \Sigma(\langle V, z\rangle)]\Theta(e, z)$
$\land [\forall e : Ee][\forall z : \Theta(e, z)]\Sigma(\langle V, z\rangle))$

(69) Σ satisfy $\ulcorner\Theta[e_i, v]\urcorner \leftrightarrow \exists E(E \simeq \Sigma(\mathbb{C}_i)$
$\land [\forall z : \Sigma(\langle v, z\rangle)][\exists e : Ee]\Theta(e, z)$
$\land [\forall e : Ee][\exists z : \Sigma(\langle v, z\rangle)]\Theta(e, z)$
$\land [\forall e : Ee][\forall z : \Theta(e, z)]\Sigma(\langle v, z\rangle))$

So defined, the θ-role requires every pizza to be eaten at some event, as it should, but that event may now overlap several of the suppers. It need not be one of them. The sum-of-plurals interpretations of (62) and (64) through (66) thus show that θ-roles are among those elements incorporating a mereological condition.[22]

Such a condition can also be seen at work in the logical form of cumulative quantification, where a second-order definite description of events relates one conjunct to the events described by an antecedent conjunct, as in (71) and (72).

(70) Exactly four turtles ate exactly four pizzas.

(71) Exactly four turtles ate pizzas, and *there* turtles ate exactly four pizzas.

(72) ... *there*$_i$, $[4! y : Py][\exists E_i : \text{eat}[e_i]]\text{OF}[e_i, y])$

Among the situations in which (70), interpreted as cumulative quantification, would be true are some where the 4 turtles each ate a quarter of every pizza. As we have seen, the description of such a context is not reducible to relations between individual turtles and pizzas, since no turtle ate any one pizza. The reference to events that holds together the cumulative quantification in (70), represented by *there* in (71), turns out to denote not just one event but whatever events there are in which an individual turtle eats pizza (see chapter 9). That is, each event denoted by *there* corresponds to the action of an individual turtle:

(73) there$(e) \leftrightarrow [\exists x : Tx]\forall z(\text{INFL}(e, z) \leftrightarrow z = x)$

If (70) is true, *there* will refer to a plurality of events.[23] How are the pizzas to be related to them? It cannot be said that for each of the 4 pizzas there is an event among them where it is eaten. In any of the events referred to, what is eaten is at best 4 quarters from different pies. The eating of any one pizza must be reconstituted from the separate actions of all 4 turtles. Note that it will *overlap* each of these. It will not be a part of any. If, as I assume, *there* in (71) divides its reference according to what the individual turtles did, then the logical form for the second conjunct, something like (72), comes out true only if at least one of the expressions following '[4! y : Py]', the event quantifier, or the θ-role itself introduces events overlapping the actions of the individual turtles.[24]

In summary, the cross-reference to events in a cumulative quantification and the sum of plurals with a collective predicate or collective adverbial show that quantification over events is second-order. I have made all reference to events mediated by the values assigned to the second-order parameters $\mathfrak{C}_i$, $i \geq 0$. In any given clause, the verb, adverbs, θ-roles, and their arguments are directed toward the events assigned to a single parameter. Depending on the structure of the clause, its various constituents comment not necessarily on the same events but on events that occupy the same event space. A mereological relation between events shows up in the semantic clauses for θ-roles, and it also belongs in the clauses defining the event quantifier that follows a first-order quantifier in order to pick out what any object did alone. This point has been demonstrated on existential event quantifiers, but it carries over to the second-order definite descriptions of events that take their place in chapter 7.

2.2 Event identity and interpretation

Recall from chapter 5, section 2, that the Davidsonian decomposition of the symmetric predicate in (74) and (77) commits one to the metaphysical claim that the Carnegie Deli's sitting opposite Carnegie Hall is not the same event or situation as Carnegie Hall's sitting opposite the Carnegie Deli.

(74)   The Carnegie Deli sits opposite Carnegie Hall.

(75) $\exists e(\text{INFL}(e, \text{CD}) \wedge \text{sit}(e) \wedge \text{opposite}(e, \text{CH}))$

(76) $\exists e(\forall z(\text{INFL}(e, z) \leftrightarrow z = \text{CD}) \wedge \text{sit}(e)$
       $\wedge \forall z(\text{opposite}(e, z) \leftrightarrow z = \text{CH}))$

(77)   Carnegie Hall sits opposite the Carnegie Deli.

(78) $\exists e(\text{INFL}(e, \text{CH}) \wedge \text{sit}(e) \wedge \text{opposite}(e, \text{CD}))$

(79) $\exists e(\forall z(\text{INFL}(e, z) \leftrightarrow z = \text{CH}) \wedge \text{sit}(e)$
       $\wedge \forall z(\text{opposite}(e, z) \leftrightarrow z = \text{CD}))$

Were these events to be identified and were (74) and (77) assigned logical forms that undertake even the simple decomposition shown in (75) and (78), they would jointly entail that the Carnegie Deli sits opposite itself and so does Carnegie Hall. Moreover, identifying these events is not consistent with logical forms (76) and (79), which represent the exhaustiveness of θ-roles, since they would then jointly entail the contradiction that in that one event the Carnegie Deli alone bears both θ-roles and Carnegie Hall bears them alone, too. Given a commitment to the Davidsonian logical forms, the Carnegie Deli's sitting opposite Carnegie Hall must not be the same event as Carnegie Hall's sitting opposite the Carnegie Deli, although it is necessarily true that the one exists if and only if the other does too.

It is thus possible for distinct events to occupy the same space and time, as with buyings and sellings. Presumably, there are abstract features of these events that allow them to remain distinct. Whatever these features are, they will have to enter the analysis of the θ-roles in (76) and (79). Suppose, for example, that every event of sitting opposite has a left side and a right side. The same stuff in the world can be viewed from many angles and thus events distinguished only by their orientation will coincide in space and time. If this is the way it goes, then the θ-roles should mean something along the lines of (80). (In the schemas (68) and (69) that interpret '$\Theta[e_i, \alpha]$', (80) glosses '$\Theta(e, z)$' on the right-hand side.)

(80) a. INFL(e, z) $\leftrightarrow$ sits(e, z) & left-side(e, z)
    b. OF(e, z) $\leftrightarrow$ sits(e, z) & right-side(e, z)

In the event of the Carnegie Deli's sitting opposite Carnegie Hall, the deli is on the left side, and it alone is on the left side. Without the abstract orientation, the purely physical circumstances ('sits(e, z)') are not enough to define a θ-role that the deli bears uniquely, as (76) and (79) require.

The fine-grained ontology has its effect on how we understand the notion of overlapping events deployed in the semantic clauses. Overlap in space and time cannot be a sufficient condition for events to overlap ('$e_i O e_j$'). If it is given that distinct events can occupy the same space and time, it follows from the axioms of a mereology (chapter 5, section 3) that spatiotemporal overlap is not sufficient for mereological overlap. Suppose spatiotemporal overlap were sufficient for $e_i O e_j$. Then, according to axiom (81a), each of the coincident events is a part of the other, from which it follows by (81b) that they are identical, contrary to the hypothesis that they are distinct (see also chapter 2, n. 8).

(81) a. $x \leq y \leftrightarrow \forall z(z\mathbf{O}x \rightarrow z\mathbf{O}y)$
     b. $x = y \leftrightarrow (x \leq y \wedge y \leq x)$

This consequence of a mereology is welcome. For, if spatiotemporal overlap were sufficient, the mereological condition that enters the interpretation of the θ-roles in (83) would make (82) true.

(82) The Carnegie Deli sits opposite the Carnegie Deli.

(83) $[\exists E_i : 1(E_i)](\text{INFL}[e_i, \text{CD}] \wedge \text{sit}[e_i] \wedge \text{opposite}[e_i, \text{CD}])$

The Carnegie Deli does, after all, sit opposite Carnegie Hall. There is thus an event that makes the conjunct 'sit[e_i]' true, and since this is the event of the Carnegie Deli sitting opposite Carnegie Hall, the first conjunct of (83) is undeniably true as well. In verifying the final conjunct, the clause interpreting the θ-role (see (68)) invites us to consider events that completely overlap the Carnegie Deli's sitting opposite Carnegie Hall. If spatiotemporal overlap were sufficient, then Carnegie Hall's sitting opposite the Carnegie Deli completely overlaps, and in this event it is indeed the Carnegie Deli that is sat opposite from, which verifies the final conjunct of (83). Fortunately, the Carnegie Deli's sitting opposite Carnegie Hall does not mereologically overlap Carnegie Hall's sitting opposite the Carnegie Deli, and (82) does not come out true.

To give sufficient mereological conditions, one would have to appeal to whatever abstract features allow the coincident events to be distinct in the first place. To continue with the example given earlier, suppose that one event of sitting opposite is part of another just in case it is a spatiotemporal part and its orientation is preserved. That is, anything on the left side of the first event remains so in the second event, and similarly for the right side. The Carnegie Deli's sitting opposite Carnegie Hall is then no part of Carnegie Hall's sitting opposite the Carnegie Deli, as desired.

The considerations that reconcile Davidsonian logical form and symmetric predicates extend to a class of examples the significance of which was pointed out to me by Peter Lasersohn. The predicates involved are not symmetric, but here too the crucial point is that the mereological notions relevant to the semantics do not coincide with spatiotemporal notions.

Suppose a psychologist tests a large and diverse population. The subjects' performance is not directed toward any goal like high achievement, and they are, of course, blind to the psychologist's purpose. Perhaps he is as well, but he develops a career sifting the corpus for statistical regularities to classify various segments of the population. His work begins with observational statements of the form X *outscores* Y, where X is some group being compared to some group Y. Needless to say, the actual performance of any one subject falls under many such observational statements. Sometimes that performance puts the subject among the outscorers and sometimes among the outscored. The corpus is replete with events of outscoring, without which the psychologist would have had no future.

Suppose now that (84) is false under its most natural interpretation.

(84) The nailbiters outscored the bedwetters.

The nailbiters and the bedwetters all scored the same, but there are three bedwetters $\mathbf{B}$, who are $\mathbf{b}_1$, $\mathbf{b}_2$, and $\mathbf{b}_3$, and only two nailbiters $\mathbf{N}$, $\mathbf{n}_1$, and $\mathbf{n}_2$. Adding up the scores on each side, we get that the bedwetters in fact outscored the nailbiters. Formula (85) should therefore turn out false, where e is this outscoring:

(85) INFL[e, N] $\wedge$ outscore[e] $\wedge$ OF[e, B]

With e an outscoring, it has to be that a θ-role conjunct is false. Their interpretation according to (68) takes into account events completely overlapping the outscoring e.

(68) Σ satisfy $\ulcorner \Theta[e_i, V] \urcorner$
$\leftrightarrow \exists E(E \simeq \Sigma(\mathbb{C}_i) \wedge [\forall z : \Sigma(\langle V, z \rangle)][\exists e : Ee]\Theta(e, z)$
$\wedge \ [\forall e : Ee][\exists z : \Sigma(\langle V, z \rangle)]\Theta(e, z)$
$\wedge \ [\forall e : Ee][\forall z : \Theta(e, z)]\Sigma(\langle V, z \rangle))$

In this connection, consider the events each of which compares the two nailbiters to only one of the bedwetters. In each of these, the nailbiters outnumber and therefore outscore the bedwetter. So we have event $\mathbf{e}_1$ of the two nailbiters $\mathbf{N}$ outscoring bedwetter $\mathbf{b}_1$, event $\mathbf{e}_2$ of $\mathbf{N}$ outscoring $\mathbf{b}_2$, and event $\mathbf{e}_3$ of $\mathbf{N}$ outscoring $\mathbf{b}_3$. There may even be observational statements attesting to these events, such as *The nailbiters outscored the five-year-old bedwetters*, *The nailbiters outscored the seven-year-old bedwetters*, and *The nailbiters outscored the nine-year-old bedwetters*. In any case, these three events certainly exist, and, taken together, they completely overlap in space and time event e where it is the bedwetters who outscore the nailbiters. All there is in space and time is the subjects' performance that one day when they were tested. Their performance in event e is the same stuff as their performance across events $\mathbf{e}_1$, $\mathbf{e}_2$, and $\mathbf{e}_3$. Suppose now that spatiotemporal overlap were sufficient for mereological overlap in the semantics. According to (68), the first conjunct of (85) is true just in case the nailbiters $\mathbf{N}$ are the outscorers among some events that completely overlap e. Since they are the outscorers in e_1, e_2, and e_3 and these events as supposed completely overlap e, the first conjunct of (85) is true. Similarly, the final conjunct is true, since the bedwetters B are the outscored in these three events. Thus (85) turns out to be true, contrary to the fact that e is an event of the bedwetters outscoring the nailbiters.

This unwanted result is avoided, however, since the supposition is mistaken. As we have seen, spatiotemporal overlap is not always sufficient for mereological overlap. Events e_1, e_2, and e_3 are not parts of event e in the relevant sense. A condition that is sufficient for mereological overlap will rely on whatever abstract feature allows events to coincide in space and time while remaining distinct. As with the symmetric predicates, the θ-roles for *outscore* mean something like (86) (glossing '$\Theta(e,z)$' on the right side of (68) and (69)).

(86) a. INFL(e,z) ↔ is-tested(e,z) & winning-side(e,z)
      b. OF(e,z) ↔ is-tested(e,z) & losing-side(e,z)

The θ-roles do not distinguish the physical performance of the outscorers and the outscored ('is-tested(e,z)'), but the event is abstract, with a winning side and a losing side that do distinguish the participants. Like the events of sitting opposite, one event of outscoring is part of another only if the sides are preserved. The winners in the one event are winners in the second, and similarly for the losers. If this is a condition for the mereological relation, then events e_1, e_2, and e_3 are indeed not parts of event e. If so, (85) is not true, despite the wider truth conditions that introducing a mereological relation into (68) and (69) has allowed.

The surfeit of events that busy the psychologist raises a point that needs to be clarified about how we understand his assertion. The most salient interpretation of (84) takes it as a report of some singular event:

(87) $[\exists E_i : 1(E_i)]([\iota X : \forall x(Xx \leftrightarrow Nx)]\text{INFL}[e_i, X] \land \text{outscore}[e_i]$
      $\land [\iota Y : \forall y(Yy \to By)]\text{OF}[e_i, Y])$

We have seen that (87) cannot truthfully be a report about event e. If, in evaluating (87), e and only e is assigned as the value of $\mathfrak{C}_i$, then the θ-role conjuncts are false, as they should be. With the notion of overlap properly understood, the semantics for (87) does not allow e to be misdescribed. As a matter of logical form, the same sentence (84) might, however, have been about a plurality of events:

(88) $\exists E_i([\iota X : \forall x(Xx \leftrightarrow Nx)]\text{INFL}[e_i, X] \land \text{outscore}[e_i]$
      $\land [\iota Y : \forall y(Yy \to By)]\text{OF}[e_i, Y])$

If so, then the three events e_1, e_2, and e_3 make the sentence true. In evaluating (88), assign these events as the values of $\mathfrak{C}_i$. The verb, according to (50), requires each of them to be an outscoring, which they are.

(50) Σ satisfy $\ulcorner V[e_i] \urcorner \leftrightarrow \exists e \Sigma(\langle \mathfrak{C}_i, e \rangle) \wedge \forall e(\Sigma(\langle \mathfrak{C}_i, e \rangle) \rightarrow Ve)$

As noted above, the nailbiters are the outscorers in these events, and the bedwetters are the outscored, with the result that (88) is true. Note that these events satisfy the θ-role conjuncts themselves without taking advantage of the mereology to reconstitute them as some other events. The second-order event quantifier in (88) with the cardinality restriction removed would have been enough for the three events to make the sentence true.

Nothing is amiss here. Sentence (84) is simply ambiguous between (87) and (88). We do not know whether the psychologist has uttered something true or false until we know which he intends. Our understanding of his intentions depends in part on what are taken to be the relevant events in the context of utterance (chapter 5, section 4). If, for example, the psychologist has been scoring nailbiters against bedwetters of a certain age, nailbiters versus five-year-old bedwetters, versus seven-year-old bedwetters, and versus nine-year-old bedwetters, then (84) is naturally taken as a true report that the nailbiters have, across the board, outscored the bedwetters. The psychologist intends to utter (88). Like examples (32) in section 1.2 and (62) in section 2.1, which show the essential use of a second-order event quantifier, no logical form other than (88) will do in this context.

In the absence of such a suggestive and structured domain of events, an utterance of (84) is indeed taken to be about a single event that adds up all the scores of the nailbiters and all the scores of the bedwetters. That is, we assume the psychologist means (87), uttering (84) out of the blue. This is not surprising to the extent that we trust him to be measuring something determinate and contingent, the results of which he intends to convey with this utterance. In the unstructured domain of events, 'The nailbiters outscored the bedwetters', 'The bedwetters outscored the nailbiters', and 'The nailbiters tied the bedwetters' are all true, given logical forms like (88) that make plural reference to events. This is sufficient grounds to reject the idea that the psychologist intends (88) when he utters (84) out of the blue (see appendix I for related discussion).

In summary, there are contexts where the truth conditions of (84) call for a second-order event quantifier. I assume that pragmatic considerations are responsible when the interpretation represented by (88) appears to be suppressed. Since a context has been constructed that makes (88) salient, this is a plausible assumption. Some predicates, however, in contrast to *outscore*, seem to exclude any construal that applies a concept of events distributively to a plurality of events. Compare (89) and (90).

(89) The elms are clustered.

(90) The elms are dense (in the middle of the forest).

Sentence (89) can be understood to mean either that the elms are in a cluster or that they are in clusters. The latter interpretation allows the elms to be distributed among clusters that may themselves be scattered. In contrast, (90) excludes such an interpretation. To account for (90), it cannot be said that any of the scattered clusters is not itself dense enough, since one could have said of its elms that they are dense. Rather, it seems that the predicate does not apply to a plurality of events distributively. One could therefore claim that the predicate *dense* does not fall under schema (50). It imposes a restriction on the number of events denoted, as in (91).

(50) Σ satisfy $\ulcorner V[e_i] \urcorner \leftrightarrow (\exists e \Sigma(\langle \mathfrak{C}_i, e \rangle) \wedge \forall e (\Sigma(\langle \mathfrak{C}_i, e \rangle) \to Ve))$

(91) Σ satisfy $\ulcorner \text{dense}[e_i] \urcorner \leftrightarrow (1(\Sigma(\mathfrak{C}_i)) \wedge \forall e (\Sigma(\langle \mathfrak{C}_i, e \rangle) \to \text{dense}(e)))$

For my purposes, it would be a small matter to concede that verbs may be organized into several classes, only one of which is properly characterized by (50). I hesitate, however, to limit (50)'s scope on the basis of the evidence of *dense* and similar predicates. The contrast in (89) and (90) is discussed by Dowty (1987) and Taub (1989) in connection with examples such as (92) and (93). The quantifier *all*, which in (92) distributes the elms among possibly distinct clusters, is ungrammatical in (93).

(92)   The elms are all clustered.

(93)   *The elms are all dense.

Notice that (91) can play no role in the explanation of (93). Presumably, the event quantifier in the scope of *all* is free to quantify over events one at a time, resulting in an assertion that for every elm there is an event where it, along with some other elms, is dense. Within the scope of *all*, the restriction to one event that (91) imposes is met. To the extent that (93) and the absent interpretation in (90) reflect the same phenomenon, we should look elsewhere than (91) for an explanation, leaving (50) intact for the time being.

2.3 Truth with respect to a context of events

I should point out that the introduction of mereological relations into the semantics obliges me to take a particular view of how the evaluation of a sentence depends on a given context of events. Recall from chapter 5 the discussion of examples similar to (94). On its semidistributive interpretation, it asserts that no more than 20 truckers participated in events of loading 3 trucks.

(94) No more than twenty truckers loaded up three trucks.

(95) $[(\leq 20)x : \text{trucker}(x)][\exists E_i : 1(E_i) \wedge \text{load-up}[e_i]]$
$(\text{Co-INFL}[e_i, x] \wedge [\exists Y : 3(Y) \wedge \forall y(Yy \rightarrow Ty)]\text{OF}[e_i, Y])$

(96) ▮ ▮ ▮ ▮ ▮ ▮ ▮   ▮ ▮   ▮

   ↑ ↑ ↑ ↑ ↑ ↑ ↑   ↑ ↑   ↑

   ○ ○ ○ ○ ○ ○ ○   ○ ○   ○

  e_1 e_2 e_3 e_4 e_5 e_6 e_7 | e_8 |

(97) $\forall e(\mathfrak{C}_0 e \leftrightarrow (e - e_1 \vee e - e_2 \vee e - e_3 \vee e = e_4 \vee e = e_5$
$\vee \, e = e_6 \vee e = e_7 \vee e = e_8))$

Given 10 atomic events of loading up a truck, as in (96), it was observed in chapter 5 that contexts will differ in what they take to be the relevant individual events. If, in a discourse, the atomic events are considered to be the individuals, then an utterance of (94) would be true. The context would contain no events of loading up 3 trucks. In (96) we imagine that their location in space and time makes it natural for context C_0 to contain 8 individual events of loading trucks. Only one of them is a loading up of 3 trucks, and so sentence (94) is expected to be true of C_0 just in case no more than 20 truckers participated in that event, e_8.

These, however, are not the truth conditions of the logical form in (95). We expect it to be true with respect to C_0 if it is satisfied by some Σ that assign to $\mathfrak{C}_i$ exactly the events of C_0. But clause (59), interpreting the event quantifier in (98), makes available any plurality of events that completely overlaps C_0.

(98) $\ldots[\exists E_i : 1(E_i) \wedge \text{load-up}[e_i]]$
$(\text{Co-INFL}[e_i, x] \wedge [\exists Y : 3(Y) \wedge \forall y(Yy \rightarrow Ty)]\text{OF}[e_i, Y])$

(59) Σ satisfy $\ulcorner[\exists E_i : \Phi]\Psi\urcorner$
$\leftrightarrow [\exists E : \exists E'(E' \simeq \Sigma(\mathfrak{C}_i) \wedge \forall e(Ee \rightarrow E'e))$
$\wedge \exists\Sigma_0(\forall e(\Sigma_0(\langle\mathfrak{C}_i, e\rangle) \leftrightarrow Ee) \wedge \Sigma_0 \approx_{\mathfrak{C}_i} \Sigma \wedge \Sigma_0 \text{ satisfy } \Phi)]$
$\exists\Sigma_0(\forall e(\Sigma_0(\langle\mathfrak{C}_i, e\rangle) \leftrightarrow Ee) \wedge \Sigma_0 \approx_{\mathfrak{C}_i} \Sigma \wedge \Sigma_0 \text{ satisfy } \Psi)$

These other ways of completely overlapping C_0 include events of loading 3 trucks other than e_8. Some will, for example, include the mereological sum $e_5 + e_6 + e_7$, which is an event of loading 3 trucks. It should be clear that every one of the atomic events in (96) will be a constituent of some event of loading 3 trucks in some context that completely overlaps C_0. Thus the logical form in (95) turns out to be true of C_0 just in case there were no more than 20 truckers among all the events of C_0.

Operators introducing a mereological relation threaten to undermine whatever boundaries on events a given context imposes. An utterance may be directed toward a particular context of events C_0. But, as we have seen, it is not enough to say that the speaker intends the sentence to be true with respect to C_0. Rather, if the speaker intends to comment on C_0, then he intends that we grasp a particular logical form, like (99), where the restriction to C_0 enters in explicitly:[25]

(99) $[(\leq 20)x : \text{trucker}(x)][\exists E_i : 1(E_i) \wedge \text{load-up}[e_i] \wedge C_0[e_i]]$
     $(\text{Co-INFL}[e_i, x] \wedge [\exists Y : 3(Y) \wedge \forall y(Yy \rightarrow Ty)]\text{OF}[e_i, Y])$

This, of course, is not novel; rather, it is one well-known way to resolve incomplete definite descriptions. It is left to the reader to verify the truth conditions of (99).

Chapter 7
First-Order and
Second-Order Quantifiers

1   First-Order Quantifiers: Distributivity

A first-order quantifier must include within its scope some kind of quantifier over events. On the distributive interpretation of (1), every boy ate his own crisp.

(1)   Every boy ate a crisp.

(2)   *$\exists e$[every $x : Bx$](INFL$[e, x]$ ∧ eat$[e]$ ...)

(3)   [every $x : Bx$]$\exists e$(INFL$[e, x]$ ∧ eat$[e]$ ...)

They could not have done this in the same event, since the intepretation of 'INFL$[e, x]$' would require absurdly that each was the unique agent in that event. Each must have his own event in which to eat his own crisp.

We have seen earlier that various descriptions can attach to their collective action. That is, what each did is part of a larger event. The larger event may be described as graceful, as in (4).

(4)   Gracefully, every boy ate a crisp.

(5)   [$\exists E_i : $ graceful$[e_i]$]][every $x : Bx$]$\exists E_i$(INFL$[e_i, x]$ ∧ eat$[e_i]$ ...)

(6)   Three video games taught every quarterback two new plays.

(7) $\exists E_i$([$\exists X : 3(X)$ ∧ $\forall x(Xx \rightarrow Gx)$]INFL$[e_i, X]$ ∧ teach$[e_i]$
          ∧ [every $y : Qy$]$\exists E_i$(TO$[e_i, y]$ ...)))

Or the description may say who the participants in another θ-role are, as in (6), an example of essential separation (see chapter 1, section 3).

In logical forms (3), (5), and (7), the existential quantifier over events following each NP first-order quantifier lets every participant seek his own part. Recall from chapter 6, section 2, that the interpreting clause (59) allows the event quantifier to quantify over the parts of the large

graceful event in (5) or over the parts of the large event in (7) of three
video games teaching quarterbacks.

Every first-order quantifier must include within its scope a quantifier
over events. Thus if logical forms follow the pattern of (3), (5), and (7),
we expect an existential quantifier over events in all the positions shown
in (9).

(8) Gracefully, every boy surrendered to every girl two crisps.

(9) $[\exists E_i : \text{graceful}[e_i]][\text{every } x : Bx]$
$\quad \exists E_i(\text{INFL}[e_i, x] \wedge \text{surrender}[e_i]$
$\quad\quad \wedge [\text{every } y : Gy] \exists E_i(\text{to}[e_i, y] \wedge [\exists Z : 2(Z) \wedge \forall z(Zz \rightarrow Cz)]$
$\quad\quad \text{OF}[e_i, Z]))$

The two crisps being handed over to any one girl are just a proper part of
any one boy's action.

With decreasing quantifiers, the above pattern fits if one intends to
speak about negative events as in (12) (see chapter 6, section 1.1). The
more likely reading of (10) is represented in (11) with a different pattern:
the only existential event quantifier falls within the scope of both first-
order quantifiers.

(10) Somebody loves nobody.

(11) $[\text{some } x : \text{person}(x)][\text{no } y : \text{person}(y)]$
$\quad \exists E_i(\text{INFL}[e_i, x] \wedge \text{love}[e_i] \wedge \text{OF}[e_i, y])$

(12) $[\text{some } x : \text{person}(x)]$
$\quad \exists E_i(\text{INFL}[e_i, x] \wedge \text{love}[e_i] \wedge [\text{no } y : \text{person}(y)]\exists E_i \text{ OF}[e_i, y])$

Note further that (9) and (12) separate the θ-roles, but (11) does not.
Rather than face the complications of a syntax that admits both patterns
but excludes others, I prefer to fix the location of the θ-roles, if possible.
Since separation is elsewhere essential, I will follow the pattern of (9) and
(12), separating θ-roles from each other but keeping them close to their
first-order quantifiers. The event quantifier that accompanies every first-
order quantifier will, however, have to be something other than the existential quantifiers that appear in (9) and (12). Logical form (12) cannot
express what (11) does, and (9) and (12) conflict with the formal constraint
(announced in chapter 6, section 1, and to be demonstrated in section 2.3)
that any clause contains no more than one existential event quantifier.
Replacing the existential event quantifier, we get '$[\hat{E} : \text{INFL}[e, x]]$' in (13)
as a second-order *definite* description of whatever events there are, if any,
in which x is the unique INFLer.

(13) ... $[\text{every } x : Bx][\hat{E} : \text{INFL}[e, x]]$ ...

With respect to (4), it describes whatever eating a boy did in the given context. The new operator quantifies over all those events that overlap events in the context (and only those in the context). Therefore, for each boy, if he did any eating at all, among the available events will be those in which he alone ate. '$[\hat{E} : \text{INFL}[e, x]]$' denotes these. Similarly, the logical form for (8) will be (14), and its intended paraphrase is (15a), or the less literal but more felicitous (15b).

(14) $[\exists E_i : \text{graceful}[e_i]]$ [every $x : Bx$]$[\hat{E} : \text{INFL}[e_i, x]]$ (surrender$[e_i]$
   $\wedge$ [every $y : Gy$]$[\hat{E} : \text{to}[e_i, y]][\exists Z : 2(Z)$
   $\wedge \forall z(Zz \rightarrow Cz)]$ OF$[e_i, Z])$

(15) a. In a graceful event, every boy is such that whatever he did, surrendering is such that every girl is such that whatever she did, being surrendered to is such that two crisps were surrendered.

   b. In a graceful event, every boy's surrendering is such that every girl's being surrendered to is such that two crisps were surrendered.

All first-order quantifiers will work this way. The LF

'$[Q_1 N'][Q_2 N'][Q_3 N'](\ldots V(e) \ldots \Theta(e, x_1) \ldots \Theta(e, x_2) \ldots \Theta(e, x_3) \ldots)$'

comes to assert that Q_1 many N's are such that whatever they did as Θ_1-ers is such that Q_2 many N's are such that whatever they did as Θ_2-ers is such that Q_3 many N's are such that whatever they did as Θ_3-ers are V-ings, or again more briefly, that Q_1-many N's Θ_1-ing is such that Q_2-many N's Θ_2-ing is such that Q_3-many N's Θ_3-ing is V-ing. The translation of the trace-binding relationship at LF puts the θ-role into the restriction of a quantifier over events. That quantifier over events then determines the context of events for the remainder of the logical form:

(16) $\text{NP}_i[_\Phi \ldots \Theta[e_k, t_i]\underline{\quad\quad}] \Rightarrow \text{NP}_i[\hat{E}_k : \Theta[e_k, v_i]][_\Phi \ldots \underline{\quad\quad}]$

It is clear that the derived logical forms do not violate the constraints on existential event quantifiers. They also realize a certain parallelism in the translation of first-order quantifiers and the second-order quantifiers that remain *in situ* in LF. The latter are translated adjacent to their Θ-roles:

(17) $\ldots \wedge [\exists V : \Phi]\Theta[e, V] \wedge \ldots$

With the new operators '$[\hat{E} : \Phi]$', this can become a general feature of translating all NPs. In evaluating any quantifier, one knows that its θ-role is disposed of next. The NPs are always construed locally with their θ-roles, the exact interpretation depending on whether it is a first- or second-order quantifier. It is at least a convenience that LF is structurally dis-ambiguating: fixing the relative scope of the NPs fixes all the other rela-tions as well.

1.1   The syntax and semantics of $[\hat{E} : \Theta[e, v]]$

Further consideration of (10) will clarify some syntactic points that affect the application of (16) and how the new operator is ultimately to be defined. Note first that we would not have obtained an adequate represen-tation if we replaced only the one existential quantifier over events:

(18) [some x : person(x)][no y : person(y)][$\hat{E}_i$: INFL[e_i, x]]
      (love[e_i] $\wedge$ OF[e_i, y])

Formula (18) asserts that someone is such that no one is the sole object of his love. The formula within the scope of the first-order quantifiers says that whatever loving x did was loving of y. This, of course, does not fit the meaning of (10). Rather, there must also be a quantifier over events dedi-cated to the first-order quantifier *nobody*:

(19) [some x : person(x)][no y : person(y)]
      [$\hat{E}_i$: INFL[e_i, x]][$\hat{E}_i$: OF[e_i, y]] love[e_i]

Formula (19) says that whatever loving x did was such that whatever part of it was loving y was loving. According to (19), there is someone whose loving is such that no one can claim a part of it as his own. This is true just in case someone loves no one, as desired.

As we have supposed, every first-order quantifier must have its own second-order definite description '[$\hat{E} : \Theta[e, v]$]', restricted by the θ-role it binds into. I arrive at this conclusion from three considerations: the general requirement that when quantifying over objects we must also somehow quantify over parts of events, a preference for a uniform trans-lation for all first-order quantifiers and the constraint, to be demonstrated, that keeps us from using existential quantifiers over events.

The rule of translation (16) derives (20), however, rather than (19):

(20) [some x : person(x)][$\hat{E}_i$: INFL[e_i, x]]
      [no y : person(y)][$\hat{E}_i$: OF[e_i, y]] love[e_i]

The favored paraphrase is

(21) Someone is such that whatever loving he did is such that no one is
      such that whatever (in it) is a loving of him is a loving.

Changing the scope of the definite description in (20) appears to make little difference, and so it is just as well that (20) is the canonical transla-tion. Interpreting the operator according to the following clause bears out the adequacy of either logical form:

(22) Σ satisfy $\ulcorner[\hat{E}_i : \Phi]\Psi\urcorner$
$$\leftrightarrow [\exists E : \forall e(Ee \leftrightarrow \exists E'\exists\Sigma_0(E' \simeq \Sigma(\mathbb{C}_i) \wedge \forall e(\Sigma_0(\langle\mathbb{C}_i, e\rangle) \to E'e)$$
$$\wedge \Sigma_0 \approx_{\mathbb{C}_i} \Sigma \wedge \Sigma_0(\langle\mathbb{C}_i, e\rangle) \wedge \Sigma_0 \text{ satisfy } \Phi))]$$
$$\exists\Sigma_0(E \simeq \Sigma_0(\mathbb{C}_i) \wedge \Sigma_0 \approx_{\mathbb{C}_i} \Sigma \wedge \Sigma_0 \text{ satisfy } \Psi)^1$$

Given that Σ assign the events C_0 to $\mathbb{C}_i$, 'E' in (22) denotes an event just in case it is among some events that are within the event space of C_0 and that Φ is true of. Adopting (20) gives us a more intuitive handle on translation. '$[Q_1 N'][Q_2 N'][Q_3 N']\Phi$' just becomes '$Q_1$ many N's are such that whatever they did as Θ_1-ers is such that Q_2 many N's are such whatever they did as Θ_2-ers is such that ...'. In sentences that combine second- and first-order quantifiers, such as (23), θ-roles remain near their arguments, as in (24).

(23) Three video games taught every quarterback every new play in five minutes.

(24) $\exists E_i([\exists X : 3(X) \wedge \forall x(Xx \to Gx)] \text{INFL}[e_i, X] \wedge \text{teach}[e_i]$
$\wedge [\text{every } y : Qy][\hat{E}_i : \text{TO}[e_i, y]][\text{every } z : Pz][\hat{E}_i : \text{OF}[e_i, z]]$
$[\exists W : 5(W) \wedge \forall w(Ww \to Mw)] \text{in}[e_i, W])$

Taking up the θ-roles into the restrictions of the new operators raises a further question of syntactic detail. Since I have assumed that the minimal domain for QR is VP, the scope of the innermost quantifier and the operator restricted by its θ-role will normally include the verb:

(25) $\dots[Qx : N'][\hat{E} : \Theta[e, x]][_{VP} V[e]\dots]$

But for the event-dependent interpretation, I have assumed VP preposing, thus deriving an immediate LF of the form in (27):

(26) No more than 10 students collaborated on 3 problems.

(27) $[VP_j[\text{no more than ten students}_i[_{IP} \text{INFL}[e, t_i]t_j]]]$

The scope of the innermost operator will be just a trace t_j unless some content is provided, which I will assume is the head of the moved constituent, the verb:

(28) $[\forall e_j : VP][(\leq 10)x : Sx][\hat{E} : \text{INFL}[e_j, x]] V[e_j]$

1.2   The interaction of '$\exists E$' and '$[\hat{E} : \Theta[e, v]]$'

Recall that second-order descriptions '$[\hat{E} : \Theta[e, v]]$' are introduced to meet both the requirement that first-order quantifiers be accompanied by quantification over the subevents in which they participated and the formal constraint that keeps us from using more than one existential quantifier over events in a clause. I assume that one existential event quantifier is underlyingly clause-initial and that QR raises quantifiers to superior positions.

Note here a crucial respect in which the event descriptions interact with the one existential quantifier over events. The logical form of at least one interpretation of (29) cannot be (30):

(29) Every boy ate two pies.

(30) [every $x : Bx$][$\hat{E} : \mathrm{INFL}[e, x]$]
    (eat[e] $\wedge$ [$\exists Y : 2(Y) \wedge \forall y(Yy \rightarrow Py)$] OF[$e, Y$])

It says that whatever each boy ate it was an eating of two pies. Recall that in the construal of any plural, it denotes exactly those that bear the θ-role to the events in the given context. Here the context is whatever each boy ate, and so the logical form in (30) ends up imposing the incorrect condition that each boy ate two and no more than two pies. The logical form neglects, however, the placement of the existential quantifier over events. With the event quantifier in place, the logical form is (31):

(31) [every $x : Bx$][$\hat{E} : \mathrm{INFL}[e, x]$]
    $\exists E$(eat[e] $\wedge$ [$\exists Y : 2(Y) \wedge \forall y(Yy \rightarrow Py)$] OF[$e, Y$])

The existential quantifier selects an event from each boy's experience that is indeed an event of eating exactly two pizzas, but which is perhaps only one among many. The single occurrence of an existential quantifier over events in the logical form allows the indefinite descriptions in the sentence to escape the implication that there are no others.[2] In all other contexts demanding a quantifier over events we are free, then, to choose '[$\hat{E} : \Phi$]'.

2 Second-Order Quantifiers

I turn now to the intepretation of singular and plural, definite and indefinite descriptions, which are all second-order quantifiers. Just prior to translation, second-order quantifiers appear in two contexts: (32), if QR has raised them, or (33), if left *in situ*.

(32) ... [$\exists V : \Theta$]$_i$ ... $\Theta[e, t_i]$ ...

(33) ... $\Theta[e, [\exists V : \Phi]]$ ...

Quantifiers left *in situ* are translated as in (34), where they are moved to a position adjacent to their θ-roles:

(34) $\Theta[e, [\exists V : \Phi]] \Rightarrow [\exists V : \Phi]\Theta[e, V]$

Thus (35) has logical form (36):

(35) Two detectives solved three crimes.

(36) $\exists E([\exists X : 2(X) \wedge \forall x(Xx \rightarrow Dx)] \text{INFL}[e, X] \wedge \text{solve}[e]$
$\wedge [\exists Y : 3(Y) \wedge \forall y(Yy \rightarrow Cy)] \text{OF}[e, Y])$

A raised second-order quantifier may result in a (semi)distributive interpretation, as in (37), or in a nondistributive interpretation, as in (38):

(37) $[\exists V : \Phi]_i(\ldots \Theta[e, t_i]\underline{\quad\quad}) \Rightarrow [\exists V : \Phi][\forall v : Vv][\hat{E} : \Theta[e, v]](\ldots\underline{\quad\quad})^3$

(38) $[\exists V : \Phi]_i(\ldots \Theta[e, t_i]\underline{\quad\quad}) \Rightarrow [\exists V : \Phi](\ldots \Theta[e, V]\underline{\quad\quad})^4$

In a way, this theory stands things on its head. It makes quick work of plurals but labors over ordinary first-order quantifiers. The following sections comment on the differences in the translation of second order and first-order quantifiers, their interactions, the occurrence of no more than one existential event quantifier in a clause, and the constraint mentioned earlier in chapter 1, section 2.4, about the nature of cross-reference in cases of essential separation.

2.1 The translation of second-order quantifiers in situ

First, I observe that logical forms for second-order quantifiers that are analogous to the translations of trace binding yield illicit interpretations:

(39) $*\ldots [\exists V : \Phi][\hat{E} : \Theta[e, V]]\Psi$

Consider (40) and the valid inference to (41), where *the children* and *the vans* refer back to the event described by (40):

(40) Six children went (to the zoo) in two vans.

(41) If one of the vans took two of the children, then the other took four.

(42) $[_{v_1} c_1, c_2] \quad [_{v_2} c_3, c_4] \quad [_{v_3} c_5, c_6]$

Now sentence (40) is false in context (42), since there is no (sub)event that puts six children in two vans. Sentence (41) is false as well, since it fails to refer to two vans. However, formula (43), an instance of (39), would make (40) true in (42).

(43) $[\exists X : 6(X) \wedge \forall x(Xx \rightarrow Cx)][\hat{E} : \text{INFL}[e, X]]$
$[\exists Y : 2(Y) \wedge \forall y(Yy \rightarrow Vy)][\hat{E} : \text{in}[e, Y]] \text{go}[e]$

Some six children's going to the zoo in three vans is such that two vans, in their part of the trip, took children to the zoo. If (43) were the logical form of (40), it would also invalidate the inference to (41). Formula (43) relates children and vans not to the same event but to events in a part-whole relation. Parallel to our understanding of first-order quantifiers, the last conjunct requires only that for some two vans what they did within the event of children going to the zoo in vans was to carry children. These conditions are too weak to translate the relation between the plurals in (40). Once particular events are taken up in the course of interpreting the first plural, later plurals must describe the participants of those events. The interpretation of the later plural cannot introduce a description that may denote only a proper part of the events presented. As a result, the quantification over parts of events that iterates with every occurrence of a first-order quantifier must not occur with second-order quantifiers.

2.2 Essential separation and the interaction of first-order and second-order quantifiers

The logical form of separation introduces into relations among particulars a crucial vagueness about who did what to whom and to how many. That there is any relation among the participants in various θ-roles is an effect of reference to events. The events in which the various θ-roles are carried out overlap in some way. The logical form for separation that has been assumed so far risks overstating the vagueness in the relation among the participants. Consider the simple case in (44) and the suggested form in (45):

(44) Three video games taught every quarterback two plays.

(45) $\exists E([\exists X : 3(X) \land \forall x(Xx \rightarrow Gx)] \text{INFL}[e, X]$
       $\land [\text{every } y : Qy][\hat{E} : \text{TO}[e, y]]$
       $(\text{teach}[e] \land [\exists Z : 2(Z) \land \forall z(Zz \rightarrow Pz)] \text{OF}[e, Z])$

Suppose that three video games taught, but only one of them taught every quarterback two new plays. The other two video games taught French to bicyclists. In this situation, (44) is false; however, (45) is presumably true. There is an event of teaching by three video games, and, by quantification over its parts, every quarterback was taught two plays there. The example is perhaps tame if it can be claimed that we understand the subject matter of the sentence to concern only events of video games teaching quarterbacks new plays. Excluding from the domain of relevant events those where French is taught will falsify (45), as required.

The problem is not so easily sidestepped. Consider a context for evaluating (46) and (48) that contains only events of video games teaching quarterbacks new plays. In (50), eight of the ten video games each taught exactly one quarterback exactly one play, while the two remaining video games taught two quarterbacks each two new plays.

(46) Ten video games taught exactly two quarterbacks (each) two new plays.

(47) $\exists E([\exists X : 10(X) \wedge \forall x(Xx \rightarrow Gx)]\ \text{INFL}[e, X]$
$\wedge\ [2!y : Qy][\hat{E} : \text{TO}[e, y]]$
$(\text{teach}[e] \wedge [\exists Z : 2(Z) \wedge \forall z(Zz \rightarrow Pz)]\ \text{OF}[e, Z]))$

(48) Ten video games taught at least two quarterbacks each two new plays.

(49) $\exists E([\exists X : 10(X) \wedge \forall x(Xx \rightarrow Gx)]\ \text{INFL}[e, X]$
$\wedge\ [\exists Y : \geq 2(Y) \wedge \forall y(Yy \rightarrow Qy)][\forall y : Yy][\hat{E} : \text{TO}[e, y]]$
$(\text{teach}[e] \wedge [\exists Z : 2(Z) \wedge \forall z(Zz \rightarrow Pz)]\ \text{OF}[e, Z]))$

(50)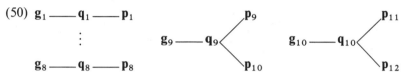

Sentences (46) and (48) are false in the context, since eight of the video games had nothing to do with the the quarterbacks who were each taught two new plays. The sentences entail that ten video games are the teachers in what happened to those quarterbacks. But logical forms (47) and (49) come out true. The context is an event of ten video games teaching quarterbacks new plays, and it is one in which each of two quarterbacks is taught two new plays. The quantification over parts of events that follows the first-order quantifier allows us to neglect the action of some of the ten video games and provide a partial description of what happened. The truth conditions of these forms are too weak. Rather, the truth conditions should require that each of the ten video games contributed to the education of those two quarterbacks. In some sense, once the teaching by ten video games is introduced, the rest of the formula ought to be a comprehensive description of what they did.

My proposal is that the cross-reference between the conjunct expressing plural predication and the quantificational conjunct that follows is not the one shown in (47) and (49). Rather, the event place exposed in the first conjunct is covered by an occurrence of a descriptive anaphor that refers to the events described by the quantificational conjunct:

(51) $\exists E([\exists X : 10(X) \wedge \forall x(Xx \rightarrow Gx)]$ INFL$[that_i, X]$
$\wedge [_i[2!y : Qy][\hat{E} : \text{TO}[e, y]]$
$(\text{teach}[e] \wedge [\exists Z : 2(Z) \wedge \forall z(Zz \rightarrow Pz)] \text{ OF}[e, Z])])$

(52) $\exists E([\exists X : 10(X) \wedge \forall x(Xx \rightarrow Gx)]$ INFL$[that_i, X]$
$\wedge [_i[\exists Y : \geq 2(Y) \wedge \forall y(Yy \rightarrow Qy)][\forall y : Yy][\hat{E} : \text{TO}[e, y]]$
$(\text{teach}[e] \wedge [\exists Z : 2(Z) \wedge \forall z(Zz \rightarrow Pz)] \text{ OF}[e, Z])])$

(53) In some events two quarterbacks were each taught two new plays,
and that was by ten video games.

The intended anaphor is just the one introduced in chapter 1, section 2.4,
to support cross-reference to events in the logical form of cumulative
quantifiers. The point of this cross-reference is to refer exactly to whatever
the two quarterbacks did. The semantics that gives the descriptive anaphor
this reference is discussed in chapter 9, section 3, on cumulative quantifiers. I note here the syntactic conditions for cross-reference in (51) and
(52). In proposing a Davidsonian logical form, one must assume that
some way of establishing cross-reference among the conjuncts is obligatory. In the simplest cases, that coreference takes the form of identical
variables in each of the conjuncts:

(54) Two video games taught two quarterbacks.

(55) $\exists E([\exists Z : 2(Z) \wedge \forall z(Zz \rightarrow Gx)]$ INFL$[e, X]$
$\wedge \text{teach}[e] \wedge [\exists Y : 2(Y) \wedge \forall y(Yy \rightarrow Qy)] \text{ OF}[e, Y])$

In contrast, the logical forms in (47) and (49) fail to make explicit any
cross-reference. The conjunct in the scope of a first-order quantifier does
not contain a free event variable. The only way to refer to the events
described by such a clause is by descriptive anaphor. Thus only (51) and
(52) are coherent Davidsonian logical forms.

Some alternative suggestions for revising (47) and (49) are worth considering, if only to confirm the view that the problem is one of cross-
reference to events. If grounds could be found to introduce copies of the
quantifier and θ-role, (56) would represent the target interpretation of
(46):

(56) $\exists E([\exists X : 10(X) \wedge \forall x(Xx \rightarrow Gx)]$ INFL$[e, X]$
$\wedge [2!y : Qy][\hat{E} : \text{TO}[e, y]] \text{ teach}[e]$
$\wedge [2!y : Qy][\hat{E} : \text{TO}[e, y]][\exists Z : 2(Z) \wedge \forall z(Zz \rightarrow Pz)] \text{ OF}[e, Z])$

The additional conjunct guarantees that exactly two quarterbacks are taught by the ten video games. A similar revision of (49) cannot simply copy the second-order quantifier and its θ-role, since the resulting logical form in (57) would continue to be true in the context (50):

(57) $\exists E([\exists X : 10(X) \land \forall x(Xx \rightarrow Gx)] \text{INFL}[e, X]$
$\land [\exists Y : \geq 2(Y) \land \forall y(Yy \rightarrow Qy)] \text{TO}[e, Y]$
$\land [\exists Y : \geq 2(Y) \land \forall y(Yy \rightarrow Qy)][\forall y : Yy][\hat{E} : \text{TO}[e, y]]$
$(\text{teach}[e] \land [\exists Z : 2(Z) \land \forall z(Zz \rightarrow Pz)] \text{OF}[e, Z]))$

The ten video games did teach at least two quarterbacks, and at least two quarterbacks were each taught two new plays there. The revised logical form requires a closer connection between the arguments to the two occurrences of the θ-role TO.

(58) $\exists E([\exists X : 10(X) \land \forall x(Xx \rightarrow Gx)] \text{INFL}[e, X]$
$\land [\exists Y : \geq 2(Y) \land \forall y(Yy \rightarrow Qy)]$
$(\text{TO}[e, Y] \land [\forall y : Yy][\hat{E} : \text{TO}[e, y]]$
$(\text{teach}[e] \land [\exists Z : 2(Z) \land \forall z(Zz \rightarrow Pz)] \text{OF}[e, Z])))$

Allowing the difference in the translation of *exactly two quarterbacks* and *at least two quarterbacks*, I find decisive the objection that the revisions undertaken are appropriate only in the context of conjuncts that cross-refer to the events described. No interpretation of (59) entails that exactly two quarterbacks were taught new plays.

(59) Exactly two quarterbacks were each taught two new plays.

(60) $[2!y : Qy][\hat{E} : \text{TO}[e, y]] \text{teach}[e]$
$\land [2!y : Qy][\hat{E} : \text{TO}[e, y]]$
$[\exists Z : 2(Z) \land \forall z(Zz \rightarrow Pz)] \text{OF}[e, Z]$

In the case of *at least two quarterbacks*, the logical form in (62) fails to represent the most salient interpretation of (61), which bears no existential commitment to an event of any kind.

(61) At least two quarterbacks were each taught not a single new play.

(62) $\exists E[\exists Y : \geq 2(Y) \land \forall y(Yy \rightarrow Qy)]$
$(\text{TO}[e, Y] \land [\forall y : Yy][\hat{E} : \text{TO}[e, y]][\text{no } z : Pz][\hat{E} : \text{OF}[e, z]] \text{teach}[e])$

Note that we cannot regard the occurrence of the additional θ-role as an unconditioned option. If it can be omitted in (62), its omission in (58) would be just the unacceptable (49).

The revisions that force the sentence to describe exactly what the ten video games did are appropriate only because there is already a conjunct saying they did something. On my view, this follows if exact description is the effect of a cross-referring descriptive anaphor.

2.3   No more than one existential event quantifier in a clause

To show that there is no more than one existential event quantifier in a clause, and thus to justify the translation of first-order quantifiers that introduces a definite description of events, we rely on an observation about the reference of descriptive anaphors.

According to the cumulative interpretation of (63), any video game and quarterback such that it taught him a new play should be among the two video games and the two quarterbacks.

(63)   Exactly two video games each taught a new play to exactly two quarterbacks.

The logical form yields this result just in case the events referred to by the descriptive anaphor in (64) or (65) includes any event where a game teaches a quarterback a new play.

(64) $[2!x : Gx][\hat{E} : \text{INFL}[e, x]]\exists E$
$(\text{teach}[e] \wedge [\exists Y : 1(Y) \wedge \forall y(Yy \rightarrow Py)] \text{OF}[e, Y]$
$\wedge [\exists Z : \forall z(Zz \rightarrow Qz)] \text{to}[e, Z])$
$\wedge \text{ } there[2!z : Qz][\hat{E} : \text{to}[e, z]] \text{ teach}[e]$

(65)   Exactly two video games each taught a new play to quarterbacks, and *there* video games taught new plays to exactly two quarterbacks.

Note that it will include the several events that any video game has participated in if these meet the description. So it would falsify (63) if, in addition to the events of (66), video game g_1 would go on to teach a new play to a third quarterback.

(66) $g_1 \text{——} p_1 \text{——} q_1 \qquad g_1 \text{——} p_2 \text{——} q_2 \qquad g_2 \text{——} p_1 \text{——} q_1$
$g_2 \text{——} p_2 \text{——} q_2$

With this observation about the reference of the descriptive anaphor in mind, consider sentences (67) and (69) and context (72).

(67)   Two video games taught exactly three quarterbacks each a new play.

(68) $\exists E([\exists X : 2(X) \wedge \forall x(Xx \rightarrow Gx)] \text{INFL}[that_i, X]$
$\wedge [_i[3!y : Qy][\hat{E} : \text{TO}[e, y]]$
$(\text{teach}[e] \wedge [\exists Z : 1(Z) \wedge \forall z(Zz \rightarrow Pz)] \text{OF}[e, Z])])$

(69) Four video games taught exactly three quarterbacks each a new play.

(70) $\exists E([\exists X : 4(X) \wedge \forall x(Xx \rightarrow Gx)]$ INFL$[that_i, X]$
$\wedge [_i[3!y : Qy][\hat{E} : \text{TO}[e, y]]$
$(\text{teach}[e] \wedge [\exists Z : 1(Z) \wedge \forall z(Zz \rightarrow Pz)]$ OF$[e, Z])])$

(71) *$\exists E([\exists X : 4(X) \wedge \forall x(Xx \rightarrow Gx)]$ INFL$[that_i, X]$
$\wedge [_i[3!y : Qy][\hat{E} : \text{TO}[e, y]]\exists E$
$(\text{teach}[e] \wedge [\exists Z : 1(Z) \wedge \forall z(Zz \rightarrow Pz)]$ OF$[e, Z])])$

(72)

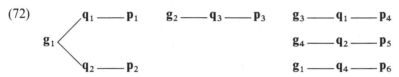

To discourage taking 'n video games' and 'exactly three quarterbacks' as cumulative, the context falsifies this interpretation. It contains four video games teaching four quarterbacks new plays. Interpretations in which 'n video games' is understood distributively are falsified as well, since only one video game is related to exactly three quarterbacks. The only chance for a true interpretation is to understand the sentences merely to assert the existence of an event of teaching by n video games. So understood, (67) is true. There is an event of teaching exactly three quarterbacks each a new play, corresponding to the first two blocks in (72), and the teachers are two video games. But (69) has no interpretation true in (72). The teaching by any four video games is not an event of exactly three quarterbacks each being taught a new play. At best, it could be said that four video games taught exactly three quarterbacks each one or more new plays. This judgment can be exaggerated. As in the first two blocks of (72), imagine that two video games taught exactly three quarterbacks each a new play, but, in addition, a hundred other video games, apart from teaching many other quarterbacks new plays, taught these three a hundred or so new plays. It cannot be said that a hundred and two video games taught exactly three quarterbacks each a new play. There is no event of teaching every quarterback each a new play in which all hundred and two video games participated.[5]

Both logical forms (70) and (71) contain a descriptive anaphor that refers to the events (among events E) described exactly by its antecedent *exactly three quarterbacks each being taught a new play*. They differ in an occurrence of the existential quantifier over events that, in (71), follows the first-order quantifier *exactly three quarterbacks*. Its occurrence is suffi-cient to make (71) true in (72), contrary to the interpretation of (69). Consider that part of (72) that excludes teaching quarterback q_4, and suppose that in evaluating the outermost existential quantifier, an event or events that coincide with that part are assigned to the parameter $\mathfrak{C}$. As for the second conjunct of (71), it is true that within this part of (72), exactly three quarterbacks can find some subevent in which he has been taught a new play. The second occurrence of the existential event quantifier invites consideration of any subevent that meets the description. Quarterbacks q_1 and q_2 happen to have more than one.

Recall from the discussion of (63) through (66) that the descriptive anaphor refers to whatever the quarterbacks did that meets the descrip-tion. In this case, it will include any subevent within the relevant part of (72) where either q_1, q_2, or q_3 is taught a new play. These subevents completely overlap that part of (72), and so the descriptive anaphor refers to it all. But that part of (72) is a teaching by four video games. The logical form (71) is therefore true in the context, mistakenly. What seems wrong is that the logical form does not give an exact description of what the four video games did there, which is not an event of three quarterbacks each being taught a new play. The action of two of the video games is lost in a description of just what the other two did. Note that this has developed even though the quantifier governing the description *exactly three quar-terbacks* does describe everyone related to the four video games in this part of (72).

Now compare (70), which omits the second occurrence of the existential event quantifier. For the part of (72) that excludes teaching q_4 to satisfy the second conjunct, it must be that what q_1 did in that part of (72) is to be taught a new play. But this is false. The reference of the definite description '$[\hat{E} : \mathrm{TO}[q_1, y]]$', all of what was done to him in this part, is a being taught two new plays. One play does not exhaust the participants in these events. Similarly for q_2's part. Any part of (72) that includes action by four video games simply fails to satisfy the second conjunct of (70), as desired. In contrast, the smaller event consisting of only the first two blocks of (72) does satisfy the second conjunct, and it will yield a truth if it is described as a teaching by two video games, as in (67) and its logical form (68).

Within the matrix scope of the matrix quantifier over events, once some events have been taken up for evaluation, the remaining constituents con-spire to produce an exact description. If it includes a first-order quantifier, then for each participant, the description must exactly fit all of what he did among the events under consideration. As we have seen, another existential quantifier over events undermines an exact fit. For this reason the translation of first-order quantifiers does not introduce them. There is only the one existential quantifier that is underlyingly clause-initial, which is sufficient for any indefinite reference to some events that a sentence may make.

Chapter 8
Semidistributivity

In semidistributive interpretations, first-order quantifiers appear to quantify over pluralities. It is the only interpretation when the verb is intrinsically collective. Thus (1) asserts that few composers are among the pluralities that each constitutes a collaboration of composers.

(1) Few composers collaborated.

Semidistributive interpretations occur also with predicates that are not intrinsically collective. Imagine that there are various teams of bakers with members highly specialized in various aspects of the art (sifting, mixing, glazing) who produce pies in such a way that no one of them can be said to bake any one pie. Suppose further that some teams have a weakness for eating their products, again in such a way that no one baker eats any one pie. Sentence (2) can then report that exactly a dozen bakers are among the weak-willed teams.

(2) Exactly a dozen bakers ate the pies that they baked.

Semidistributivity is not confined to subject positions. The appearance of quantifying over pluralities can occur at other θ-roles, and the distribution of semidistributivity among the θ-roles of a sentence seems to be free. Thus in (3) either or both quantifiers may be understood semidistributively.

(3) Three trellises (each) isolated no more than five banquet areas.

(4) case 1: $\textcircled{$\mathbf{a}_i$}$ $\mathbf{t}_j$ $\mathbf{t}_j$ isolates $\mathbf{a}_i$

 case 2: $\textcircled{$\mathbf{a}_{ij}$}$ $\mathbf{t}_j$–$\mathbf{t}_k$ $\mathbf{t}_j$–$\mathbf{t}_k$ isolate $\mathbf{a}_i$ & $\forall t \neg (t$ isolates $\mathbf{a}_i)$

 case 3: $\textcircled{$\mathbf{a}_i$–$\mathbf{a}_l$}$ $\mathbf{t}_j$ $\mathbf{t}_j$ isolates $\mathbf{a}_i$–$\mathbf{a}_l$ & $\forall a \neg (\mathbf{t}_j$ isolates $a)$

 case 4: $\textcircled{$\mathbf{a}_i$–$\mathbf{a}_l$}$ $\mathbf{t}_j$–$\mathbf{t}_k$ $\mathbf{t}_j$–$\mathbf{t}_k$ isolate $\mathbf{a}_i$–$\mathbf{a}_l$ & $\forall a \forall t \neg (t$ isolates $a)$

In the catering business, trellises are used to subdivide floor space into banquet areas. Suppose that trellises are layered to enhance privacy. For example, the banquet areas for one convention might be separated from each other by a thickness of one trellis, but many trellises enclose the group of them so that they are undisturbed by a neighboring convention. The caterer is taking stock of how his trellises have been deployed when he utters (3). The context is rich enough to support four-way ambiguity. Without any semidistributivity, the only relevant relation is where an individual trellis isolates an individual banquent area, case 1 in (4). Sentence (3) then reports that each of three trellises stood in this relation to no more than five banquets areas. If this is not a remark about how each trellis has been used over several occasions, then, of course, any one trellis would have to be a folding one to completely isolate more than one banquet area. When both quantifiers are understood semidistributively, then all the cases shown in (4) are relevant. Sentence (3) reports that each of three trellises, with perhaps some other trellises, isolated no more than five banquet areas from some other areas. In cases 3 and 4, the trellises isolate the banquet areas from the other convention but not from each other. Suppose we apply semidistributivity only to the second quantifier and fully distribute the first. We want to know how many banquet areas the individual trellis can surround, isolating them from outside banquets but not necessarily each other. This interpretation is concerned only with cases 1 and 3. Each trellis is asserted to contain no more than five areas. Finally, if only the first quantifier *three trellises* is understood semidistributively, the relevant cases are just the first two. Here the sentence reports how many trellises were involved in completely isolating an individual banquet area. Each of three trellises participated (on various occasions) in completely isolating no more than five banquet areas. We thus see that (3) has four distinct interpretations, each making a different choice of relevant cases from those shown in (4). This possibility for a four-way ambiguity fits the view adopted here that semidistributivity, however it is eventually formalized, may occur at any θ-role.[1]

As first remarked in chapter 1, section 3, semidistributive quantification over pluralities appears to be quite robust. It can have scope over other quantifiers, as in (5), where the relevant interpretation is that no more than ten students are among collaborations on three problems, and it can appear to bind plural pronouns, as in (6).[2]

(5) No more than ten students collaborated on three problems.

(6) Few composers agreed that they should collaborate.

On my view of pluralities, we might expect semidistributivity to engage a second-order quantifier.[3] The logical form of (1) would then be equivalent to (7).

(7) [few $x : Cx$][$\exists X : Xx \wedge \forall x(Xx \rightarrow Cx)$]$\exists E$(INFL[$e, X$] $\wedge$ V[e])

It says that few composers, with some others, collaborate. The second-order quantifier does the work of quantifying over pluralities. In the logical form for (5) in (8), it includes within its scope *three problems*, and in (9), the logical form for (6), it binds the plural pronoun.

(8) [($\leq$ 10)$x : Sx$][$\exists X : Xx \wedge \forall x(Xx \rightarrow Sx)$]
    $\exists E$(INFL[e, X] $\wedge$ V[e] $\wedge$ [$\exists Y : 3(Y) \wedge \forall y(Yy \rightarrow Py)$] on[$e, Y$])

(9) [few $x : Cx$][$\exists X : Xx \wedge \forall x(Xx \rightarrow Cx)$]
    $\exists E$(INFL[e, X] $\wedge$ OF(e, [$_s$ that ... (ιZ)($\forall z(Zz \leftrightarrow Xz)$) ...]))

This syntax for a covert second-order quantifier becomes untenable, however, in the face of two considerations. The first is that its possible scope assignments do not coincide with those of its overt counterpart, *with other composers*, in (10).

(10) Few composers collaborated with other composers.

The second consideration is that semidistributive scope and semidistributive binding cannot both be served. In some cases, the scope necessary to bind a pronoun is not consistent with the interpretation of the covert quantifier relative to other quantifiers in the sentence. I will spell out these considerations in more detail after presenting the proposal in section 1. This proposal introduces the operator *Co-*, modifying θ-roles, which fixes the scope properties of semidistributivity. The modifier fails to provide an antecedent for the semidistributively bound pronouns, which are to be treated as descriptive anaphors.

1   The Semidistributive Operator *Co-*

Recall that both distributive and semidistributive interpretations are derived by a translation of the LF in (11):

(11) [$Qv : N'$]$_i$ (... $\Theta[e, t_i]$____)

The semidistributive modifier applies to θ-roles, as in (12). The rule for translating first-order quantifiers then derives (13). Sentence (1), for example, has the logical form in (14):

(12) [QN']$_i$ (... Co-$\Theta[e_k, t_i]$____)

(13) $[Qv_i : \text{N}'][\hat{E}_k : \text{Co-}\Theta[e_k, v_i]](\ldots \underline{\qquad})$

(14) $[\text{few } x : Cx][\hat{E} : \text{Co-INFL}[e, x]] \exists E \text{ collaborate}[e]$

The derived θ-role can be fulfilled with the help of other things. The reference to others is concealed in the semantic clause in (15), which makes (14) equivalent to (17):

(15) $\Sigma \text{ satisfy } {}^\ulcorner\text{Co-}\Theta[e, v]{}^\urcorner \leftrightarrow [\exists X : \forall x(\Sigma(\langle v, x \rangle) \to Xx)]$
$\exists \Sigma_0(\Sigma_0 \approx_v \Sigma \wedge \forall x(\Sigma_0(\langle v, x \rangle) \leftrightarrow Xx) \wedge \Sigma_0 \text{ satisfy } {}^\ulcorner\Theta[e, v]{}^\urcorner)$

(16) $\Sigma \text{ satisfy } {}^\ulcorner\text{Co-}\Theta[e, V]{}^\urcorner \leftrightarrow \Sigma \text{ satisfy } {}^\ulcorner\Theta[e, V]{}^\urcorner)^4$

(17) $[\text{few } x : Cx][\hat{E} : [\exists X : Xx] \text{ INFL}[e, X]] \exists E \text{ V}[e]$

Formula (17) says, in effect, that not many a composer is such that whatever he did as a collaborator with perhaps other things was in fact to collaborate with other things. This is, of course, not the sense of (1), which concerns only collaborations with other composers. The refinement I adopt recasts the semidistributive operator as a binary one, adding a restriction whose content is dependent on the antecedent quantifier, as in (18).

(18) $[Qv : \text{N}'_j]_i ([\text{Co} : \text{N}'_j]\text{-}\Theta[e, t_i]\Psi)$

The semantic clause is then (19).

(19) $\Sigma \text{ satisfy } {}^\ulcorner[\text{Co} : \text{N}']\text{-}\Theta[e, v]{}^\urcorner$
$\leftrightarrow [\exists X : \forall x(\Sigma(\langle v, x \rangle) \to Xx)$
$\wedge \forall x(Xx \to \exists \Sigma_0(\Sigma_0 \approx_v \Sigma \wedge \forall z(\Sigma_0(\langle v, z \rangle) \leftrightarrow z = x)$
$\wedge \Sigma_0 \text{ satisfy } \text{N}')]$
$\exists \Sigma_0(\Sigma_0 \approx_v \Sigma \wedge \forall x(\Sigma_0(\langle v, x \rangle) \leftrightarrow Xx) \wedge \Sigma_0 \text{ satisfy } {}^\ulcorner\Theta[e, v]{}^\urcorner)$

The refinement may be unnecessary if it is assumed that pragmatic considerations restrict the relevant events to those of composers collaborating. In any case, although I will assume a binary operator, the logical forms that appear suppress the restriction.

2 Semidistributively Bound Pronouns

This view of semidistributivity requires a different treament of the anaphoric relation in (20).

(20) Few composers$_i$ agreed that they$_i$ should collaborate.

Since the scope of the semidistributive operator includes only the modified θ-role, it is in no position to bind pronouns. Thus there is no analogue to (21), where the one operator both binds the pronoun and expresses semidistributivity.

(21) [few $x : Cx$][$\exists X : Xx \wedge \forall x(Xx \rightarrow Cx)$]
  $\exists E$(INFL$[e, X] \wedge$ V$[e]$
    $\wedge$ OF$(e, [_s$ that $\ldots (\iota Z)(\forall z(Zz \leftrightarrow Xz))\ldots])$)

Instead, the anaphoric relation is one that assigns to the descriptive content of the pronoun the θ-role bound by its antecedent.[5] The logical form of (20) is (22), which is paraphrased by the *de re* reading of (23):[6]

(22) [few $x : Cx$][$\hat{E} : $ Co-INFL$_i[e, x]$]
  $\exists E$(agree$[e]$
    $\wedge$ OF$(e, [_s$ that $\ldots (\iota Z)(\forall z(Zz \leftrightarrow$ Co-INFL$_i[e, z]))\ldots])$)

(23) Few composers ever agreed that those then agreeing should collaborate.

To become the descriptive content of the pronoun, the θ-role, 'Co-INFL', must be separable. The analysis of semidistributivity thus provides another argument for separation.

3 Evidence against a Covert Occurrence of '$[\exists V : \Phi]$' in the Logical Form of Semidistributivity

We turn now to the two considerations that further this analysis of semidistributivity: first, that the covert second-order quantifier, exemplified in (21), cannot have the same scope has its overt counterpart, and second, that semidistributive scope and the semidistributive binding of plural pronouns cannot both be served by the same operator. The latter point is especially important if we are to maintain the somewhat unexpected treatment of the pronoun in (20).

3.1 Semidistributive scope
The covert second-order quantifier makes (24) similar in structure to (10), where a second-order quantifier occurs overtly.

(24) Few composers collaborated.

(25) [few $x : Cx$][$\exists X : Xx \wedge \forall x(Xx \rightarrow Cx)$]$\exists E($ ... INFL$[e, X]$ ... $)$

(10) Few composers collaborated with other composers.

(26) [few $x : Cx$][$\exists Z : $some$(Z) \wedge \neg Zx \wedge \forall x(Zx \rightarrow Cx)$]
  $\exists E($ ... INFL$[e, x]$ ... with$[e, Z]$ ... $)$[7]

The only difference is that the first-order and second-order quantifier in (24) articulate the one θ-role assigned to the subject, but in (10) they bind distinct θ-roles. The similarity in structure makes it unexpected that (27) and (28) should diverge in interpretation:

(27) Few composers collaborated on no more than three operas.

(28) Few composers collaborated with (some) others on no more than three operas.

On the relevant interpretations of (28) and (29), *(some) others* and *any others* include within their scope *no more than three operas*.

(29) Few composers collaborated with any others on no more than three operas.

Sentence (28) asserts that few composers are such that there are some composers with whom they have collaborated on no more than three operas. It is false, since for every composer we can surely find composers with whom he has had no collaboration. This interpretation of (28) is represented by (30):

(30) $[\text{few } x : Cx][\exists Z : \text{some}(Z) \wedge \neg Zx \wedge \forall x(Zx \rightarrow Cx)][(\leq 3)y : Oy]$
       $\exists E(\ldots \text{INFL}[e, x] \ldots \text{with}[e, Z] \ldots \text{on}[e, y] \ldots)$

Sentence (27) does not, however, permit the covert second-order quantifier to have scope over *no more than three operas*. If *few composers* includes in its scope *no more than three operas*, its only interpretation is that few composers collaborated on no more than three operas. For most composers, there are more than three operas that they collaborated on with other composers. Thus the interpretations available to (27) diverge from its overt counterpart in (28). We have (32) but not (31).[8]

(31) *$[\text{few } x : Cx][\exists X : Xx \wedge \forall x(Xx \rightarrow Cx)][(\leq 3)y : Oy]$
       $\exists E(\ldots \text{INFL}[e, X] \ldots \text{on}[e, y] \ldots)$

(32) $[\text{few } x : Cx][(\leq 3)y : Oy]$
       $\exists E[\exists X : Xx \wedge \forall x(Xx \rightarrow Cx)](\text{INFL}[e, X] \ldots \text{on}[e, y] \ldots)$

One attempt at an explanation seeks to reduce the contrast to the difference in θ-roles noted above. The thought is that semidistributivity modifies a θ-role and so there is a locality condition that the covert quantifier it introduces must remain close to the modified θ-role. Thus (31) is excluded, because *no more than three operas* intervenes between the semidistributing quantifier and the θ-role. The locality condition, however it is to be formulated, is respected in (32). Since the overt NP *some others* in (28) is an argument in its own right, the locality condition does not apply, and (30) is simply one way to assign scope.[9]

I have taken the view that semidistributive operators attach to θ-roles. Note that applying a locality condition to a second-order quantifier '$[\exists X : \Phi]$' will have an effect exactly the opposite of what is needed if θ-roles appear where I have put them, in a position adjacent to their quantifiers. The locality condition requires (33):

(33) [few $x : Cx$][$\exists X : Xx \land\ \le 2(X) \land \forall x(Xx \to Cx)$]
$\quad\quad$ [$\hat{E} :$ INFL[e, X]][$(\le 3)y : Oy$] ...

In fact, my translation rules, independent of the locality condition, will not permit *no more than three operas* to intervenc. But (33) is just my version of the intepretation to be excluded, (31). Given the placement of θ-roles, the facts of semidistributivity seem to require an *anti*locality condition. It is obligatory for the interpretation of (27) that *no more than three operas* intervene:

(34) [few $x : Cx$][$(\le 3)y : Oy$][$\exists X : Xx \land\ \le 2(X) \land \forall x(Xx \to Cx)$]
$\quad\quad$ [$\hat{E} :$ INFL[e, X]] ...

I have abandoned the covert second-order quantifier rather than face the challenge of formulating such a condition. Note that the more inviting locality condition, discriminating successfully between (31) and (32), does not keep the unwanted interpretation from surfacing in (33) unless θ-roles are fixed in the positions found in (31) and (32). But this would contradict the evidence that θ-roles can separate (see chapter 1, section 2.3, and chapter 4).

3.2 Interactions of scope and binding

The second consideration for rejecting the covert quantifier is less theory-internal. There is no element that can both articulate the scope properties of semidistributivity and at the same time bind the plural pronouns in semidistributive interpretations like those discussed for (2) and (6). My remarks here are divided between the two sections that follow. I first show that the additional burden of pronominal binding adds to the challenge of formulating a syntactic condition on scope assignment. I then go on to show that in some cases it is impossible for an occurrence of '$[\exists X : \Phi]$' both to represent semidistributive scope and to bind a pronoun.

3.2.1. Sentence (35) shows further complexities that will dog any syntactic condition intended to exclude the unwanted scope assignment in (31) to (27):

(35) Few comrades reenacted (together) some struggles they had endured together for fewer than a hundred young pioneers.

Sentence (35) allows the assignment of scope to the quantifiers that coincides with their order in the sentence. The sentence reports, in effect, that
most struggles are reenacted by their original participants for large cap-
tive audiences:

(36) [few $x : Cx$][$\exists X : Xx \wedge \forall x(Xx \rightarrow Cx)$]
$\quad$ [$\exists Y : \text{some}(Y) \wedge \ldots Sy \ldots \wedge \ldots (\imath Z)(\forall z(Zz \leftrightarrow Xz)) \ldots$]
$\quad$ [$(\leq 100)u : Pu$]$\ldots$

Note that the covert quantifier occupies a position from which it can
bind the plural pronoun, identifying those who endured the struggles with
those who performed the reenactment. The resulting structure in (36) is
then one in which the covert quantifier includes within its scope *fewer than
a hundred young pioneers*. We thus cannot impose any constraint against
the unwanted scope assignment for (27) that is not sensitive to other
aspects of the context, such as the plural pronoun in (35).

$\quad$3.2.2. I now turn to a case where no operator can both represent semidistributive scope and bind a plural pronoun that is nevertheless understood as dependent on the pluralities quantified over. Consider the
sentences in (37):

(37) a. Few vaudevillians$_i$ danced together to most ballads that they$_i$
$\qquad$ sang together.
$\quad$ b. Few vaudevillians$_i$ danced together to every ballad that they$_i$
$\qquad$ sang together.

(38) a. Few vaudevillians danced to most ballads that they sang with
$\qquad$ some vaudevillians, with other vaudevillians.
$\quad$ b. Few vaudevillians danced to every ballad that they sang with
$\qquad$ some vaudevillians, with other vaudevillians.

They pay attention to song and dance routines where the singers are the
dancers. They are distinct from (38), where there is no anaphoric connection between the singers and dancers. Consider a vaudevillian who has
sung, say, four ballads with one troupe of vaudevillians, danced to them
with another troupe, and danced to nothing else:

(39) Dancers: $\mathbf{v}, \mathbf{d}_1, \ldots, \mathbf{d}_n$ $\quad$ $\mathbf{v}, \mathbf{d}_1, \ldots, \mathbf{d}_n$ $\quad$ $\mathbf{v}, \mathbf{d}_1, \ldots, \mathbf{d}_n$ $\quad$ $\mathbf{v}, \mathbf{d}_1, \ldots, \mathbf{d}_n$

$\quad$ Ballads: $\quad$ $\mathbf{b}_1$ $\qquad\qquad$ $\mathbf{b}_2$ $\qquad\qquad$ $\mathbf{b}_3$ $\qquad\qquad$ $\mathbf{b}_4$

$\quad$ Singers: $\quad$ $\mathbf{v}, \mathbf{s}_1, \ldots, \mathbf{s}_n$ $\quad$ $\mathbf{v}, \mathbf{s}_1, \ldots, \mathbf{s}_n$ $\quad$ $\mathbf{v}, \mathbf{s}_1, \ldots, \mathbf{s}_n$ $\quad$ $\mathbf{v}, \mathbf{s}_1, \ldots, \mathbf{s}_n$

Many vaudevillians like $\mathbf{v}$ in (39) would falsify the sentences in (38) but
not those in (37). Each of such vaudevillians has danced with vaudevil-

lians to every ballad that he sang with vaudevillians. Sentences (38a) and (38b) allow few of these. However, since these ballads are not danced to by their singers, vaudevillians like **v** who danced to nothing else danced to no ballads relevant for (37). Sentences (37a) and (37b) are then vacuously true. A similar contrast holds between (40) and (41).

(40) Few vaudevillians$_i$ danced together to no more than three ballads that they$_i$ sang together.

(41) Few vaudevillians danced to no more than three ballads that they sang with some vaudevillians, with other vaudevillians.

Many vaudevillians like **v** falsify (40) but not (41). For (41), each vaudevillian like **v** has danced with vaudevillians to more than three ballads that he sang with vaudevillians, and many such vaudevillians are no counterexample to (41). But again, since these ballads are not danced to by their singers, vaudevillians like **v** who danced to nothing else danced to no more than three of the ballads relevant for (40), and many such vaudevillians therefore falsify (40).

The interpretation of (37) is paraphrased in (42), which is close to how I view the pronoun's connection to its antecedent.

(42) a. Few vaudevillians danced together to most ballads that *the dancers* sang together.
      b. Few vaudevillians danced together to every ballad that *the dancers* sang together.

Using instead a second-order quantifier to bind the plural pronoun, we can obtain a paraphrase only if we rearrange the constitutents, as in (43):

(43) [few $x : Vx$][$Qy : By$][$\exists X : Xx \wedge \forall x(Xx \rightarrow Vx)$]
      ($\exists E(\text{INFL}[e, X] \wedge \text{dance}[e] \wedge \text{to}[e, y])$
      $\wedge \ \exists E(\text{INFL}[e, X] \wedge \text{sing}[e] \wedge \text{OF}[e, y])$)

Note that (43) extraposes the relative clause, as in (44), but it also lowers the clause into the scope of the second-order quantifier.

(44) a. Few vaudevillians danced to most ballads together that they sang together.
      b. Few vaudevillians danced to every ballad together that they sang together.

Without this dislocation, binding and scope cannot be reconciled. Thus (45) fails to bind the pronoun, and (46) makes the wrong scope assignment:

(45) *[few $x : Vx$][$Qy : By \land \exists E(INFL[e, X] \land sing[e] \land OF[e, y])$]
      [$\exists X : Xx \land \forall x(Xx \rightarrow Vx)$]$\exists E(INFL[e, X] \land dance[e] \land to[e, y])$)

(46) *[few $x : Vx$][$\exists X : Xx \land \forall x(Xx \rightarrow Vx)$]
      [$Qy : By \land \exists E(INFL[e, X] \land sing[e] \land OF[e, y])$)]
      $\exists E(INFL[e, X] \land dance[e] \land to[e, y])$)

It may seem reasonable, in light of (44), to suppose that extraposition and perhaps lowering is freely available when translating into logical form and that binding the plural pronoun makes it obligatory in the case of (37). But in fact the extraposed relative clauses in (44) must be restored in logical form to their original position. First, note that the meaning of such an extraposition does not join the relative clause to the quantifier's second term. Thus (47) and (49) do not mean (48) and (50), respectively.[10]

(47) Most ballads were danced to that were good.

(48) *[most $x :$ ballad(x)]$(danced-to(x) \land good(x))$

(49) Every ballad was danced to that was good.

(50) *[every $x :$ ballad(x)]$(danced-to(x) \land good(x))$

Second, *every* and *most*, which license negative polarity items, such as *ever* or *any* (in its existential sense), in the first term only, as in (51) and (52), nevertheless license their occurrence in an extraposed relative clause in (53), indicating that the relative clause, when it contains a negative polarity item, is restored in logical form to its position within the first term.

(51) a. Most ballads about any national heroes were danced to.
     b. Every ballad that was ever influential was danced to.

(52) a. *Most ballads about national heroes were danced to any marches.
     b. *Every ballad that was influential was ever danced to.

(53) a. Most ballads were danced to that were about any national heroes.
     b. Every ballad was danced to that was ever influential.

A negative polarity item may be added to the relative clauses in (37) without affecting the sense or grammaticality of these sentences:

(54) a. Few vaudevillians$_i$ danced together to most ballads that they$_i$ ever sang together.
     b. Few vaudevillians$_i$ danced together to every ballad that they$_i$ ever sang together.

The relative clauses in (54) cannot be extraposed in logical form, thereby excluding (43).

In a last attempt to maintain the extraposition in logical form, one could consider ternary quantifiers, e.g., 'few(N', S, S')', where the relative clause itself becomes a term. The suggestion, however, undermines the pronominal binding in (43). Recall the earlier observation that extraposition there is combined with a lowering of the clause. It contains a bound variable that must fall within the scope of a quantifier that belongs to the second term, S.

I conclude, then, that the logical form in (43), which is an ad hoc paraphrase, is not derivable for either (37) or (44). As (45) and (46) show, a second-order quantifier cannot both represent semidistributivity and bind pronouns whose reference depends on the composers quantified over.

In my proposal, I sever any anaphoric connection between pronouns and the semidistributive operator, whose scope includes only a θ-role. The pronoun is related by its descriptive content to its antecedent, as in (55). Its content is the θ-role bound by its antecedent.

(55) Few vaudevillians danced together to most ballads that the dancers
     (= they) sang together.

In constructing the logical form, I presume that a theory of sequence of tense makes available a predicate like 'coincide(e, e')' to express a relation between dancings and singings.[11] Sequence of tense will in general determine how the events of an embedded predicate or clause are related to the events of its immediate context. Thus it is invoked twice in the logical form for (55): once to relate the predicate of the relative clause to the matrix predicate and once again to relate the pronoun's content, 'dancer at e', to the relative clause. The dependencies are shown in (56).

(56) Few vaudevillians danced(e) together to most ballads that the

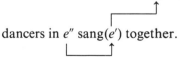

     dancers in e'' sang(e') together.

In (57) the translation of *most ballads that they sang together* occupies the middle three lines, and it is paraphrased as follows: most ballads such that any one among them is, among the singings that coincide with dancings, sung in a singing by the dancers in the coincident dancing.

(57) [few x : Vx] [$\hat{E}$: Co-INFL$_i$[e, x]]
      [most y : By $\wedge$ [$\hat{E'}$: OF[e', y]]][$\exists E'$: $\exists E$ coincide(e', e)]
        ([$\imath Z$: [$\exists E$: coincide(e, e')] Co-INFL$_i$[e, Z]] INFL[e', Z]
          $\wedge$ sing[e'])]
      [$\hat{E}$: to[e, y]] dance[e]

An event on stage is relevant only if its dancers and its singers are the same, as required. Note that in translating the pronoun, on the third line, I have assumed the minimal content. Whatever is there answers either to sequence of tense or to the interpretation of anaphora, which copies a θ-role.

The logical form in (57) represents one of the more difficult cases for the interaction of semidistributive scope and binding. The semidistributive operator has scope only over the modified θ-role. The quantifier *no more than three ballads that they sang together* is not within the scope of any quantifier over groups of vaudevillians, and yet the logical form is concerned only with the acts where the singers are the dancers, as if the pronoun *they* were bound by a quantifier over groups. Instead, the effect is achieved by a θ-role that enters into the pronoun's descriptive content and is separated from the other θ-roles.

Chapter 9
Cumulative Quantification

The collective interpretation of (1) is distinct from any distributive interpretation derived by assigning scope to the quantifiers in (4):

(1) Two detectives solved three crimes.

(2) The detectives solved the crimes.

(3) Some detectives solved some crimes.

(4) a. $[2x : Dx][3y : Cy]$ solve(x, y)
    b. $[3y : Cy][2x : Dx]$ solve(x, y)

It can, however, be given an unexceptional logical form if there are plural objects:

(5) $[\exists x : 2(x) \wedge \forall z(z \in x \rightarrow Dz)][\exists y : 3(y) \wedge \forall z(z \in y \rightarrow Cz)]$ solve(x, y)

Two detectives and *three crimes* are translated as existential quantifiers over plural objects. The interpretation is thus rendered without any novel way of forming sentences from quantifiers. All are restricted, unary quantifiers lined up in some assignment of scope, and the formula within their scope is simply the predicate 'solve(x, y)'. The apparent independence from scope assignment is reduced to the fact that existential quantifiers can be permuted without a change in meaning.

The term *cumulative quantification*, which I owe to Remko Scha (1981), classifies interpretations that present the problem that they cannot be represented by logical forms that fall within the strictures noted above. The troublesome class includes all those interpretations where nonincreasing quantifiers, such as *exactly two detectives* in (6) and *no more than three crimes* in (7), are independent.

(6) Exactly two detectives solved exactly three crimes.

(7) No more than two detectives solved no more than three crimes.

Their independence excludes the logical forms in (8) and (9), respectively, where relative scope is assigned.

(8) a. $[2!x : Dx][3!y : Cy]$ solve(x, y)
    b. $[3!y : Cy][2!x : Dx]$ solve(x, y)

(9) a. $[(\leq 2)x : Dx][(\leq 3)y : Cy]$ solve(x, y)
    b. $[(\leq 3)y : Cy][(\leq 2)x : Dx]$ solve(x, y)

With the quantifiers interpreted independently, (6) asserts that exactly two detectives solved crimes, and exactly three crimes were solved. This corresponds to neither of the distributive interpretations represented in (8). The fact that the quantifiers are nonincreasing also excludes the logical forms available to collective interpretations, (10) and (11).

(10) *$[\exists x : 2!(x) \wedge \forall z(z \in x \rightarrow Dz)][\exists y : 3!(y) \wedge \forall z(z \in y \rightarrow Cz)]$
    solve(x, y)

(11) *$[\exists x : \leq 2(x) \wedge \forall z(z \in x \rightarrow Dz)][\exists y : \leq 3(y) \wedge \forall z(z \in y \rightarrow Cz)]$
    solve(x, y)

Quantifiers are nonincreasing if they impose an upper bound on the extension of the predicate. The sentence in (6) entails that some two detectives solved some three crimes, but it also asserts that no other detectives solved any other crimes. Thus there is an upper bound on what detectives solved what crimes. But logical forms (10) and (11) impose no such bound.[1]

The problem that independent, nonincreasing quantifiers present recurs for me in a similar form. As we have seen, the increasing quantifiers of (1) are second-order descriptions, and they are independent in the logical form in (12):

(12) $\exists E([\exists X : 2(X) \wedge \forall x(Xx \rightarrow Dx)]$ INFL$[e, X] \wedge$ solve$[e]$
    $\wedge [\exists Y : 3(Y) \wedge \forall y(Yy \rightarrow Cy)]$ OF$[e, Y])$

I have, of course, rejected primitive polyadicity. There is no predicate 'solve(x, y)' in (12). But the quantifers, second-order in this case, are unary and restricted, and appear in a strictly linear order. Translation does not yet derive an interpretation for nonincreasing quantifiers in which they are independent. Translation as second-order descriptions, in the pattern of (12), will mistake their meaning. The remaining translation, by QR and interpretation of the trace-binding relation, yields only distributive or semidistributive interpretations.

1   The Logical Form of Cumulative Quantification

The independent, nonincreasing quantifiers call for some enlargement of logical form. Prior to quantifier raising or any rule of translation, the syntactic structure of (7) is something like (13):

(13) $[_S$ INFL(e, no more than 2 detectives)
        $[_{VP}$ solve(e) OF(e, no more than 3 crimes))]]

The first step in deriving the distributive interpretations of (13) is to assign scope to the first-order quantifiers by QR. It is also the first step in deriving the cumulative interpretation, since the same grammatical constraints apply, a point to which I return in section 5. But unlike QR's earlier application, I allow that QR assigns to distinct quantifiers the same scope (compare May 1985), which I will indicate using the familiar syntax of branching quantification:

(14)   [no more than two detectives]

$>[_S \ldots]$

       [no more than three crimes]

(15) $[Q_1 \ N'_1]$

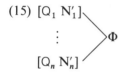

       $[Q_n \ N'_n]$

The LF in (15) is merely a schema for certain scope relations. It indicates that the quantifiers on branches are independent of one another and not within the scope of elements occurring in Φ. There is a broad consensus that at least this much is involved in cumulative quantification.[2] What is unsettled is the meaning that these scope relations give rise to, which for me becomes the question of how to translate into logical form the LFs that fall under (15).

The n accumulated quantifiers assigned identical scope are rewritten as a conjunction of n quantified clauses, related to each other by cross-reference to the same context of events:

(16) $[Q_1 \ N'_1]$

$>[_\Phi \text{——} \Theta_1[e, t_1] \ldots \Theta_n[e, t_n] \text{——}] \Rightarrow$

       $[Q_n \ N'_n]$

$$[_{\Phi'_i} [Q_1\ N'_1][_{\Phi}\text{———}\Theta_1[e, t_1][\exists X_2 : \forall x(Xx \rightarrow N'_2(x))]\ \Theta_2[e, X_2]\ldots$$
$$[\exists X_n : \forall x(Xx \rightarrow N'_n(x))]\ \Theta_n[e, X_n]\text{———}]]$$
$$\wedge\ [\hat{E} : \Phi''_i][Q_2 N'_2]\ \Theta_2[e, t_2] \wedge \cdots \wedge [\hat{E} : \Phi''_i][Q_n\ N'_n]\ \Theta_n[e, t_n]$$

The descriptive content Φ'' of the cross-referencing device is anaphorically linked, in a way to be made precise, to the syntactic scope assigned by QR. The scope proper for the quantifiers is reduced to a θ-role in the cross-referencing conjuncts.[3] Quantifier-trace binding is spelled out in the usual way. Thus the cumulative intepretation of (17) has logical form (18), and its intended paraphrase is (19):

(17) Exactly two detectives solved exactly three crimes.

(18) $[_{\Phi_i} [2!x : Dx][\hat{E} : \text{INFL}[e, x]]$
　　　　$\exists E(\text{solve}[e] \wedge [\exists Y : \forall y(Yy \rightarrow Cy)]\ \text{OF}[e, Y])]$
　　$\wedge\ [\hat{E} : \Phi''_i][3!y : Cy][\hat{E} : \text{OF}[e, y]]\ \text{solve}[e]^4$

(19) Exactly two detectives solved crimes, and *there* exactly three crimes were solved.

Note that the meaning of (17) is not (20).

(20) Exactly two detectives solved things, and *there* exactly three crimes were solved.

Nothing is implied about the detectives solving linguistics problem sets, and so the exported quantifiers in (16) are assumed to leave behind a copy of their descriptive contents and their θ-roles. Perhaps this is unnecessary if pragmatic considerations restrict the domain of relevant events to those of detectives' solving crimes. Nevertheless, the restriction seems to be an obligatory feature of branching quantifiers that distinguishes them from structures with similar logical forms that do not derive from a branching LF, as section 5.1.2 will suggest.

Intuitions confirm the paraphrase in (19), but I have yet to make good on the meaning of *there*. For the moment, let us assume that a semantics for '$[\hat{E} : \Phi'']$' will be delivered to underwrite the cross-reference paraphrased by *there*. The logical form of cumulative quantification is distinguished by the following features:

1. The first-order quantifiers are always unary and restricted.

2. *$\hat{E}$-anaphora.* The conjuncts are related by a device of cross-reference, '$[\hat{E} : \Phi'']$'.

3. *Cumulative asymmetry.* In any conjunct where this device appears, the scope of the first-order quantifier includes its θ-role but excludes any of

the quantifiers occurring within Φ, the scope assigned by QR to the accumulated quantifiers.[5]

The first two features are closely related. It is the device of cross-reference, '$[\hat{E} : \Phi'']$', that allows me to maintain that first-order quantifiers are always unary and restricted. To illustrate this, chapter 12, section 1, presents my view of a class of sentences that has figured prominently in discussions that would discover a need for n-ary quantifiers on the basis of an interaction of independent quantifiers with adverbial conditions like that imposed by the reciprocal in (21):

(21) Most stars and most dots are all connected to each other.

The third feature in my treatment of cumulative quantification is justified in section 2. Cumulative asymmetry is just a case of separation. The truth conditions for sentences with cumulative quantifiers show that the scope independence among these quantifiers derives from separating all but one of the independent quantifiers from the main body of the sentence. Separation leaves behind the other, dependent quantifiers the sentence may contain. Thus the logical form for a case of essential separation such as (22), where *no more than two detectives* and *no more than five agencies* are cumulative and *exactly two crimes* is dependent, is paraphrased as in (23):

(22) No more than two detectives (each) solved exactly two crimes, for no more than five agencies.

(23) No more than two detectives (each) solved exactly two crimes for agencies, and *there* for no more than five agencies did detectives solve crimes.

The cumulative interpretation is crucially vague about the number of crimes that were solved for any one agency. It must be that *no more than five agencies* and its θ-role is separated from the other arguments. In particular, *exactly two crimes* occurs only within the first conjunct. This is the essential asymmetry in the scopes of the cumulative quantifiers. In section 2 (and chapter 4) I show that the intended interpretation is not represented by any logical form where *no more than two detectives* and *no more than five agencies* have scope over identical formulas:

(24) *No more than two detectives (each) solved exactly two crimes for agencies, and (*there*) for no more than five agencies did detectives (each) solve exactly two crimes.

All such symmetric logical forms impose a condition on how many crimes are related to each agency that is absent from the cumulative interpretation of (22), which is essentially vague on this point, as I expect from separation, as in (23).[6]

Assuming, then, the third feature of logical form, that it is asymmetric, leads straightaway to the second feature, the need for a device of cross-reference to events. Contrary to the paraphrase in (25), which omits the cross-referential *there*, the cumulative interpretation does not entail that no more than five agencies were the beneficiaries of detectives' solving crimes:

(25) No more than two detectives (each) solved exactly two crimes for agencies, and for no more than five agencies did detectives solve crimes.

It entails only that no more than five agencies were the beneficiaries of detectives' (each) solving *exactly two* crimes. More agencies may have benefited from the detectives solving some other number of crimes. The paraphrase in (23) is appropriately restricted by *there* referring to just those events of detectives (each) solving exactly two crimes.

The semantics of cross-reference to events is developed in section 3. The fundamental observation is that cross-reference to events is just like the reference of the descriptive anaphors in (26), each of which refers cumulatively to the donkeys that the farmers bought. (The clash in number agreement in (26a) bothers some speakers. See chapter 1, n. 14.)

(26) a. Every farmer bought a donkey. They were then hitched together in a mule train.
     b. Every farmer bought a donkey. The donkeys were then hitched together in a mule train.
     c. Every farmer bought (some) donkeys. They were then all hitched together in a mule train.

The idea is that the reference of the anaphor in (18) and (19) is to the events that the detectives acted in as solvers of crimes. At least this analogy should hold up, even if I am mistaken about other aspects of the anaphoric relation. Following Evans (1977) as amended by Davies (1981), and others,[7] I suppose that that relation depends on the descriptive content of the anaphor, which is a definite description of some sort. Section 3 discusses both the descriptive content necessary for the cumulative reference illustrated in (26) and the semantics of the definite-description operator appropriate for cross-reference to events—event concepts, like mass nouns, are often nonsortal. Treatments based on definite descriptions and descriptive anaphora must face the problem of nonmaximal reference, where what is referred to appears to be less than what the descriptive content describes. My account of the problem is given in chapter 10.

Chapter 11 continues to track down interpretations that demonstrate cumulative asymmetry and that therefore demand some form of separation and cross-reference to events. But the class of interpretations found there, strictly speaking, fall outside the system of logical form developed so far. The suggestion is that they involve a different construction more akin to free relatives, the semantics of which is similar in crucial respects to that of quantifying into questions. My remarks consists mainly in pointing to the similarities and providing a provisional semantics. For if the speculations are correct, providing the semantics requires a full-fledged discussion of the semantics of questions, which is beyond the scope of this work.

As noted earlier, Scha (1981) observes in a framework with plural objects that independence among increasing quantifiers takes on an unexceptional logical form. The increasing quantifiers are just existential quantifiers over plural objects, linearly ordered. Special efforts are necessary only to represent independence among nonincreasing quantifiers.[8] I agree with Scha's bifurcation. It coincides more or less with my classification of NPs into second-order and first-order quantifiers, and only independence among the latter requires the special syntax of branching.[9] Since, as will be seen in section 5, the conditions on movement distinguish the two classes, the bifurcation in how they represent independence also seems to be justified on purely syntactic grounds.

In contrast, discussions advocating *n*-ary quantifiers propose that quantificational independence looks the same for both increasing and nonincreasing quantifiers. It has the syntax of branching quantifiers. In a theory without plural objects, reference to events, or second-order expressions in the object language, certain interactions with adverbial conditions, such as those imposed by the reciprocals in (27) and (28), do argue that branching is essential to represent independence among increasing and among nonincreasing quantifiers.

(27) Most stars and most dots are all connected to each other.

(28) Few stars and few dots are all connected to each other.

Confined to singular predication and unaware of the relevance of events, such a theory cannot cope with essential plurals or essential separation. In Barwise 1979, the difference between increasing and nonincreasing quantifiers turns up anyway, in the interpretation of the branching structures. Increasing quantifiers that branch are interpreted along the lines of (29), but the decreasing branching quantifier must be assigned the distinct interpretation in (30).

(29) $\exists X \exists Y([most\ x : N'_1(x)]\ Xx \land [most\ y : N'_2(y)]\ Yy$
$\land\ \forall x \forall y((Xx \land Yy) \rightarrow \Phi(x, y)))$

(30) $\exists X \exists Y([few\ x : N'_1(x)]\ Xx \land [few\ y : N'_2(y)]\ Yy$
$\land\ \forall x \forall y(\Phi(x, y) \rightarrow (Xx \land Yy)))$

Given the empirical considerations that the addition of plural predication raises and the syntactic evidence from conditions on movement, one might just conclude that a conceded difference has been mistakenly located in the clauses interpreting branching. It is more pervasive and enters into the syntax of the object language.

More recently Sher (1990) and Westerståhl (1987), accepting Barwise's conclusions about representation, have proposed a uniform interpretation for branching quantifiers. Thus, in their view, quantificational independence has one look and one meaning. Were this so, it would generate the small worry that no difference in syntactic structure seems to correlate with the fact that only first-order quantifiers are constrained in their movements. More worrisome is what it is about the introduction of plurals and plural predication that should suddenly force onto the object language the syntactic and semantic distinctions between second-order and first-order quantifiers that I have been assuming. Chapter 12 takes up the question of whether there is a unified semantics of branching quantifiers. To be fair to the other views, I confine my discussion to just those paradigms, interactions with adverbs, that first gave evidence of branching quantifiers. My conclusion is that there is no way for n-ary quantification to unify the semantics of increasing and nonincreasing branching. The proposals fail in fact to give a correct semantics for branching with nonincreasing quantifiers, and so there is no uniform account of quantificational independence even within this limited domain.

2 Cumulative Asymmetry

Sentence (32) is the suggested paraphrase for the cumulative quantification in (31).

(31) No more than two detectives solved no more than three crimes.

(32) No more than two detectives solved crimes, and *there* detectives solved no more than three crimes.

The example on its own does not justify the cross-reference indicated by *there*, since the paraphrase without it does just as well:

(33) No more than two detectives solved crimes, and detectives solved
      no more than three crimes.

Moreover, the cross-reference, if there is one, has not been fixed. We know only that it cannot presuppose the existence of relevant events, since none might exist if no detective solved any crimes. In this section I turn to a class of cases that will help determine what the cross-referring device must denote. This section will also demonstrate the need for cross-reference and what I have called cumulative asymmetry, that in any conjunct where cross-reference appears, the scope of the first-order quantifier excludes all the other quantifiers of the sentence.

We consider sentences, with (at least) three quantifiers, that combine cumulative quantification with a standard assignment of scope. Such combinations, I argued in chapter 4, provide the essential cases of separation. Thus the relevant interpretations of (34) to (36) assign narrow scope to 'exactly two crimes' and 'exactly two criminals' but take 'exactly two detectives' and 'exactly one N'' cumulatively, as in (37).

(34) Exactly two detectives (each) solved exactly two crimes for exactly
      one agency (between them).

(35) Exactly two detectives (each) reported exactly two crimes to exactly
      one agency (between them).

(36) Exactly two detectives (each) gave exactly two criminals exactly one
      alibi (between them).

(37)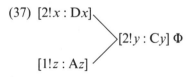
$$[2!x : Dx]$$
$$[2!y : Cy]\ \Phi$$
$$[1!z : Az]$$

Paraphrasing (34) through (36) gives (38) through (40):

(38) Exactly two detectives (each) solved exactly two crimes for
      agencies, and *there* detectives solved crimes for exactly one agency.

(39) Exactly two detectives (each) reported exactly two crimes to
      agencies, and *there* detectives reported crimes to exactly one agency.

(40) Exactly two detectives (each) gave exactly two criminals alibis, and
      there detectives gave criminals exactly one alibi.

Sentence (34) is about detectives each solving exactly two crimes for agencies, and it asserts that exactly two detectives did this and they did it for a total of exactly one agency. Similarly, the relevant interpretation of (36) asserts that exactly two detectives and exactly one alibi were involved in incidents of detectives each giving exactly two criminals alibis.

Making precise the conditions under which this interpretation of (34) is true will show that cumulative asymmetry is essential. Consider the following sort of context for (34):

(41)

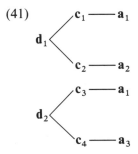

Two detectives and only two each solve their own two crimes and no others. Each crime is solved for a different agency with the exception indicated. The two detectives each solve one of their crimes for the same agency. Similar contexts about reporting crimes or giving criminals alibis can be provided for sentences (35) and (36) (the diagrams are the same as (41)). Now it seems that (42) to (44) are true in the given context on their intended cumulative interpretations.

(42) Exactly two detectives (each) solved exactly two crimes for exactly three agencies (between them).

(43) Exactly two detectives (each) reported exactly two crimes to exactly three agencies (between them).

(44) Exactly two detectives (each) gave exactly two criminals exactly three alibis (between them).

After all, in the case of (42), exactly two detectives are each related to exactly two crimes, and exactly three agencies had anything to do with it. Of course, if this is so, then (34) through (36) must be false, which accords with intuition, since they claim that exactly one agency is involved.

To demonstrate cumulative asymmetry, suppose to the contrary that the accumulated quantifiers have the same scope. Then (34) to (36) will go over into (45) to (47), where *exactly two crimes* or *exactly two criminals* falls within the scope of both of the accumulated quantifiers:

(45) Exactly two detectives (each) solved exactly two crimes for agencies, and exactly one agency had detectives solve exactly two crimes for it.

(46) Exactly two detectives (each) reported exactly two crimes to agencies, and exactly one agency had detectives report exactly two crimes to it.

(47) Exactly two detectives (each) gave exactly two criminals alibis, and exactly one alibi was given by detectives to exactly two criminals.

These paraphrases, however, are all true in the contexts corresponding to (41). There is exactly one agency that detectives solved exactly two crimes for. These paraphrases thus do not descend from the logical forms for sentences (34) to (36), which are all false in (41). One might imagine that symmetric scope could be preserved if an appropriate condition could be found to falsify the second conjunct. Keep in mind that symmetric scope and the appropriate condition will also govern the interpretation of (42) to (44), which must remain true in context (41). Suppose, for example, that something compelled *exactly one agency* to be understood semidistributively, so that each agency in (41) is related with other agencies to exactly four crimes. As required, (45) is falsified. But so is (48), which paraphrases what would be the logical form for (42) in (49):

(48) Exactly two detectives (each) solved exactly two crimes for agencies, and exactly three agencies had detectives solve exactly two crimes for it.

(49) $[2!x : Dx][\hat{E} : \text{INFL}[e, x]][2!y : Cy][\hat{E} : \text{OF}[e, y]]$
  $\exists E(\text{solve}[e] \land [\exists Z : \forall z(Zz \rightarrow Az)] \text{Co-for}[e, Z])$
  $\land [3!z : Az][\hat{E} : \text{Co-for}[e, z]][2!y : Cy][\hat{E} : \text{OF}[e, y]]$
  $\exists E([\exists X : \forall x(Xx \rightarrow Dx)] \text{INFL}[e, X] \land \text{solve}[e])$[10]

These observations suggest that there will be no way of assigning symmetric scope that yields appropriate truth conditions for both (34) to (36) and (42) to (44). This point is in fact a corollary to chapter 4, which shows separation to be essential. What these sentences with three quantifiers have allowed us to do is to construct examples of essential separation that involve cumulative quantification. If there were a way of assigning symmetric scope to the cumulative quantifiers in these sentences, it would show that separation could in general be eliminated via *n*-ary quantifiers.

The schema in (50) by no means fixes the interpretation of *n*-ary quantifiers, but it marks plainly the property that all interpretations share.

(50) 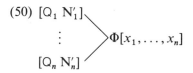 $\Phi[x_1, \ldots, x_n]$

The n-ary quantifier applies to (the extension of) the n-place relation that Φ expresses. The internal structure of the formula Φ does not interact with the quantifier. This was the crucial property that, in chapter 4, kept polyadic logical form from doing the work of separation, even when augmented by n-ary quantifiers. If there were a way of assigning symmetric scope to the accumulated quantifiers, it would demonstrate that the n-ary quantifier interpreted as in (51) is adequate to express cases of essential separation.

(51) a formula that falls under schema (50) is true
$$\leftrightarrow [Q_1 x : N'_1] \exists x_2 \ldots \exists x_n \, \Phi \wedge \cdots \wedge [Q_n x : N'_n] \exists x_1 \ldots \exists x_{n-1} \, \Phi$$

Not all n-ary quantifiers defined on the relation expressed by Φ are symmetric. In fact, the n-ary quantifier defined in (52) is just fine, despite the obviously asymmetrical scope relations (see Higginbotham and May 1981).[11]

(52) a formula that falls under scheme (50) is true
$$\leftrightarrow [Q_1 x : N'_1] \ldots [Q_n x : N'_n] \, \Phi$$

But if one is limited to quantifying into the n-place relation, all the reasonable n-ary quantifiers that might be fielded to represent (34) to (36) and (42) to (44) will be paraphrasable in terms of symmetric scope assignment.

If the n-ary quantifiers augment a theory of plurals, as they do in Scha 1981, the domain for the variables includes plural objects. The existential quantifiers introduced in (53) quantify, in effect, over groups of agencies and over groups of detectives. The interpretation derived is exactly that paraphrased in (45).

(34) Exactly two detectives (each) solved exactly two crimes for exactly one agency (between them).

(37) $[2!x : Dx]$

$$[2!y : Cy] \, \Phi$$

$[1!z : Az]$

(53) (37) is true
$$\leftrightarrow [2!x : Dx][\exists z : Az][2!y : Cy] \, \Phi \wedge [1!z : Az][\exists x : Dx][2!y : Cy] \, \Phi$$

(45) Exactly two detectives (each) solved exactly two crimes for agencies, and exactly one agency had detectives solve exactly two crimes for it.

Inviting n-ary quantifiers into a theory of plurals thus introduces an interpretation that we have seen the sentence does not have, while it misses the targeted interpretation.

Most discussions of n-ary quantifiers do not offer an account of plural predication, and in the context of purely singular predication, the interpretation of n-ary quantifiers amounts to something rather different. In (34), it would be an interpretation concerned only with those pairs of individual detective and individual agency where the detective solved exactly two crimes for the agency. The question of whether n-ary quantifiers might be defined for predicates denoting only individual objects is taken up in section 4.

3   The Interpretation of '$[\hat{E} : \Phi]$'

If the accumulated quantifiers do not have the same scope, it becomes obvious that some cross-reference device is required. If we omit such a device in (55), then (55) entails that no more than that two agencies benefited from detectives solving any number of crimes, but sentence (54) is only concerned with detectives solving exactly two crimes.

(54) No more than two detectives (each) solved exactly two crimes for no more than two investigating agencies (between them).

(55) No more than two detectives (each) solved exactly two crimes for agencies, and *there* detectives solved crimes for no more than two agencies.

To present the matter more concretely, the following contexts show detectives solving crimes in such a way that the first conjunct of (55) is true. In (56), no detective solves exactly two crimes. The two of them each solve three.

(56)

In (57), there are two but no more than two detectives each solving exactly two crimes.

(57)

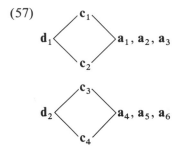

Sentence (54) tells the two contexts apart. It is false in (57) but true in (56), where there are no detectives solving exactly two crimes. The cross-reference carried by *there* in (55) is, as it were, to events described by the first conjunct. But the events described cannot simply be all those in a context that make it true. If they were, (56) too would falsify (54), since more than two agencies are involved there. Instead, *there* in (55) should denote all and only events of detectives each solving exactly two crimes. In (57), these events are coextensive with the context. In (56), however, there are no such events, and so no more than two agencies benefited from such events.

My view of the cross-reference in (55) is in effect that *there* expresses something like what *whatever they did* expresses when *they* is a descriptive anaphor related to *no more than two detectives*:

(58) No more than two detectives$_i$ (each) solved exactly two crimes for agencies, and whatever they$_i$ did is such that detectives solved crimes for no more than two agencies.

(59) ..., and whatever the detectives that (each) solved exactly two crimes did ...

Since there are no detectives that solved exactly two crimes in (56), whatever they did is nothing at all, as required.

The construction required for cross-reference to events is one that also occurs with more familiar examples of descriptive anaphora:

(60) a. Few farmers bought a donkey, and they came with no guarantees. (The donkeys that were not bought were under warranty but too expensive.)

 b. Few farmers bought a donkey, and the donkeys came with no guarantees. (The donkeys that were not bought were under warranty but too expensive.)

(61) a. Few farmers bought a donkey, but the livestock trailer was packed with them anyway.

b. Few farmers bought a donkey, but the livestock trailer was packed with the donkeys anyway.

(62) a. Every farmer fed a donkey. Then they were hitched together in a mule train.

b. Every farmer fed a donkey. Then the donkeys were hitched together in a mule train.

The meaning of (60a) is that whatever donkeys were bought, if any, came with no guarantees. The reference of the pronoun collects the various donkeys that various farmers bought. My main point is that the logical form of cumulative quantification contains a pronoun whose reference collects, in much the same way, the various events in which various detectives were solvers. The semantics of cumulative quantification reveals a tacit occurrence of a pronoun bearing cumulative reference to events. Because speakers have a rather robust understanding of the conditions for cumulative reference, some of which I survey below, this conclusion about the logical form of cumulative quantifiers is warranted despite doubts that may attend any particular analysis of pronominal reference. The problem of cumulative quantification is at least reducible to the problem of cumulative reference in pronouns. At present it seems unavoidable that pronouns will have a rather rich descriptive content, since the only general method for fixing the reference of an unbound anaphor is to specify its content.[12]

Like unbound anaphora in general, anaphora with cumulative reference appears to distinguish cases where the antecedent is governed by a nonincreasing quantifier. If, as in (60), it is governed by a nonincreasing quantifier, cumulative reference must be maximal. The donkeys referred to in (60) include all those that farmers bought. It cannot be that some farmers bought donkeys with some guarantees. Similarly for the cumulative interpretation of (63), the cross-reference to events must include all the events in which a farmer buys a donkey in a department store.

(63) Few farmers bought a donkey in few department stores.

(64) Few farmers bought a donkey in a department store, and *there* farmers bought donkeys in few department stores.

If the governing quantifier is not nonincreasing, then at least an appearance of nonmaximal reference becomes possible. Thus in a context for (62) some farmers may have each fed many donkeys. Sentence (62) is still true even if each farmer is represented in the mule train by only one of his donkeys. Similarly for cross-reference to events, (65) can be true in contexts where it took thirty minutes for all the farmers to have fed one of their donkeys but perhaps longer for them to have fed all their donkeys:

(65) Every farmer fed a donkey in thirty minutes.

(66) Every farmer fed a donkey, and *there* farmers fed donkeys in thirty minutes.

The exact conditions for nonmaximal reference and its account in a theory that treats all unbound anaphora as definite descriptions is the subject of chapter 10. Here I simply note the similarities between the tacit pronoun referring to events and its overt counterparts and between cumulative reference and the more familiar unbound anaphora.

As a first approximation, it seems that the translation of the pronoun in (60) must itself contain a descriptive anaphor linked to *few farmers*:

(67) ..., and whatever donkeys *they* bought came with no guarantees.

(68) ..., and whatever donkeys that farmers who each bought a donkey bought came with no guarantees.

The description of the donkeys must not be construed to require of any one of them that the farmers bought *it*. The description denotes a donkey if *some* farmer bought it. So it appears that the pronoun referring to farmers in (67) is an *indefinite* description in this context, in contrast to the more familiar translation as a definite description. As it turns out, the effect of quantifying existentially over farmers is essential, which I will show shortly, but this example admits a more straightforward translation whose exact failings should be noted before we accept more elaborate schemes.

Keeping in mind that the descriptions of the donkeys and of the farmers are second-order, one might suggest that they both remain definite, as in (69) and in (70) if one ignores any existential commitment inherent in the latter:

(69) ..., and whatever donkeys that whatever farmers that each bought a donkey bought came with no guarantees.

(70) ..., and the donkeys that the farmers who each bought a donkey bought came with no guarantees.

(71) ... and $[\imath Y : \forall y(Yy \rightarrow Dy)$
$\qquad \land \exists E([\imath X : [\forall x : Xx](Fx \land \ldots)] \text{INFL}[E, X]$
$\qquad \land \text{buy}[e] \land \text{OF}[E, Y])]$
$\quad Y$ came with no guarantees

The abstraction of the second-order variable 'Y' allows that the relation between the donkeys and the farmers is a sum of plurals, which, of course, does not require that each donkey be bought by the farmers. Thus there is apparently no need to consider a description that replaces *the farmers* with the indefinite *some farmers*.[13]

The success of this translation is, however, an artifact of the abbreviated example, where the relevant events include all those of farmers buying donkeys. It fails once the relevant events are further restricted by the description in the antecedent clause. In (72) and in (73) the relevant events are not all those where farmers feed donkeys bags of oats but only those where a farmer feeds two donkeys one bag.

(72) a. Exactly two farmers each fed two donkeys one bag of oats. The oats weighed two pounds, and the donkeys ate for twenty minutes.

    b. Exactly two farmers each fed two donkeys one bag of oats. They were two pounds of rolled grain, and they ate for twenty minutes.

(73) Exactly two farmers each fed two donkeys one bag of oats in twenty minutes.

The restriction excludes that event in (74) where farmer f_1 feeds bag of oats b_2 to just the one donkey d_3, and this event is not included in assessing the reference of the tacit and overt anaphors in (72) and (73).

(74)

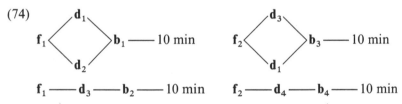

Thus discourses (72) and (73) are true in (74) if it depicts all there is of farmers' feeding donkeys and if a single bag of oats weighs one pound. Then indeed the oats in events of farmers' each feeding two donkeys one bag weighed a total of two pounds, and it all took twenty minutes. Cross-reference is to the donkeys, the oats, and the events in that part of (74) that excludes f_1's feeding d_3 and f_2's feeding d_4. In this context, it would be correct for a pronoun or incomplete description referring to the bags of oats to stand for *the bags of oats each of which a farmer fed two donkeys*, but one cannot construct an equivalent description containing definite descriptions of the farmers and the donkeys, as in *the bags of oats that they, the farmers, fed them, the donkeys*. Since f_1 and d_3 in the first excluded event are among the farmers and donkeys of the relevant events, the bags of oats that farmers f_1 and f_2 fed donkeys d_1, d_2, and d_3 will include the extra bag b_2 and weigh more than two pounds. An appropriate description of the donkeys referred to in (72) is also not forthcoming if one is constrained to refer to the farmers with a definite description. A description such as *the donkeys that the farmers fed bags of oats to* would fail the intended reference of *the donkeys* in (72a) and the second pronoun in (72b), since it includes d_4, which is one of the donkeys that the farmers feed. Reproducing more faithfully the antecedent clause does no better. *The donkeys that the farmers fed one bag of oats to* does not refer to d_1, d_2, and d_3 in (74). *One bag of oats* describes neither the individual farmer's gifts nor the collective action of the farmers.[14] If *one bag of oats* is meant to describe a donkey's receipts (or those of a group of donkeys), it describes d_4's and thus *the donkeys that the farmers fed one bag of oats to* would fail to refer, as (72) requires, to just the donkeys in those events where farmers each feed two donkeys one bag of oats.[15] It appears that reference to these donkeys requires a description containing an existential quantifier over farmers: *the donkeys such that a farmer fed one bag of oats to two of them.* Similar considerations show that the descriptive content of the tacit pronoun referring to events in (73) must also change the character of reference to the farmers. Cross-reference is to the events in each of which a farmer feeds two donkeys a bag of oats, and there is no description referring to these events that begins 'the events in which the farmers...'.

These observations raise a puzzle. While it is fair to say that the tacit pronouns referring to events behave just like their overt counterparts and it is sure that cumulative reference behaves as it does in the examples discussed, there ought to be more to the explanation of cumulative reference than an algorithm that introduces indefinite descriptions ad hoc into an already elaborate notion of descriptive content. Could the next language we look at opt for one of the rejected translations?[16] In a sense, the explanation will ask us to take more seriously the line diagrams that have been used to depict the various contexts in which sentences are evaluated.

In his 1976 paper "States of Affairs," Barry Taylor develops a notion of the state of affairs that corresponds to a sentence. I will shy away from the question of whether such a correspondence should replace the standard view that a sentence denotes a truth value.[17] It suffices for us to grant that the question would not have been entertained if an intuitive grasp of the state of affairs described by a sentence had not already presented itself. Suppose that f's buying d is an atomic state of affairs, which could be represented by $\langle\langle f, d \rangle, \text{'buy'}\rangle$. The state of affairs described by the first sentence of (75) is naturally a collection of atomic states of affairs of farmers' buying donkeys where, for every farmer f, there is some donkey d such that $\langle\langle f, d \rangle, \text{'buy'}\rangle$ is among those atomic states of affairs.

(75) Every farmer bought a donkey. They were hitched to the mule train.

Such states of affairs have an obvious affinity to the line diagrams I have used to depict contexts of events. If speakers have a notion of the state of affairs described by the sentence, then it is not difficult to imagine that they might refer to the donkeys bought *in that state of affairs*. Construing the pronoun in (75) in this way, we obtain cumulative reference. Note that to describe the donkeys without referring to the state of affairs, we would have to say, 'the donkeys each of which *some* farmer bought'. The apparent introduction of an indefinite description is to be explained in this way. Speakers do grasp a notion of the state of affairs described by a sentence, and in using an unbound anaphor to bear cumulative reference, they understand that its content takes the unexceptional form just noted, including the descriptive content of the antecedent, *donkey* in (75), the θ-role bound by the antecedent, and a reference to the states of affairs described by the antecedent clause. If one were to neglect the fact that sentences correspond in a general way to states of affairs, then indeed the descriptive content of pronouns bearing cumulative reference would appear to introduce indefinite descriptions ad hoc. The translation is, however, not arbitrary, and languages shouldn't differ on this. How cumulative reference is translated must answer to an account of the speaker's grasp of the states of affairs described by a sentence.

The correspondence between sentences and states of affairs is a new semantic relation. For Taylor, the relation is *state of affairs Σ is assigned sentence s*, which, like the definition of satisfaction, is characterized by recursive clauses. Each clause states how a particular operator affects the construction of the relevant state of affairs. In my construction, events take the place of states of affairs. Recursive clauses characterize the events that are described by, or *render*, a sentence. The interpretation of the operator '$[\hat{E}:\Phi]$' is based on the new semantic relation. Thus $\ulcorner[\hat{E}:\Phi]\Psi\urcorner$ is true just in case the events that render Φ make Ψ true:

(76) Σ satisfy $\ulcorner[\hat{E}_i:\Phi]\ \Psi\urcorner$

$\leftrightarrow [\imath E : \mathrm{render}(E,\Phi,\Sigma)][\exists\Sigma_0 : \Sigma_0 \approx_{\mathbb{C}_i} \Sigma \wedge \Sigma_0(\mathbb{C}_i) \simeq E]\Sigma_0$ satisfy Ψ

(77) $[\imath E : \Phi]\ \Psi$

$\leftrightarrow_{\mathrm{df}} [\exists E : \Phi \wedge \forall e(\exists E(Ee \wedge \Phi) \rightarrow \forall e'(e'\mathbf{O}e \rightarrow \exists e''(e'\mathbf{O}e'' \wedge Ee'')))]\ \Psi$

As we will see below, distinct events E and E' can render a given sentence in a given context, and so the operator must itself be a definite description operator if reference is to be definite. As defined in (77), the events E are events that are Φ, and they completely overlap any other events that are Φ.[18]

Recall that, in addition to its use in cross-reference, the operator also appears in the translation of first-order quantifiers restricted only by a θ-role, '$[\hat{E}_i : \Theta[e_i, v]]$'. Under the clause for rendering a θ-role in (78) together with (76), the term continues to denote whatever v did as a θ-er in the given context:

(78) $\text{render}(E, \ulcorner\Theta[e_i, v]\urcorner, \Sigma)$
    $\leftrightarrow \forall e(Ee \leftrightarrow \exists E(Ee \wedge \Sigma(\mathbb{C}_i) \simeq E \wedge \forall z(\Theta(e, z) \leftrightarrow \Sigma(\langle v, z \rangle))))$

(79) $\text{render}(E, \ulcorner\Theta[e_i, V]\urcorner, \Sigma)$
    $\leftrightarrow \forall e(Ee \leftrightarrow \exists E(Ee \wedge \Sigma(\mathbb{C}_i) \simeq E \wedge \exists z\, \Theta(e, z)$
    $\wedge \forall z(\Theta(e, z) \rightarrow \Sigma(\langle V, z \rangle))))$

That is, the events rendering a θ-role are all those overlapping only events assigned to $\mathbb{C}_i$ in which the object assigned to v is the bearer of that θ-role. The rendering events correspond to whatever the object did in the given context as a Θ-er.[19]

In the logical form of cumulative quantification, the cross-reference is to the events that render the antecedent clause. The logical form for (54) is (80):

(54) No more than two detectives (each) solved exactly two crimes for no more than two investigating agencies (between them).

(80) $(_{\Phi} [(\leq 2)x : Dx][\hat{E}_i : \text{INFL}[e_i, x]][2!y : Cy][\hat{E} : \text{OF}[e_i, y]]$
    $\exists E_i(\text{solve}[e_i] \wedge [\exists Z : \forall z(Zz \rightarrow Az)] \text{for}[e_i, Z]))$
    $\wedge [\hat{E}_i : \Phi][(\leq 2)z : Az][\hat{E}_i : \text{for}[e_i, z]] \text{solve}[e_i]$

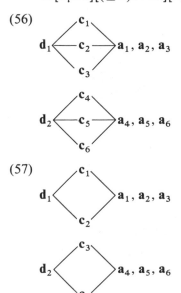

(56)

d_1 — c_1, c_2, c_3 — a_1, a_2, a_3

d_2 — c_4, c_5, c_6 — a_4, a_5, a_6

(57)

d_1 — c_1, c_2 — a_1, a_2, a_3

d_2 — c_3, c_4 — a_4, a_5, a_6

Recall that (54) tells apart the two contexts in (56) and (57). The sentence is false in (57), since there are six agencies that are the beneficiaries of detectives each solving exactly two crimes. It is true, however, in (56), where no events correspond to detectives each solving exactly two crimes. That is, no events are among the events that render the antecedent clause in (80). Note in particular that the reference to events must not include, for example, d_1's solving c_1 and c_2, although this might be described as a solving of exactly two crimes. For each detective, what he did is included just in case he solved exactly two crimes, and then the rendering events include any crimes he solved. These conditions are spelled out in the clause for rendering a quantificational formula:

(81) $\text{render}(E, \ulcorner [Qv : \Phi] \Psi \urcorner, \Sigma)$
  $\leftrightarrow \Sigma \text{ satisfy } \ulcorner [Qv : \Phi] \Psi \urcorner$
    $\wedge \forall e(Ee$
      $\leftrightarrow [\exists x : \exists \Sigma_0(\Sigma_0 \approx_v \Sigma \wedge \forall z(\Sigma_0(\langle v, z \rangle) \leftrightarrow z = x)$
        $\wedge \Sigma_0 \text{ satisfy } \Phi)]$
      $[\exists \Sigma_0 : \Sigma_0 \approx_v \Sigma \wedge \forall z(\Sigma_0(\langle v, z \rangle) \leftrightarrow z = x)$
        $\wedge \Sigma_0 \text{ satisfy } \Psi]$
      $\exists E(Ee \wedge \text{render}(E, \Psi, \Sigma_0)))$

Some events render the antecedent clause *no more than two detectives each solved exactly two crimes for agencies* only if it is true, which it is in both (56) and (57). The rendering events comprise the events that render any detective's solving exactly two crimes. In (57), but not in (56), there are detectives who each solved exactly two crimes. So the rendering events only in (57) will include, for each detective, his solvings of any crimes. The events in (57) that render the antecedent clause completely overlap the context, and these events then falsify the assertion that no more than two agencies are involved.

The other clauses required for the interpretation of (80) are just those one would expect. An event is among those that render a conjunction just in case it is among the events rendering each conjunct:[20]

(82) $\text{render}(E, \ulcorner \Phi \wedge \Psi \urcorner, \Sigma)$
  $\leftrightarrow \forall e(Ee$
    $\leftrightarrow [\exists E_0 : \text{render}(E_0, \Phi, \Sigma)][\exists E_1 : \text{render}(E_1, \Psi, \Sigma)](E_0 e \wedge E_1 e))$

Event concepts can be assumed to be rendered by their satisfiers:

(83) $\text{render}(E, \ulcorner V[e_i] \urcorner, \Sigma) \leftrightarrow \forall e(Ee \leftrightarrow (\Sigma \text{ satisfy } \ulcorner V[e_i] \urcorner \wedge \Sigma(\langle \mathfrak{C}_i, e \rangle)))$

Events that render an existential second-order quantification over events, '$[\exists E_i : \Phi] \Psi$', render its matrix Ψ for some events that Φ:

(84) $\text{render}(E, \ulcorner[\exists E_i : \Phi]\,\Psi\urcorner, \Sigma)$
  $\leftrightarrow\ [\exists E' : \forall e(E'e \to \Sigma(\langle \mathbb{C}_i, e\rangle))$
  $\land\ \exists\Sigma_0(\Sigma_0 \approx_{\mathbb{C}_i} \Sigma \land \forall e(\Sigma_0(\langle\mathbb{C}_i, e\rangle) \leftrightarrow E'e) \land \Sigma_0 \text{ satisfy } \Phi)]$
  $[\exists\Sigma_0 : \Sigma_0 \approx_{\mathbb{C}_i} \Sigma \land \Sigma_0(\mathbb{C}_i) \simeq E' \land \Sigma_0 \text{ satisfy } \Psi]\ \text{render}(E, \Psi, \Sigma_0)$

Similarly, events that render a formula prefixed by the definite description operator for events render its matrix for the events that meet the description:

(85) $\text{render}(E, \ulcorner[\hat{E}_i : \Phi]\,\Psi\urcorner, \Sigma)$
  $\leftrightarrow\ \forall e(Ee \leftrightarrow [\iota E_0 : \text{render}(E_0, \Phi, \Sigma)][\exists\Sigma_0 : \Sigma_0 \approx_{\mathbb{C}_i} \Sigma \land \Sigma_0(\mathbb{C}_i) \simeq E_0]$
  $(\Sigma_0 \text{ satisfy } \Psi \land \exists E_1(\text{render}(E_1, \Psi, \Sigma_0) \land E_1 e)))$

In evaluating the sentences in (86), recall that the events in (89) that render the antecedent clause ought to exclude farmer f_1's feeding donkey d_3 and f_2's feeding d_4.

(86) a. Exactly two farmers each fed two donkeys one bag of oats. The bags weighed two pounds, and the donkeys ate for twenty minutes.

  b. Exactly two farmers each fed two donkeys one bag of oats. They were two lbs. of rolled grain, and they ate for twenty minutes.

(87) Exactly two farmers each fed two donkeys one bag of oats in twenty minutes.

(88) $[2!x : Fx][\hat{E} : \text{INFL}[e, x]]$
  $\exists E(\text{feed}[e] \land [\exists Y : 2(Y) \land \forall y(Yy \to Dy)]\,\text{TO}[e, Y]$
  $\land\ [\exists Z : 1(Z) \land \forall z(Zz \to Bz)]\,\text{OF}[e, Z])$

(89)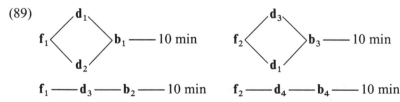

The logical form of the antecedent clause is shown in (88). With the addition of a clause for second-order descriptions in (90), the definition of rendering applies to (88) and excludes the unwanted events.

(90) $\text{render}(E, \ulcorner[\exists V : \Phi]\,\Psi\urcorner, \Sigma)$
  $\leftrightarrow\ [\exists X : \exists\Sigma_0(\Sigma_0 \approx_V \Sigma \land \forall x(\Sigma_0(\langle V, x\rangle) \leftrightarrow Xx) \land \Sigma_0 \text{ satisfy } \Phi)]$
  $[\exists\Sigma_0 : \Sigma_0 \simeq_V \Sigma \land \forall x(\Sigma_0(\langle V, x\rangle) \leftrightarrow Xx) \land \Sigma_0 \text{ satisfy } \Psi]$
  $\text{render}(E, \Psi, \Sigma_0)$

Some events render a formula prefixed by a second-order description just in case they render its matrix for some objects that meet the description. In (89), $\mathbf{d}_3$'s feeding is not among any events rendering $\mathbf{f}_1$'s feeding two donkeys one bag of oats, and $\mathbf{d}_4$'s feeding is not among the rendering events for $\mathbf{f}_2$.

Given cross-reference to the events that render the antecedent clause, cumulative reference by the overt pronouns in (86) is a simple matter. It is sufficient for the descriptive content of the pronoun to contain the θ-role bound into by its antecedent and the descriptive content of its antecedent:

(86) $\Phi. [\hat{E}:\Phi]([\imath Z:\forall z(Zz \rightarrow Bz) \wedge \text{OF}[e, Z]]$ weighed two lbs.,
       and $[\imath Y:\forall y(Yy \rightarrow Dy) \wedge \text{TO}[e, Y]]$ ate for twenty minutes)[21]

The cumulative interpretation of (91) puts every buying of a donkey by a farmer among those that took place in few department stores. Even if a farmer has bought many donkeys, they all must come from those few stores.

(91) Few farmers bought a donkey in few department stores.

(92) $(_\Phi$ [few $x : Fx]$
       $(_\Psi [\hat{E}:\text{INFL}[e, x]]\exists E(\text{buy}[e]$
       $\wedge [\exists Y:1(Y) \wedge \forall y(Yy \rightarrow Dy)]\,\text{OF}[e, Y]$
       $\wedge [\exists Z:\forall z(Zz \rightarrow Sz)]\,\text{in}[e, Z])))$
       $\wedge [\hat{E}:\Phi][\text{few } z:Sz][\hat{E}:\text{in}[e, z]]\,\text{buy}[e]$

The events that render the antecedent clause in (92) include all those that for any farmer are among some events that render the formula bracketed as Ψ. Some events render that formula for a given farmer just in case they are his buying one donkey. But rendering Ψ is not a unique property of some events; the events that are that farmer's buying another donkey also render Ψ. The events rendering the clause collect all such events rendering Ψ, and so all donkey buyings are included, as they should be.

I remarked above that the definiteness of the operator in (76) had to be made explicit, since rendering did not in all cases provide a unique description of some events.

(76) Σ satisfy $\ulcorner[\hat{E}_i:\Phi]\,\Psi\urcorner$
       $\leftrightarrow [\imath E:\text{render}(E, \Phi, \Sigma)][\exists \Sigma_0:\Sigma_0 \approx_{\mathfrak{C}_i} \Sigma \wedge \Sigma_0(\mathfrak{C}_i) \simeq E]\,\Sigma_0$ satisfy Ψ

(77) $[\imath E:\Phi]\,\Psi$
       $\leftrightarrow_{\text{df}} [\exists E:\Phi \wedge \forall e(\exists E(Ee \wedge \Phi) \rightarrow \forall e'(e'Oe \rightarrow \exists e''(e'Oe'' \wedge Ee'')))]\,\Psi$

The concern that the operator be definite is that it not subvert maximal reference in those unbound pronouns that seem to demand it. Thus Evans's (1977) observation that the pronoun in (93) refers to all the sheep that John owns would not be borne out if, as in (95), one could cross-refer to only some events that render the antecedent clause.

(93) John owns some sheep, and Harry vaccinated them.

(94) John owns some sheep,
and $[\hat{E} : \Phi]$, Harry vaccinated $[\iota Y : \forall y(Yy \rightarrow Sy) \wedge \text{OF}[e, Y]]$

(95) John owns some sheep,
and $[\exists E : \exists \Sigma \text{ render}(E, \Phi, \Sigma)]$ Harry vaccinated
$[\iota Y : \forall y(Yy \rightarrow Sy) \wedge \text{OF}[e, Y]]$

Of the ten sheep John owns, his owning two is an event or events that renders the antecedent clause. Harry did vaccinate the sheep owned in these events, but not all the sheep John owns. The definite-description operator in (94) will, however, require that the events referred to be John's owning some sheep and that they overlap all events of his owning sheep. If Harry vaccinated all the sheep owned in these events, then he vaccinated all of John's sheep, and the maximal reference of the pronoun is restored. The device for cross-reference to events is a definite description, no different from any other unbound anaphor. Chapter 10 discusses the conditions under which unbound anaphora, both tacit and overt, appear not to bear maximal reference.

   None of the examples discussed so far shows a decreasing quantifier in the scope of the cumulative quantifiers. Usually the interpretation of such cases is unexceptional. Thus (96), like (54), is true in (56) but false in (57):

(96) No more than two detectives (each) solved no more than two
crimes for no more than two investigating agencies (between them).

(97) $(_{\Phi} [(\leq 2)x : Dx][\hat{E}_i : \text{INFL}[e_i, x]][(\leq 2)y : Cy][\hat{E} : \text{OF}[e_i, y]]$
   $\exists E_i(\text{solve}[e_i] \wedge [\exists Z : \forall z(Zz \rightarrow Az)] \text{for}[e_i, Z]))$
   $\wedge [\hat{E}_i : \Phi][(\leq 2)z : Az][\hat{E}_i : \text{for}[e_i, z]] \text{solve}[e_i]$

(54) No more than two detectives (each) solved exactly two crimes for
no more than two investigating agencies (between them).

(56)

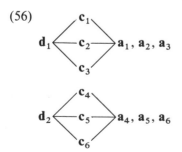

(57)

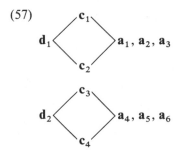

The events that render the antecedent clause in (97) are those where a detective that solved no more than two crimes for agencies solved crimes for agencies. In (56) there are no such events, and so crimes are solved for no more than two agencies among them. In (57) the rendering events overlap the entire context, where in fact six agencies are the beneficiaries and (96) is false.

In the cases that deserve special mention, a narrow-scope decreasing quantifier or negation precludes the existence of rendering events:

(98) Exactly two detectives solved no crimes for exactly two agencies.

(99) Exactly two detectives solved no crimes, and *there* detectives solved crimes for exactly two agencies.

(100) No more than two detectives solved no crimes for no more than two agencies.

(101) No more than two detectives solved no crimes, and *there* detectives solved crimes for no more than two agencies.

(102) Exactly two detectives did not talk to exactly two agencies.

(103) Exactly two detectives did not talk to agencies, and *there* detectives talked to exactly two agencies.

(104) No more than two detectives did not talk to no more than two agencies.

(105) No more than two detectives did not talk to agencies, and *there* detectives did not talk to no more than two agencies.

The logical form for cumulative quantification would attribute to these sentences interpretations that are anomalous in one way or another. The events cross-referred to in (99) are those where a detective that solved no crimes for agencies solved crimes for agencies. There are, of course, no such events, and so the cross-referring term does not denote any. But (99) is then a contradiction, since it asserts that in these events crimes were solved for two agencies.[22] Sentence (101) is not contradictory, but it is infelicitous. Given that no events render the antecedent clause, it is like an assertion that no crimes were solved for agencies and crimes were solved for no more than two agencies. Similar remarks apply to the interpretations paraphrased in (103) and (105).

It should be clear that sentences (98), (100), (102), and (104) have no such anomalous interpretations. Indeed, they have fairly normal cumulative interpretations. These have so far not been represented; they are the subject of the next section. To set them aside for the moment, it remains unexplained why the anomalous interpretations attributed to the sentences should go undetected.

I do not, however, see this as a challenge to the logical forms assumed. The behavior of filtering out contradictions or infelicities also occurs in the interpretation of overt unbound anaphora:

(106) No senators voted for JFK, and they supported no democratic bill.

(107) No farmers bought donkeys. They came with no guarantees.

Why is it impossible to hear the pronouns as *whatever senators voted for JFK* and *whatever donkeys farmers bought*? It is not that the plural pronouns imply existence:

(108) Few senators voted for JFK, and they supported no Republican bill.

(109) Few farmers bought donkeys. They came with no guarantees.

Here the pronouns can be heard that way, and they leave open the possibilities that in fact no senators voted for JFK and no farmers bought donkeys. The first possibility would arise if, for example, the speaker knows, as a general proposition, that anyone who votes for JFK does not vote for a Republican bill and his grounds for asserting (108) are the partial results of a Senate roll call, taken at a point when no senators had as yet voted for JFK and only a few remained to be counted. The speaker could say of that vote that at most few, and perhaps no, senators voted for JFK, and whichever senators did supported no Republican bill. Such a possible construal of the pronoun does not, however, redeem (106). The speaker knows that there are no relevant senators, and it is infelicitous to speak of a possible reference that is known to be foreclosed. The infelicity persists even if doubts about the existence of such senators are made explicit:

(110) No senators voted for JFK, and whichever senators (if any) voted for JFK supported no Republican bill.

Presumably, all of this would go into an account of the behavior that filters out the excluded interpretations of the pronouns in (106) and (107), but it leaves unanswered the following question: given the descriptive analysis of the pronouns, why can't one hear (106) as expressing the same, albeit infelicitous, thought as (110)?[23] On my view, the lingering question and the effects that distinguish the pronouns in (106) and (107) from those in (108) and (109) do not, however, threaten the descriptive analysis that unifies them.

Sentences (98), (100), (102), and (104) lack the contradictory or infelicitous interpretations that the logical form of cumulative quantifiers would attribute to them. I do, however, expect tacit pronouns that cross-refer to events to share all the properties of overt unbound pronouns. The absent interpretations of these sentences would all contain a tacit pronoun that refers to events that the speaker knows do not exist, from sense alone. Such interpretations are apparently filtered out. The parallel with the overt pronouns would tend to support this analysis.

I have yet to define *rendering* for a negated formula. That definition should bear out the similarity between (98) and (102).

(98)　Exactly two detectives solved no crimes for exactly two agencies.

(99)　Exactly two detectives solved no crimes, and *there* detectives solved crimes for exactly two agencies.

(102)　Exactly two detectives did not talk to exactly two agencies.

(103)　Exactly two detectives did not talk to agencies, and *there* detectives talked to exactly two agencies.

In (99) the cross-reference is to events where detectives that solved no crimes for agencies solved crimes for agencies. As we have seen, the interpretation fails as a result. The interpretation paraphrased by (103) should fail in the same way. The events that render the antecedent clause should include those where detectives that did not talk to agencies talked to agencies. The definition in (111) has this effect when applied to the logical form in (112):

(111)　$\text{render}(E, \ulcorner \neg \Phi \urcorner, \Sigma)$

$\leftrightarrow \forall e(Ee \leftrightarrow (\Sigma \text{ satisfy } \ulcorner \neg \Phi \urcorner \land \exists E(Ee \land \text{render}(E, \Phi, \Sigma))))$

(112)　$[(\leq 1)x : Dx][\hat{E} : \text{INFL}[e, x]]$

$\quad \neg \exists E(\text{talk}[e] \land [\exists Y : \forall y(Yy \to Ay)] \text{to}[e, Y])$

$\quad \land [\hat{E} : \Phi][(\leq 1)y : Ay][\hat{E} : \text{to}[e, y]] \text{ talk}[e]$

4   Apparent Counterexamples to Cumulative Asymmetry

In his discussion of scope assignment to branching and linear quantifiers, Robert May (1985) cites an interpretation that at first appears to be a counterexample to the view that distinct quantifiers never have identical scope in logical form. The example is similar to the following, and we may imagine it uttered when we want to know about what official sold defense documents to what superpower:

(113) Two officials each sold two defense documents to two superpowers.

An accessible interpretation is that two officials and two superpowers were among the pairs in which an official sold two defense documents to a superpower. The interpretation requires the quantifiers to branch and to include within their scope *two defense documents*, since it appears that the quantifier *two defense documents* is dependent on the choice of both the individual official and superpower:

(114) $[2x : Ox]$

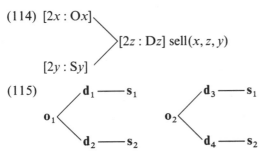

$[2z : Dz]$ sell(x, z, y)

$[2y : Sy]$

(115)

Note that the interpretation is false in the context shown in (115), where no one official sold two defense documents to any one superpower. It contrasts with the interpretation of (113) that is true in (115) simply because two officials did each sell two defense documents and two superpowers were indeed involved. This latter interpretation is a case of essential separation, and in the logical form of (113), *two defense documents* falls within the scope of only one of the NP quantifiers:

(116) $\exists E(_\Phi [\exists X : 2(X) \wedge \forall x(Xx \to Ox)][\forall x : Xx][\hat{E} : \text{INFL}[e, x]]$
        $(\text{sell}[e] \wedge [\exists Z : 2(Z) \wedge \forall z(Zz \to Dz)] \text{OF}[e, Z]))$
        $\wedge [\hat{E} : \Phi][\exists Y : 2(Y) \wedge \forall y(Yy \to Sy)] \text{to}[e, Y]$

(117) There is a selling where two officials each sold two defense
        documents to superpowers and that was to two superpowers.

This contrast between interpretations with asymmetric scope and those apparently with symmetric scope also emerges where the independent quantifiers are cumulative:

(118) No more than one official sold two defense documents to no more than two superpowers.

(119) No more than two officials each sold two defense documents to no more than one superpower.

The cumulative asymmetric interpretations of (118) and (119) are false in (115), where more than one official has sold two defense documents to superpowers and more than one superpower has received documents:

(120) No more than one official sold two defense documents to superpowers, and *there* officials sold defense documents to no more than two superpowers.

(121) $[(\leq 1)x : Ox][\hat{E} : INFL[e, x]]$
  $\exists E(sell[e] \wedge [\exists Z : 2(Z) \wedge \forall z(Zz \rightarrow Dz)] OF[e, Z])$
  $\wedge [\hat{E} : \Phi][(\leq 2)y : Sy][\hat{E} : \iota o[e, y]] sell[e]$

(122) No more than two officials each sold two defense documents to superpowers, and *there* officials sold defense documents to no more than one superpower.

In contrast, one can also imagine uttering (118) and (119) with the intention that they be true in (115), since that context contains no pairs of an official and a superpower where the official sells two documents to the superpower. This is another instance of the interpretation that May suggests results from a symmetrical logical form, as in (123).

(123) $[(\leq 1)x : Ox]$
  $>[2z : Dz] sell(x, z, y)$
  $[(\leq 2)y : Sy]$

In the logical forms appropriate to May's interpretation, predication is always singular, as one would expect if it is to represent a dependency on n-tuples of individual objects. Chapter 4 showed that the symmetrical logical forms of n-ary quantification cannot represent essential cases of separation, even when supplemented with plural predication. Here the question is whether a theory adequate to represent separation must admit, along with such logical forms as (116) and (121), an alternative ad hoc translation for branching quantifiers. How else to represent those distinct interpretations of (113), (118), and (119) that seem to quantify over pairs of an official and a superpower?[24]

To admit such an alternative translation would make quantification over n-tuples of individual objects a fully general resource. In the examples cited so far, the narrow-scope quantifier, *two defense documents*, has been increasing. It could just as well have been decreasing or nonmonotonic:

(124) $[Qx : Ox]$

$$[(\leq n)z : Dz] \text{ sell}(x, z, y)$$

$[Qy : Sy]$

(125) $[(\leq 1)x : Ox]$

$$[n!z : Dz] \text{ sell}(x, z, y)$$

$[(\leq 2)y : Sy]$

(126) Two officials (each) sold no more than six defense documents to two superpowers.

(127) No more than two officials (each) sold six defense documents to no more than two superpowers.

(128) Exactly two officials (each) sold no more than six defense documents to exactly two superpowers.

(129) Two officials (each) sold exactly six defense documents to two superpowers.

(130) No more than two officials (each) sold exactly six defense documents to no more than two superpowers.

(131) Exactly two officials (each) sold exactly six defense documents to exactly two superpowers.

Thus sentences (126) to (128) should have a reading that quantifies over pairs of individual official and superpower such that the official sold the superpower no more than six defense documents. Similarly, (132) and (133) should be able to quantify over pairs of a detective and an agency where the detective solved exactly six, or no more than six, crimes for the agency. We will see that such readings obtain only under special circumstances.[25]

(132) Exactly two detectives (each) solved no more than six crimes for exactly two agencies.

(133) Exactly two detectives (each) solved exactly six crimes for exactly two agencies.

The difference between increasing and nonincreasing quantifiers in this position favors an account of apparent quantification over n-tuples that manages to avoid the additional translation scheme for branching quantifiers.

How a speaker comes to understand that sentences (113) and (118) have the force May identifies can be explained without recognizing a distinct semantic interpretation. As we have seen in chapter 5, a context of utterance brings with it a domain of relevant events. We will rely on the pragmatics of this domain to explain how sentences can be understood in the way reported even though in their logical forms distinct quantifiers never have identical scope.

The truth-conditional force of May's readings is arrived at when the speaker presupposes or understands that the relevant events comprise just those that are about what an individual official did for an individual superpower. Such a context partitions what happened in (115) into the four events C in (134a):

(134) a.

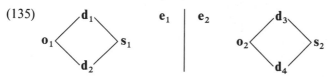

$$\forall e(Ce \leftrightarrow (e = e_1 \vee e = e_2 \vee e = e_3 \vee e = e_4))$$

b. $[(\leq 1)x : Ox][\hat{E} : \mathrm{INFL}[e, x]][\exists E : 1(E) \wedge C[e]]$
    $(\mathrm{sell}[e] \wedge [\exists Z : 2(Z) \wedge \forall z(Zz \rightarrow Dz)] \, \mathrm{OF}[e, Z]])$
    $\wedge [\hat{E} : \Phi][(\leq 2)y : Sy][\hat{E} : \mathrm{to}[e, y]] \, \mathrm{sell}[e]$

If this is the understood context of events, then indeed no official has an event in which he sells two defense documents. The logical form (121) becomes true here, as May's reading requires, if its existential event quantifier is restricted to individual events in the context, as in (134b).[26] It is hardly unnatural to suppose that a discourse has been directed toward the individual actions of officials and superpowers. In reaching for this reading of the sentences, one assumes such a context of discourse.

The logical form and paraphrases cited in (116) and (117) for sentence (113) are false, as required, when the event quantifier is restricted in the same way, $[\exists E : 1(E) \wedge C[e]]$, and the events are partitioned as in (134). The reason, again, is that there is no one event in which two officials participated. But (116) and (117) still do not capture the intended reading, since they are also false in (135), where no event includes both officials.

(135)

The events in this context are, however, exactly the sort of individual actions that the intended reading is a report of.

I accept that the speaker entertains a reading of the sentence (113) that is false in (134) but true in (135). What is required is that the speaker have in mind a logical form that will yield this result when the relevant events are those he presupposes. The following serves the purpose. In its second conjunct it has a cumulative cross-reference to the events where each of the two officials is involved in an event in which he sells two defense documents to superpowers.

(136) $[\exists X : 2(X) \wedge \forall x(Xx \rightarrow Ox)]$
$\quad [\forall x : Xx][\hat{E} : \text{INFL}[e, x]][\exists E : 1(E) \wedge C[e]]$
$\quad (\text{sell}[e] \wedge [\exists Z : 2(Z) \wedge \forall z(Zz \rightarrow Dz)] \text{OF}[e, Z]$
$\quad \wedge [\exists Y : \forall y(Yy \rightarrow Sy)] \text{to}[e, Y])$
$\quad \wedge [\hat{E} : \Phi][\exists Y : 2(Y) \wedge \forall y(Yy \rightarrow Sy)] \text{to}[e, Y]$

(137) In whatever two officials did as sellers, each is involved in an event
      in which he sold two defense documents to superpowers, and
      those sales were to two superpowers.

The cumulative cross-reference eschews the condition that the officials participate in the same event. The presupposed context supports the inference that any event of selling to superpowers is a selling to one super-power.[27] Logical form (136) is thus true in (135) and false in (134). The account of these readings for sentences (113), (118), and (119) thus appears to eliminate quantifying over n-tuples.

An alternative to this pragmatic account recognizes May's readings as semantically distinct but fits the added logical forms within the frame-work of cumulative asymmetry. Thus it too recovers apparently symmet-rical interpretations without proposing an entirely new translation scheme for branching quantifiers. Recall that the extraposed quantifiers leave be-hind a copy of their descriptive contents in the antecedent clause. The copies restrict the assertion of the antecedent clause to the relevant events:

(138) No more than two officials sold no more than two defense
      documents.

(139) a.   No more than two officials sold defense documents, and *there*
           no more than two defense documents were sold.
      b.   *No more than two officials sold things, and *there* no more
           than two defense documents were sold.

I have assumed that the copies in the antecedent clause serve only this purpose and are otherwise inert, but perhaps they behave as other second-order descriptions and can therefore be assigned scope by QR. In the logical form for (118) in (140), *some superpowers* is raised in the antecedent clause to include within its scope *exactly two defense documents*, where it is interpreted distributively :

(118) No more than one official sold two defense documents to no more than two superpowers.

(140) $[(\le 1)x : Ox][\hat{E} : \text{INFL}[e, x]][\exists Z : \forall z(Zz \rightarrow Sz)][\forall z : Zz][\hat{E} : \text{to}[e, z]]$
$\exists E(\text{sell}[e] \wedge [\exists Y : 2(Y) \wedge \forall y(Yy \rightarrow Dy)] \text{OF}[e, Y])$
$\wedge [\hat{E} : \Phi][(\le 2)z : Sz][\hat{E} : \text{to}[e, z]] \text{sell}[e]$

(141) No more than one official sold superpowers each two defense documents, and *there* defense documents were sold to no more than two superpowers.

The events described by the antecedent clause in (140) overlaps exactly those events where a single official sells to a single superpower two defense documents, as required for May's interpretation. The description of the relevant events is determined entirely by the antecedent clause and doesn't deviate from an asymmetric logical form. As before, the antecedent clause is about events of an official's selling two defense documents to superpowers, but now there is a formal ambiguity concerning whether *selling two defense documents* applies to the superpowers collectively or individually.

In the representation of the asymmetric interpretation of (42), discussed in section 2, the copied *agencies* remains *in situ* in the antecedent clause, as reflected in the paraphrase in (142).

(42) Exactly two detectives (each) solved exactly two crimes for exactly three agencies.

(142) Exactly two detectives (each) solved exactly two crimes for agencies, and *there* crimes were solved for exactly three agencies.

Exactly two crimes is not dependent on the individual agency but applies to whatever solving of crimes for agencies a detective did. A symmetric logical form for the symmetric interpretation of (42) would make *exactly two crimes* dependent on both the individual detective and the individual agency in both clauses, as in (143). A curious gap then arises if both (142) and (143) correspond to possible logical forms for (42).

(143) Exactly two detectives (each) solved for an agency exactly two crimes, and (there) exactly three agencies are each such that a detective solved exactly three crimes for it.

(144) *Exactly two detectives (each) solved exactly two crimes for agencies, and (there) exactly three agencies are each such that detectives solved exactly two crimes for it.

As remarked in section 2, the symmetric logical form corresponding to (144), where the copies of *agencies* and *detectives* remain in their respective clauses undistributed, represents an interpretation that (42) does not have. But why should that be, given that the copied material may be left *in situ*, as attested by the asymmetric (142)? Symmetric logical forms are obligatorily distributed with respect to all the argument positions related to the cumulative quantifiers. At least this question does not arise in either the pragmatic or semantic accounts, which deploy only asymmetric logical forms.

Neither the pragmatic nor semantic account, however, can straightforwardly explain away readings where the narrow scope quantifier is decreasing or, more generally, nonincreasing, if such exist. May does not report such cases, but I assume that in the right context one could utter (145), intending that two officials and two superpowers are among the pairs where the official sold no defense documents to the superpower:

(145) Two officials sold no defense documents to two superpowers.

(146) Two officials sold few defense documents to two superpowers.

(147) No more than one official sold no defense documents to no more than two superpowers.

Similarly, one could utter (148), intending that no more than one official and no more than one superpower are among the pairs where the official did not talk to the superpower:

(148) No more than one official did not talk to no more than one superpower.

Recall from the previous section that the logical forms I expect to assign (145) and (148) in fact represent anomalous interpretations:

(149) Two officials sold no defense documents to superpowers, and *there* officials sold defense documents to two superpowers.

(150) No more than one official did not talk to superpowers, and *there* officials sold defense documents to no more than two superpowers.

Let us examine more closely the circumstances under which the intended interpretation of (145) to (147) can be uttered truthfully. Consider (151):

(151) Two officials sold no more than one defense document to two superpowers.

Sentence (151) has a number of easy interpretations sharing some of the features of May's symmetric quantification, from which they have to be distinguished. One interpretation makes all three quantifiers independent. *No more than one defense document* measures the accumulation of what the two officials sold to the two superpowers:[28]

(152) Two officials and two superpowers are such that they sold them
       no more than one defense document.

This interpretation lacks, of course, the dependence of the decreasing quantifier on the choice of the individual official and superpower. But in yet two other interpretations, we may combine dependence with apparent independence between the increasing quantifiers without resorting to branching quantification:

(153) Two officials (each) sold (a certain) two superpowers (each) no
       more than one defense document.

(154) Two officials (each) sold no more than one defense document to
       (a certain) two superpowers.

Although *two superpowers* falls within the distributed scope of *two officials*, the indefinite NP may still be understood as if it were independent. So understood, (151) could assert, for example, that two officials each sold no more than one defense document to the same two superpowers, as in (153).[29] These interpretations shadow very closely the scope relations May would assume. My worry is that the speaker not call on these interpretations when he readily affirms May's reading. To set them and all other extraneous interpretations aside, consider the following context, which falsifies (151) in all its readings except for May's:[30]

(155) o_1 —— d_1 —— s_1 o_2 —— d_6 —— s_2

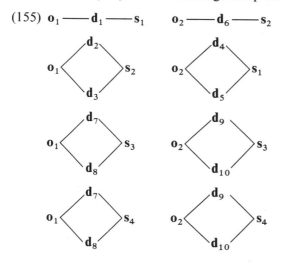

Note in particular that for any official there is only one superpower to which he sold no more than one defense document. He fails to stand in that relation to each of the other three. Branching quantification is, however, true here, since there are pairs of an individual official and superpower where the official sold the superpower no more than one defense document, and two officials and two superpowers are among these pairs. A yet simpler context will distinguish branching in (145) from its non-branching interpretations. Suppose that the officials and superpowers shown in (156) are all there are, and (156) shows all that happened between them:

(145) Two officials sold no defense documents to two superpowers.

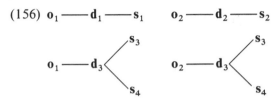

Then since the first official sold nothing to the second superpower and the second official sold nothing to the first superpower, the branching interpretation is true. All other interpretations of (145), however, are false.

It seems to me that the readings of (151) and (145) that are true in contexts (155) and (156) demand some priming. They are accessible just in case one imagines that to sell no more than one (no) defense document is something that one does to another. Then, indeed, one official did it once to one superpower, and another official did it once to another superpower. Attributing actions of this kind, the sentences assert that two officials did that to two superpowers. May's reading is appropriate under conditions similar to those where it would make sense to assert (157) or (159):

(157) Angleton has a picture of Philby not selling the Soviets documents.

(158) ... $[\exists x : P(x) \land [\exists E : \neg (INFL[e, p] \land sell[e]$
          $\land [\imath Y : \forall y(Yy \to Sy)] TO[e, Y] \land [\exists Z : \forall z(Zz \to Dz)]$
        $OF[e, Z])] of[x, E]] ...$

(159) Philby was in an event of selling the Soviets no documents.

(160) ... $[\exists E : 1(E) \land \forall e(Ee \to event(e))$
          $\land [\exists E' : [no\ z : Dz][\hat{E}' : OF[e', z]] \exists E'(INFL[e', PRO_i]$
            $\land sell[e'] \land [\imath Y : \forall y(Yy \to Sy)] TO[e', Y])]$
        $of[e, E']] ...$

It is plain that the logical form for (157) will include an existential quantifier over pictures and that the logical form for (159) will include an existential quantifier over events. It is also plain that in any of the pictures that make (157) true, Philby does not sell the Soviets documents and, similarly, that in any event that makes (159) true, he does not sell them documents. These conditions are not enough, however, to explicate the meaning of these sentences. Philby is not selling documents in Angleton's picture of his favorite hound, but this is not a picture *of* Philby not selling the Soviets documents. Sentences (157) and (159) belong to an idiom that appears at least to talk of so-called negative events or acts. As many have discussed, event-based treatments of adverbs and the complements to perception verbs and causatives appear prima facie to refer to such events:[31]

(161) Gracefully, no one stirred.

(162) John saw no one leave.

(163) It resulted in no one's being elected.

If we are unwilling to embrace negative events, the idiom must be explained away somehow. It is beyond the scope of this work to join that discussion. Nevertheless, it is fair to suggest that May's reading of (145) and (151) calls upon that idiom, in which case the logical form in (164) is not too far off. It gives (145) an asymmetric logical form, where there is *de re* quantification over superpowers into the complement of *event of*:[32]

(164) $[\exists X : 2(X) \wedge \forall x(Xx \rightarrow Ox)][\forall x : Xx][\hat{E}' : \text{INFL}[e', x]]$
$[\exists Y : \forall y(Yy \rightarrow Sy)]$
$\exists E(C[e]$
    $\wedge [\exists E' : [\text{no } z : Dz][\hat{E}' : \text{OF}[e', z]](\text{sell}[e'] \wedge \text{to}[e', Y])] \text{ of}[e, E'])$
$\wedge [\hat{E} : \Phi][\exists Y : 2(Y) \wedge \forall y(Yy \rightarrow Sy)] \text{ to}[e', Y])$

(165) Two officials are such that there are events in the given context of their selling some superpowers no documents, and those events of selling no documents were to two superpowers.

The success of logical form (164) depends on a number of features. First, the nonextensionality of the idiom noted above is essential. An event in which o_1 sells no documents to s_2 is not an event *of* o_1 selling no documents to s_2; otherwise, (164) would be vacuously true. Second, the interpreted relation *is an event of* creates an embedded context from which *to two superpowers* is extracted in (164) and (165). The extraposed clause is elliptical. It requires the surrounding context for the θ-role to be reconstructed as in (166) and (167), following the general pattern for long-distance separation, to be discussed in section 5.1.1.

(166) $\dots[\hat{E}:\Phi][\exists Y:2(Y) \wedge \forall y(Yy \rightarrow Sy)]$
$\quad\quad \exists E(C[e]$
$\quad\quad\quad \wedge\ [\exists E':[\text{no }z:Dz][\hat{E}':OF[e',z]](\text{sell}[e'] \wedge \text{to}[e',Y])]\text{ of}[e,E'])$

(167) Two officials are such that there are events in the given context of their selling some superpowers no documents, and among those events of selling no documents, two superpowers are such that there are events of selling them no defense documents.

Note that *no documents* remains in the complement of *events of*. The embedding allows the cross-reference in the extraposed conjunct to properly refer to events of selling no documents. The cross-referring term abstracts on 'E' rather than 'E'', which makes it irrelevant that no events render the subformula '$[\text{no }z:Dz]\Psi[e']$'.

The virtue in appealing to the idiom of so-called negative events or acts is that the conditions for talking sensibly about negative events match those where May's reading of (145) and (151) is accessible.[33] My logical forms do not straightforwardly deliver the dependence of *no defense documents* on pairs of individual officials and superpowers. The effect is obtained indirectly by quantifying over events that meet an appropriate description. But when the dependent quantifier is nonincreasing, as is *no defense documents*, the events described are negative events. In that case, May's reading is grasped only under the priming conditions discussed above. Thus the effort to assimilate his reading into the present framework has some promise, despite the concession to an unanalyzed idiom. The structure it assumes gains in plausibility to the extent that there is independent evidence that the underlying structure of all polyadic verbs fairly closely resembles causative constructions.[34] If 'x sells y to z' is more like 'x acts (as a seller) so that y is sold to z', then it would not be unnatural for a quantifier to remain within the complement to the causative: 'x acts (as a seller) so that no documents are sold to z'. As remarked earlier, the alternative to the enriched structure is a special translation of branching quantifiers that delivers the symmetric readings.

5 Quantifier Raising Assigns the Same Scope to Distinct Quantifiers

The first step in deriving the distributive interpretations of (168) is to assign scope to the first-order quantifiers by QR.

(168) No more than two detectives solved no more than three crimes.

(169) [$_S$ INFL(e, no more than 2 detectives)
     [$_{VP}$ solve(e) OF(e, no more than 3 crimes)]]

It is also the first step in deriving the cumulative interpretation. The same grammatical constraints apply. A cumulative quantification is acceptable just in case its nonincreasing quantifiers can each be raised to a position from which they have scope over the same clause. Thus there is a cumulative interpretation of (170) just in case (171) can be understood to assert that for no more than three crimes did Marlowe identify the victim that they had ruined.

(170)   No more than two detectives identified the victim that no more
        than three crimes had ruined.

(171)   Marlowe identified the victim that no more than three crimes had
        ruined.

(172)   *[no more than 3 crimes]$_j$ ...
        [$_S$ Marlowe identified [$_{NP}$ the victim [$_{S'}$ that t_j had ruined]]]

Both interpretations are impossible, and this is attributed to conditions on grammar that prohibit the movement shown in (172). The cumulative interpretation of (170) requires that both quantifiers be raised to include the matrix clause within their scope, but *no more than three crimes* is too deeply embedded.

In contrast, there is no such constraint against construing the indefinite descriptions in (173) as independent, which is expected if their independence follows from just the linear arrangement of existential quantifiers:

(173) Two detectives identified two victims that three crimes had ruined.

(174) $\exists E([\exists X : 2(X) \wedge \forall x(Xx \rightarrow Dx)]$ INFL$[e, X] \wedge$ identify$[e]$
     $\wedge [\exists Y : 2(Y) \wedge \forall y(Yy \rightarrow Vy)$
         $\wedge \exists E'([\exists Z : 3(Z) \wedge \forall z(Zz \rightarrow Cz)]$ INFL$[e', Z] \wedge$ ruin$[e']$
         $\wedge$ OF$[e', Y])]$ OF$[e, Y])$

The distributive interpretations do not follow from the *in situ* interpretation of the quantifiifiers. The optional application of QR to derive the distributive interpretations is subject to grammatical constraints. In particular, *three crimes* cannot be raised to include within its scope either *two victims* or *two detectives*:[35]

(175) *$\exists E([\exists X : 2(X) \wedge \forall x(Xx \rightarrow Dx)]$ INFL$[e, X] \wedge$ identify$[e]$
     $\wedge [\exists Z : 3(Z) \wedge \forall z(Zz \rightarrow Cz)][\forall z : Zz]$
         $[\exists Y : 2(Y) \wedge \forall y(Yy \rightarrow Vy) \wedge [\hat{E'} :$ INFL$[e', z]]\exists E'($ruin$[e']$
         $\wedge$ OF$[e', Y])]$ OF$[e, Y])$

(176) *[∃Z : 3(Z) ∧ ∀z(Zz → Cz)][∀z : Zz]
        ∃E([∃X : 2(X) ∧ ∀x(Xx → Dx)] INFL[e, X] ∧ identify[e]
           ∧ [∃Y : 2(Y) ∧ ∀y(Yy → Vy)
              ∧ [Ê′ : INFL[e′, z]]∃E′(ruin[e′] ∧ OF[e′, Y])] OF[e, Y])

(Nondistributive readings of the indefinites are another matter. See n. 35 for discussion.)

QR and the conditions on movement are to explain the noted correlation between the cumulative interpretation and scope assignment in related interpretations. To extend QR to cumulative quantification, we require that it allow first-order quantifiers to be assigned the same scope, which yields structures that conform to the patterns in (177) and (178):

(177) [Q₁ N′₁] ... [Qₙ N′ₙ] Φ

(178) [Q₁ N′₁]
          ⋮   ⟩Φ
      [Qₙ N′ₙ]

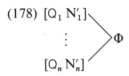

If the conditions that constrain QR are understood as conditions on extraction from Φ, the noted correlation between cumulative and distributive interpretations follows. A cumulative interpretation is acceptable only if the movements involved in (178) are attested by linear interpretations, (177), that extract the quantifiers from the same domain.[36]

5.1   Long-distance cumulative quantifiers

5.1.1   Ellipsis and reconstruction   Cumulative quantification is not confined to a single clause, and as we will see, neither is cumulative asymmetry. The cumulative interpretations of the following sentences raise 'no more than five N'' either out of an NP or an embedded clause:

(179)   No more than two detectives found solutions to no more than five crimes.

(180)   No more than two detectives tried to work for no more than five agencies.

(181)   No more than two detectives seemed to have worked for no more than five agencies.

I claim that the cumulative interpretation of these sentences have the *same* logical form as the corresponding sentences (182) through (184) and that their logical form closely resembles the latter group of sentences in showing cross-reference.

(182) No more than two detectives found solutions to crimes, and that was to no more than five crimes.

(183) No more than two detectives tried to work for agencies, and that was for no more than five agencies.

(184) No more than two detectives seemed to work for agencies, and that was for no more than five agencies.

Whatever the logical form of (182) to (184) may be, it is obvious that the second conjunct does not apply to events denoted by the the matrix verb in the antecedent clause. In (182), *to no more no than five crimes* applies not to findings but to solutions. The second conjunct asserts that no more than five crimes are among those that detectives found solutions to. It is elliptical for something like (185), which reconstructs enough of the antecedent conjunct to interpret the θ-role stranded in the second conjunct:

(185) ..., that was such that to no more than five crimes were solutions found.

(186) ..., that $[(\leq 5)y : Cy]\exists E(\text{find}[e] \land [\exists Z : \forall z(Zz \rightarrow Sz \land \text{to}[z, y])]$ OF$[e, Z])$

Note that even if sense permitted, it would not be enough to reconstruct only the predicate that the stranded θ-role is lexically dependent on. That is, (180) and (183) cannot be paraphrased by (187).

(187) No more than two detectives tried to work for agencies, and that was such that no more than five agencies were worked for.

Contrary to (180) and (183), (187) is true when detectives have tried to work for many agencies but succeeded with no more than five. The reconstruction must include *try*, as in (188):

(188) No more than two detectives tried to work for agencies, and that was such that no more than five agencies did any detective try to work for.

(189) ..., that $[(\leq 5)y : Ay]\exists E(\text{try}[e]$
$\land [\exists E' : \text{INFL}[e', \text{PRO}_i] \land \text{work}[e'] \land \text{for}[e', y]]$ OF$[E, E'])^{37}$

Minimally, the reconstruction is closed under lexical government, including a chain of predicates that head the governed phrases and end with the stranded preposition. This much is required just to properly construe the stranded θ-role. Formula (189) shows a more extensive reconstruction, including the infinitival subject. The thought is that once *try* is reconstructed to accommodate the stranded θ-role, its selectional restrictions (and those of any other reconstructed element) must be satisfied. Hence *try* appears with a full complement clause projecting a subject position.

A more extensive reconstruction is justified by those cases of cumulative quantification that more plainly quantify into opaque domains:[38]

(190) No more than two prosecutors believed that few witnesses could give alibis to no more than five suspects.

(191) No more than two prosecutors believed that few witnesses could give alibis to some suspects, and that was to no more than five suspects.

(192) $[(\leq 2)x : Px][\hat{E}' : \text{INFL}[e, x]]$
       $\exists E(\text{believe}[e] \wedge [\exists Z : \forall z(Zz \rightarrow Sz)]$
       $\text{OF}[e, \text{₍[few } x : Wx][\hat{E}' : \text{INFL}[e', x]]$
       $\exists E'(\text{give}[e'] \wedge [\exists Y : \forall y(Yy \rightarrow Ay)] \text{ OF}[e', Y] \wedge \text{to}[e', Z])]\text{₎})$
       $\wedge [\hat{E} : \Phi][(\leq 5)z : Sz][\hat{E} : \text{to}[e', z]] \text{ give}[e']$

For the relevant interpretation, prosecutors entertain object-dependent beliefs about suspects, such as Giuliani's belief that few witnesses could possibly come forth with alibis for Gotti. On this interpretation, *few witnesses* is *de dicto* and so occurs in the subject position of the complement clause for *belief*. To faithfully represent the meaning of (190) or its paraphrase in (191), it is plain that the subject *few witnesses* must be included in the reconstruction:

(193) No more than two prosecutors believed that few witnesses could give alibis to some suspects, and *there*, of no more than five suspects was it believed that few witnesses could give them alibis.

Omitting the subject mistakes the meaning of (190):

(194) *No more than two prosecutors believed that few witnesses could give alibis to some suspects, and *there*, no more than five suspects were such that it was believed that they could be given alibis.[39]

As we have seen, the translation of branching quantifiers introduces clauses, corresponding to all but one of the quantifiers, that consist of a cross-reference to events, a quantifier, and the θ-role it binds. If the branching involves a long-distance extraction, the stranded θ-role is improperly related to the events described by the matrix, antecedent clause:

(195) ... $\wedge\ [\hat{E}_i : \Phi][Qv_j : \mathrm{N}']\ \Theta[e_k, v_j]$

Such cases call for a reconstruction of the surrounding context for the stranded θ-role. It reconstructs much of the antecedent clause. Starting with the predicate that selects the stranded θ-role, it reconstructs a chain of predicates that is closed under government and selection. But we have also seen that for any element so introduced, the reconstruction must include its full complement, such as the complement clause for *believe* in (192).

I now consider cases of long-distance cumulative quantifiers that demonstrate cumulative asymmetry. In these examples, two quantifiers quantify into embedded clauses. In (196a), the detectives' thoughts are about which crimes are solved for which agencies.

(196) a. Exactly two detectives (each) thought that exactly two crimes were solved for exactly one agency.
   b. Exactly two detectives tried to (each) solve exactly two crimes for exactly one agency.
   c. Exactly two detectives seemed to have (each) solved exactly two crimes for exactly one agency.

(197) a. Exactly two detectives (each) thought that exactly two crimes were solved for exactly three agencies.
   b. Exactly two detectives tried to (each) solve exactly two crimes for exactly three agencies.
   c. Exactly two detectives seemed to have (each) solved exactly two crimes for exactly three agencies.

Spade thinks that the theft of the Maltese Falcon was solved for the Pinkerton agency. Sentence (196a) entails that for each of two detectives, there are exactly two crimes for which there are some agencies that he thinks they were solved for. The logical form of the complement is shown in (198), where both *exactly two crimes* and *exactly three agencies* have been extracted from the embedded clause.

(198) $[2!x : Dx][\hat{E} : \mathrm{INFL}[e, x]][2!z : Cz][\exists Y : \forall y(Yy \rightarrow Ay)][\forall y : Yy]$
   $\exists E(\mathrm{thought}[e] \wedge \mathrm{OF}[e, {}_\lbrack[\hat{E}' : \mathrm{INFL}[e', z]]\exists E'(\mathrm{solve}[e']$
   $\wedge\ \mathrm{for}[e', y])]_\rbrack) \wedge [\hat{E} : \Phi][k!y : Ay]\ \mathrm{for}[e', y]$

In the complements to *try* and *seem* in (196b) and (196c), the *de re* construal of *exactly two crimes* is, of course, easier. The sentences in (196) and (197) and the context in (199) reproduce the paradigm from section 2 ((34), (42), and context (41)) illustrating cumulative asymmetry. In (199), detective d_1 thinks that crime c_1 was solved for agency a_1 and that c_2 was solved for a_2, and similarly for the rest of the diagram.

(199)

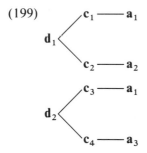

Sentence (197a) is true in this context. Exactly two detectives each thought of exactly two crimes that they were solved, and there were exactly three agencies that their thoughts were about. In contrast, (196a) falsely asserts that their thoughts were about exactly one agency. As in the previous section, a symmetric treatment of the cumulative quantifiers, giving them identical scope, would mistakenly assign (196a) an interpretation that is true in (199):

(200)   Exactly two detectives each thought of exactly two crimes that
        they were solved for some agencies, and *there* exactly one agency
        was such that exactly two crimes were thought to have been solved
        for it.

Notice, however, that the reconstruction of the context for the stranded θ-role in (198) will not reconstruct *exactly two crimes* into the scope of *exactly k agencies*. Since *exactly two crimes* has been extracted, it does not occur in the complement clause for *believe*. Reconstructing the complement will therefore not get in the way of cumulative asymmetry. When we view the contrast betweeen (190) and (197a) schematically in (201) and (202), we see that after translation *few witnesses* ends up in the scope of both cumulative quantifiers, but *exactly two crimes* shows the effects of cumulative asymmetry. It will not appear in the second conjunct.

(201) $[(\leq 2)x : \text{prosecutor}(x)]$

x believes that few witnesses could
give alibis to y

$[(\leq 5)y : \text{suspect}(y)]$

(202) $[2!x : \text{detective}(x)]$

$[2!y : \text{crime}(y)]$ x thought that y was
solved for z

$[k!z : \text{agency}(z)]$

These remarks on reconstruction are speculative at best. It is important to keep in mind, however, that they are driven by the meaning of the ordinary English sentences in (182) to (184). Any speaker of English is sure to recognize that the simple structure of the second conjunct—pronoun, copula, and prepositional phrase—belies a complex interpretation that depends on certain features of the antecedent clause not revealed in the surface structure of the second conjunct. This is simply a fact about these English sentences. My claim is that the logical form for the cumulative interpretations of (179) through (197) is just the same as these sentences. The translation of branching quantifiers assumed so far is enough to put (179) through (197) into that form. The two sets of sentences then face the same problem of undoing the apparent ellipsis, and they end up with the same range of meanings. The reconstruction in the second conjunct is not ad hoc to the translation of cumulative quantifiers. Rather, the interpretation of cumulative quantifiers is the same as sentences that bear the target logical form overtly, and these sentences clearly implicate some process of ellipsis and reconstruction, even if its syntax remains obscure.

5.1.2 Adjuncts The antecedent conjunct in the logical form for cumulative quantification must include the θ-roles and the descriptive contents of all the arguments. In particular, those that are separated leave behind copies. That is, (203) comes out as (204) rather than (205) if it is not to imply that few detectives solved crosswords.

(203)   No more than two detectives solved no more than three crimes.

(204)   No more than two detectives solved crimes, and *there* no more than three crimes were solved.

(205)   *No more than two detectives solved things, and *there* no more than three crimes were solved.

Adjunct phrases give rise to an ambiguity that distinguishes interpretations with independent quantifiers. One interpretation of (206) and (209), which unmistakably contain adjunct phrases, derives from the branching of the two quantifiers, which are cumulative.

(206)   No more than two victims died because of no more than two good samaritans.

(207)   No more than two victims died, and *that* was because of no more than two good samaritans.

(208)   No more than two victims died because of good samaritans, and *there* victims died because of no more than two good samaritans.

(209) No more than two politicians were running for office with no more than two endorsements.

(210) No more than two politicians were running for office, with there being no more than two endorsements.

(211) No more than two politicians were running for office with endorsements, and *there* politicians were running for office with no more than two endorsements.

So understood, (206) is about victims dying because of well-intentioned but counterproductive good samaritans. As the paraphrase in (208) reports, there were no more than two victims and no more than two good samaritans involved in such events. This interpretation requires that the adjunct phrase and the descriptive content of its argument appear in the first conjunct, since there is no implication that no more than two victims died. The second interpretation of (206), paraphrased in (207), asserts that a death toll of no more than two victims was due to the efforts of no more than two good samaritans. Heroic action on their part limited the number of fatalities. On this interpretation, the adjunct relates to an assertion that absolutely no more than two victims died. The sentence does not mean that because of no more than two good samaritans, no more than two victims died because of good samaritans. On this interpretation, the quantified NP *no more than two good samaritans* remains entirely within the adjunct phrase, which modifies the whole main clause.[40] The logical form of the main clause contains no trace of the adjunct phrase or its quantifier.

The ambiguity just noted also occurs with phrases that are not overtly sentential adjuncts. The nonbranching, noncumulative interpretation, where the quantifier remains within the adjunct phrase, becomes salient when the branching interpretation results in infelicity or contradiction:

(212) No more than two detectives solved crimes for no licensed agencies.

(213) *No more than two detectives solved crimes for licensed agencies, and *there* detectives solved crimes for no licensed agencies.

(214) Two detectives solved two crimes for no licensed agencies.

(215) *Two detectives solved two crimes for licensed agencies, and *there* detectives solved crimes for no licensed agencies.

The branching interpretation of (212), which leaves *for licensed agencies* behind in the antecedent clause in (213), is infelicitous, since anyone who can assert it can assert, more to the point, that no detectives solved crimes for no licensed agencies. The sentence is felicitous, however, when it is taken to assert that no more than two detectives solved crimes, and the beneficiaries, if any, included no licensed agencies. This latter interpretation parallels the cases above where the quantifier remains within the adjunct phrase.

The apparent generalization is that quantifier raising out of the phrase is obligatory unless the phrase in question can occur separately at s-structure. The stars in the first sentence of the following couplets indicates that any interpretation where the quantifiers are independent is infelicitous or contradictory. Since the direct object in (216a) is not separable, as (216b) attests, the only way for the quantifiers to be independent is by raising *no nice roses* into a branching structure with *few boys*. But, the interpretation of that LF is the infelicitous assertion that few boys gave girls nice roses and boys gave girls no nice roses.

(216) a. *Few boys gave girls no nice roses.
     b. *Few boys gave girls, and it was of no nice roses.

(217) a. *Two boys gave two girls no nice roses.
     b. *Two boys gave two girls, but it was of no nice roses.

The branching LF for (218a) is equally infelicitous, but since the indirect object is separable, as in (218b), a felicitous interpretation for the sentence is available by extraposing the PP. The separability of the phrase is presumably a consequence of larger differences in the internal structure of VP.[41]

(218) a. Few boys gave roses to no nice girls.
     b. Few boys gave roses, and it was to no nice girls.

(219) a. Two boys gave some roses to no nice girls.
     b. Two boys gave some roses, but it was to no nice girls.

Further examples in support of the generalization are found in (220) to (227):

(220) a. *Few teachers taught freshmen no exotic languages.
     b. *Few teachers taught freshmen, and it was of no exotic languages.

(221) a. *Two teachers taught freshmen no exotic languages.
     b. *Two teachers taught freshmen, and it was of no exotic languages.

(222) a. Few teachers taught French to no freshmen.
     b. Few teachers taught French, and it was to no freshmen.

(223) a. Two teachers taught French to no freshmen.
   b. Two teachers taught French, and it was to no freshmen.

(224) a. ?No more than two linguists entered into none of these book exhibits.
   b. ?No more than two linguists entered, and it was into none of these book exhibits.

(225) a. ?Two linguists entered into none of these book exhibits.
   b. ?Two linguists entered, and it was into none of these book exhibits.

(226) a. *No more than two linguists entered into no discussions.
   b. *No more than two linguists entered, and it was into no discussions.

(227) a. *Two linguists entered into no discussions.
   b. *Two linguists entered, and it was into no discussions.

Chapter 10
Cumulative Quantifiers and
Nonmaximal Reference

In earlier sections, the events referred to by '$[\hat{E}:\Phi]$' were those described by an antecedent clause that contained a nonincreasing quantifier. The events referred to are maximal, comprising, as they do in (1) and (2), all events of a detective solving two crimes.[1]

(1) Few detectives solved two crimes for exactly three agencies.

(2) Few detectives solved two crimes, and *that* was for exactly three agencies.

In this respect, cross-reference to events is the same as all other cases of descriptive anaphora to a nonincreasing antecedent. Evans (1977) observes that the pronoun in (3) refers maximally to all the MPs that came to the party:

(3) Few MPs came to the party, but they had a marvelous time.

In contrast, maximal reference sometimes disappears when the antecedent is increasing.[2] A parallel between descriptive anaphora and the cross-reference to events will hold here as well. On the most natural reading of (4), which modifies an example due to Donnellan (1978), there is no suggestion that all the men that came to the office today tried to sell encyclopedias:

(4) Two men came to the office today. They tried to sell me an encyclopedia.

The nonmaximal reference of the pronoun is more than can be attributed to a contextual restriction on the domain of the quantifier, *two men*. Presumably, any domain accessible to *two men* in (5) is also accessible to *few men* in (6).

(5) Two men came to the office today. They tried to sell encyclopedias. Perhaps there were even others who did the same.

(6) *Few men came to the office today. They tried to sell encyclopedias. Perhaps there were even others who did the same.

Yet there remains a difference. The pronoun in (6) refers maximally to all the men, whatever the context, that came to the office today, and thus there could be no others. But (5) allows that men other than the two may have come to the office today and tried to sell encyclopedias.[3]

The noted contrast between increasing and nonincreasing quantifiers extends to cumulative reference. The pronoun in (7), whose antecedent falls within the scope of a nonincreasing quantifier, must refer to all the donkeys that any farmers bought.

(7) a. Few farmers bought a donkey, and they were led out of the corral together.
     b. Few farmers bought a donkey, and the donkeys were led out of the corral together.

In (8), it is sufficient for the pronoun to refer to some donkeys among which for every farmer there is a donkey he bought.

(8) a. Every farmer bought a donkey, and they were led out of the corral together.
     b. Every farmer bought a donkey, and the donkeys were led out of the corral together.

It allows that the farmers may have bought other donkeys that were not led out of the corral together.

When the antecedent clause contains increasing quantifiers, reference to the events described shows a similar pattern of nonmaximal reference. Consider sentences (9), (11), and (12) in context (14):

(9) The 2 students were shown four movies in 10 hours.

(10) $\exists E([\iota X : 2(X) \wedge \forall x(Xx \rightarrow Sx)] \text{INFL}[e, X] \wedge \text{show}[e]$
$\wedge [\exists Y : 4(Y) \wedge \forall y(Yy \rightarrow My)] \text{OF}[e, Y] \wedge \ldots \text{in}[e, 10 \text{ hours}])$

(11) Every one of the 2 students was shown 2 movies in 10 hours.

(12) Every student was shown 2 movies, and it took 10 hours.

(13) $[\text{every } x : [\iota X : 2(X) \wedge \forall x(Xx \rightarrow Sx)] Xx][\hat{E} : \text{INFL}[e, x]]$
$\exists E(\text{show}[e] \wedge [\exists Y : 2(Y) \wedge \forall y(Yy \rightarrow My)] \text{OF}[e, Y])$
$\wedge [\hat{E} : \Phi] \text{in}[e, 10 \text{ hours}]$

(14)

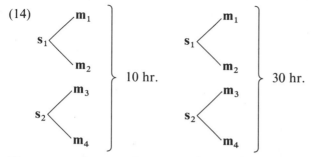

The context is a continuous period of 40 hours. In exactly 10 of those hours the two students each saw 2 movies, and in the remaining 30 hours they saw them again. Describing the whole scene, one could say that the 2 students were shown 4 movies in 40 hours, but it is also true to say that in 10 hours, the students were shown 4 movies, or to say that they were shown 4 movies in 30 hours. An observer of (14) would not use (9), (11), or (12), for they report less than he knows. But if one were to hear or come to believe these sentences and later to discover that (14) is the complete picture, then surely what one heard or believed turns out to have been true. Sentence (9) is made true by the existence of an event that coincides with the 10 hour portion depicted in (14). On the interpretation where the adverb modifies the entire clause, the truth conditions of (11) and (12) are the same as those of (9).

In the way characteristic of separation, the adverbial modifying the clause in (11) refers back to the events described, and it must be possible for the reference to include some but not all the events of a student being shown 2 movies:

(15) [$_{s_i}$ Each of the 2 students was shown 2 movies], and that$_i$ took 10 hours

Pronominal reference provides examples identical in structure in a more familiar setting. Suppose, for example, that the context is similar to (14), but the second time around the students are shown 4 different movies:

(16)

Suppose also that only the first 4 movies receive devastating reviews in *The New Yorker*. In this context, sentences (17) and (19) can both be true, and the pronoun refers *collectively* to some of the movies shown to the students:

(17) Every student was shown 2 movies, and then they were panned together in *The New Yorker*.

(18) [every $x : Sx$][$\exists Y : 2(Y) \wedge \forall y(Yy \rightarrow My)$]$_i$ ... they$_i$ ...

(19) Every student was shown a movie, and then they were panned together in *The New Yorker*.

(20) [every $x : Sx$][$\exists y : My$]$_i$ ... they$_i$ ...

However, (17) and (19) are true in this context not because the pronoun is glossed as an indefinite: *some of the movies that the students were shown*. Such a gloss would make (17) and (19) true in contexts where they are plainly false, if, for example, only the first 2 movies in (14) were panned. The panned movies must include movies from each student's experience.[4]

If the pronoun has definite reference, it of course cannot be to all the movies that students were shown in (14). Rather, from all that happened in (14), the antecedent clause describes something that happened, and it is this context that supports definite reference in the pronouns. *They* refers to all the movies found there. It must turn out that the antecedent clause in (17) describes some events in (14) just in case for every student, an event of his being shown 2 movies is among them.

That cross-reference to events and pronominal anaphora both distinguish increasing and nonincreasing antecedents fits the observational claim that they are the same phenomenon. But a uniform analysis in terms of the descriptive content of the anaphor will appear to some to violate the distinction between increasing and nonincreasing antecedents. For it is sometimes held that to view pronouns as definite descriptions is to be committed to maximal reference in every case. It is difficult, however, to imagine how pronouns bearing cumulative reference, maximal or not, could be treated by something other than descriptions, and so most of this section will defend an account of nonmaximal reference where unbound anaphors of all kinds are always definite descriptions.

Besides nonmaximal reference, cross-reference when the antecedent is governed by an increasing quantifier presents a further problem: that of exact description. In contrast to (11) and (12), the sentences in (21) are false in the context (16), even if it took the students each 15 hours to see their third and fourth movies.

(21) a. Every student was shown 2 movies in 25 hours.

    b. Every student was shown 2 movies, and it took 25 hours.

A part of (16) that took 25 hours would include the first set of movies that the students were shown and two of the movies being shown to the students in the second set. These events, however, are not exactly described by the antecedent clause. The events referred to ought to include, for each student, no more than his being shown two movies. The same constraint applies to a pronoun bearing cumulative reference. Suppose that all the movies in (16) were panned, each by a different reviewer. Sentence (22) is true and requires nonmaximal reference, but (23) is false.

(22) Every student was shown 2 movies, and then 4 reviewers panned them in a single issue of *The New Yorker*.

(23) Every student was shown 2 movies, and then 6 reviewers panned them in a single issue of *The New Yorker*.

The pronoun must refer to the movies shown in some events that are exactly described by the antecedent clause. To get 6 reviewers, the events referred to would have to include some student's seeing more than two movies. The problem of exact description was first encountered in chapter 7, section 2.3, and an analogous solution is given in section 2 below.

1 Nonmaximal Reference and Unbound Anaphora

There are broadly two approaches to the distribution of maximal and nonmaximal reference. One, which I will call the linked-variable view, sees it as a difference of logical form.[5] Nonmaximal reference obtains when an existential quantifier includes within its scope both the pronoun and its increasing antecedent. As in (24), the existential quantifier will, if necessary, take scope over an entire discourse. In the case of a nonincreasing antecedent, it is stipulated that a nonincreasing quantifier cannot be related to the existential quantifier enabling nonmaximal reference:

(24) $\exists C([\exists X : 2(X) \land \forall x(Xx \leftrightarrow (Mx \land Cx))]$

    $[_\Phi X$ came to the office today]

        $[\iota X : \forall x(Xx \leftrightarrow (Mx \land Cx \land \Phi))] X$ tried to sell me encyclopedias)

(25) *$\exists C([\text{few } x : Mx \land Cx][_\Phi x$ came to the office today]

        $[\iota X : \forall x(Xx \leftrightarrow (Mx \land Cx \land \Phi))] X$ tried to sell me encyclopedias)

Formula (25) does not exclude contextual restrictions on the domain of quantification, only existential quantification over such restrictions. Without the existential quantifier, the reference of the pronoun will be maximal, as required.

Apart from its stipulation in logical form, there is a well-known objection to this approach.[6] In holding that nonmaximal reference is intrinsic to the logical form of pronouns whose antecedents are increasing quantifiers, this method neglects those cases where a pronoun dependent on an increasing quantifier has maximal reference:

(26) John owns some sheep, and Harry vaccinated them. (Evans 1977)

(27) Socrates owned a dog, and it bit Socrates. (Evans 1977)

(28) Some children are allergic to cats; cats have an adverse effect on them. (Sommers 1982)

(29) Leif has a chair. It is in the kitchen. (Kadmon 1990)

Evans (1977) observes of (26) that Harry must have vaccinated all the sheep that John owns. And as Kadmon (1990) emphasizes, if (30) is the only logical form assigned to (26), then it effaces the maximality felt to distinguish (26) from (31).[7]

(30) $\exists C([\exists X : (\geq 2)(X) \wedge \forall x(Xx \leftrightarrow (Sx \wedge Cx))][_\Phi$ John owns $X]$, and $[\iota X : \forall x(Xx \leftrightarrow (Sx \wedge Cx \wedge \Phi))]$ Harry vaccinated $X)$

(31) Some sheep are such that John owns them and Harry vaccinated them.

The objection can be partly answered, at least to defend the claim that logical form formally distinguishes maximal and nonmaximal reference. The discourse-level existential quantifier can still be considered necessary for nonmaximal reference, which continues to be excluded by nonincreasing quantifiers, but its occurrence with increasing quantifiers is now only optional. Thus the desired interpretation of (26) is obtained by omitting '$\exists C$' and 'Cx' in (30). Some further explanation is required to sort out the preference for maximal reference in (26) through (29) from its nonmaximal opposite in (4).[8]

A rival approach finds nothing in the facts of nonmaximal reference that merits a distinction in logical form.[9] The pronoun is simply another definite description, and like all definite descriptions, an incompletely specified one will give the appearance of nonmaximal reference. If more than two men came to the office, the conditions under which it would be felicitous to utter (32) are, according to this view, just those of a felicitous utterance of (33).

(32) Two men came to the office. They tried to sell encyclopedias.

(33) The two men that came to the office tried to sell encyclopedias.

Proponents of this approach, where the pronoun is an absolute definite description, take pains to survey the variety of factors drawn from the context of utterance and the common knowledge of the discussants that can be called upon to secure maximal reference.[10] They all meet Evans's criterion that the user of a definite description or descriptive pronoun must be "*prepared to answer upon demand*, the question 'He? Who?' or 'It? Which?'" if the description is itself incomplete (1977, 130).

So long as we are generous with the speaker's means to complete the description, Evans's criterion correctly represents the conditions for using a definite description or descriptive pronoun. I will take exception, however, to the equation suggested by (32) and (33). A pronoun whose antecedent is an indefinite may fail to refer to all the things referred to by its translation as an absolute definite description, and yet a speaker may felicitously use it without being "prepared to answer on demand" Evans's question.

I return shortly to the substantive conditions of use. Let me first acknowledge that a virtue in the view that pronouns are absolute definite descriptions, with its turn toward pragmatics for an account of nonmaximal reference, is its wariness of more formal methods. This wariness, however, leaves it unprepared for the systematic difference between increasing and nonincreasing antecedents, illustrated above by (5) and (6). Recall that the anaphoric connection between pronoun and antecedent indicates only that the antecedent determines the pronoun's descriptive content. In effect, (5) and (6) are (34) and (35), respectively.

(34)   Two men came to the office today. The (two) men that came to the office today tried to sell encyclopedias. Perhaps there were even others who did the same.

(35)   *Few men came to the office today. The (few) men that came to the office today tried to sell encyclopedias. Perhaps there were even others who did the same.

The first two sentences of (34) and (35), as they are, do not conceal any relevant structure. This approach will exclude, for example, a discourse-level operator that binds a variable in the shared descriptive content. Now when a speaker coherently asserts (5), the pronoun, which corresponds to the definite description in (34), is used to refer not to all the men that came to the office today but to some two, whom the speaker is prepared upon demand to specify completely. But this account of the felicity of the pronoun in (5) would also lend coherence to (6). The speaker uses the definite description taking the place of the pronoun to refer not to all of the few men that came to the office today but only to some fewer few, whom the speaker is prepared upon demand to specify completely. Sentence (6) does not admit such a reading. There must be some other account of non-maximal reference in (5) or else some other explanation of its absence in (6).[11]

Absolute definite descriptions also rely on a mistaken pragmatics. Pronouns with increasing and indefinite antecedents may be used felicitously without the speaker being prepared to complete a description upon demand. Because of its importance for the analysis to follow, I first consider an example where tense serves as a pronoun to establish a cross-reference to events:[12]

(36) Once (no one knows when) John fell ill. He recovered quickly.

The discourse, with or without the parenthetical, does not imply that John fell ill only once or that he recovered quickly every time he did fall ill. Thus *the time that John fell ill* or *the time or times that John fell ill* are incomplete descriptions of the events referred to by the tense of the last sentence. Without injury to felicity, the parenthetical makes it clear that no one is prepared to give a complete description. Alongside demonstrative uses of the past tense, it can also be used, of course, as a completely general term to quantify existentially over events or times. This is how it is interpreted in the first sentence in (36).[13] There is nothing in the continuation of the discourse to suggest that the speaker has grounds to assert anything other than the existential proposition in (37):

(37) There was a time when John fell ill and he recovered quickly.

Conditions do not change if the cross-reference is made explicit:

(38) Once John fell ill. That time, he recovered quickly.

But if the tense introducing the discourse is not existential, then Evans's criterion applies:

(39) The time that John fell ill, he recovered quickly.

(40) The time that John fell ill, no one knows when it was, he recovered quickly.

If the time that John fell ill is not unique, then the speaker must be prepared to say which one he means, and if a parenthetical remark precludes this, then indeed it must be that John fell ill only once.

The system governing tense and reference to events permits existential quantification across sentences, as the above considerations would seem to show.[14] If so, and even if the discourse level is restricted to quantifiers over times or events, it undermines for all pronouns, whatever they refer to, the claim that they have the pragmatics of absolute definite descriptions. Thus, to Geach's objection that the pronoun in (41) does not carry an implication of uniqueness, the logical form implicit in Evans's reply (1980, 223, n. 7) is unavoidable:[15]

(41) Socrates kicked a dog and it bit him, and then Socrates kicked another dog and it did not bite him.

(42) $\exists e_1 \exists e_2 \exists e_3 (e_1 \leq e_2 \leq e_3 \land [\exists y : Dy] \, kick(s, y, e_1)$
$\land [\imath y : Dy \land kick(s, y, e_1)] \, bite(y, s, e_2)$
$\land [\exists z : Dz \land \neg [\imath y : Dy \land kick(s, y, e_1)] y = z] \, kick(s, z, e_3)$
$\land \, | [\exists e_4 : R(e_3, e_4)]$
$[\imath z : Dz \land \neg [\imath y : Dy \land kick(s, y, e_1)] \, y = z \land kick(s, z, e_3)]$
$bite(z, s, e_4))$

The speaker is entitled not to know whether or not Socrates has kicked dogs on other occasions and to be unprepared to answer which kickings he means, having no further particulars in mind. Since the existential quantifiers over events have scope over the discourse, what is to exclude (42), where the definite description specifies a unique referent relative to the unknown events? In that case the pronoun *it* would not refer to a unique dog, as Geach first observes, and yet the speaker need not meet Evans's condition for using either of the absolute definite descriptions: *the dog that Socrates kicked* and *the dog that Socrates kicked which bit him*. Note that if indeed speakers of (41) had to know more about the dogs, it would be a mystery what compels the pronouns to be absolute descriptions, unrelativized to the accessible events. Thus the view that the pronouns in these examples must be absolute definite descriptions is either outrageous, if it denies the existential force of the cross-sentential temporal reference in (36) and (41), or it is incoherent, if it is meant to apply only to anaphora between NPs.[16]

The problem of tense and the conclusion that existential quantifiers over events have discourse scope also compromise the explanation for the maximal reference that the pronouns in (26) through (29) are felt to bear. The explanation relies on translating the pronouns as absolute definite descriptions. When they are relativized to events, however, the contrast between (26) and (31) is lost. The same conditions warrant asserting (31) and (26) when they are given the logical form in (43):

(31) Some sheep are such that John owns them and Harry vaccinated
      them.

(26) John owns some sheep, and Harry vaccinated them.

(43) $\exists e \exists e'([\exists Y : (\geq 2)(Y) \wedge \forall y(Yy \rightarrow Sy)]$ owns(j, Y, e)
      $\wedge [\iota Y : (\geq 2)(Y) \wedge \forall y(Yy \rightarrow Sy) \wedge$ owns$(j, Y, e)]$
      vaccinate(h, Y, e'))

But perhaps compromise is deserved. It is not all that difficult for pronouns to lack maximal reference in discourses very close to (26) through
(29):

(44) In the salon there is a chair. It is a Regency or Biedermeier. There is
      another chair. It is a Biedermeier. And there are other chairs in
      various European styles.

(45) In the salon there was a chair. It was covered with silk brocade.
      There was also another chair, from a matching set, and so it too was
      covered with silk brocade. Other chairs were newer but less grand.

(46) Leif has a chair. It is a Regency or Biedermeier. He has another
      chair. It is a Biedermeier. His other chairs are in various European
      styles.

The speaker need not be prepared to say more about the chairs. Suppose
that he has no acquaintance or causal connection to the chairs and that,
in any case, he cannot tell one style of furniture from another. It is sufficient grounds for (44) that the speaker knows that there are some chairs
of which one is a Regency or Biedermeier, a second is a Biedermeier, and
the others European. Similar remarks hold of (45). In contrast, maximal
reference in Kadmon's example (29) is, to my ear, difficult to deflect, for
reasons to be discussed below. Geach's strategy, as reported in Evans
(1980), produces a coherent discourse that precludes it, but there is a
difference between (46) and the pair in (44) and (45). Except perhaps for
a very strange context that I will discuss later, (46) is felicitous only if the
speaker is enumerating chairs that he can distinguish if pressed.

    Contexts where reference is felt to be maximal are more special than the
proposed account of (26) through (29) would suggest. Defending an absolute definite description in (47),

(47) A wine glass broke last night. It had been very expensive (Heim 1982,
      28),

Kadmon argues that the speaker must be prepared to say in what way the
wine glass is unique, citing the following context: "Suppose I broke two

identical wine glasses, owned by the same person, at the same time. I am completely unable to distinguish between them. In this situation, I cannot felicitously use [(47)], not even if the number of broken glasses (one or two) is irrelevant, one being enough to make me lose my job. In contrast, I can truthfully and felicitously report my tragedy, in the same situation, using [(48)]. There doesn't have to be any unique glass associated with [(48)]" (1990, 282).[17]

(48) A wine glass that had been very expensive broke last night.

The example speaks to the pronoun in (47) only if *A wine glass broke last night* is felicitous in the situation. This is perhaps doubtful if Gricean considerations urge me to report that two glasses broke last night. Nevertheless, the force of the example granted, it still does not demonstrate that the pronoun is an absolute definite description. It warrants instead a more narrow claim. If the speaker bears a certain epistemic attitude toward the situation reported, then the pronoun is used felicitously only if the speaker is prepared to describe its referent uniquely. In the example, I report what I know by acquaintance. I saw it, I was there and participated.

Unique reference is absent if we deviate from Kadmon's context in at least one of two ways. Suppose that it was not I who broke glasses, that I was not a witness, and that I have no direct causal connection to the reported incident. I have formed the general belief that there was an expensive wine glass broken last night. Perhaps I have found a shard in my soup or noticed the empty space in the stemware cupboard and the sign in the window advertising for a new sommelier. There may have been more than one glass, but I do not know this or any further particulars about broken wine glasses. I may say (47) or (48) with equal felicity. To indicate that I lack singular grounds for my assertion, I might prefer to say (49) or (50), but this does not affect the status of the pronoun.

(49) There was a wine glass broken last night. It was very expensive.

(50) Some wine glass or other was broken last night. It was very expensive.

I am simply unaware of any property that uniquely identifies its referent. In this context, I am unable to meet the conditions for an absolute definite description.[18]

Geach's strategy contributes the other way around unique reference. Let us return to where I am acquainted with the incident and suppose that in fact three expensive wine glasses were simultaneously broken when

I dropped them. In a lugubrious frame of mind, I could go on as in (51):

(51) A wine glass broke last night. It was *very* expensive. And another
wine glass broke last night. It too was *very* expensive. And a third
one. Count 'em! Three glasses, cut crystal, Czechoslovakia. Any
more and I'll have to sell the business.

Although I suffer from the loss of each glass, I am in no better position to
individuate them. The discourse in (51) may not be felicitous as a sober
report of the incident, but it is effective for one so distraught as me—a
point to which I will return with an explanation.

For the account to follow, I essentially assume the soundness of everyone's examples for the contexts they discuss. Those put forth to show
convincing cases where pronominal reference must be maximal, e.g., (26)
through (29), do so. There are equally compelling contexts that show
pronouns behaving as if they were bound by discourse-level existential
quantifiers, e.g., (32), (36), (41), and (47).[19] The apparent conflict is to be
resolved by appeal to a theory of aspect and its interaction with the speaker's point of view.

Quite independent of the problems of anaphora, it is well known that
the conditions imposed by some aspects can be met by the speaker's perspective on the events reported. This is true of the progressive, whatever
the favored theory is.[20] Thus, planning a vacation from our home in
California, I am obliged to say (53) rather than (52).

(52) I-80 is leading to the George Washington Bridge.

(53) I-80 leads to the George Washington Bridge.

The state of I-80 is not sufficient for the progressive, nor is my perspective
on that state. If, however, we are driving east on I-80, then my perspective
licenses me to use the progressive. The situation does not change how
things are with I-80. Rather, how things are with me at the time of utterance is crucial. Pronominal reference, it turns out, is similarly dependent
on the conditions under which the reported events are thought to be
observed.

To draw out what distinguishes (44) and (45) from (29), imagine that
(44) or (45) is the narration to a film as the camera slowly sweeps around
the salon.[21]

(29) Leif has a chair. It is in the kitchen.

(44) In the salon there is a chair. It is a Regency or Biedermeier. There is
another chair. It is a Biedermeier. And there are other chairs in
various European styles.

(45) In the salon there was a chair. It was covered with silk brocade. There was also another chair, from a matching set, and so it too was covered with silk brocade. Other chairs were newer but less grand.

No one would doubt the felicity of the discourses in (44) and (45), given this perspective on the chairs. We must assume that when the narration reaches *It is a Regency or Biedermeier*, the camera's attention is directed toward a unique chair. The camera sweep is crucial to the felicitous use of the pronoun *it*, which I will take to be a singular, definite description relativized in some way to the speaker's perspective. It should be pointed out that perspective does not much change the facts. The first sentence in (44) or (45) does not assert that in the salon, there is a chair in scene 1 or in a particular corner of the salon, or that in the spatiotemporal slice of the salon bounded by scene 1, there is a chair. It asserts that there is a chair in the salon, *tout court*, and it says nothing to hinder the belief that the chair's being there coincides with the other chairs' also being there.

Perspectives classify but are not themselves mental or psychophysical states. They involve abstract objects like planar projections and angles of observation.[22] Like a phrase marker, another abstract object, their empirical bite is their role in a psychological theory. Let $\Pi(e^p, e^o)$ be the camera's perspective, characterized as a relation between abstract percepts, that is, images or scenes, and the events that they are images or scenes *of*. In this context, one understands the first sentence in a form akin to (54):[23]

(54) $\exists e(\exists e'[\exists x : Cx](\text{be}(e', x) \wedge \Pi(e, e') \wedge \text{in}(e', s)))$

As required, (54) says just that a chair was in the salon, with the further remark that its being there was observed in a certain way. This perspective on the salon provides a new route to singular reference for the pronoun. Assuming that the quantifier over perceptual events has discourse scope allows the relativized definite description in (55) (the periods mark the ends of sentences):

(55) $\exists e^p([\exists x : Cx]\exists e'(\text{INFL}(e', x) \wedge \text{be}(e') \wedge \Pi(e^p, e') \wedge \text{in}(e', s)).$
$[\imath x : Cx \wedge \exists e'(\text{INFL}(e', x) \wedge \text{be}(e') \wedge \Pi(e^p, e') \wedge \text{in}(e', s))]$
$\exists e''(\text{be}(e'') \wedge \text{Regency}(e'', x) \vee \text{Biedermeier}(e'', x))).)$

To be sure, a camera sweep that lingers on various things in a room achieves a special effect. It is not a neutral mode of presentation. With this in mind, I return to (44) and (45), about chairs, and to (47) and (49) to (51), about broken wine glasses. Compare (44) and (45) to (56) through (58), which carry a uniqueness implication:

(56) There is a chair in the salon. It is a Biedermeier.

(57) A chair is in the salon. It is a Biedermeier.

(58) The salon has a chair in it. It is a Biedermeier.

If, as in the most ordinary setting for (56) to (58), I report knowledge from my acquaintance with the salon, then, for the sake of verisimilitude, I report it from a perspective that I know fits my experience of the salon and what I have to say about it. Suppose that there were other chairs in the salon, Biedermeiers or not. Of course, there exist perspectives that present exactly one chair, a close-up of a Biedermeier, for example. But such a perspective does not coincide with my experience of the salon. A perspective Π that presents only one of the chairs takes in the salon only if the other chairs are concealed from me. With perspective Π appropriate only under these circumstances, relativizing unique reference to perspective is harmless in (56) through (58). For these are circumstances that in any case license the use of an absolute definite description, since I refer to the only chair to which I was causally connected. Thus (56) through (58) are understood to be about a unique chair.

Four premises underlie this account. First, if the speaker is delivering a report of what he knows first-hand, then it is normally assumed that the perspective adopted is causally related to the speaker's experience of the events reported. Second, it makes sense to speak of a perspective that *coincides* with or *covers* the speaker's experience. We do not doubt that a speaker may take a close-up of just one of the salon chairs, but that is just one of the perceptual events in the speaker's perspective on how things are in the salon. The third premise addresses the correspondence between perspective and the sentences of a discourse. Suppose that Π coincides with the speaker's experience, as required. We do not want a passing glance at a Biedermeier, e^p, to render (56) to (58) felicitous, despite a perspective Π that takes in the other chairs:

(59) $\exists e^p([\exists x : Cx]\exists e'(\text{INFL}(e', x) \wedge \text{be}(e') \wedge \Pi(e^p, e') \wedge \text{in}(e', s)).$
$\quad\quad [\iota x : Cx \wedge \text{INFL}(e', x) \wedge \exists e'(\text{be}(e') \wedge \Pi(e^p, e') \wedge \text{in}(e', s))]$
$\quad\quad\quad \exists e''(\text{be}(e'') \wedge \text{Biedermeier}(e'', x)).)$

The third premise is a condition on completed discourses. It is that the perspective contain perceptual events corresponding to the sentences, and it contain nothing else. That is, if (59) is a completed discourse, Π is a perspective where exactly one e^p is such that $\exists e'\Pi(e^p, e')$. (Compare (60) below, where Π contains exactly three perceptual events.) With just the one perceptual event, Π in (59) takes in no other chairs, or unique reference will fail. Fourth, determining that the speaker's experience and perspective is of the salon is itself a context-dependent decision. Earlier discourse, how we carve up reality, our expectations about what medium-sized objects or events need accounting for all enter into the thought that this discourse is about how things are in the salon. On this view, the implication of uniqueness in (56) through (58) is felt just in case the discourses are taken to be complete and to report what the speaker knows first-hand of how things are in the salon—the most pedestrian circumstances under which one might encounter (56) to (58).

For examples (44) and (45), where the perspective must sweep across the salon to realize singular reference, we need not suppose that the context for the discourse is any different, since the sequence of perceptual events do cover a speaker's experience of the salon. The only remarkable feature is the choice of that perspective. It may very well be one the speaker has lived through, but a snapshot may better fit how he organizes the facts, or at least it is the neutral perspective conventionally assumed. Departures from the neutral perspective produce special effects. Consider the breaking of three wine glasses reported in (51) with a sweeping perspective. Recall that the glasses broke simultaneously when the speaker dropped them. Nevertheless, it is narrated as three distinct perceptual events:

(60) $\exists e_1^p \exists e_2^p \exists e_3^p$

$([\exists x : Gx]\exists e(\text{INFL}(e, x) \wedge \text{break}(e) \wedge \Pi(e_1^p, e) \wedge \text{last night}(e)).$

$[\imath x : Gx \wedge \exists e(\text{INFL}(e, x) \wedge \text{break}(e) \wedge \Pi(e_1^p, e) \wedge \text{last night}(e))]$
$\quad \exists e(\text{be}(e) \wedge \text{expensive}(e, x)).$

$[\exists y : Gy]\exists e(\text{INFL}(e, y) \wedge \text{break}(e) \wedge \Pi(e_2^p, e) \wedge \text{last night}(e)).$

$[\imath y : Gy \wedge \exists e(\text{INFL}(e, y) \wedge \text{break}(e) \wedge \Pi(e_2^p, e) \wedge \text{last night}(e))]$
$\quad \exists e(\text{be}(e) \wedge \text{expensive}(e, y)).$

$[\exists z : Gz]\exists e(\text{INFL}(e, z) \wedge \text{break}(e) \wedge \Pi(e_3^p, e) \wedge \text{last night}(e)).$

$[\imath z : Gz \wedge \exists e(\text{INFL}(e, z) \wedge \text{break}(e) \wedge \Pi(e_3^p, e) \wedge \text{last night}(e))]$
$\quad \exists e(\text{be}(e) \wedge \text{expensive}(e, z)).)$

Of course, this is not an individuation achieved by normal observation. A close-up of one glass breaking is followed by a close-up of another simultaneous with the first. But the distortion afforded by this perspective accords well with the speaker's obsession with each glass. This is the perspective causally active in the speaker's psychology, as Hitchcock might attest.

We have seen a felt implication of maximal or unique reference lost in two ways. One, Geach's strategy of asserting nonunique reference (see Evans 1980), as in (44) and (45), is accommodated in a theory where discourse pronouns are definite descriptions relativized to perspective. In the other way, the discourse is not understood as the report of a witness.

The speaker is not taken to have any causal connection to the incident reported. In the example cited, the speaker forms a general belief that there was an expensive wine glass broken last night and knows of no further particulars. In that context, the truth conditions and the felicity of the following examples are the same:

(61) A wine glass that was expensive broke last night.

(62) a. There was a wine glass broken last night. It was very expensive.
     b. Some wine glass or other was broken last night. It was very expensive.

In such circumstances, there is no question of a perspective that is related to the speaker's experience of the events reported. All that is expected is that there is some perspective on true events:

(63) $\exists\Pi\exists e^{\mathrm{p}}([\exists x : Gx]\exists e'(\mathrm{break}(e') \wedge \Pi(e^{\mathrm{p}}, e') \wedge \mathrm{OF}(e', x))$.
     $[\iota x : Gx \wedge \exists e'(\mathrm{break}(e') \wedge \Pi(e^{\mathrm{p}}, e') \wedge \mathrm{OF}(e', x))]$
     $\exists e''(\mathrm{be}(e'') \wedge \mathrm{expensive}(e'', x))$.)

The existential quantifier over perspectives provides those cases where a discourse pronoun behaves like a variable bound by an existential quantifier. The pronoun is, however, a definite description. But because it is relativized to perspectives, which are existentially quantified over, the speaker need not be prepared to identify a broken glass.

In a context where (56) through (58) are infelicitous, a perspective consisting only of a close-up of a Biedermeier's being in the salon fails to cover a speaker's relevant experience. In Kadmon's (1990) original example, the implication of uniqueness is more difficult to sidestep:

(64) Leif has a chair. It is in the kitchen.

Suppose that Leif has many chairs, several of which are in the kitchen. Sentence (64) is felicitous just in case an appropriate narrow perspective can be found so that the definite description in (65) refers uniquely:

(65) $[\exists x : Cx]\exists e'(\mathrm{INFL}(e', \mathrm{l}) \wedge \mathrm{have}(e') \wedge \Pi(e^{\mathrm{p}}, e') \wedge \mathrm{OF}(e', x))$.
     $[\iota x : Cx \wedge \mathrm{INFL}(e', \mathrm{l}) \wedge \exists e'(\mathrm{have}(e') \wedge \Pi(e^{\mathrm{p}}, e') \wedge \mathrm{OF}(e', s))]$
     $\exists e''(\mathrm{INFL}(e'', x) \wedge \mathrm{be}(e'') \wedge \mathrm{in}(e'', \mathrm{k}))$.

The description refers only if some chair is the only one in events or situations of having chairs observed in e^{p}. Now, to observe that a chair is in the salon, it suffices to observe it in the salon. But what is an observation of a chair's belonging to Leif? Moreover, even if there were such a percept, unique reference in (65) demands that we be able to individuate the sight of one chair's belonging to Leif from the sight of any other chair's belonging to him. Ownerships, unlike locations, are not observed situations.[24] We might then expect it to be absurd for '$\Pi(e^p, e^o)$' to occur with *have*. The matter of perspective does not arise in Kadmon's example, and thus its implication of uniqueness is more robust:[25]

(66) $[\exists x : Cx]\exists e'(\text{INFL}(e', l) \wedge \text{have}(e') \wedge \text{OF}(e', x))$.
$\quad [\iota x : Cx \wedge \text{INFL}(e', l) \wedge \exists e'(\text{have}(e') \wedge \text{OF}(e', s))]$
$\quad\quad \exists e''(\text{INFL}(e'', x) \wedge \text{be}(e'') \wedge \text{in}(e'', k))$.

At the other end of the spectrum, there is faint implication of maximal reference in an example such as (67):

(67) Two men came to the office yesterday. They tried to sell encyclopedias.

When the salon contains other Biedermeiers, it is a special circumstance to imagine that the speaker experienced a perspective containing one chair's being in the salon but not the contemporaneous events of other chairs' being there. Ordinarily, he would have seen a room and what's in it, and so ordinarily the truth is that the Biedermeier is the only chair there. Even if the speaker is acquainted with the events reported by (67), these events may be so distant in time from others like them that a perfectly ordinary perspective on how things passed in the office allowed the speaker to encounter only the two men. It surely must be that he saw no others while brushing off these two, but the others may have appeared while he was in the washroom. Assuming that the speaker's experience was ordinary will not let us conclude that only two men came to the office yesterday. Actions, unlike states, are over in an instant. They are easy to miss.

To return to formal considerations, I will say nothing more to explicate Π or to make more precise how it classifies predicates of events. Note, however, that the existence of effects such as those just discussed is an argument that there is some appropriate Π that will allow discourse anaphora to follow schema (68):

(68) $\exists \Pi \exists e^p([\exists a : \Phi] \ldots \Pi(e^p, e^o) \ldots \underline{\quad}[\iota a : \Phi \wedge \ldots \Pi(e^p, e^o) \ldots]\underline{\quad})$

I argued above that there must be *some* discourse-level existential quantifier, if only to obtain the undeniably existential force of cross-sentential temporal reference. In this respect, I agree with the linked-variable approaches. It was also argued above that restricting the discourse level to quantifiers over events will not contain the existential force, should one wish to dispense with Π and offer (69) and (70) as instances of what is to take the place of (68):

(69) $\exists e([\exists y : \text{chair}(y)] \text{INFL}(e, \text{l}) \land \text{have}(e) \land \text{OF}(e, y)$.
   $[\imath y : \text{chair}(y) \land \text{INFL}(e, \text{l}) \land \text{have}(e) \land \text{OF}(e, y)]$
   $\exists e'(\text{INFL}(e', y) \land \text{be}(e') \land \text{in}(e', \text{k})).$)

(70) $\exists e([\exists y : \text{chair}(y)](\text{INFL}(e, y) \land \text{be}(e) \land \text{in}(e, \text{s}))$.
   $[\imath y : \text{chair}(y) \land \text{INFL}(e, y) \land \text{be}(e) \land \text{in}(e, \text{s})]$
   $\exists e'(\text{INFL}(e', y) \land \text{be}(e') \land \text{Biedermeier}(e', y)).$)

The quantification over events in (69) and (70) nullifies any implication that Leif has a unique chair or that only one chair is in the salon.[26] The existence of such implications is recovered by introducing Π, as in (68), and it is left to the theory of that relation to sort out their distribution. Note that it is not enough simply to make perspectives available. It must also be the case that the quantifier over events denoted by the verb is largely excluded from joining the other quantifiers at the discourse level. Recall that not all events are observed events (see (66) above). In the case of unobserved events $\Pi(e^p, e^o)$ does not occur with the verb, and in general we would not want to make a relation to perspectives obligatory in the logical form of every sentence. Then such variants of (69) and (70) that vacuously affix perspectival quantifiers will arise unless '$\exists e^o$' is simply denied discourse scope or allowed it only when perspective is nonvacuous:

(71) $*\exists \Pi \exists e^p \exists e^o([\exists \alpha : \Phi] \ldots V(e^o) \ldots \underline{\quad}[\imath \alpha : \Phi \land \ldots V(e^o) \ldots] \underline{\quad})$

If '$\exists e^o$' is allowed to have discourse scope, then substantive conditions on the relation '$\Pi(e^p, e^o)$' will play a larger role. Suppose that a witness hears two cars crash but did not see them. The witness is certain from the sound of the collision that there were two cars and that they were both totaled, but he cannot tell them apart. He did not, for example, hear one start to fold up before the other. It would be strange for the witness to say either (72) or (73):

(72) A car crashed, and another one did too.

(73) A car crashed. It was totaled. Another car crashed, and it was totaled too.

The definite description in (74) does not refer to a unique car if the witness's only percept was of two cars crashing.

(74) $[\imath x : Cx \land \exists e(\text{INFL}(e, x) \land \text{crash}(e) \land \Pi(e^p, e))]$

But if the quantifier over observed events had discourse scope, the undiscerning nature of the witness's percept would become irrelevant:

(75) $\exists e^p \exists e([\exists x : Cx](\text{INFL}(e, x) \land \text{crash}(e) \land \Pi(e^p, e))$.
   $\ldots [\imath x : Cx \land \exists e(\text{INFL}(e, x) \land \text{crash}(e) \land \Pi(e^p, e))] \ldots$)

The objection is answered if this witness's perception of two cars crashing is not a percept of either car crashing, since he cannot discern them. Then neither car would meet the description in (75). This is not to say that any percept is of a unique event (which, in this case, would presumably be the event that coincides with the auditory impression). It should remain possible for distinct events such as those described by (76) and (77) to be grounded in the same percept.

(76) The foreground is black.

(77) The background is white.

Rather, what needs to be said is that if a percept is not fine-grained enough to resolve some events or objects x and y on which it causally depends, then it is not a percept of them, i.e., $\neg\Pi(e^p, x)$ and $\neg\Pi(e^p, y)$. If we do not wish to bother with such conditions that allow '$\exists e^o$' to occur occasionally at the discourse level, it can be excluded altogether.

In the case of an existential NP, exclusion from the discourse-level is obvious. If discourse pronouns can be formal bound variables, any implication of uniqueness is undermined, whatever Π may say. The point is that perspectival quantifiers are the only existential quantifiers through which to avoid the uniqueness implications of an absolute definite description. No quantifiers introduced by lexical elements are allowed discourse scope. The possible exception for $\exists e^o$ occurring with a nonvacuous $\exists\Pi$ is entirely superfluous. It can therefore be maintained that QR is strictly sentential.

Since there are perspectival quantifiers at the discourse level, cross-sentential temporal reference is accommodated without any implication of uniqueness, as desired:

(78) Once upon a time John fell ill. He recovered.

(79) $\exists\Pi\exists e^p([\exists e : Pe](\text{INFL}(e,j) \wedge \text{fall-ill}(e) \wedge \Pi(e^p, e)).$
$[\imath e : Pe \wedge \text{INFL}(e,j) \wedge \text{fall-ill}(e) \wedge \Pi(e^p, e)][\exists e' : e \leq e']$
$(\text{INFL}(e',j) \wedge \text{recover}(e').)$

(80) Once upon a time John had a used car. He was broke.

(81) $\exists\Pi\exists e^p([\exists e : Pe][\exists y : Cy]$
$(\text{INFL}(e,j) \wedge \text{have}(e) \wedge t(e^p) \subseteq t(e) \wedge \text{OF}(e,y)).$
$[\imath e : Pe \wedge t(e^p) \subseteq t(e)$
$\wedge [\exists y : Cy](\text{INFL}(e,j) \wedge \text{have}(e) \wedge t(e^p) \subseteq t(e) \wedge \text{OF}(e,y))]$
$[\exists e' : e \leq e'](\text{be}(e') \wedge \text{broke}(e',j)).)$

In a case where the event referred to is not observable, as in (80), we assume that other relations of a purely temporal nature relate it to a perceptual event and thus avoid the implication that it was the only time that John had a used car. The availability of temporal relations is not surprising if the perceptual quantifiers belong to the analysis of tense and aspect. We might identify the perceptual events with Reichenbach's reference events as presented in Partee 1984b, which follows Hinrichs 1981.[27] But whereas they deploy reference events only to determine temporal relations, and they attribute to them no further content, I have added perspective.

Some formal constraint on the distribution of '$\Pi(e^p, e^o)$' must be assumed to account for the systematic difference between increasing and nonincreasing quantifiers discussed earlier:

(82) Two men came to the office today. They tried to sell encyclopedias. Perhaps there were even others who did the same.

(83) $\exists\Pi\exists e^p([\exists X : 2(X) \land \forall x(Xx \to Mx)]$
$\quad \exists e(\text{INFL}(e, X) \land \text{come}(e) \land \Pi(e^p, e) \land \text{to}(e, o) \land \text{today}(e)).$
$\quad [\iota X : (_\Phi 2(X) \land \forall x(Xx \to Mx)$
$\quad\quad \land \exists e(\text{INFL}(e, X) \land \text{come}(e) \land \Pi(e^p, e) \land \text{to}(e, o)$
$\quad\quad \land \text{today}(e))_\Phi)]\exists e' \dots.$
$\quad\quad \text{Perhaps } [\exists Y : \exists y Yy \land \forall y(Yy \to My \land \neg[\iota X : \Phi]Xy)]$
$\quad\quad \exists e(\text{INFL}(e, X) \land \text{come}(e) \land \text{to}(e, o) \land \text{today}(e)) \land \dots))^{28}$

(84) *Few men came to the office today. They tried to sell encyclopedias. Perhaps there were even others who did the same.

(85) *$\exists\Pi\exists e^p([\text{few } x : Mx]$
$\quad \exists e(\text{INFL}(e, x) \land \text{come}(e) \land \Pi(e^p, e) \land \text{to}(e, o) \land \text{today}(e))\dots)$

The formal constraint is made more palatable if we accept the following desideratum.

CONSTRAINT ON PERSPECTIVE   Perspective, whatever its use in securing reference, should not intrude on the description of how things are in the world. That is, a perspective-laden assertion should always yield a perspective-free truth.

With this in mind, note that the following conditionals distinguish quantifiers:[29]

(86) $\exists\Pi\exists e^p[\exists x : Nx \land \exists e(\dots V_i e \land \Pi(e^p, e)\dots)]\exists e(\dots V_j e \dots)$
$\quad \to [\exists x : Nx \land \exists e(\dots V_i e \dots)]\exists e(\dots V_j e \dots)$

(87) $\exists\Pi\exists e^p[\exists x : Nx \land \exists e(\dots V_i e \dots)]\exists e(\dots V_j e \land \Pi(e^p, e)\dots)$
$\quad \to [\exists x : Nx \land \exists e(\dots V_i e \dots)]\exists e(\dots V_j e \dots)$

(88) $*\exists\Pi\exists e^{P}[\forall x : Nx \wedge \exists e(\ldots V_i e \wedge \Pi(e^{P}, e)\ldots)]\exists e(\ldots V_j e \ldots)$
  $\rightarrow [\forall x : Nx \wedge \exists e(\ldots V_i e \ldots)]\exists e(\ldots V_j e \ldots)$

(89) $\exists\Pi\exists e^{P}[\forall x : Nx \wedge \exists e(\ldots V_i e \ldots)]\exists e(\ldots V_j e \wedge \Pi(e^{P}, e)\ldots)$
  $\rightarrow [\forall x : Nx \wedge \exists e(\ldots V_i e \ldots)]\exists e(\ldots V_j e \ldots)$

(90) $*\exists\Pi\exists e^{P}[\text{few } x : Nx \wedge \exists e(\ldots V_i e \wedge \Pi(e^{P}, e)\ldots)]\exists e(\ldots V_j e \ldots)$
  $\rightarrow [\text{few } x : Nx \wedge \exists e(\ldots V_i e \ldots)]\exists e(\ldots V_j e \ldots)$

(91) $*\exists\Pi\exists e^{P}[\text{few } x : Nx \wedge \exists e(\ldots V_i e \ldots)]\exists e(\ldots V_j e \wedge \Pi(e^{P}, e)\ldots)$
  $\rightarrow [\text{few } x : Nx \wedge \exists e(\ldots V_i e \ldots)]\exists e(\ldots V_j e \ldots)$

The existential quantifier in (86) and (87) yields a perspective-free truth, whether or not perspective has been invoked in either the relative clause or in the matrix—a consequence of the fact that the existential quantifier is increasing with respect to both terms. In contrast, the universal quantifier in (88), which is not increasing with respect to the restricting term, does not yield a perspective-free truth if perspective restricts the domain. The decreasing quantifier *few*, decreasing in both its terms, excludes any perspective-laden assertion if the constraint on perspective is accepted.

The formal statement that realizes this constraint cannot simply exclude Π from those positions where Π would derail a perspective-free truth according to the above patterns. The reason is that Π can occur in the restriction to a decreasing quantifier, for example, if it is introduced there by an anaphoric relation:

(92) Twenty men came to the office today. Few could sell encyclopedias.

The discourse in (92) asserts that few of the twenty could sell encyclopedias. Other men that came to the office today may have been more successful:

(93) $\exists\Pi\exists e^{P}([\exists X : 20(X) \wedge \forall x(Xx \rightarrow Mx)]\exists e(\ldots \text{came}(e) \wedge \Pi(e^{P}, e)\ldots).$
  $[\text{few } x : [\iota X : 20(X) \wedge \forall x(Xx \rightarrow Mx) \wedge \exists e(\ldots \text{came}(e)$
  $\wedge \Pi(e^{P}, e)\ldots)] Xx].\ldots)$

The constraint can, however, stipulate that the relevant domains are opaque to binding, that is, to c-commanding local antecedents:

(94) $*\exists\Pi\exists e^{P}([\text{few} : \ldots \Pi \ldots].\ldots)$

(95) $\exists\Pi\exists e^{P}(\ldots \Pi \ldots. \quad [\text{few} : \ldots \Pi \ldots].\ldots)$

Under this notion of opacity, a determiner renders its restriction or its matrix opaque to perspective just in case the determiner is nonincreasing with respect to that term. This at least gives the extension of the constraint on perspective. The additional cases that linking admits are exactly those where the presence of an antecedent clause in the discourse allows one to grasp a perspective-free truth. Corresponding to (92), the perspective-free truth is that twenty men are such that they came to the office today and few of them could sell encyclopedias.

Note that Heim's (1982) observations that she attributes to a familiarity condition on definite descriptions fall under the constraint on perspective as a special case. The felicity conditions for the use of the definite description in (96) are not those of the indefinite in (97), because the constraint on perspective excludes (98).

(96) *The man that telephoned earlier came to the office today.

(97)   A man that telephoned earlier came to the office today.

(98) *$\exists\Pi\exists e^P([\iota x : \text{man}(x) \wedge \exists e(\ldots\text{telephone}(e) \wedge \Pi(e^P, e)\ldots)]\ldots)^{30}$

It allows (99) and (100), however.

(99)   A man telephone earlier. {He/The man} came to the office today.

(100) $\exists\Pi\exists e^P(\ldots\text{telephone}(e) \wedge \Pi(e^P, e)\ldots.$
          $[\iota x : \text{man}(x) \wedge \exists e(\ldots\text{telephone}(e) \wedge \Pi(e^P, e)\ldots)]\ldots.)$

A residual problem concerns antecedents that are increasing in their first term, the existential (and cardinal) quantifiers. Consider a mathematical discourse that can reasonably be asserted without an appeal to perspective:

(101) But there does exist a number that is F. So the unique F is G.

The definite description in (101) is *not* anaphoric to the indefinite. It stands alone as a fully general, complete definite description. As such, (102) is anomalous:

(102) *But there does exist a number that is F. So the unique F is G.
          Perhaps there is also another number that is F and G.

Unrestricted by perspective, (101) would mean something like (103):

(103) $\exists\Pi\exists e^P([\exists x : Nx]\exists e F(x, e). [\iota x : Nx \wedge \exists e F(x, e)]\exists e G(x, e).)$

Now if an anaphoric element replaces the definite description, as in (104) and (105), its descriptive content should be identical to the one in (103), and the content of the entire discourse should be unchanged.

(104) But there does exist a number that is F. So that number is G.

(105) But there does exist a number that is F. So it is G.

It is however impossible to find readings of (106) and (107) that are contradictory:

(106) But there does exist a number that is F. So that number is G. Perhaps there is also another number that is F and G.

(107) But there does exist a number that is F. So it is G. Perhaps there is also another number that is F and G.

This would suggest that the indefinite *must* be perspective-dependent in some way. That dependence is reproduced in the anaphor, which forcibly copies the entire content of its antecedent:

(108) $\exists\Pi\exists e^{p}([\exists x : \exists e(N(x, e) \wedge \Pi(e^{p}, e))]\exists e\ F(x, e).$
$[\iota x : \exists e(N(x, e) \wedge \Pi(e^{p}, e)) \wedge \exists e\ F(x, e)]\exists e\ G(x, e))$

A *non*anaphoric definite description, whose content is not copied, is free to omit perspective:[31]

(109) $\exists\Pi\exists e^{p}([\exists x : \exists e(N(x, e) \wedge \Pi(e^{p}, e))]\exists e\ F(x, e).$
$[\iota x : \exists e N(x, e) \wedge \exists e\ F(x, e)]\exists e\ G(x, e))$

2   Exact Description

Anaphors that refer cumulatively acquire nonmaximal reference by falling within the scope of a discourse-level quantifier over perspectives, just like unbound anaphora in general:

(8) a. Every farmer bought a donkey, and they were led out of the corral together.

  b. Every farmer bought a donkey, and the donkeys were led out of the corral together.

(110) $\exists\Pi\exists e^{p}([\text{every } x : Fx][\hat{E} : \text{INFL}[e, x]]$
   $\exists E(\text{buy}[e] \wedge \Pi(e^{p}, e) \wedge [\exists Y : 1(Y) \wedge \forall y(Yy \rightarrow Dy)]\ \text{OF}[e, Y])$
  $\wedge\ [\hat{E} : \Phi]\exists E'([\iota Y : \forall y(Yy \rightarrow Dy) \wedge \text{OF}[e, Y]]$
   were-led-out-of-the-corral-together$[e'])$

(11) Every student was shown two movies in ten hours.

(111) $\exists\Pi\exists e^{p}([\text{every } x : Sx][\hat{E} : \text{INFL}[e, x]]$
   $\exists E(\text{show}[e] \wedge \Pi(e^{p}, e)$
   $\wedge\ [\exists Y : 2(Y) \wedge \forall y(Yy \rightarrow My)]\ \text{OF}[e, Y])$
  $\wedge\ [\hat{E} : \Phi][\exists Z : 10(Z) \wedge \forall z(Zz \rightarrow Hz)]\ \text{in}(e, z))$

The pronoun in (8) refers to just those donkeys that farmers bought in events perceived in e^{p}. In the logical form in (110), the description of events '$[\hat{E} : \Phi]$' contains an occurrence of '$\Pi(e^p, e)$', along with the rest of the antecedent clause.[32] Any percept that misses some of the donkeys that some farmers bought will allow the pronoun to refer, nonmaximally, to fewer donkeys than were bought by farmers.

In the introductory remarks to this chapter, it was observed that when the antecedent is not within the scope of any nonincreasing quantifiers, the unbound anaphor is not merely nonmaximal in its reference; it also meets the further condition of exact description.

(22) Every student was shown 2 movies, and then 4 reviewers panned them in a single issue of *The New Yorker*.

(23) Every student was shown 2 movies, and then 6 reviewers panned them in a single issue of *The New Yorker*.

Sentence (23) was found to be false in a context where the antecedent events corresponding to reviews by 6 reviewers would have to include some student's being shown more than 2 movies. In contrast, (22) is true, since there were some events which, for each student, include his being shown only 2 movies, and the movies in these events were panned by 4 reviewers.

(16)

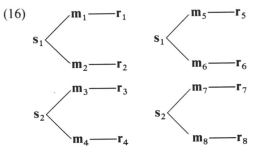

The logical form in (112), although it includes perspective, does not provide an exact description.

(112) $\exists\Pi\exists e^p([\text{every } x : Sx][\hat{E} : \text{INFL}[e, x]]$
$\exists E(\text{show}[e] \wedge \Pi(e^p, e)$
$\wedge [\exists Y : 2(Y) \wedge \forall y(Yy \to My)] \text{ OF}[e, Y]) \ldots)$

Surely, if a student is shown, say, 6 movies, there are percepts of his being shown 3, 4, 5, or 6 of them. Given a larger percept, the cross-reference to events will refer to all the events it surveys where a student is shown 2 movies. Sentence (23) comes out true if it is represented by (112). The percept of all that happens to s_1 in (16) and half of what happens to s_2 is of events where every student is shown 2 movies and 6 reviewers panned the movies in those events.

The distribution of exact description is independent of nonmaximal reference. It applies to any antecedent not within the scope of a non-increasing quantifier. Recall from the preceding section that an implication of maximal reference was strongest felt in the class of examples due to Kadmon in (113):

(113) a. Leif has a chair. It is in the kitchen.
      b. Leif has some chairs. They are in the kitchen.
      c. Leif has two chairs. They are in the kitchen.

These are not easily relativized to perspective, or at least not to one that individuates one chair's belonging to Leif from another's belonging to him.[33] The implication of (113c) is that Leif has only two chairs and they are all in the kitchen. A similar implication is felt with cumulative reference in (114):

(114) a. Every roommate has a chair. They are in the kitchen all together.
      b. Every roommate has some chairs. They are all in the kitchen all together.
      c. Every roommate has two chairs. They are in the kitchen all together.

The sentences in (114c) suggest that each roommate has only two chairs and that they and the other roommates' chairs are together in the kitchen. Note that the simple account treating the pronoun in (113) as an absolute definite description obtains maximal reference there, but this is no help in (114), which we might wish to view as the same phenomenon. For (113c), it suffices that the discourse is not relativized to perspective and that the pronoun is translated as *the two chairs that Leif has*, which includes the cardinal adjective in the description. The discourse then implies that Leif has only two chairs, although the antecedent sentence alone would be true if he had more. In (114), the absence of perspective is also sufficient to make *they* have maximal reference, which implies that all chairs that roommates have are in the kitchen. But in (114c) there is no obvious way to derive the implication that every roommate has only two chairs, at least not by translating the pronoun as a definite description containing a cardinal adjective.

As in earlier examples, exact description does not apply when the antecedent is within the scope of a nonincreasing quantifier:

(115) Few roommates have a chair, but they are in the kitchen all together.

(116) Few roommates have two chairs, but they are in the kitchen all
together.

Any roommates who have any chairs are potential counterexamples to
(115), and, however many chairs they have, they must all be in the kitchen
for the sentence to be true.[34]

The interaction of perspective with such apparent nonobservables as an
event of a boy giving girls no toys raises some further questions about
exact description and nonmaximal reference, both of which obtain in
(117) and (118):

(117) a. Every boy gave a girl none of his toys. They abandoned the
boors and shared their own toys among themselves.

b. Every boy gave a girl none of his toys. The girls abandoned the
boors and shared their own toys among themselves.

(118) a. Every boy gave two girls none of his toys. They abandoned the
boors and shared their own toys among themselves.

b. Every boy gave two girls none of his toys. The girls abandoned
the boors and shared their own toys among themselves.

The pronoun's reference in (118a) and the reference of the definite description in (118b) include just two girls for each boy. If these girls abandoned the boors and shared their toys, then the discourse allows that
there are other girls whom boys gave no toys to but who did not abandon
them. The reference is also not maximal. In contrast, the pronoun in
(119a) and the description in (119b) refer to all the girls that some boy or
another gave none of the toys to:

(119) a. Few boys gave a girl none of the toys, and in any case, they
abandoned the boors and shared their own toys among
themselves.

b. Few boys gave a girl none of the toys, and in any case, the girls
abandoned the boors and shared their own toys among
themselves.

(120) a. Few boys gave two girls none of the toys, and in any case,
they abandoned the boors and shared their own toys among
themselves.

b. Few boys gave two girls none of the toys, and in any case, the
girls abandoned the boors and shared their own toys among
themselves.

I consider two accounts of exact description, neither of which extends
unsupplemented to examples about negative events, such as (117) through

(120). I make some suggestions but ultimately leave the problem unsolved. The first account of exact description revises the definition of rendering. It introduces separate clauses for increasing and nonincreasing quantifiers, in effect stipulating the difference between environments within the scope of a nonincreasing quantifier and those not within. The second account attempts with limited success to characterize the difference syntactically. This account appears preferable because it promises a definition of rendering that treats the first-order quantifiers uniformly.

2.1 The first account of exact description

The definition of *rendering* in chapter 9, section 3, took nonincreasing quantifiers to be the defining instance for all first-order quantifiers. As we have seen, all events that meet the description in the scope of a nonincreasing quantifier are among the rendering events. So the clause in (121) states that the rendering events include any events that render 'I' for anything that is Φ:

(121) $\text{render}(E, \ulcorner[Qv : \Phi] \Psi\urcorner, \Sigma)$
$\leftrightarrow \Sigma$ satisfy $\ulcorner[Qv : \Phi] \Psi\urcorner$
$\wedge \forall e(Ee \leftrightarrow$
$[\exists x : \exists \Sigma_0(\Sigma_0 \approx_v \Sigma \wedge \forall z(\Sigma_0(\langle v, z \rangle) \leftrightarrow z = x) \wedge \Sigma_0 \text{ satisfy } \Phi]$
$[\exists \Sigma_0 : \Sigma_0 \approx_v \Sigma \wedge \forall z(\Sigma_0(\langle v, z \rangle) \leftrightarrow z = x) \wedge \Sigma_0 \text{ satisfy } \Psi]$
$\exists E(Ee \wedge \text{render}(E, \Psi, \Sigma_0)))$

I now restrict this definition to nonincreasing quantifiers. As in chapter 9, n. 1, a quantifier is classified as *increasing* just in case (122) is true for all Φ and Ψ:

(122) $[Qv : \Phi] \Psi \leftrightarrow [\exists X : [Qv : \Phi] Xv][\forall v : Xv] \Psi$

Otherwise, a quantifier is nonincreasing. Here, then, is the restricted definition:

(123) $\text{render}(E, \ulcorner[Q^{ni}v : \Phi] \Psi\urcorner, \Sigma)$
$\leftrightarrow \Sigma$ satisfy $\ulcorner[Q^{ni}v : \Phi] \Psi\urcorner$
$\wedge \forall e(Ee \leftrightarrow$
$[\exists x : \exists \Sigma_0(\Sigma_0 \approx_v \Sigma \wedge \forall z(\Sigma_0(\langle v, z \rangle) \leftrightarrow z = x) \wedge \Sigma_0 \text{ satisfy } \Phi]$
$[\exists \Sigma_0 : \Sigma_0 \approx_v \Sigma \wedge \forall z(\Sigma_0(\langle v, z \rangle) \leftrightarrow z = x) \wedge \Sigma_0 \text{ satisfy } \Psi]$
$\exists E(Ee \wedge \text{render}(E, \Psi, \Sigma_0)))$

Recall that the clause for second-order descriptions in (124) states that the events rendering a formula headed by a second-order description render the formula in the scope of the description for some things it describes:

(124) render$(E, \ulcorner[\exists V : \Phi]\ \Psi\urcorner, \Sigma)$

$\leftrightarrow [\exists X : \exists\Sigma_0\ (\Sigma_0 \approx_V \Sigma \wedge \forall x(\Sigma_0(\langle V, x\rangle) \leftrightarrow Xx) \wedge \Sigma_0\ \text{satisfy}\ \Phi)]$

$[\exists\Sigma_0 : \Sigma_0 \approx_V \Sigma \wedge \forall x(\Sigma_0(\langle V, x\rangle) \leftrightarrow Xx) \wedge \Sigma_0\ \text{satisfy}\ \Psi]$

render(E, Ψ, Σ_0)

The rendering events do not collect events from everything that fits the description. In general, distinct events E_i and E_j will render a formula headed by a second-order description. The choice of two movies determines what events render *two movies were shown*. But if a second-order description heads a formula within the scope of a nonincreasing quantifier, '$[\exists V : \Phi]\ \Psi$', (123) will have the effect of collecting events from every V that is Φ and Ψ. Thus the events rendering *few students were shown two movies* includes any events of students being shown two movies.

The new definition of *rendering* for first-order, increasing quantifiers makes them more like second-order descriptions. In general, there will be distinct events E_i and E_j that render a formula headed by an increasing quantifier. The definition states that the rendering events collect a single plurality of rendering events for each relevant individual:

(125) render$(E, \ulcorner[Q^i v : \Phi]\ \Psi\urcorner, \Sigma) \leftrightarrow$

$[\exists X :$

$\quad [Q^i x : \exists\Sigma_0(\Sigma_0 \approx_v \Sigma \wedge \forall z(\Sigma_0(\langle v, z\rangle) \leftrightarrow z = x)$

$\quad\quad \wedge \Sigma_0\ \text{satisfy}\ \Phi)]Xx$

$\quad \wedge \forall x\exists\Sigma_0(Xx \rightarrow (\Sigma_0 \approx_v \Sigma \wedge \forall z(\Sigma_0(\langle v, z\rangle) \leftrightarrow z = x)$

$\quad\quad \wedge \Sigma_0\ \text{satisfy}\ \Phi))]$

$([\forall e : Ee][\exists x : Xx]\exists E_0$

$\quad [\exists\Sigma_0 : \Sigma_0 \approx_v \Sigma \wedge \forall z(\Sigma_0(\langle v, z\rangle) \leftrightarrow z = x) \wedge \Sigma_0\ \text{satisfy}\ \Psi]$

$\quad (\text{render}(E_0, \Psi, \Sigma_0) \wedge E_0 e)$

$\wedge [\forall x : Xx]\exists E_0$

$\quad [\exists\Sigma_0 : \Sigma_0 \approx_v \Sigma \wedge \forall z(\Sigma_0(\langle v, z\rangle) \leftrightarrow z = x) \wedge \Sigma_0\ \text{satisfy}\ \Psi]$

$\quad (\text{render}(E_0, \Psi, \Sigma_0) \wedge \forall e(E_0 e \rightarrow Ee)$

$\quad\quad \wedge \forall e \forall E_1[\forall\Sigma_1 : \Sigma_1 \approx_v \Sigma \wedge \forall z(\Sigma_1(\langle v, z\rangle) \leftrightarrow z = x)$

$\quad\quad\quad \wedge \Sigma_1\ \text{satisfy}\ \Psi]$

$\quad\quad ((\text{render}(E_1, \Psi, \Sigma_1) \wedge E_1 e \wedge Ee) \rightarrow E_0 e)))$

In evaluating *every student was shown two movies*, one chooses for each student one pair of movies, and only the events of his being shown these two movies are added to those rendering the entire sentence. Of course, if some students have each been shown more than two movies, there will be distinct events E_i and E_j rendering the sentence. Choosing a different two movies for a student changes the rendering events.

Exact description now follows from the interaction of (125) with the operator that fixes the cross-reference to events rendered by an antecedent clause. Recall that this operator is a definite description.

(126) Σ satisfy $\ulcorner[\hat{E}_i : \Phi] \Psi\urcorner$

$\qquad \leftrightarrow [\imath E : \text{render}(E, \Phi, \Sigma)][\exists \Sigma_0 : \Sigma_0 \approx_{\mathfrak{C}_i} \Sigma \wedge \Sigma_0(\mathfrak{C}_i) \simeq E]$
$\qquad \Sigma_0$ satisfy Ψ

(127) $[\imath E : \Phi] \Psi \leftrightarrow_{\text{df}}$
$\qquad [\exists E : \Phi \wedge \forall e(\exists E(Ee \wedge \Phi) \rightarrow \forall e'(e'\mathbf{O}e \rightarrow \exists e''(e'\mathbf{O}e'' \wedge Ee'')))] \Psi$

The events that render *every student was shown two movies* are some events E in which each student is shown just two movies, and they overlap all such pluralities of events. This can be only if every student was shown exactly two movies; that is, if the antecedent clause is an exact description. Of course, if the antecedent clause and the cross-reference to the rendering events are restricted by perspective, then the description is exact relative to that perspective, as required.

Consider now the apparent cross-reference to negative events in (117) and (118). Nonmaximal reference suggests that the discourse should be relativized to some perspective that contains a percept of some relevant events.

(117) a. Every boy gave a girl none of his toys. They abandoned the boors and shared their own toys among themselves.

  b. Every boy gave a girl none of his toys. The girls abandoned the boors and shared their own toys among themselves.

(118) a. Every boy gave two girls none of his toys. They abandoned the boors and shared their own toys among themselves.

  b. Every boy gave two girls none of his toys. The girls abandoned the boors and shared their own toys among themselves.

The logical form in (128) is, however, illicit, since the assertion does not yield a perspective-free truth, which contradicts the constraint on perspective of section 1.[35] There is always a perspective from which it appears that the boys gave the girls no toys.

(128) $\exists \Pi \exists e^{\text{p}}[\hat{E}' : \Pi(e^{\text{p}}, e')]$
$\qquad ([\text{every } x : \mathbf{B}x][\hat{E}' : \text{INFL}[e', x]][\exists Y : 2(Y) \wedge \forall y(Yy \rightarrow Gy)][\forall y : Yy]$
$\qquad [\hat{E}' : \text{TO}[e', y]][\text{no } z : \mathbf{T}z][\hat{E}' : \text{OF}[e', z]]\exists E' \text{ give}[e'].$
$\qquad [\hat{E}' : \Phi]\ldots[\imath Y : \forall y(Yy \rightarrow Gy) \wedge \text{TO}[e', Y]]\ldots)$

Furthermore, within (128) cross-reference to the events that render the antecedent, '$[\hat{E} : \Phi[e']]$', would refer to whatever events there are of boys' giving girls their toys. There are none, and therefore there are no girls to refer to as the recipients in such events—a problem discussed earlier in chapter 9, section 4. Recall from the discussion of negative events in chapter 6, section 1.1, and in chapter 9, section 4, that it is coherent to say things like (129).

(129) Once, every boy gave two girls none of his toys.

We must assume that there is a substantive relation, '$C[e] \wedge \Theta[e, e']$', that makes it significant that nothing much happens in the events E' related to the events or occasions that the adverb quantifies over:

(130) $[\exists E : 1(E) \wedge C[e]][\hat{E}' : \Theta[e, e']][\text{every } x : Bx]$
$\quad [\hat{E}' : \text{INFL}[e', x]][\exists Y : 2(Y) \wedge \forall y(Yy \rightarrow Gy)][\forall y : Yy]$
$\quad [\hat{E} : \text{TO}[e', y]][\text{no } z : Tz][\hat{E} : \text{OF}[e', z]]\exists E' \text{ give}[e']$

The events that the adverb quantifies over are solid enough ground for perspective. Formula (131) entails the perspective-free (130):

(131) $\exists \Pi \exists e^{p}[\hat{E} : \Pi(e^{p}, e)]$
$\quad ([\exists E : 1(E) \wedge C[e] \wedge \Pi(e^{p}, e)][\hat{E}' : \Theta[e, e']][\text{every } x : Bx]$
$\quad [\hat{E}' : \text{INFL}[e', x]][\exists Y : 2(Y) \wedge \forall y(Yy \rightarrow Gy)][\forall y : Yy]$
$\quad [\hat{E} : \text{TO}[e', y]][\text{no } z : Tz][\hat{E} : \text{OF}[e', z]]\exists E' \text{ give}[e'])$

Cross-reference is now to occasions on which every boy gives two girls none of his toys. The definite description '$[\hat{E} : \Phi[e]]$' in (132) makes it *the* such occasions, but it is relativized to perspective and so does not necessarily include all such occasions.

(132) $\exists \Pi \exists e^{p}[\hat{E} : \Pi(e^{p}, e)]$
$\quad ([\exists E : 1(E) \wedge C[e] \wedge \Pi(e^{p}, e)][\hat{E}' : \Theta[e, e']][\text{every } x : Bx]$
$\quad [\hat{E}' : \text{INFL}[e', x]][\exists Y : 2(Y) \wedge \forall y(Yy \rightarrow Gy)][\forall y : Yy]$
$\quad [\hat{E} : \text{TO}[e', y]][\text{no } z : Tz][\hat{E} : \text{OF}[e', z]]\exists E' \text{ give}[e'].$
$\quad [\hat{E} : \Phi[e]] \ldots [\imath Y : \forall y(Yy \rightarrow Gy) \wedge \text{TO}[e', Y]] \ldots)$

The pronoun refers to the girls that the boys gave none of their toys to on the perceived occasions. Thus reference is nonmaximal. But exact description is likely lost. Recall how the definite-description operator obtains it. First, rendering is not an increasing relation to events. Some events that render *show two movies* and some other events that render *show two movies* together do not render *show two movies*, unless the movies are the same. The reference to *the* events that render *show two movies* is therefore proper only if there are just two movies. I can claim that rendering is not an increasing relation, because I think I understand something about the θ-roles and event concepts that make up the descriptions of the rendering events. I do not understand so much about '$C[e] \wedge \Theta[e, e']$', however. Suppose that on some occasion every boy gave four girls none of his toys. We may allow that there are distinct (sub)occasions on which every boy gave two girls none of his toys. But a definite description referring to the relevant events will simply refer to the largest occasion, including all four girls for every boy, unless it can be claimed that this occasion at which every boy gives two girls none of his toys is nevertheless not an occasion *of* every boy's giving two girls none of his toys. Below I return to this problem with some suggestions.

2.2   The second account of exact description

The account of exact description that would spare us the new semantic clauses dividing first-order quantifiers into increasing and nonincreasing was suggested in chapter 7, section 2.3, the first time exact description was encountered. In the context in (135), where four video games teach four quarterbacks new plays, there is an event verifying (133).

(133)   Two video games taught exactly three quarterbacks each a new play.

(134)   Four video games taught exactly three quarterbacks each a new play.

(135)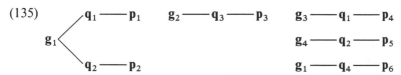

This event, which corresponds to the first two blocks, is an event of two video games' teaching, and it is a teaching of exactly three quarterbacks each a new play. In contrast, it was observed that (134) is false in the context, since the teaching by any four video games is not an event of exactly three quarterbacks each being taught a new play. Rather, there is an event of teaching by four video games that could be described as an event of exactly three quarterbacks each being taught one or more new plays. In the logical form for (134) in (136), the cross-referring expression 'that$_i$' must refer to events that are described exactly as *exactly three quarterbacks each being taught a new play*.

(136) $\exists E([\exists X : 4(X) \wedge \forall x(Xx \rightarrow Gx)] \text{INFL}[\text{that}_i, X]$
         $\wedge [_i [3! y : Q y][\hat{E} : \text{TO}[e, y]]$
         $(\text{teach}[e] \wedge [\exists Z : 1(Z) \wedge \forall z(Zz \rightarrow Pz)] \text{OF}[e, Z])])$

Exact description in this case led to the conclusion that a clause contains no more than one occurrence of an existential event quantifier. The logical forms in (136) and (137) differ only in the second occurrence of the existential event quantifier that follows the first-order quantifier in (137).

(137) $*\exists E([\exists X : 4(X) \wedge \forall x(Xx \rightarrow Gx)]\ \text{INFL}[\text{that}_i, X]$
$\wedge\ [_i\ [3!\ y : Q y][\hat{E} : \text{TO}[e, y]]$
$\exists E\ (\text{teach}[e] \wedge [\exists Z : 1(Z) \wedge \forall z(Zz \rightarrow Pz)]\ \text{OF}[e, Z])])$

Formula (137), but not (136), is true in the context, contrary to the interpretation of (134). Consider any event of four video games' teaching. If it is to verify (136), then for each of the three quarterbacks, all of what he did in that event is an event of being taught just one play. There is no such event, and (136) turns out false, as required. That event of teaching by four video games does, however, verify (137), since it merely requires that for each of the three quarterbacks, the event has a subpart, '$\exists E$', that is an event of his being taught one play. Formula (137) allows the verifying event to contain a quarterback's being taught more than one play.

Once some events have been introduced, as they are by the matrix event quantifier in (136), the remainder of the sentence is committed to an exact description. The description in the scope of a first-order quantifier must describe, for any participant, all of what he did. Another existential quantifier over events spoils it. Exact description obtains whenever the antecedent clause does not contain '$\exists E$'. One is tempted by this example to treat the distribution of exact description with a syntactic condition on the distribution of '$\exists E$'. Certainly one could extend the contexts excluding '$\exists E$' so that it is also excluded if the domain of events is restricted by perspective. This would accommodate (23).

(23) Every student was shown 2 movies, and then 6 reviewers panned them in a single issue of *The New Yorker*.

Exact description obtains in (138), where the antecedent clause contains no occurrence of '$\exists E$':

(138) $\exists\Pi\exists e^p[\hat{E} : \Pi(e^p, e)]([\text{every } x : Sx][\hat{E} : \text{INFL}[e, x]]$
$(\text{show}[e] \wedge [\exists Y : 2(Y) \wedge \forall y(Yy \rightarrow My)]\ \text{OF}[e, Y])\ldots)$

As required, (138) entails that every student within the object of the given percept is shown two movies. Sentence (23), if represented by (138), is false in the context given in (16).

(16)

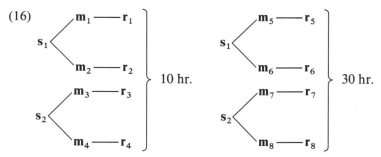

The movies in the events described by the first conjunct are reviewed by 4 reviewers.

Once we take up, in the mind's eye, the events that fall under a certain percept, we appear to be constrained to give an exact description of those events, which would be undermined, however, if an occurrence of '$\exists E$' intervened in (138). If, as suggested at the end of section 1, an assertion that can be perspective-dependent must be, then (139) will take the place of (136), and crucially (138) is the only logical form for (23).

(139) $\exists \Pi \exists e^{P}[\hat{E} : \Pi(e^{P}, e)]([\exists X : 4(X) \wedge \forall x(Xx \rightarrow Gx)]$ INFL[that$_i$, X]
$\wedge [_i [3! y : Q y][\hat{E} : \text{TO}[e, y]]$
$(\text{teach}[e] \wedge [\exists Z : 1(Z) \wedge \forall z(Zz \rightarrow Pz)]$ OF$[e, Z])])$

Exact description, in (23) in particular, is then a consequence of the obligatory perspective and the constraint that a clause contain no more than one existential event quantifier. If only it were also the case that exact description entailed perspective, we could explain why exact description does not apply within the scope of nonincreasing quantifiers. It would require perspective, but perspective does not occur with nonincreasing quantifiers when a perspective-free truth cannot be grasped. We have seen in (114), however, that exact description obtains even where perspective is presumably absent and reference is maximal.

(114) a. Every roommate has a chair. They are in the kitchen all together.
b. Every roommate has some chairs. They are in the kitchen all together.
c. Every roommate has two chairs. They are in the kitchen all together.

Exact description in (114) can be represented, as in (140a), simply by omitting '$\exists E$' from the antecedent clause (compare (140b)). However, it cannot be said of (140) that a perspectival quantifier has preempted the place for an existential event quantifier, which should remain an option.

(140) a.　[every x : Rx][$\hat{E}$: INFL[e, x]]
　　　　　　　(have[e] $\land$ [$\exists Y$: 2(Y) $\land$ $\forall y(Yy \rightarrow Cy$)] OF[$e, Y$]).
　　　　　　　[$\hat{E}$: Φ]($\ldots$[ιY : $\forall y(Yy \rightarrow Cy$) $\land$ OF[e, Y]]$\ldots$).

　　　　b.　*[every x : Rx][$\hat{E}$: INFL[e, x]]
　　　　　　　$\exists E$(have[e] $\land$ [$\exists Y$: 2(Y) $\land$ $\forall y(Yy \rightarrow Cy$)] OF[$e, Y$]).
　　　　　　　[$\hat{E}$: Φ]($\ldots$[ιY : $\forall y(Yy \rightarrow Cy$) $\land$ OF[e, Y]]$\ldots$).

Recall that perspective has been presumed to be absent from (114), so the reference of the pronoun will be maximal. Such a presumption seems fair enough whenever the events described are not readily observable. What, after all, is a percept of a roommate having a chair? And even if there were such a percept, we can still be confident that the reference of the pronoun includes all the chairs belonging to a roommate, unless there are also percepts to individuate a roommate's having a chair from his having another. No doubt the accessible perspectives depend on the nature of the events to be perceived, but perhaps the inaccessibility of perceiving someone's having a chair should not be expressed formally as the absence of perspectival operators, as in (140). We could leave it entirely to the meaning of Π to sort it out, in which case the logical form for (114) would be (141).

(141) $\exists\Pi\exists e^{\mathrm{p}}[\hat{E}$: $\Pi(e^{\mathrm{p}}, e)$]([every x : Rx][$\hat{E}$: INFL[e, x]]
　　　　（have[e] $\land$ [$\exists Y$: n(Y) $\land$ $\forall y(Yy \rightarrow Cy$)] OF[$e, y$]).
　　　　[$\hat{E}$: Φ]($\ldots$[ιY : $\forall y(Yy \rightarrow Cy$) $\land$ OF[e, Y]]$\ldots$).)

A percept of a roommate may be sufficient to count as a percept of his states. If so, the first sentence of (141) will turn out to be true where expected. However, it should follow from the conditions on perspective imposed by Π that there are no percepts of a roommate fine-grained enough to individuate events of his having chairs. The only state to be perceived is the one in which he has whatever chairs he has, and therefore the reference of the pronoun to the chairs in the perceived event is nevertheless maximal, as required.

If such an account is plausible, then the contrast between the nonmaximal reference in (23) and the maximal reference felt in (114) need not amount to a difference in their logical forms. Their similar quantificational structure allows them both to be relativized to perspective, and they both must be if we are to follow the suggestion from section 1. In the logical forms for (23) and (114), the perspectival operators exclude a later occurrence of '$\exists E$', which results in exact description. Contexts of exact description thus coincide with the distribution of perspectival operators.

In (115) and (116), the nonincreasing quantifiers exclude perspective, and the antecedent clauses do not provide exact descriptions of the relevant events. A roommate who has many chairs rather than one or two is nevertheless relevant to (115) and (116). He must be among the few, and all of his many chairs must be in the kitchen.

(115) Few roommates have a chair, but they are in the kitchen all together.

(116) Few roommates have two chairs, but they are in the kitchen all together.

(142) [few $x : Rx$][$\hat{E}$: INFL[e, x]]
$\quad \exists E(\text{have}[e] \wedge [\exists Y : n(Y) \wedge \forall y(Yy \rightarrow Cy)] \text{ OF}[e, Y])$
$\quad \wedge [\hat{E} : \Phi](\dots [\imath Y : \forall y(Yy \rightarrow Cy) \wedge \text{OF}[e, Y]] \dots)$.

There remains a problem if exact description is to follow the distribution of perspectival operators. Exact description in (114a) and the entailment that every roommate has exactly one chair are the effects of pronominal reference in the second sentence, which are absent when the first sentence is considered in isolation:

(143) Every roommate has a chair.

(144) $\exists \Pi \exists e^{p}[\hat{E} : \Pi(e^{p}, e)]([\text{every } x : Rx][\hat{E} : \text{INFL}[e, x]]$
$\quad (\text{have}[e] \wedge [\exists Y : 1(Y) \wedge \forall y(Yy \rightarrow Cy)] \text{ OF}[e, y]))$

The roommates with more than one chair do not falsify (143). Yet I have supposed that there are no percepts smaller than the percept of a roommate's having whatever chairs he has. The logical form (144) then says of this percept that there is one chair in the perceived event, and so it entails that every roommate has only one. To seek a way out from this unwelcome result, let us reconsider the distribution of perspectival operators. I have assumed that they enclose every discourse, subject to the constraint that any perspective-laden assertion should yield a perspective-free truth. The constraint serves a crucial distinction between increasing and nonincreasing quantifiers. It should be noted that in doing so, it does not rely on any substantive properties of perspectives. Recall from section 1 that the quantifier *few*, decreasing in both its terms, upholds neither (90) nor (91), and therefore was said to exclude perspective. The conditionals in (90) and (91) are false, whatever relations '$\exists \Pi$' quantifies over and not because we think of them as perspectives.

(90) *$\exists \Pi \exists e^{p}[\text{few } x : Nx \wedge \exists e(\dots V_i e \wedge \Pi(e^{p}, e) \dots)]\exists e(\dots V_j e \dots)$
$\quad \rightarrow [\text{few } x : Nx \wedge \exists e(\dots V_i e \dots)]\exists e(\dots V_j e \dots)$

(91) $*\exists\Pi\exists e^{P}[\text{few } x : Nx \land \exists e(\dots V_i e \dots)]\exists e(\dots V_j e \land \Pi(e^P, e)\dots)$
$\rightarrow [\text{few } x : Nx \land \exists e(\dots V_i e \dots)]\exists e(\dots V_j e \dots)$

Let us, then, reject the idea that the domain of the discourse-level operator '∃Π' is restricted a priori to perspectives. The constraint will still distinguish increasing and nonincreasing quantifiers (and notice that we have
come that much closer to the purely formal proposals of Heim 1982 and
Kamp 1981). If Π can be any arbitrary relation, (144) escapes the entailment that every roommate has exactly one chair. If a roommate has
several chairs and there are therefore several events of his having a chair,
then there is sure to be some relation Π that relates at least one of these to
some (arbitrary) event e^P. If we would like an operator with more content,
we could well imagine that the operator quantifies over relations restricted
to abstract perspectives, formulated in a vocabulary of, say, the geometry
of planar projections but free of any epistemic conditions. Thus the
domain of the quantifier includes many abstract perspectives that are
inaccessible.

I have, of course, relied on epistemic notions about perspective to explain when a descriptive anaphor bears maximal or nonmaximal reference. Having removed them as conditions on the domain of '∃Π', I need
to reintroduce them in the context of descriptive anaphora. As in Burge
1973, 1974, names, demonstratives, and all singular (or plural) terms may
be considered as varieties of definite descriptions that differ in their conditions of use (see Burge 1973, 1974, Taylor 1980, and Davies 1982 for
discussions of how these conditions are to enter the semantic theory). The
rather specific conditions on perspective that govern the use of the demonstratives, 'this N'' and 'that N'' obviously differ from the more subtle
epistemic conditions on the use of names that Higginbotham (1988) has
discussed. I will assume that the general sorts of conditions on perspectives that I have relied on to classify some as accessible to observers join
the list governing the use of referring expressions, including the pronouns
and definite descriptions that occur as descriptive anaphors. A large
domain for '∃Π' in (144) keeps (143) from entailing that every roommate
has exactly one chair, but if Π in (141) is to play a role in determining
the reference of the pronouns in (114), then the percepts of roommates'
having chairs must be accessible. Presumably, there are no accessible
percepts that individuate a roommate's having some of his chairs from
his having others of his chairs. From this maximal reference will follow.
These suggestions are tentative, but they offer an approach that relates
exact description to perspective while allowing that exact description and
maximal reference arise only when there is descriptive anaphora.

As noted in section 2.1, cross-reference to negative events shows non-maximal reference and exact description, just like cross-reference to ordinary events. The exact description of negative events is not, however, straightforwardly represented:

(117) a. Every boy gave a girl none of his toys. They abandoned the boors and shared their own toys among themselves.
     b. Every boy gave a girl none of his toys. The girls abandoned the boors and shared their own toys among themselves.

(118) a. Every boy gave two girls none of his toys. They abandoned the boors and shared their own toys among themselves.
     b. Every boy gave two girls none of his toys. The girls abandoned the boors and shared their own toys among themselves.

(131) $\exists \Pi \exists e^{p}[\hat{E} : \Pi(e^{p}, e)]$
$([\exists E : 1(E) \wedge C[c] \wedge \Pi(c^{p}, c)]$
$[\hat{E}' : \Theta[e, e']][\text{every } x : Bx][\hat{E}' : \text{INFL}[e', x]]$
$[\exists Y : 2(Y) \wedge \forall y(Yy \rightarrow Gy)][\forall y : Yy][\hat{E} : \text{TO}[e', y]]$
$[\text{no } z : Tz][\hat{E} : \text{OF}[e', z]]\exists E' \text{ give}[e'])$

There is a perspective on some events that an adverb would denote. The logical form asserts that every boy has two girls to whom he gives no toys in the neighborhood of these events. Nothing keeps the neighborhood of these events from including his giving some other two girls no toys. The pronoun then refers to the more than two girls that a boy gives no toys to in the neighborhood of these events. What may be missing is a direct relation between the events that the adverb '$C[e]$' denotes on the one hand and the boys and girls on the other.

In addressing this problem, one might adopt a richer structure for perspectives, essentially to draw an analogy between (118) and (145):[36]

(145) For every boy, there are two girls, and every boy gave the girls none of his toys...

Perspective makes available a presentational predicate with its own cluster of dependent θ-roles, just like the first clause of (145). Since I have conceived of percepts as abstract objects, angles of observation, planar projections, etc., it is not unnatural to suppose that they are rich enough to, in effect, diagram functions. A relevant percept for (145) marks off a region for each boy within which he is related to two girls. Here I identify the copula with a predicate denoting percepts:

(146) $\exists\Pi\exists e^{P}([$every $x : Bx][\hat{E}^{P} : for[e^{P}, x]][\exists Y : 2(Y) \wedge \forall y(Yy \rightarrow Gy)]$

$\quad(INFL[e^{P}, Y] \wedge be[e^{P}])$

$\quad\wedge [\hat{E}^{P} : \Phi][$every $x : [\iota X : \forall x(Xx \rightarrow Bx) \wedge for[e^{P}, X]] Xx]\ldots$

In the given percept, whatever each boy is mapped onto is associated with exactly two girls. Exact description can be obtained just from the structured percept. The idea is a logical form for (118) that could be paraphrased as in (147):

(118) Every boy gave two girls none of his toys. They abandoned the boors and shared their own toys among themselves.

(147) For every boy, there were two girls, and *there* every boy gave the two girls *there* for him none of his toys. The girls that were *there* abandoned the boors *there* and shared their own toys among themselves.

The percept of the boys and girls being there is not a percept of boys giving girls anything, but their being there is a reference point for the latter assertion. As in section 1, substantive conditions on perspective determine where nonmaximal reference is possible. In (147), some (spatio-temporal) relation holds between the events perceived, at which for every boy there were two girls, and the events relevant to the assertion that every boy gave two girls none of his toys. The effect of such a relation is observed in (149) and (151).

(148) Every one of the lines intersects a polygon.

(149) a. Every one of the lines intersects a polygon, and they form the surface of a regular solid.

   b. Every one of the lines intersects a polygon, and the polygons form the surface of a regular solid.

(150) Every one of the lines intersects two polygons.

(151) a. Every one of the lines intersects two polygons, and together they form the surface of a regular solid.

   b. Every one of the lines intersects two polygons, and together the polygons form the surface of a regular solid.

A line intersects infinitely many polygons, and so (148) and (150) are simply judged true. Since exact description applies, (149) and (151) are true only if reference is nonmaximal. What context of lines intersecting polygons is properly related to a percept of there being one or two such polygons for every line? In the absence of such a context, the speaker is taken to have some particular polygons in mind or some way to complete the description, as he would have in uttering (152) or (153):

(152) For every one of the lines there is a polygon, and every line intersects that polygon.

(153) For every one of the lines there are two polygons, and every line intersects those polygons.

The sentences could be true and felicitous if, for example, they were comments on the behavior of some machine that graphed for each line one or two polygons that it intersected. These sentences are felicitous only in special contexts. In (117) and (118), however, the possibility of nonmaximal reference is obvious, since a percept of there being boys and girls can readily locate an occasion where the boys acted so as to give the girls none of their toys.

The evidence of a substantive relation between the events perceived and the dependent assertion supports, to some extent, the view of exact description in these cases. Exact description always involves cross-reference to an antecedent clause, and nonmaximal reference always involves a discourse-level perspective. The novelty in these cases is tacitly introducing a presentational structure as the antecedent clause. The antecedent clause may then be restricted by perspective, but the presentational assertion coheres with the matrix only if certain conditions similar to conditions on the sequence of tense and location in a discourse are met.

This view contrasts with an obvious alternative that would simply make Skolem functions available to express various dependencies. Tantamount to assigning discourse-level scope to any indefinite NP, this alternative would vacate any conditions on nonmaximal reference. The sentences in (149) would then simply be judged true because every one of the lines intersects some polygon such that these polygons form the surface of a regular solid:

(154) $\exists f([\text{every } x : Lx] \text{ intersect}(x, f(x))$
$\qquad \& \ldots [\iota Z : \forall z(Zz \leftrightarrow \exists x(z = f(x)))] \ldots)$

Chapter 11
The Cumulative Interpretation of Dependent Quantifiers

This chapter tracks down one last construction that demonstrates separation in its logical form. At this point, some aspects of the construction remain obscure, including the extent to which its semantics can be made to coincide with that of the earlier constructions. I suggest that the construction is similar to questions and their semantics.

The construction is a form of cumulative quantification, which measures the accumulated work of many. In chapters 9 and 10, we have seen it with quantifiers that were independent. They appear in separate conjuncts, related by cross-reference to the events described by the first. Each quantifier is then a comment on the total number of participants in those events. Cumulative quantification is not confined, however, to independent quantifiers. In the relevant interpretation of (1), no more than a dozen pizzas is the total amount eaten by the two boys.

(1) Two boys ate no more than a dozen pizzas (between them).

This reading corresponds to neither distributive interpretation, and yet the quantifiers are not independent. Nor is it equivalent to the conjunction in (2).

(2) Two boys ate some pizzas, and *there* no more than a dozen pizzas were eaten.

Sentence (2) implies the boys ate some pizzas, and (1) does not.

Consider instead a logical form where *no more than a dozen pizzas* falls entirely within the scope of *two boys* but the latter is not distributed. *Two boys* binds into an occurrence of '$[\hat{E} : \Theta[e, X]]$'. This is the first time we have seen the operator restricted by a formula with a free second-order variable. According to (3), whatever they *all* did involves no more than a dozen pizzas:

(3) $[\exists X : 2(X) \wedge \forall x(Xx \rightarrow Bx)][\hat{E} : \text{INFL}[e, X]][(\leq 12)y : Py]$
$[\hat{E} : \text{OF}[e, y]]\exists E \text{ eat}[e]$

(4) Two boys are such that whatever they all did as eaters is such that
    no more than a dozen pizzas were eaten.

No more than a dozen pizzas is plainly dependent on *two boys* and at the
same time is cumulative. Yet the operator '$[\hat{E} : \Phi]$' is not apt here. According to the interpretation offered in chapter 9, section 3, the events denoted
by '$[\hat{E} : \text{INFL}[e, X]]$' are just those where the boys, X, both ate:

(5) $\forall e(Ee \leftrightarrow \exists E'(E'e \wedge \text{INFL}[e', X]))$

Suppose that one of them ate several dozen pizzas but the other ate
none. The intended interpretation of (1) is false. Formula (3), however,
would be true, since there are no events among which the boys both can
be found eating. The revision should include whatever the boys did *jointly
or severally*. The operator '$[\hat{E} : \text{INFL}[e, X]]$' denotes the eating done by at
least some of them:

(6) $\forall e(Ee \leftrightarrow \exists x(\text{INFL}(e, x) \wedge \forall x(\text{INFL}(e, x) \rightarrow Xx)))$

The one boy's eating several dozen pizzas will then falsify (3), as required.

Revising the meaning of the operator along the lines suggested will not
disturb the other contexts where it has appeared so far. In translating
distributivity, the singular variable 'x' in '$[\hat{E} : \Theta[e, x]]$' makes harmless the
extension to events done by a proper subset of x. In its other contexts, it
provides the cross-reference between the conjuncts of independent quantifiers, as in (7).

(7) Two detectives each solved two crimes, and *that* was for three
    agencies.

There is reason to expect that weakening the operator to include what was
done jointly or severally will not affect the cross-reference in these cases.
While the operator allows that some events are referred to even if only one
of the two detectives solved any crimes, the antecedent asserts that both
detectives each solved two. The truth of the antecedent clause guarantees
that the cross-reference is in fact to events of two detectives each solving
two crimes. It appears, then, that a revised meaning for the operator
allows us to include dependent, cumulative quantifiers at little expense.

A great variety of interpretations can be obtained simply by allowing
the operator to take up the θ-role governed by any plural term. The
operator could iterate, as in (10), to obtain that interpretation of (8) and
(9) where whatever the two girls gave the two boys amounted to no more
than a dozen pizzas.

(8) Two girls gave two boys no more than a dozen pizzas.

(9)   The girls gave the boys no more than a dozen pizzas.

(10) $[\exists X : \ldots Gx \ldots][\hat{E} : \text{INFL}[e, X]][\exists Y : \ldots By \ldots][\hat{E} : \text{TO}[e, Y]]$
      $[(\leq 12)z : Pz][\hat{E} : \text{OF}[e, z]]\exists E \text{ give}[e]$

As with (1), the interpretation is falsified if one of the girls gave one of the boys more than a dozen pizzas, even though no other pizzas passed between them.

The cumulative interpretation can mix with quantifiers understood distributively:

(11) Two girls gave no more than a dozen boys (each) two pizzas.

(12) The girls gave no more than a dozen boys (each) two pizzas.

(13) $[\exists X : \ldots Gx \ldots][\hat{E} : \text{INFL}[e, X]][(\leq 12)y : By][\hat{E} : \text{TO}[e, y]]$
      $\exists E(\text{give}[e] \wedge [\exists E : 2(Z) \ldots Pz \ldots] \text{OF}[e, Z])$

According to the intended interpretation, whatever pizzas the girls gave boys, no more than a dozen boys ended up with two. Similarly, (14) and (15) first accumulate whatever the two girls gave the two boys, and of that it is asserted that the boys were each given no more than a dozen pizzas:

(14) Two girls gave two boys each no more than a dozen pizzas.

(15) The girls gave the boys each no more than a dozen pizzas.

(16) $[\exists X : \ldots Gx \ldots][\hat{E} : \text{INFL}[e, X]][\exists Y : \ldots By \ldots][\forall y : Yy][\hat{E} : \text{TO}[e, y]]$
      $[(\leq 12)z : Pz][\hat{E} : \text{OF}[e, z]]\exists E \text{ give}[e]$

It would appear from the above examples that '$[\hat{E} : \Theta[e, X]]$' can occur wherever its singular counterpart '$[\hat{E} : \Theta[e, x]]$' does. This turns out not to be true, and the difference in its syntactic distribution leads me to doubt whether the representation of dependent, cumulative quantification should involve the same operator. First, the plural '$[\hat{E} : \Theta[e, X]]$' occurs only in connection with a cumulative quantifier. The sentences in (17) cannot be true if just one boy arrived, unlike the logical form in (18), which asserts that whatever the boys did jointly or severally was an arriving:

(17) a. Two boys arrived.
      b. The boys arrived.

(18) $[\exists X : \ldots Bx \ldots][\hat{E} : \text{INFL}[e, X]]\exists E \text{ V}[e]$

Of course, the syntactic context is appropriate for the singular counterpart:

(19) Every boy arrived.

(20) [every $x : Bx$][$\hat{E} : \text{INFL}[e, x]$]$\exists E \ V[e]$

A second restriction peculiar to the plural version is that it does not occur within the scope of an existential event quantifier. As in (22), suppose that three children rode in two vans to two zoos, and suppose further that there are no other children or vans:

(21) a. Three children rode in two vans to one zoo.

    b. Three children rode in two vans to no more than one zoo.

(22) $[_{v_1} \mathbf{c}_1, \mathbf{c}_2, \mathbf{c}_3] \longrightarrow \mathbf{z}_1 \qquad [_{v_2} \mathbf{c}_1, \mathbf{c}_2, \mathbf{c}_3] \longrightarrow \mathbf{z}_2$

(23) a. $\exists E([\exists X : 3(X) \wedge \forall x(Xx \rightarrow Cx)] \text{INFL}[e, X]$
$\wedge [\exists Y : 2(Y) \wedge \forall y(Yy \rightarrow Vy)][\hat{E} : \text{in}[e, Y]]$
$(\text{ride}[e] \wedge [\exists W : 1(W) \wedge \forall w(Ww \rightarrow Zw)] \text{to}[e, W]))$

    b. $\exists E([\exists X : 3(X) \wedge \forall x(Xx \rightarrow Cx)] \text{INFL}[e, X]$
$\wedge [\exists Y : 2(Y) \wedge \forall y(Yy \rightarrow Vy)][\hat{E} : \text{in}[e, Y]][(\leq 1)w : Zw]$
$[\hat{E} : \text{to}[e, w]] \text{ride}[e])$

In the given situation, the sentences in (21) are plainly false, but the logical forms in (23), where '$[\hat{E} : \text{in}[e, Y]]$' occurs within the scope of an existential event quantifier, are true: there is an event, the first trip to a zoo, in which three children ride and two vans, $\mathbf{v}_1$ and $\mathbf{v}_2$, are such that whatever they did there jointly or severally is a ride to one zoo.[1] In contrast, the interpretation of (21) shown in (24) is false in the situation.

(24) a. $[\exists X : 3(X) \wedge \forall x(Xx \rightarrow Cx)][\hat{E} : \text{INFL}[e, X]]$
$[\exists Y : 2(Y) \wedge \forall y(Yy \rightarrow Vy)][\hat{E} : \text{in}[e, Y]]$
$(\text{ride}[e] \wedge [\exists W : 1(W) \wedge \forall w(Ww \rightarrow Zw)] \text{to}[e, W])$

    b. $[\exists X : 3(X) \wedge \forall x(Xx \rightarrow Cx)][\hat{E} : \text{INFL}[e, X]]$
$[\exists Y : 2(Y) \wedge \forall y(Yy \rightarrow Vy)][\hat{E} : \text{in}[e, Y]]$
$[(\leq 1)w : Zw][\hat{E} : \text{to}[e, w]] \text{ride}[e]$

These children are such that whatever they did as riders jointly or severally is such that whatever these two vans did jointly or severally were rides to two zoos, and there are no other children or vans to consider. Recall that it was such illicit interpretations as (23) that led us in chapter 7, section 2, to exclude quantification over parts of events from the translation of plurals. If we are now to admit that plurals do bind into '$[\hat{E} : \Theta[e, V]]$', as in (24), it is difficult to imagine a principled basis for allowing (24) and the singular analogue to (23) in (25) while excluding (23).

(25) a. Three children rode two vans each to one zoo.

b. $\exists E([\exists X : 3(X) \wedge \forall x(Xx \rightarrow Cx)] \text{INFL}[e, X]$
$\wedge [\exists Y : 2(Y) \wedge \forall y(Yy \rightarrow Vy)][\forall y : Yy][\hat{E} : \text{in}[e, y]]$
$(\text{ride}[e] \wedge [\exists W : 1(W) \wedge \forall w(Ww \rightarrow Zw)] \text{to}[e, W]))$

Given the syntactic restrictions, my current inclination is to consider dependent, cumulative quantification to be a distinct construction, similar to *wh*-clefts. Thus the target interpretation of (26) has a form similar to (27):

(26) Two boys gave two girls no more than twelve pizzas.

(27) What two boys gave two girls was no more than twelve pizzas.

Assuming a clefted structure at LF would exclude the interpretation of (17) asserting that what two boys did jointly or severally was arrive. There is no appropriate position for the *wh-* to bind. Note that in (28), the *wh-* binds the object position of the main verb *do*, which does not occur in the s-structure of (17) and, one assumes, is not freely inserted at LF:[2]

(28) What two boys did was arrive.

Since the *wh*-phrase is restricted by the entire matrix sentence with only an NP removed, it also seems reasonable to assume that the *wh*-phrase will never fall within the scope of the existential event quantifier, which then rules out the misconstrual of (25). If indeed these interpretations are derived by *wh*-clefting, there is no possibility of iterative structure, as in (10). The interpretation would be represented only by a structure similar to (27), where the one *wh*-cleft contains all the arguments that jointly or severally performed the relevant actions.

To support this view, I show first that, on semantic grounds, the relevant operator must sometimes be restricted by the entire sentence minus the clefted NP. Second, I show that overt *wh*-phrases, questions and relative clauses, and the tacit *wh*-clefts share some interpretations and some idiosyncratic properties.

The cumulative interpretations of (29) and (30) extend beyond what can be expressed by operators whose only descriptive content is a θ-role: '$[\hat{E} : \Theta[e, V]]$'.

(29) Two girls (each) gave two boys no more than a dozen pizzas (between them).

(30) Two girls (each) gave the boys no more than a dozen pizzas (between them).

The relevant interpretation of (29) says that there are two girls and for each of them there are two boys such that the pizzas that the girls gave their boys added up to no more than a dozen. What is crucial about the example is that *two boys* is dependent on a distributed occurrence of *two girls* and it is independent of *no more than a dozen pizzas*.[3] Its logical form must follow closely the paraphrase in (31), where the restriction on the operator includes much more than a single θ-role:

(31) Whatever some two girls (each) gave some two boys, no more than a dozen pizzas were given.

The pattern of dependencies and the correct cumulative interpretation cannot be recovered by other means. While not amounting to a proof, the following considerations should be argument enough. Let us suppose that the operator takes up only θ-roles. Then since the interpretation is cumulative with respect to *two girls*, we expect the logical form to be a continuation of (32).

(32) $[\exists X : \ldots Gx \ldots][\hat{E} : \text{INFL}[e, X]] \ldots$

(33) Two girls are such that whatever they gave . . .

Since each girl is related to two boys, *two boys* must occur within the scope of a distributing quantifier:

(34) $[\exists X : \ldots Gx \ldots][\hat{E} : \text{INFL}[e, X]] \ldots [\forall x : Xx] \ldots$
      $[\exists Y : 2(Y) \ldots By \ldots] \ldots$

There is now no appropriate placement for *no more than a dozen pizzas*. Within the scope of '$[\forall x : Xx]$', it becomes dependent on the individual girls rather than cumulative. If instead *no more than a dozen pizzas* includes within its scope '$[\forall x : Xx]$', pizzas are relevant just in case they are related to all the girls. But our interest in this interpretation is that it accumulates the pizzas related to either girl.

A best approximation in the pattern of (32) that nevertheless fails is obtained by resorting to semidistributivity and assuming that there are other means, such as Skolem functions, to stipulate dependencies. Consider the paraphrase in (35):

(35) Two girls each had two boys such that no more than a dozen pizzas are such that each girl with perhaps the other girl gave pizzas to her boys and perhaps the other girl's boys.

The paraphrase fails because it cannot be false if one of the girls gave no boys pizzas. The other girl is free in that case to exceed twelve pizzas, contrary to the cumulative interpretation. A similar paraphrase following the alternative placement for *no more than a dozen pizzas* turns out nearly to succeed with this particular example:

(36) Two girls each had two boys such that each girl with perhaps the other girl gave no more than a dozen pizzas to her boys and perhaps the other girl's boys.

Although *no more than a dozen pizzas* falls within the scope of *each girl*, cumulativity is approximated by interpreting the dependency semidistributively. The paraphrase nevertheless deviates from the cumulative interpretation of (29). Suppose that one chooses for the girls disjoint groups of boys: girl 1 is related to boys 1 and 2, and girl 2 to boys 3 and 4. These boys and girls verify the cumulative interpretation just in case no more than a dozen pizzas are among those that girl 1 has given to boys 1 and 2 and those that girl 2 has given to boys 3 and 4. If either of the girls has also given pizzas to the other girl's boys, these pizzas are irrelevant. But (36) incorrectly counts them among the no more than a dozen.

With other examples, we can point to a more immediate failing of a form like (36):

(37) Two girls (each) gave two boys exactly twelve pizzas (between them).

(38) Two girls each had two boys such that each girl with perhaps the other girl gave exactly twelve pizzas to her boys and perhaps the other girl's boys.

Interpretation (38) implies that both girls gave pizzas, but the cumulative interpretation of (37) allows that the twelve pizzas may have been the gift of only one of them. We have thus seen the cumulative interpretation escape the more desperate efforts to fit it into the formal constraints of (32). A language in which the descriptive content of '$[\hat{E} : \Phi]$' is restricted to θ-roles is insufficient to express this interpretation.

The content of '$[\hat{E} : \Phi]$' should include longer phrases, as the paraphrase in (31) suggests. Taking the paraphrase seriously, I view occurrences of '$[\hat{E} : \Phi]$' to be tacit free relatives: 'whatever Φ'. The semantics of the relative clauses is, in turn, related to the semantics of questions, as I will show. I will not, however, introduce a semantics of questions.

The question in (39) is ambiguous.

(39) What did everyone buy?

One interpretation is obtained simply by extracting the *wh*-phrase, with the universal quantifier remaining within its scope. An object is an answer just in case everyone bought it. Question (39) may also be understood to present an alternative question, one that can be answered with a list pairing each person with what he bought. An object appears on the list if someone, not necessarily everyone, has bought it. The connection between this question and the free relative *what everyone bought* is drawn out as follows. According to many discussions,[4] the reference of a question is its answers, and the semantics for this question will construct the list pairing each person with his purchase.[5] Then the reference of the free relative is, in effect, to those objects that are bought according to the list, the referent of the question. In this way the semantics of the relative clause is parasitic on the semantics of the question, which accounts for their common properties. In the example of *what everyone bought*, the relation to the list of answers has two crucial properties: an object is denoted if anyone bought it, and everyone need not have bought something. An answer to the question may include that so-and-so bought nothing.

I assume that there is quantifying into questions, '$[Qx : \Phi][$wh- $: \Psi]\Sigma$', and that the semantics of such an interrogative "constructs" the pair list. The suggestion that free relatives are parasitic on the semantics of questions is pointless if this assumption is mistaken. I know of two proposals that attempt to explain answering with pairs, without resorting to a construction that interprets '$[Qx : \Phi][$wh- $: \Psi]\Sigma$'. Karttunen (1977) proposes that *everyone* quantifies into a matrix performative:

(40) Everyone-x (I ask) what did x buy

Engdahl (1986) observes, however, that the proposal is insufficiently general, citing M. Bennett 1979 for (41) and Belnap 1982 for (42):

(41) John wonders where two unicorns live.

(42) The average grade depends on what grade each student gets.

Sentence (41) may convey that John wants to know about two unicorns where they each live. Short of analyzing *wonder* as the biclausal *want-to-know*, quantifying into a performative clause commits John to *de re* questions about unicorns, which is not the intended reading of (41):

(43) Two-unicorns-x (John wonders where x lives)

More to the point for our discussion is Engdahl's discussion of (42). Since, the average depends on the collected grades, the scope of *each student* cannot include more than the indirect question:

(44) *Each-student-x (the average grade depends on what grade x gets)[6]

Nor can (42) be represented by (45), where *each student* remains within the scope of the question and *wh-* quantifies over individual grades.

(45) The average grade depends on what-grade-y each-student-x
  x gets y.

A grade is averaged in if some student, not necessarily every one, gets it. As we have already seen, this interaction with a *wh*-element is not peculiar to indirect questions. It also occurs with heads of relative clauses. In (46) and (47), the description refers to the papers turned in by any student:

(46) John made a pile out of what papers each student turned in.

(47) John made a pile out of what papers the students turned in.[7]

Engdahl (1986, 163 ff.), though she rejects Karttunen's proposal, endorses not quantifying into questions but another proposal. She observes first that there are natural interpretations of the following examples that do not involve quantifying into questions:

(48) *Q*: Who do you expect every Englishman to admire most?
  A: His mother.

(49) *Q*: What should few men forget?
  A: Their wife's birthday.

In (48), *every Englishman* may be construed *de dicto*. It does not elicit for every Englishman an answer to the question who do you expect him to admire most. In (49), quantifying into the question is simply incoherent. It would demand that the respondent answer questions concerning few men, which could be complied with by saying nothing at all.

Since there cannot be quantifying into questions in these examples, Engdahl concludes that the answers to (48) and (49) answer a question quantifying over functions (The λ-notation in (50) and (51) represents functional abstraction.):[8]

(50) *Q*: [Wh *F*] you expect every Englishman to admire *F* most?
  A: $\lambda x(x$'s mother)

(51) *Q*: [Wh *F*] should few men forget *F*?
  A: $\lambda x(x$'s wife's birthday)

Engdahl's proposal, then, is to eliminate apparent cases of quantifying into questions in favor of quantifying over functions. The pair-list answer thought to be elicited by quantifying into a question is just another way to specify a function in answer to a question that quantifies over functions.

Were it true, Engdahl's proposal could save me much hand waving and eliminate questions from the semantics of such referring expressions as *what everyone bought*. Its reference would be to those things in the range of the function F such that everyone bought F. This function can be referred to without invoking the semantics of questions. Groenendijk and Stokhof (1984) observe, however, that questions like (51) where quantifying in is incoherent are those that permit a functional answer but no pair-list answer: *Ricky { forgot/didn't forget} Lucy's birthday, and Fred { forgot/didn't forget} Ethel's. For Engdahl, this divergence of functional answer and pair list answer is unexpected. The pair-list should be just another way of delivering an acceptable functional answer. Yet its unacceptability as an answer to (51) is accounted for if there is quantifying into questions and pair-list answers are tied to the family of questions it generates.[9] Quantifying into a question is incoherent in (51), and so is a pair-list answer to (51). It appears that quantifying over functions cannot take the place of quantifying into questions in an account of pair-list answers. (See n. 10 for further discussion of pair-list answers and quantifying over functions).

In cases where functional and pair-list answers diverge, the cumulative interpretation of the referring expression corresponding to a question fits the pattern of the pair-list answers. It refers to objects in a pair-list, if such an answer to the question is acceptable, but not to the range of a functional answer. The functional answer available to the underlying question in (52) or (53) does not yield a coherent cumulative interpretation of the referring expression.

(52) John made a pile out of what books no students read.

(53) John made a pile out of the books that few students read.

Suppose that the books their teachers recommend is a true functional answer to the question of what books no students read. The range of that function does not coincide with the reference of the expression in (52), not if, for example, those books were read by students to whom they were not recommended. In the absence of a pair-list answer, there is no cumulative interpretation. The only reference is to books described by a conventional relative clause: those books that were each read by no students.[11] Since we have seen the cumulative interpretation of the referring expression correlate with a pair-list answer, it is plausible that its semantics is parasitic on the semantics of quantifying into questions. I turn now to survey other properties that the two constructions share.

The quantifiers that can quantify into questions are limited. The dialogue in (51) illustrates that decreasing quantifiers are excluded, and (52) and (53) show the effect of this on the corresponding referring expressions. In general, quantifying into questions is restricted to definite and indefinite descriptions and universal quantifiers.[12] The dialogue in (54) is an example of an indefinite description quantifying in and eliciting a pair-list answer.

(54) Q: Don't bother with them all. Tell me what topics {some/a few/two} students wrote about?

    A: Elena wrote about extraposition in German, and Liliana about *ser* versus *estar*.

Alongside it, (55) has an interpretation that is true only if there are two students and John made a pile out of whatever papers they turned in jointly or severally:[13]

(55) John made a pile out of what papers two students turned in.
John made a pile out of the papers two students turned in.

Other quantifiers will not support a pair-list answer.

(56) *Q: Don't bother with them all. Tell me what topics {many/most/exactly two} students wrote about?[14]

    A: Elena wrote about extraposition in German, and Liliana about *ser* versus *estar*.

(57) a. John made a pile out of what papers {many/most/exactly two} students turned in.

    b. John made a pile out of the papers {many/most/exactly two} students turned in.

(53) John made a pile out of {what/the} papers that few students turned in.

When these quantifiers appear in relative clauses, the most salient interpretation is perhaps the one where the quantifier is dependent on the objects denoted by the head. Thus reference in (53) would be to the papers each turned in by few students. Nondistributive interpretations in (57) and (53) are also possible, but these do not require the resources of quantifying in. We may understand, for example, that many students turned in papers and John made a pile out of the papers that they in fact turned in. The relative clause involves cross-reference to an *independent* antecedent:[15]

(58) ... [ιX : many students turned in papers
    $\wedge$ [$\hat{E}$: INFL[e, the students that turned in papers]] in[e, X]] ...

The NP, crucially, does not allow that any of the many students did *not* turn in papers, and it refers to those papers collected from those who did.

However they are interpreted there, this class of quantifiers must remain within the relative clause or question. These quantifiers will also prevent a description or universal quantifier they c-command from quantifying into a question. In (59), the c-commanding pronoun may quantify in, as the pair-list answer indicates.

(59) Q: What did they recommend to few students?
     A: Russell recommended *Principia Ethica* to few students, and
          Moore recommended *Principia Mathematica* to few students.

Similarly for the relative clause in (60), since one interpretation the NP has is that it refers to the works that one or the other don recommended to few students.

(60) Ludi sought out {the/what} works they recommended to few
     students.

(61) Q: Who did they recommend them to?
     A: Russell recommended *Principia Mathematica* to Ludi, and
          Moore recommended *Principia Ethica* to David.

(62) The librarian found the books for the students they recommended
     them to.

In contrast, the pronoun in (63), c-commanded by the decreasing quantifier, cannot quantify into the question. The pair-list answer is unacceptable.

(63) *Q: Who did few dons recommend them to?
      A: Few dons recommended *Principia Mathematica* to Ludi, and
           few recommend *Principia Ethica* to David.

Similarly, the NP in (64) cannot refer to the group of students that includes those that few dons recommended *Principia Ethica* to and those that few dons recommended *Principia Mathematica* to.

(64) The librarian found the books for the students few dons
     recommended them to.

It would, for example, exclude any student to whom few dons recommended *Principia Ethica* but many dons recommended *Principia Mathematica*.

The two classes of quantifiers with respect to quantifying into questions and the opacity effect induced by the one are reflected in the distribution and behavior of cumulative quantification with a dependent quantifier. According to the relevant interpretation of (65), no more than two students are such that Russell recommended to him few books or Moore recommended to him few books.

(65) The dons recommended few books to no more than two students.

(66) $[\hat{E}:$ the dons recommended few books to students]
$[(\leq 2)y : Sy][\hat{E} : \text{to}[e, y]]$ recommend$[e]$

(67) Whatever the events where the dons recommended few books, no more than two students were those to whom books were recommended.

No more than students thus accumulates those, if any, to whom either don recommended few books. This interpretation is obtained by including what is shown in (66) in the restriction on the event operator. *The dons* is understood to quantify in. Thus the expression refers to those events each of which is a recommending of few books by one or the other don. As in chapter 9, section 4, we must assume that there is a nonvacuous way of quantifying over events of recommending few books. Examples such as (68) suggest there must be.

(68) Russell twice recommended few books.

It must also turn out that if, as in (66) and (67), no more than two students were in such events of being recommended few books, then the many other students who were not in events of being recommended few books were in an event where one or the other don recommended to him many books. Under these assumptions about quantifying over events, (66) and (67) express the interpretation that no more than two students were recommended few books by one or the other don.[16]

A parallel interpretation is not available to (69).

(69) Few dons recommended the books to no more than two students.

(70) $[\hat{E}:$ few dons recommended the books to students]
$[(\leq 2)y : Sy][\hat{E} : \text{to}[e, y]]$ recommend$[e]$

(71) *Whatever the events where few dons recommend the books, no more than two students were those to whom books were recommended.

The cumulative quantifier *no more than two students* does not collect any student to whom either *Principia Ethica* or *Principia Mathematica* was recommended by few dons. The reason is that the definite description *the books*, c-commanded by *few dons*, cannot quantify in.

There are other grounds on which to compare quantifying into questions, quantifying into relative clauses, and quantifying into the tacit relative clauses introduced by cumulative quantifiers. The comparison is imperfect, however. May (1985) reports the condition that the quantifier quantifying into a question must c-command (at s-structure) the *wh*-trace. The effect disappears when the *wh*-phrase is plural (Kuno and Robinson 1972, Krifka 1992b):

(72) Tell me what everyone bought. Answer (A) below.
(73) ?Tell me who bought everything. Answer (B) below. (This is ok if *who* is thought of as a plural.)

(74) Tell me what appliance every customer bought. Answer (A).
(75) ?Tell me what customer bought every appliance. Answer (B).

(76) Tell me what appliances every customer bought. Answer (A).
(77) Tell me what customers bought every appliance. Answer (B).

(78) Tell me what the customers bought. Answer (A).
(79) ?Tell me who bought the appliances. Answer (B).

(80) Tell me what appliance the customers bought. Answer (A).
(81) ?Tell me what customer bought the appliances. Answer (B).

(82) Tell me what appliances the customers bought. Answer (A).
(83) Tell me what customers bought the appliances. Answer (B).

(A)   Hilary bought the fridge, Robin the range, Sandy the dishwasher, and Terry bought nothing.

(B)   Hilary bought the fridge, Robin the range, Sandy the dishwasher, and no one the Vegematic.

In judging whether the effect is observable in relative clauses, we must pay particular attention to the cumulative interpretation. On that interpretation, (84) and (85) do *not* imply that all the customers bought appliances.

(84) The clerk put in one consignment {what/the} appliances every customer bought.

(85) The clerk put in one consignment {what/the} appliances the customers bought.

The clerk put in one consignment the appliances of those that did.

Now consider examples where the expression quantifying in does not c-command the *wh*-trace:

(86) The dealer gathered together {what/the} customers {∅/that} bought every appliance.

(87) The dealer gathered together {what/the} customers {∅/that}
     bought the appliances.

That (86) and (87) do not require each customer to buy every appliance is
irrelevant, since the relative clause surely has a nondistributed interpretation. The crucial consideration for quantifying in is whether or not the
dealer's gathering together some customers entails that every appliance
was bought. There does seem to be some contrast between these examples
and those in (84) and (85). There may be appliances that *what appliances
the customers bought* refers to without every customer buying an appliance. If, however, there are customers referred to by *what customers
bought the appliances*, then the appliances were all bought.[17]

At least then, there is some evidence from May's c-command effect for
a similarity between quantifying into questions and quantifying into relative clauses. It seems, however, that the subject-object asymmetry shown
above does not have an equivalent in the tacit relative clauses of cumulative quantification. Sentences (88a) and (88b) allow that not all the customers were involved in buying whatever appliances were bought, as do
sentences (88c) and (88d), which make explicit the underlying relative
clauses.

(88) a. The ten customers bought no more than a dozen appliances.
     b. The ten customers bought exactly a dozen appliances.
     c. What appliances the ten customers bought were no more than a
        dozen.
     d. What appliances the ten customers bought were exactly a dozen.

And counting against the subject-object asymmetry, the sentences in (89)
allow that not all the appliances were bought by the customers who were
buying.

(89) a. No more than ten customers bought the appliances.
     b. Exactly ten customers bought the appliances.
     c. What customers bought the appliances were no more than ten.
     d. What customers bought the appliances were exactly ten.

Sloan (1991) claims that in addition to May's c-command condition there is a further locality condition that requires the quantifier
quantifying-in to fall within the governing category of the *wh*-trace.
The following examples are unambiguous in excluding a pair-list answer:

(90) Who do you think everyone saw Mary talk to?

(91) Who does everyone think saw you?

(92) Who did everyone say that Bill saw?

(93) Who did everyone see Bill's picture of?

My own judgments are that quantifying in is perhaps clause-bound and therefore marginal only in (90) (May (1985), however, accepts cases similar to (90). See (xx), n. 10). Question (93) is marginal because of a specificity condition on extraction. If the condition applies weakly, then in general the extraction succeeds, and in particular the acceptability of a pair-list answer improves:

(94) What subject did everyone want your opinion about?

The clause-mate condition applies also to quantifying into relative clauses and to cumulative quantification. In (95) and (96), the books will include those that any of the teachers thought Johnny should read, yet these sentences do not imply that every teacher thought he should read something.

(95) The principal made a pile out of {what/the} books {∅/that} the teachers thought Johnny should read.

(96) The teachers thought Johnny should read no more than a dozen great books.

In contrast, (97) and (98) do not allow *the students* to quantify in.

(97) The principal made a pile out of {what/the} books Bloom thought the students should read.

(98) Bloom thought the students should read no more than a dozen great books.

Were it possible, the books referred to would be those collected from diverse *de re* thoughts that Bloom has had about any of the students, and there would be no implication that he has thought about them all. Here the various types of quantifying in all behave alike.

My semantics for dependent, cumulative quantification is strictly provisional. It does not realize the connection to the semantics of questions. A formal semantics for quantifying into questions can be found in the references cited. The reference of a free relative is straightforward if one can recover the pair-list answers from the referent of the question. Here I introduce a new semantic relation: *schmender*. Its recursive clauses will have the effect of accumulating whatever was done jointly or severally, if at all, by the relevant participants. The point of this exercise is to show what stands in the way of assimilating dependent, cumulative quantification to those constructions based on rendering. First, the schmendering operator '$[?E : \Phi]$' has those syntactic properties attributed earlier to *wh*-clefts. It does not iterate, it has matrix scope and will not fall within the scope of any other event quantifier, and it may be restricted by complex phrases. The schmendering operator is existential. According to (105), at the end of the chapter, it requires just that there are some schmendering events. In *Two boys ate no more than a dozen pizzas*, we want some events that correspond to what some two boys ate. There is no implication of maximal reference, that the events should overlap whatever any two boys ate, and so the schmendering operator is not the definite description necessary for rendering. Could the schmendering operator turn out to be the indefinite counterpart to the rendering operator, albeit with an unusual syntactic distribution? That depends on the extent to which the semantic relations of rendering and schmendering can be made to coincide. Schmendering assumes as given a classification of quantifiers into those that do and those that do not quantify in. The classification nearly coincides with rendering's classification of quantifiers into increasing and nonincreasing quantifiers, with the exception of *many* and *most*, increasing quantifiers that do not quantify in (see (56) above). This discrepancy aside, it is interesting to note that the clauses for schmendering could replace the corresponding clauses defining rendering. I observed at the beginning of this chapter that a more inclusive reference to events done jointly or severally by some or all would not undermine the cross-reference to events in an example like (7).

(7) Two detectives each solved two crimes, and that was for three agencies.

The truth of the antecedent clause guarantees that the cross-reference is in fact to events of two detectives each solving two crimes.

There remains, however, an important difference between the schmendering and rendering operators in how nonincreasing or non-quantifying-in quantifiers and negation are treated. Recall that the cross-reference in (99) is to whatever crime solving was done by the detectives who solved no more than two crimes:

(99) Exactly two detectives (each) solved no more than two crimes for exactly five agencies.

(100) Exactly two detectives (each) solved no more than two crimes for agencies, and *there* crimes were solved for exactly five agencies.

But the events denoted in (101) must be events of solving no more than two crimes.

(101) a. Two detectives (each) solved no more than two crimes for
exactly five agencies.

b. "Whatever some two detectives (each) solved no more than two
crimes for involved exactly five agencies."

(102) $[?E : [\exists X : 2(X) \wedge \forall x(Xx \rightarrow Dx)][\forall x : Xx][\hat{E}' : \text{INFL}[e', x]]$
$[\exists Z : \forall z(Zz \rightarrow Az)][\forall z : Zz][\hat{E}' : \text{for}[e', z]]$
$\exists E(C[e] \wedge (_\Delta [\exists E' : [(\leq 2)y : Cy][\hat{E}' : \text{OF}[e', y]] \text{ solve}[e']] \text{ of}[e, E'])]$
$[5!z : Az][\hat{E}' : \text{for}[e', z]] \text{ solve}[e']^{18}$

Because schmendering is undefined for these quantifiers, they can occur in
the restriction of the schmendering operator only if the logical form explicitly introduces a relation to negative events, as in (102). I earlier discussed the difficulties and the apparent need for such negative events.
When we come to evaluate what schmenders Δ in (102), only the satisfaction, and not the schmendering, of 'no more than two crimes Γ' is relevant, according to (110). The logical form in effect keeps the quantifier
that doesn't quantify in from interacting with the definition of schmendering. Note that all quantifiers that fall within the scope of *no more than
two crimes* are similarly removed, and they do not quantify in.

If schmendering is to be unified with rendering, we can no longer rely
on its being undefined for nonincreasing quantifiers to correctly interpret
(101). The rendering clause for nonincreasing quantifiers becomes available
to interpret logical forms for (101) that do not introduce negative events:

(103) $[?E : [\exists X : 2(X) \wedge \forall x(Xx \rightarrow Dx)][\forall x : Xx][\hat{E} : \text{INFL}[e, x]]$
$[(\leq 2)y : Cy][\hat{E} : \text{OF}[e, y]]$
$\exists E (\text{solve}[e] \wedge [\exists Z : \forall z(Zz \rightarrow Az)] \text{ for}[e, Z])]$
$[5!z : Az][\hat{E} : \text{for}[e, z]] \text{ solve}[e]$

The derived interpretation is paraphrased in (104).

(104) Whatever agencies either of two detectives solved crimes for, as a
detective that solved no more than two crimes for agencies, were
exactly five agencies.

Unlike independent, cumulative quantification, (103) does not assert that
two detectives in fact each solved no more than two crimes for agencies.
Rather, it allows that one did not, provided that the other that did
meet the description solved crimes for exactly five agencies. We get an
unacceptable interpretation of (101), and some other means must be
found to exclude it, if schmendering and rendering are unified.

Here, then, is the satisfaction clause for the operator '$[?E_i : \Phi]$' and the
definition of schmendering:

(105) Σ satisfy $\ulcorner[?E_i : \Phi]\ \Psi\urcorner$

$\leftrightarrow [\exists E : \text{schmender}(E, \Phi, \Sigma)][\exists\Sigma_0 : \Sigma_0 \approx_{\mathfrak{C}_i} \Sigma \wedge \Sigma_0(\mathfrak{C}_i) \simeq E]$
Σ_0 satisfy Ψ

(106) $\text{schmender}(E, \ulcorner V[e]\urcorner, \Sigma)$

$\leftrightarrow \forall e(Ee \leftrightarrow (\Sigma \text{ satisfy } \ulcorner V[e]\urcorner \wedge \Sigma(\langle\mathfrak{C}, e\rangle)))^{19}$

(107) $\text{schmender}(E, \ulcorner\Theta[e_i, v]\urcorner, \Sigma)$

$\leftrightarrow \forall e(Ee \leftrightarrow \exists E(Ee \wedge \Sigma(\mathfrak{C}_i) \simeq E \wedge \forall z(\Theta(e, z) \leftrightarrow \Sigma(\langle v, z\rangle))))$

(108) $\text{schmender}(E, \ulcorner\Theta[e_i, V]\urcorner, \Sigma)$

$\leftrightarrow \forall e(Ee \leftrightarrow \exists E(Ee \wedge \Sigma(\mathfrak{C}_i) \simeq E \wedge \exists z\Theta(e, z)$
$\wedge \forall z(\Theta(e, z) \rightarrow \Sigma(\langle V, z\rangle))))$

(109) $\text{schmender}(E, \ulcorner\Phi \wedge \Psi\urcorner, \Sigma)$

$\leftrightarrow \forall e(Ee \leftrightarrow [\exists E_0 : \text{schmender}(E_0, \Phi, \Sigma)]$
$[\exists E_1 : \text{schmender}(E_1, \Psi, \Sigma)](E_0 e \wedge E_1 e))$

(110) $\text{schmender}(E, \ulcorner[\exists V : \Phi]\ \Psi\urcorner, \Sigma)$

$\leftrightarrow [\exists X : \exists\Sigma_0(\Sigma_0 \approx_V \Sigma \wedge \forall x(\Sigma_0(\langle V, x\rangle) \leftrightarrow Xx) \wedge \Sigma_0 \text{ satisfy } \Phi)]$
$[\exists\Sigma_0 : \Sigma_0 \approx_V \Sigma \wedge \forall x(\Sigma_0(\langle V, x\rangle) \leftrightarrow Xx)] \text{schmender}(E, \Psi, \Sigma_0)$

(111) $\text{schmender}(E, \ulcorner[Q^i v : \Phi]\ \Psi\urcorner, \Sigma) \leftrightarrow$
$[\exists X :$
$\quad [Q^i x : \exists\Sigma_0(\Sigma_0 \approx_v \Sigma \wedge \forall z(\Sigma_0(\langle v, z\rangle) \leftrightarrow z = x)$
$\quad \wedge \Sigma_0 \text{ satisfy } \Phi)]Xx$
$\quad \wedge \forall x \exists\Sigma_0(Xx \rightarrow (\Sigma_0 \approx_v \Sigma \wedge \forall z(\Sigma_0(\langle v, z\rangle) \leftrightarrow z = x)$
$\quad \wedge \Sigma_0 \text{ satisfy } \Phi))]$
$([\forall e : Ee][\exists x : Xx]\exists E_0$
$\quad [\exists\Sigma_0 : \Sigma_0 \approx_v \Sigma \wedge \forall z(\Sigma_0(\langle v, z\rangle) \leftrightarrow z = x) \wedge \Sigma_0 \text{ satisfy } \Psi]$
$\quad (\text{schmender}(E_0, \Psi, \Sigma_0) \wedge E_0 e)$
$\wedge [\forall x : Xx]\exists E_0$
$\quad [\exists\Sigma_0 : \Sigma_0 \approx_v \Sigma \wedge \forall z(\Sigma_0(\langle v, z\rangle) \leftrightarrow z = x) \wedge \Sigma_0 \text{ satisfy } \Psi]$
$\quad (\text{schmender}(E_0, \Psi, \Sigma_0) \wedge \forall e(E_0 e \rightarrow Ee)$
$\quad \wedge \forall e \forall E_1$
$\quad\quad [\forall\Sigma_1 : \Sigma_1 \approx_v \Sigma \wedge \forall z(\Sigma_1(\langle v, z\rangle) \leftrightarrow z = x) \wedge \Sigma_1 \text{ satisfy } \Psi]$
$\quad\quad ((\text{schmender}(E_1, \Psi, \Sigma_1) \wedge E_1 e \wedge Ee) \rightarrow E_0 e)))$

(112) $\text{schmender}(E, \ulcorner[\exists E_i : \Phi]\ \Psi\urcorner, \Sigma)$

$\leftrightarrow [\exists E' : \forall e(E'e \rightarrow \Sigma(\langle\mathfrak{C}_i, e\rangle))$
$\quad \wedge \exists\Sigma_0(\Sigma_0 \approx_{\mathfrak{C}_i} \Sigma \wedge \forall e(\Sigma_0(\langle\mathfrak{C}_i, e\rangle) \leftrightarrow E'e) \wedge \Sigma_0 \text{ satisfy } \Phi)]$
$[\exists\Sigma_0 : \Sigma_0 \approx_{\mathfrak{C}_i} \Sigma \wedge \Sigma_0(\mathfrak{C}_i) \simeq E'] \text{schmender}(E, \Psi, \Sigma_0)$

(113) $\text{schmender}(E, \ulcorner[\hat{E}_i : \Phi]\ \Psi\urcorner, \Sigma)$

$\leftrightarrow \forall e(Ee \leftrightarrow [\iota E : \text{schmender}(E, \Phi, \Sigma)]$
$[\exists\Sigma_0 : \Sigma_0 \approx_{\mathfrak{C}_i} \Sigma \wedge \Sigma_0(\mathfrak{C}_i) \simeq E](\text{schmender}(E, \Psi, \Sigma_0) \wedge Ee))$

Chapter 12
Cumulative Quantification Is Not *n*-ary

Quantifiers distinguish themselves syntactically and semantically. They are first divided between first- and second-order quantifiers. Furthermore, when first-order quantifiers are scope independent of one another, they require the special syntax of branching and its translation. Independence among second-order quantifiers is the rule, however, since they are all existential quantifiers. Since we have seen in chapter 9, section 5, that the conditions on movement distinguish the two classes, the bifurcation in how they represent independence seems to be justified on syntactic grounds. Semantically, we have seen in chapter 10 that nonmaximal cross-reference and exact description force us to recognize some distinction between increasing and nonincreasing quantifiers.

In contrast, discussions advocating *n*-ary quantifiers have proposed that quantificational independence looks the same for both increasing and nonincreasing quantifiers. It has the syntax of branching quantifiers. In a theory without plural objects, reference to events, or second-order expressions in the object language, certain interactions with adverbial conditions, such as those imposed by the reciprocals in (1) and (2), argue that branching is essential to represent independence both among increasing quantifiers and among nonincreasing quantifiers.

(1) Most stars and most dots are all connected to each other.

(2) Few stars and few dots are all connected to each other.

Confined to singular predication and not dealing with events, such a theory cannot cope with essential plurals or essential separation, and in Barwise 1979 the difference between increasing and nonincreasing quantifiers turns up anyway in the interpretation of the branching structures. Increasing quantifiers that branch are interpreted along the lines of (3), but decreasing branching quantifiers must be assigned the distinct interpretation in (4).

(3) $\exists X \exists Y([\text{most } x : N'_1(x)] \, Xx \, \wedge \, [\text{most } y : N'_2(y)] \, Yy$
$\wedge \, \forall x \forall y ((Xx \, \wedge \, Yy) \rightarrow \Phi(x, y)))$

(4) $\exists X \exists Y([\text{few } x : N'_1(x)] \, Xx \, \wedge \, [\text{few } y : N'_2(y)] \, Yy$
$\wedge \, \forall x \forall y (\Phi(x, y) \rightarrow (Xx \, \wedge \, Yy)))$

Given the empirical considerations that the addition of plural predication raises, the syntactic evidence from conditions on movement, and the different effects of increasing and nonincreasing quantifiers on unbound anaphora, one might just conclude that a conceded difference has been mistakenly located in the clauses interpreting branching. It is more pervasive and enters into the syntax of the object language.

Recently Sher (1990) and Westerståhl (1987), accepting Barwise's conclusions about representation, have proposed a uniform interpretation for branching quantifiers. Thus, in their view, quantificational independence has one look and one meaning. Were this so, it would give rise to a worry that no difference in syntactic structure seems to correlate with the fact that only objectual quantifiers are constrained in their movements. More worrisome is that it would cause us to wonder again what it is about the introduction of plurals and plural predication that should suddenly force onto the object language the syntactic and semantic distinctions between second-order and objectual quantifiers that I have been assuming. This chapter takes up the question of whether there is a unified semantics of branching quantifiers. To be fair to the argument, the discussion is confined to just those paradigms, interactions with adverbs, that first gave evidence of branching quantifiers. The difficulties that n-ary quantifiers have with plural predication have already been dealt with in chapter 4.

1 An Interaction between Cumulative Quantifiers and Adverbial Phrases

The examples of cumulative quantification in (5) and (6) do not by themselves justify cross-reference.

(5) Exactly two detectives solved exactly three crimes.

(6) No more than two detectives solved no more than three crimes.

The paraphrases in (7), without the cross-referential *there*, express the interpretation as well as those in (8).

(7) a. Exactly two detectives solved crimes, and exactly three crimes were solved by detectives.

  b. No more than two detectives solved crimes, and no more than three crimes were solved by detectives.

(8) a. Exactly two detectives solved crimes, and *there* exactly three
   crimes were solved by detectives.
   b. No more than two detectives solved crimes, and *there* no more
   than three crimes were solved by detectives.

We have seen that several sorts of examples can be called upon to argue
for cross-reference. Here I consider a particular class of examples, familiar
from the literature on *n*-ary quantification, that show an interaction between independent quantifiers and adverbial phrases:

(9) Most dots and most stars are connected to each other.[1]

(10) Most dots and most stars are connected, each of the one to all of
   the others.

(11) Most dots are connected to most stars, pairwise completely.

(12) Most dots are connected to most stars, in all possible combinations.

(13) Most dots are connected, each dot to every star, to most stars.

If the quantifiers are independent, these examples assert that most dots
are connected to stars, and most stars are connected to dots. The adverbial phrase stipulates the further condition that every one of that group of
most dots be connected to every one of that group of most stars. In other
words, the described relation contains the Cartesian product of dots and
stars.

In all the discussions that uncover *n*-ary quantifiers in such examples,
slight consideration is given to the meaning of the adverbial phrase or to
the details of its composition with the rest of the sentence. In joining this
discussion, I too will not attend to the semantics of the reciprocal and
adverbial phrases except to note the following. The composition of all
of these phrases must yield predicates of events to fit into Davidson's
scheme. Thus we will have 'to(e, each other)', 'each-of-the-one-to-all-of-
the-others(e)', 'pairwise-completely(e)', 'in-all-possible-combinations(e)',
and 'each-dot-to-every-star(e)'. These adverbial phrases mean what
they must, given their customary Davidsonian form. They are true of an
event just in case participation in that event meets the intended Cartesian-
product condition. Thus, 'pairwise-completely(e)' in (11) is true of an
event if and only if every one of the dots in that event is connected to every
one of its stars. The semantics of 'pairwise-completely(e)' will say how the
given context fixes the relevant pairs and relation. Perhaps the adverb is
to be understood attributively, with implicit arguments, e.g.,

pairwise-completely(e, 'connect(e)', 'INFL(e, x)', 'to(e, y)'), which is to say, e is pairwise complete with respect to the connectors and the connected.

I am committed to the Davidsonian form of these adverbial phrases as predicates of events. Once their meaning is fixed in this way, their interaction with cumulative quantifiers can be a matter only of scope. Let us consider what interpretations we derive if the adverbs are left entirely within the scope of the branching quantifiers. The interpretation derived for (11) is paraphrased in (16):

(14) [most $x : Dx$]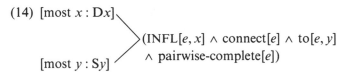

$$\text{(INFL}[e, x] \wedge \text{connect}[e] \wedge \text{to}[e, y]$$
$$\wedge \text{ pairwise-complete}[e])$$

[most $y : Sy$]

(15) [most $x : Dx$][$\hat{E} : \text{INFL}[e, x]$]
 $\exists E(\text{connect}[e] \wedge [\exists Y : \forall y(Yy \rightarrow Sy)]$
 to$[e, Y] \wedge \text{pairwise-complete}[e])$
 $\wedge$ there$_i$ [most $y : Sy$][$\hat{E} : \text{to}[e, y]$] connect$[e]$

(16) Most dots are connected to some stars pairwise completely, and *there* most stars are connected to some dots.

(17)

Suppose that in (17), $\mathbf{d}_1$, $\mathbf{d}_2$, and $\mathbf{d}_3$ are most dots and $\mathbf{s}_1$, $\mathbf{s}_2$, and $\mathbf{s}_3$, most stars. The interpretation derived from assigning the adverbial phrase narrow scope is true in (17), but the intended interpretation of (11) is false there. The connections fail to form a Cartesian product of most dots and most stars.

The intended interpretation of (9) through (13) will be derived only if the adverbial phrase is outside the scope of the cumulative quantifiers. That is, (11) asserts that most dots are connected to stars, and most stars are connected to dots, and *those connections* are pairwise complete. The adverb 'pairwise-complete(e)' applies to those events that have been asserted to involve most dots and most stars. The device of cross-reference, '[$\hat{E} : \Phi$]' in (18), makes this possible:

(18) [most $x : Sx$][$\hat{E} : \text{INFL}[e, x]$]
 $\exists E(\text{connect}[e] \wedge [\exists Y : \forall y(Yy \rightarrow Sy)]$ to$[e, Y])$
 $\wedge [\hat{E} : \Phi]$[most $y : Dy$][$\hat{E} : \text{to}[e, y]$] connect$[e]$
 $\wedge [\hat{E} : \Phi]$ pairwise-complete$[e]$

(19) a. Most stars are connected to dots, and *there* stars are connected
       to most dots, and that is pairwise complete.
     b. Most stars are connected to dots, and *there* stars are connected
        to most dots, and *there* every star *there* is connected to every dot
        there.

This view makes the relation between adverbial phrases and cumulative
quantifiers one of scope. We are able to fix the meaning of cumulative
quantifiers and the meaning of the adverbial phrases, which I assume are
predicates of events. An adverbial phrase may occur within or outside
the scope of the cumulative quantifiers. I assume that there is a way to
refer back to the events described by an antecedent clause. When the
adverbial phrase is outside the scope of the cumulative quantifiers,
the cross-reference to those events will bind the exposed event variable.
The interesting interpretation of (9) through (13), the one prominent in
the literature on *n*-ary quantifiers, is the case where the adverb has outside scope.

Not surprisingly, questions of scope are sensitive to surface structure.
Thus it seems that (20), more than (11), lets the adverb fall within the
scope of the quantifiers:

(20) Most dots are connected pairwise completely to most stars.

(11) Most dots are connected to most stars pairwise completely.

Of particular interest is an observation that Sher (1990) notes is implicit
in Barwise's (1979) translation. In my terms, the observation is that
the adverb prefers narrow scope when the cumulative quantifiers are
decreasing:

(21) Fewer than three dots are connected pairwise completely to fewer
     than three stars.

(22) Fewer than three dots are connected to fewer than three stars
     pairwise completely.

As a result of the assignment of narrow scope to the adverb, these sentences assert that fewer than three dots and fewer than three stars are distributed among pairwise-complete connections of dots and stars.[2] They
are therefore false in (23), despite the absence of a Cartesian product of all
the dots and all the stars:

(23)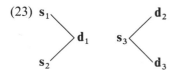

On my view, this property of decreasing quantifiers reduces to a problem that is more familiar if not solved. We expect descriptive anaphora (Evans 1977, 1980) to a decreasing antecedent to be more difficult. The device of cross-reference that we rely on when the adverb has outside scope is a descriptive anaphor. Note that with appropriate intonation, dislocating the adverb in (22), it becomes possible to understand (22) to assert that:

(24) Fewer than three dots are connected to stars, and fewer than three stars are connected to dots, and that is pairwise complete.

The adverbial phrase then entails that at least some dots are connected to stars and that whatever dots and stars are connected are connected pairwise completely.

2 Cumulative Quantifiers as *n*-ary Quantifiers

A unary restricted quantifier is a two-place relation whose arguments are one-place predicates:

(25) $Q(A(x), B(x))$

(26) no more than 2 (detective(x), x solved crimes)

The notion of a quantifier can be extended to include *n*-place relations with arguments that are *m*-place predicates. We need to consider only one type of *n*-ary quantifier:[3]

(27) $Q(A_1(x_1), \ldots, A_n(x_n), B(x_1, \ldots, x_n))$

It expresses an $(n + 1)$-place relation whose arguments are n one-place predicates and one *n*-place predicate.

One approach to cumulative quantification supposes that there is a process of lexical compounding, as it were, that forms an *n*-ary quantifier of the type shown in (27) from n unary restricted quantifiers:[4]

(28) $[Q_1\ N'_1]$
      $\vdots$ Φ
      $[Q_n\ N'_n]$

(29) $Q_1 \ldots Q_n(N'_1, \ldots, N'_n, \Phi)$

Which *n*-ary quantifier the compound expresses is determined by a definition schema. The following, which defines *independent n-ary quantifiers* in Sher (1990), serves examples of cumulative quantification uncomplicated by an interaction with adverbs (see (5) and (6)):

(30) $Q_1 \ldots Q_n(N'_1, \ldots, N'_n, \Phi)$
$\quad \leftrightarrow_{df} [Q_1 x_1 : N'_1][\exists x_2 : N'_2] \ldots [\exists x_n : N'_n] \Phi \wedge \ldots$
$\quad\quad \wedge [Q_n x_n : N'_n][\exists x_1 : N'_1] \ldots [\exists x_{n-1} : N'_{n-1}] \Phi$

On this view, the cumulative quantification in (31) asserts, in effect, that exactly two detectives solved crimes and exactly three crimes were solved by detectives.[5]

(31) Exactly two detectives solved exactly three crimes.

(32) 2!3!(detective(x), crime(y), solve(x, y))
$\quad \leftrightarrow [2!x : Dx][\exists y : Cy] \text{ solve}(x, y) \wedge [3!y : Cy][\exists x : Dx] \text{ solve}(x, y)$

(33) No more than two detectives solved no more than three crimes.

Sher's independent *n*-ary quantifiers in (30) are equivalent to what Scha (1981) takes to be the meaning of cumulative quantifiers. Scha points out that the schema in (30) is adequate for both increasing and nonincreasing quantifiers and for cumulative quantifiers that mix both types:

(34) More than 500 Dutch firms bought no more than 600 American computers.

(35) $[(> 500)x : Fx][\exists y : Cy] \text{ buy}(x, y)$
$\quad \wedge [(\leq 600)y : Cy][\exists x : Fx] \text{ buy}(x, y)$

After one revises the schema to incorporate the effects of adverbs, the increasing and nonincreasing quantifiers start to pull apart.

2.1 Essentially *n*-ary quantifiers

Sher (1990) recognizes a class of exceptions to the simple, independent quantifiers defined by (30), which she calls *complex quantifiers*. If one ignores or denies an argument place for events in natural-language predicates, branching quantifiers interacting with adverbs have to be translated as complex quantifiers, which take the form in (36):

(36) $Q_1 \ldots Q_n(N'_1, \ldots, N'_n, \Phi)$
$\quad \leftrightarrow_{df} \exists X_1 \exists X_2 \ldots X_n([Q_1 x_1 : N'_1] X_1 x_1 \wedge [Q_2 x_2 : N'_2] X_2 x_2 \wedge \ldots$
$\quad\quad \wedge [Q_n x_n : N'_n] X_n x_n \wedge \Psi[X_1, \ldots, X_n])$

In (36), Ψ embeds Φ in a larger formula that spells out the interaction with the adverb. The simple independent quantifiers defined by (30) will emerge from (36) in a moment. First, what is remarkable about (36) as a general schema for all complex quantifiers is that there is an *n*-ary condition, '$\Psi[X_1, \ldots, X_n]$', to which all the constituent quantifiers are related.

The interaction between adverbial phrase and quantifiers is not represented by a form that allows separate conditions on the constituent quantifiers. Where I have introduced a device of cross-reference between such separate conditions, *n*-ary quantification proposes that the quantifiers are all related to the same *n*-ary condition.

This view considers the schema in (36) essential for interactions with adverbs, and, assuming a uniform treatment of branching, it then extends it to all cumulative quantifiers, simple or complex. Thus, for *n* quantifiers to be cumulative is for them all to be related by second-order quantification to an *n*-ary condition. To a first approximation, the definition of a simple cumulative quantifier such as (31) then turns out to be something like (37):

(37) $\exists X \exists Y([2!x : Dx]\, Xx \wedge [3!y : Cy]\, Yy$
$\wedge\ [\forall x : Xx][\exists y : Yy]\, \text{solve}(x, y)$
$\wedge\ [\forall y : Yy][\exists x : Xx]\, \text{solve}(x, y)$
$\wedge\ [\forall x : Dx][\forall y : Cy](\text{solve}(x, y) \rightarrow (Xx \wedge Yy)))$

Note that the *n*-ary condition in (37) is (38):

(38) $[\forall x : Xx][\exists y : Yy]\, \text{solve}(x, y) \wedge [\forall y : Yy][\exists x : Xx]\, \text{solve}(x, y)$
$\wedge\ [\forall x : Dx][\forall y : Cy](\text{solve}(x, y) \rightarrow (Xx \wedge Yy))$

The quantifiers *exactly two detectives* and *exactly three crimes* "bind" the variables X and Y, which occur free in (38). Thus in place of (30) we have (39) as a special case of (36):

(39) $Q_1 \ldots Q_n(N'_1, \ldots, N'_n, \Phi)$
$\leftrightarrow_{\text{df}} \exists X_1[Q_1 x_1 : N'_1]\, X_1 x_1 \wedge \ldots \wedge \exists X_n[Q_n x_n : N'_n]\, X_n x_n$
$\wedge\ [\forall x_1 : X_1 x_1][\exists x_2 : N'_2]\ldots[\exists x_n : N'_n]\, \Phi$
$\wedge\ \ldots \wedge [\forall x_n : X_n x_n][\exists x_1 : N'_1]\ldots[\exists x_{n-1} : N'_{n-1}]\, \Phi$

Now a moment's reflection will reveal that the *n*-ary conditions that fall under (39) are too weak to capture the cumulative interpretation of *Exactly two detectives solved exactly three crimes*. Schema (37) requires only that some two detectives solved some three crimes and fails to stipulate that there were no other detectives solving other crimes. The existential, second-order quantifiers will undermine any nonincreasing quantifiers unless the conditions are strengthened. Schema (39) similarly misinterprets *Few detectives solved few crimes* as saying that a few detectives solved a few crimes. Sher proposes that the schema in (36) be modified so that the quantifiers apply to *maximal* sets:

(40) $\quad Q_1 \ldots Q_n(N'_1, \ldots, N'_n, \Phi)$

$\quad\quad \leftrightarrow_{\mathrm{df}} \exists X_1 \exists X_2 \ldots \exists X_n([Q_1 x_1 : N'_1] X_1 x_1 \wedge [Q_2 x_2 : N'_2] X_2 x_2 \wedge \ldots$

$\quad\quad\quad \wedge [Q_n x_n : N'_n] X_n x_n \wedge \Psi[X_1, \ldots, X_n]$

(max) $\quad\quad \wedge [\forall X'_1 : \forall x (X'_1 x \rightarrow N'_1 x)] \ldots [\forall X'_n : \forall x (X'_n x \rightarrow N'_n x)]$

$\quad\quad\quad ([\forall x_1 : X_1 x_1] \ldots [\forall x_n : X_n x_n](X'_1 x_1 \wedge \ldots \wedge X'_n x_n$

$\quad\quad\quad \wedge \Psi[X'_1, \ldots, X'_n])$

$\quad\quad\quad \rightarrow [\forall x_1 : X'_1 x_1] \ldots [\forall x_n : X'_n x_n](X_1 x_1 \wedge \ldots \wedge X_n x_n)))$

Thus the two detectives and three crimes that satisfy the *n*-ary condition must not be among any other detectives and crimes that do the same. Here the *n*-ary condition Ψ is (38), just that of a simple branching quantifier: detectives solve some crimes, and crimes are solved by detectives. The maximality condition guarantees that the two detectives are all those solving crimes and the three crimes are all those solved by detectives, as required.[6]

So far we have considered only how a departure from the schema for simple, independent quantifiers in (30) recovers these quantifiers as a special case. The generalization to complex quantifiers in (40) is justified by an appeal to the interactions with adverbial phrases already seen in section 1, in particular, to the interpretations of (41) to (43), where the adverbial occurs outside the scope of the cumulative quantifiers:

(41) Most dots are connected to most stars, each dot to every star.

(42) Most dots and most stars are all connected to each other.[7]

(43) Most dots are connected to most stars, pairwise completely.

Sentences (41) to (43) assert that most dots are connected to stars, and most stars are connected to dots, and every one of that group of most stars is connected to every one of that group of most dots. The adverbial phrases *each dot to every star* and *pairwise completely* and the reciprocal *all . . . to each other* impose the condition that the relation of dots to stars be a Cartesian product.

In the standard discussion of such interpretations, one free of event arguments and certainly of any devices that cross-refer to a context of events, the interpretations of (41) to (43) demonstrate that the quantifiers are essentially *n*-ary. Recall that rewriting the complex, independent quantifiers along the lines suggested by the paraphrases in (44) will fail. Suppose that in (46) $\mathbf{d}_1$, $\mathbf{d}_2$, and $\mathbf{d}_3$ are most dots and $\mathbf{s}_1$, $\mathbf{s}_2$, and $\mathbf{s}_3$ most stars. The paraphrases in (44) and the logical form in (45) are true in (46), but (9) and (11) are false there:

(44) a. Most dots and some stars are connected to each other, and most stars and some dots are connected to each other.

b. Most dots are all connected to some stars (each dot to every star), and most stars are all connected to some dots (each star to every dot).

(45) $[\exists Y : \exists y \ Yy \wedge \forall y (Yy \rightarrow Sy)][\text{most } x : Dx][\forall y : Yy] \ Cxy$
$\wedge \ [\exists X : \exists x \ Xx \wedge \forall x (Xx \rightarrow Dx)][\text{most } y : Dy][\forall x : Xx] \ Cxy$

(46)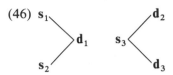

What is required is that *most dots* and *most stars* be related to a single *n*-ary condition:

(47) $\exists X \exists Y([\text{most } x : Dx] \ Xx \wedge [\text{most } y : Sy] \ Yy \wedge [\forall x : Xx][\forall y : Yy] \ Cxy)$

The logical form in (47) is false in (46), since not all the dots are connected to all the stars.

The complex interpretations for such sentences as (9) through (13) require an *n*-ary condition if the predicate is a primitive two-place '*x* is connected to *y*'. Given such essential cases, it is a short step to further suppose that all cumulative quantification fits schema (36).

3   The Interaction between Cumulative Quantifiers and Adverbial Phrases

An analogue to the scope relation between adverb and quantifier emerges from Sher's (1990) discussion of the schema for *n*-ary quantification. The contribution of the branching structure is fixed in (40). The various interpretations are distinguished by their *n*-ary conditions, and these are determined by adverbs:

(40) $Q_1 \ldots Q_n(N'_1, \ldots, N'_n, \Phi)$
$\leftrightarrow_{df} \exists X_1 \exists X_2 \ldots \exists X_n([Q_1 x_1 : N'_1] \ X_1 x_1 \wedge [Q_2 x_2 : N'_2] \ X_2 x_2 \wedge \ldots$
$\wedge \ [Q_n x_n : N'_n] \ X_n x_n \wedge \Psi[X_1, \ldots, X_n]$

(max) $\wedge \ [\forall X'_1 : \forall x(X'_1 x \rightarrow N'_1 x)] \ldots [\forall X'_n : \forall x(X'_n x \rightarrow N'_n x)]$
$([\forall x_1 : X_1 x_1] \ldots [\forall x_n : X_n x_n](X'_1 x_1 \wedge \ldots \wedge X'_n x_n$
$\wedge \ \Psi[X'_1, \ldots, X'_n])$
$\rightarrow [\forall x_1 : X'_1 x_1] \ldots [\forall x_n : X'_n x_n](X_1 x_1 \wedge \ldots \wedge X_n x_n)))$

Thus, in the complex quantification corresponding to (50) below, the adverb governing the *n*-ary condition is *pairwise completely*, which spells out the Cartesian-product condition in (52) (I suppress the maximality condition):

(48) Most dots are connected to most stars, pairwise completely.

(49) $[Qx : Dx][\hat{E} : \mathrm{INFL}[e, x]]$
$\qquad \exists E(\mathrm{connect}[e] \wedge [\exists Y : \forall y(Yy \rightarrow Sy)] \mathrm{to}[e, Y])$
$\qquad \wedge [\hat{E} : \Phi][Qy : Sy][\hat{E} : \mathrm{to}[e, y]] \, \mathrm{connect}[e]$
$\qquad \wedge [\hat{E} : \Phi] \, \mathrm{pairwise\text{-}completely}[e]$

(50) Q dots are connected to stars, and *there* dots are connected to Q stars, and that is pairwise complete.

(51) $Q_1 \ldots Q_n(N'_1, \ldots, N'_n, \mathrm{pairwise\ completely}\ \Phi) \leftrightarrow_{\mathrm{df}}$
(Q) $\exists X_1 \exists X_2 \ldots \exists X_n([Q_1 x_1 : N'_1] X_1 x_1 \wedge [Q_2 x_2 : N'_2] X_2 x_2 \wedge \ldots$
$\qquad \wedge [Q_n x_n : N'_n] X_n x_n$
(Ψ) $\wedge \, \mathrm{pairwise\text{-}completely}(X_1, \ldots, X_n, \Phi))$

(52) $Q_1 \ldots Q_n(N'_1, \ldots, N'_n, \mathrm{pairwise\text{-}completely}\ \Phi) \leftrightarrow_{\mathrm{df}}$
(Q) $\exists X_1 \exists X_2 \ldots \exists X_n([Q_1 x_1 : N'_1] X_1 x_1 \wedge [Q_2 x_2 : N'_2] X_2 x_2 \wedge \ldots$
$\qquad \wedge [Q_n x_n : N'_n] X_n x_n$
(Ψ) $\wedge \, [\forall x_1 : X x_1] \ldots [\forall x_n : X_n x_n] \, \Phi(x_1, \ldots, x_n))$

The remaining, narrow-scope interpretation of the adverb in (53) is paraphrased in (54). A dot or a star is relevant if it belongs to some pairwise-complete connection of dots and stars. It is not required that there be one, large Cartesian product of all the dots and stars:

(53) Most dots are connected pairwise completely to most stars.

(54) Q_1 dots are connected pairwise completely to stars, and Q_2 stars are connected pairwise completely to dots.

This last remark keeps the interpretation from falling under the rule for complex quantifiers in (52). This interpretation is an instance of simple, cumulative quantifiers, where the adverb *pairwise completely*, as in (58), is left inside Φ in (55).

(55) $Q_1 \ldots Q_n(N'_1, \ldots, N'_n, \mathrm{simply}\ \Phi) \leftrightarrow_{\mathrm{df}}$
(Q) $\exists X_1 \exists X_2 \ldots \exists X_n([Q_1 x_1 : N'_1] X_1 x_1 \wedge [Q_2 x_2 : N'_2] X_2 x_2 \wedge \ldots$
$\qquad \wedge [Q_n x_n : N'_n] X_n x_n$
(Ψ) $\wedge \, \mathrm{simply}(X_1, \ldots, X_n, \Phi))$

The immediate scope of the quantifiers is governed by what we may regard as the tacit adverb *simply*. The condition it imposes is spelled out in (56) (again, I suppress the maximality condition):

(56) $Q_1 \ldots Q_n(N'_1, \ldots, N'_n, \mathrm{simply}\ \Phi) \leftrightarrow_{\mathrm{df}}$
(Q) $\exists X_1 \exists X_2 \ldots \exists X_n([Q_1 x_1 : N'_1] X_1 x_1 \wedge [Q_2 x_2 : N'_2] X_2 x_2 \wedge \ldots$
$\qquad \wedge [Q_n x_n : N'_n] X_n x_n$
(Ψ) $\wedge \, [\forall x_1 : X_1 x_1][\exists x_2 : X_2 x_2] \ldots [\exists x_n : X_n x_n] \, \Phi(x_1, \ldots, x_n) \wedge \ldots$
$\qquad \wedge [\forall x_n : X_n x_n][\exists x_1 : X_1 x_1] \ldots [\exists x_{n-1} : X_n x_{n-1}] \, \Phi(x_1, \ldots, x_n))$

The simple, cumulative interpretation of (53) derives (58) from (57):

(57) most most(dot(x), star(x), simply(pairwise-completely(x, y, x is connected to y)))

(58) $\exists X \exists Y($[most $x : \text{dot}(x)$] Xx $\wedge$ [most $y : \text{star}(y)$] Yy
        $\wedge$ [$\forall x : Xx$][$\exists y : Yy$] x is connected pairwise completely to y
        $\wedge$ [$\forall y : Yy$][$\exists x : Xx$] x is connected pairwise completely to y)

   Ambiguity in (48) or (53) corresponds to the alternative forms (51) and (57). The adverb *pairwise completely* may govern the immediate scope of the quantifiers; otherwise, a default adverb is supplied, and its scope contains *pairwise completely*.[8] Note that the adverbs always occur in the scope of the second-order quantifiers that translate branching. We will see that this feature undermines a uniform treatment of increasing and nonincreasing quantifiers.

   The schema for complex cumulative quantifiers will misinterpret examples, like (59) and (60), with nonincreasing quantifiers.

(59) Few dots are connected to few stars, pairwise completely.

(60) Exactly two dots are connected to exactly two stars, pairwise completely.

My point is not that the schema falls short of some of the interpretations that I have identified by varying the scope of the adverbial. It is rather that the schema, intended to represent essential cases of complex branching quantifiers, derives for these sentences novel interpretations that are completely unacceptable. Consider the instances of the schema in (61) and (62):

(61) $\exists X \exists Y($[few $x : Dx$] Xx $\wedge$ [few $y : Sy$] Yy
(Ψ) $\wedge$ [$\forall x : Xx$][$\forall y : Yy$] Cxy
(max) $\wedge$ $\forall X' \forall Y'($[$\forall x : Xx$][$\forall y : Yy$]$(X'x \wedge Y'y)$
                $\wedge$ [$\forall x : X'x$][$\forall y : Y'y$] Cxy
                    $\rightarrow$ [$\forall x : X'x$][$\forall y : Y'y$]$(Xx \wedge Yy)))$

(62) $\exists X \exists Y($[2!$x : Dx$] Xx $\wedge$ [2!$y : Sy$] Yy
(Ψ) $\wedge$ [$\forall x : Xx$][$\forall y : Yy$] Cxy
(max) $\wedge$ $\forall X' Y'($[$\forall x : Xx$][$\forall y : Yy$]$(X'x \wedge Y'y)$
                $\wedge$ [$\forall x : X'x$][$\forall y : Y'y$] Cxy
                    $\rightarrow$ [$\forall x : X'x$][$\forall y : Y'y$]$(Xx \wedge Yy)))$

There is a context where all acceptable interpretations of (59) and (60) are false but the interpretations represented by (61) and (62) are true:

(63)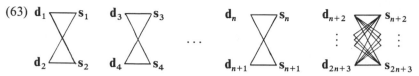

·In (63) there are $(n + 1)/2$ Cartesian products of two dots and two stars, and there is a Cartesian product of $n + 1$ stars and $n + 1$ dots. If $n + 1$ is more than a few, (59) and (60) are false on any interpretation. Note that more than a few dots and more than a few stars are distributed among the pairwise complete connections. Thus the simple cumulative interpretation, (54), is false. So is the interpretation where *pairwise completely* has outside scope, (50). This last interpretation requires that few dots and few stars are connected, which is false in (63), and that those dots and stars that are connected be pairwise complete, which is also false.[9] But (61) and (62) are true in (63). Note that each of the Cartesian products in (63) is maximal. They cannot be embedded in larger Cartesian products. So all but the last provide dots X and stars Y that meet the quantifier condition. For example, d_1 and d_2 are few (exactly two) dots, and s_1 and s_2 are few (exactly two) stars, and they are connected in a maximal Cartesian product. Thus (61) and (62) come out true.

The schema in (40) derives an unacceptable interpretation when a complex adverbial is mixed with nonincreasing quantifiers. Sher (1990) observes in her discussion of a related example that the intended interpretation of (59) and (60) can be represented if the existential second-order quantifiers are replaced by a quantifier that asserts the uniqueness of the sets that meet the maximal adverbial condition:

(64) [the (only) $\langle X, Y \rangle : [\forall x : Xx][\forall y : Yy](Dx \wedge Cxy \wedge Sy)$
$\wedge \forall X' \forall Y'(([\forall x : Xx][\forall y : Yy](X'x \wedge Y'y)$
$\wedge [\forall x : X'x][\forall y : Y'y](Dx \wedge Cxy \wedge Sy))$
$\rightarrow [\forall x : X'x][\forall y : Y'y](Xx \wedge Yy))]$
$([Qx : Dx] Xx \wedge [Qy : Sy] Yy)$

As required, uniqueness renders the interpretation false in (63), where there are many pairs $\langle X, Y \rangle$ of dots and stars connected pairwise completely. The interpretation continues, as expected, to be true in context (65) and false in context (66).

(65)

(66) $\mathbf{d}_1$ ——— $\mathbf{s}_1$

$\mathbf{d}_2$ ——— $\mathbf{s}_2$

The interaction with such adverbs as *pairwise completely* forces us to recognize two distinct schemas for interpreting cumulative quantifiers. Note that the schema for nonincreasing quantifiers, exemplified by (64), cannot serve as the interpretation of increasing quantifiers. The uniqueness requirement would make (67) false in (63), though the sentence is obviously true in that context:

(67) Some dots are connected to some stars, pairwise completely.

Thus one schema, (36), is correct only for increasing quantifiers, and another is dedicated to nonincreasing quantifiers. There is no uniform interpretation for branching quantifiers and no unified account of quantificational independence. Given the syntactic evidence from movement (chapter 9, section 5) and the semantic considerations raised by plural predication and separation, there is no reason to pursue different schemas for branching quantifiers. Rather, the distinction should be drawn in the syntax, between second-order (in)definite descriptions and cumulative, first-order quantifiers.

Attention to the truth conditions of complex, independent quantifiers also undermines the only other attempt at a uniform treatment I know of. Westerståhl (1987) shows that all natural-language quantifiers can be decomposed as the conjunction of an increasing quantifier and a decreasing quantifier. *Exactly two dots*, for example, is decomposed into *at least two dots* and *no more than two dots*. The decreasing component of the natural-language *some dots* and the increasing component of *no dots* are vacuous.[10] The *n*-ary condition then contains two conjuncts, one appropriate for increasing quantifiers and one for decreasing quantifiers. Schema (68) is the interpretation of branching quantifiers in Westerståhl's notation, where Q^+ and Q^- indicate the increasing and decreasing components, respectively:

(68) $Q_1 A$
$$\genfrac{}{}{0pt}{}{}{}\!\!\diagdown\atop\diagup \;R \Rightarrow$$
$Q_2 B$

$\exists X_1 X_2 \subseteq A, \exists Y_1 Y_2 \subseteq B\, [Q_1^+ A\, X_1\, \&\, Q_2^+ B\, Y_1\, \&\, Q_1^- A\, X_2\, \&\, Q_2^- B\, Y_2$
     $\&\, X_1 \times Y_1 \subseteq R \subseteq X_2 \times Y_2]$

Paraphrasing the interpretation of (69), we get (70):

(69) Exactly two dots are connected to exactly two stars, pairwise completely.

(70) At least two dots are connected to two stars, pairwise completely, and no more than two dots are connected to stars, and no more than two stars are connected to dots.

The paraphrase correctly renders the target interpretation. It is equivalent to assigning the adverb *pairwise completely* outside scope: exactly two dots are connected to stars, and exactly two stars are connected to dots, and the stars are connected to the dots pairwise completely.

The success of schema (68) is an artifact, however, of the quantifiers chosen in this example. There are two cases to consider. For the first case, it is necessary to dislocate the adverb with an appropriate intonation so that it occurs outside the scope of some *decreasing* quantifiers, as in (71) and (72):

(71) No more than ten dots are connected to no more than twenty stars—pairwise completely.

(72) No more than ten dots are connected to no more than twenty stars —every one of the dots to every one of the stars.

In these examples, the adverbs strongly suggest the existence of at least some dots connected to some stars, but there is no reason to think that the quantifiers have anything other than their customary sense as decreasing quantifiers. In Westerståhl's schema (68), observe that what should guarantee that there is a Cartesian product of some dots connected to some stars is just the assertion that $X_1 \times Y_1 \subseteq R$, where R is the relation $\{\langle x, y \rangle : \text{connect}(x, y)\}$. But the terms X_1 and Y_1 are related only to the increasing components of quantifiers, which are vacuous in the case of decreasing quantifiers, like *no more than ten dots* and *no more than twenty stars*. In particular, the increasing component Q^+ of a decreasing Q meets the condition that Q^+ A B $\leftrightarrow$ Q A $\varnothing$. Then, simply by choosing X_1 and Y_1 to be the empty set, it is always true, that

$$\exists X_1 \subseteq A, \exists Y_1 \subseteq B \,[(\leq 10^+)A \, X_1 \,\& \,(\leq 20^+)B \, Y_1 \,\& \, X_1 \times Y_1 \subseteq R].$$

In effect, the schema applies the adverbial condition only to the increasing constituents (see the paraphrase in (70)), and since these are vacuous in decreasing quantifiers, the effect of the adverb is lost altogether. The interpretation represented in (73) could be true even if the connected dots and stars failed to be a Cartesian product, with every dot connected to every star.

(73) $\exists X_1 X_2 \subseteq \{x : Dx\}, \exists Y_1 Y_2 \subseteq \{y : Sy\}[(\leq 10^+)\{x : Dx\} X_1$
    $\& (\leq 20^+)\{y : Sy\} Y_1 \& (\leq 10^-)\{x : Dx\} X_2$
    $\& (\leq 20^-)\{y : Sy\} Y_2 \& X_1 \times Y_1$
    $\subseteq \{\langle x, y \rangle : \text{connect}(x, y)\} \subseteq X_2 \times Y_2]$

The schema thus fails examples (71) and (72), which require a Cartesian product.

The second case that the schema fails involves quantifiers that are non-increasing and nondecreasing, like 'exactly n dots', but where the increasing and decreasing components set different limits. Consider (74) and (75), where interpretation according to schema (68) yields the paraphrase in (76):

(74) Between n and m dots are connected to between n and m stars, pairwise completely.

(75) No more than m but at least n dots are connected to no more than m but at least n stars, pairwise completely.

(76) At least n dots are connected to at least n stars, pairwise completely, and no more than m dots are connected to stars, and no more than m stars are connected to dots.

The result is a rather strange hybrid of *complex* increasing quantifiers with a *simple* cumulative interpretation of decreasing quantifiers. Consider contexts (77) to (79), which show dots and stars in connections that do form Cartesian products and those that do not. The resulting interpretation is true in (77), where there is the required Cartesian product of at least n dots and at least n stars, and *in toto* no more than m dots connected to m stars.

(77)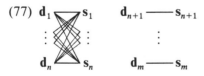

This latter condition, imposed by the decreasing component, is violated in (78), a context where the interpretation is false.

(78)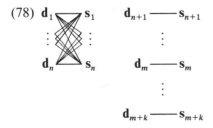

These truth conditions show that the interpretation obtained from (68) is not equivalent to a conceivable reading of sentences (74) and (75) where the quantifiers are understood as increasing, as if glossed 'some group of between *n* and *m* dots'. That reading, true in (77), is true in (78) as well.

The interpretation derived from (68) also fails to be equivalent to any interpretation of sentences (74) and (75) where the quantifiers are properly understood as nonincreasing. Placing the adverb *pairwise completely* within the scope of the cumulative quantifiers, we understand the sentences to allow the stars and dots to be distributed among distinct Cartesian products. This interpretation is true in (77) and false in (78), but it is also true in (79), where the *n* dots and the *n* stars are divided among distinct Cartesian products.

(79)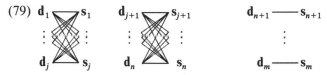

Recall that this interpretation is equivalent to the simple, cumulative quantification: between *n* and *m* dots are connected to stars, and between *n* and *m* stars are connected to dots. In contrast, the interpretation from schema (68) is false in (79). That interpretation requires a Cartesian product of at least *n* dots and at least *n* stars. Thus it is not equivalent to the narrow-scope construal of *pairwise completely*. It is also not equivalent to the target interpretation of (74) and (75), where the adverb is outside the scope of the cumulative quantifiers. This interpretation is false in all three contexts (77) through (79). In (77) it is false because all the dots and stars are not connected pairwise completely.

The patterns of star-dot connections where (74) and (75) are true are the same as those for (69).

(69) Exactly two dots are connected to exactly two stars, pairwise completely.

(74) Between *n* and *m* dots are connected to between *n* and *m* stars, pairwise completely.

(75) No more than *m* but at least *n* dots are connected to no more than *m* but at least *n* stars, pairwise completely.

They differ only in the quantity of stars and dots required. But Westerståhl's schema (68) makes them look very different. The target interpretations for (74) and (75) are obtained from schema (80), which emends (68) so that X_1 and X_2 are made identical (and replaced with X) and similarly for Y_1 and Y_2:

(80) $Q_1 A$
$$\searrow$$
$$\qquad R \Rightarrow$$
$$\nearrow$$
$Q_2 B$

$\exists X \subseteq A, \exists Y \subseteq B[Q_1^+ A\ X\ \&\ Q_2^+ B\ Y\ \&\ Q_1^- A\ X\ \&\ Q_2^- B\ Y$
$\quad \&\ X \times Y \subseteq R \subseteq X \times Y]$

It must be stipulated that the increasing and decreasing components of the quantifier apply to the same things. This stipulation will also repair the schema's first failure, where the adverb is outside the scope of decreasing quantifiers, as in (71) and (72)—a point that I leave for the reader to verify.

The apparent success of (68) in interpreting (69) is an artifact of the quantifier 'exactly n'. If its components Q^+ and Q^- apply, for example, to X_1 and X_2, (68) will be true just in case $X_1 = X_2$. This is an effect of the lower bound imposed by Q^+ being identical to the upper bound imposed by Q^-, namely n. When the upper and lower bounds differ, as in 'between n and m', (68) allows X_1 and X_2 to differ, and this results in truth conditions for (74) and (75) that differ too much from those of (69).[11]

Note that the emended schema, like Sher's suggestion in (64) for nonincreasing quantifiers, is inappropriate for interpreting increasing quantifiers. It would, for example, make (67) false in (77), where the connections between all the dots and stars do not form a Cartesian product.

(67) Some dots are connected to some stars, pairwise completely.

Westerståhl's decomposition thus either fails decreasing quantifiers and nonincreasing quantifiers such as 'between n and m', or it does not provide a uniform treatment of branching for increasing and nonincreasing quantifiers.

We have seen that when the branching quantifiers in (67), (81), and (82) are interpreted as complex, the nonincreasing and the increasing quantifiers diverge.

(67) Some dots are connected to some stars, pairwise completely.

(81) Few dots are connected to few stars, pairwise completely.

(82) Exactly n dots are connected to exactly m stars, pairwise completely.

The nonincreasing quantifiers in (81) and (82) entail that there is a Cartesian product of all dots connected to stars and all stars connected to dots. Of course, such an entailment is absent when the quantifiers are increasing, as in (67).

(50) Q stars are connected to dots, and *there* stars are connected to Q dots, and that is pairwise complete.

In Sher's and Westerståhl's schemas, where any adverb is part of the *n*-ary condition within the scope of the second-order quantfiers translating branching, this divergence requires increasing and nonincreasing branching to be interpreted by different schemas.

My view allows us to give a uniform treatment of the interaction of the adverb with the antecedent clause, whether the antecedent quantifiers are cumulative and properly branching or merely independent in virtue of being second-order (in)definite descriptions. We can derive the relevant interpretation of (67), (81), and (82) if we provide the adverb with an expression that refers back to the events described by an antecedent clause, as in (50). In the above contrast between increasing and nonincreasing quantifiers, I discern the familiar effects of descriptive anaphora, discussed in chapter 10. Only increasing antecedents license nonmaximal reference:

(83) Few farmers bought a couple of donkeys, and yet they hitched them all together in a mule train.

(84) Some farmers each bought a couple of donkeys, and they hitched them all together in a mule train.

Appendix I
Ambiguity in Logical Form

A common view of the classes of interpretations surveyed in chapter 1, section 3, one that I share, is that they are formally distinguished. Thus, if a sentence admits several of these interpretations, there is a genuine ambiguity in its logical form, and a speaker will utter it with one of its logical forms in mind. In a challenge to this view, Verkuyl and van der Does (1991) observe that the semidistributive interpretation of (1), paraphrased in (2), is entailed by both its sum-of-plurals interpretation in (3) and its fully distributive interpretation in (4):

(1) Four boys lifted three pianos.

(2) Four boys, each perhaps with some of the other boys, lifted three pianos. (Semidistributive)

(3) Four boys lifted pianos, and three pianos were lifted by boys. (Sum of plurals)

(4) Four boys each lifted (by himself) three pianos. (Distributive)

That is, (3) implies (2), and (4) implies (2). Seizing the opportunity to root out ambiguity, Verkuyl and van der Does propose that (1) has only one logical form, and it conveys semidistributivity, the weakest interpretation.[1] They suggest that the vagueness of this interpretation can be reduced in a particular context of use to convey stronger truth conditions. Their proposal is reminiscent of those attempts to eliminate scope ambiguities that exploited the fact that $\exists\forall\Phi$ entails $\forall\exists\Phi$.[2] But unlike the earlier attempts, Verkuyl and van der Does's proposal does not run up against the plain evidence of movement at LF, surveyed by May (1985, chap. 1) and Longobardi (1991) among others. Conflating (2) through (4) slights no distinction derived from movement. All three interpretations can be obtained from logical forms where *four boys* includes within its scope *three pianos*. It is thus of some interest whether vagueness can take the place of ambiguity, especially in light of the widespread sentiment that ambiguity is obnoxious, no matter how systematic. The question that Verkuyl and van der Does raise is also a crucial one for me, since I have so much riding on the integrity of the sum-of-plurals interpretation. Davidsonian logical form looks like it is made for this interpretation, which makes me think that the interpretation exists.

Van der Does (1992) already notes that reduction to the semidistributive interpretation is not a fully general strategy.[3] For in sentences like (5) and (11), the semidistributive interpretation is not the weakest.

(5) Fewer than four boys lifted three pianos.
(6) Fewer than four boys, each perhaps with others, lifted three pianos. (Semidistributive)
(7) Fewer than four boys each lifted three pianos. (Distributive)

(8) Four boys lifted fewer than three pianos.
(9) Four boys, each perhaps with others, lifted fewer than three pianos. (Semidistributive)
(10) Four boys each lifted fewer than three pianos. (Distributive)

(11) Exactly four boys lifted three pianos.
(12) Exactly four boys, each perhaps with others, lifted three pianos. (Semidistributive)
(13) Exactly four boys each lifted three pianos. (Distributive)

(14) Four boys lifted exactly three pianos.
(15) Four boys, each perhaps with others, lifted exactly three pianos. (Semidistributive)
(16) Four boys each lifted exactly three pianos. (Distributive)

The decreasing quantifiers in (5) and (8) reverse the entailment, so that it is the distributive interpretation that is entailed. The nonincreasing, nondecreasing quantifiers in (11) and (14) block entailment in either direction, so that neither interpretation can serve as the unique meaning of these sentences. This lack of generality should not, however, deter us from considering the plausibility of an unambiguous (1). One might still be drawn to it, since it is not uncommon to give a separate treatment to plural definite and indefinite descriptions (see chap. 1, n. 15, and the references cited there). The claim would be that the interactions of plural descriptions are never a source of ambiguity. Within this domain, the semidistributive interpretation is consistently the weakest. My reasons for holding to ambiguity even in the case of (1) are partly anticipated by van der Does (1992), who has rethought the conclusions of Verkuyl and van der Does 1991.

In presenting their proposal that the semidistributive interpretation of (1) subsumes the distributive and sum-of-plurals interpretations, Verkuyl and van der Does (1991) also entertain the denial of scope ambiguity. That is, it could be denied that (1) has a semidistributive interpretation or any other interpretation where *three pianos* includes within its scope *four boys*. For expository purposes, I first formulate an objection to conjoining their proposal with any such denial. I then recast the objection as an objection to the proposal itself, whether or not one denies scope ambiguity.

Taken together, the proposal and the denial lead straightaway to the result that the purported unambiguous interpretations of (17) and (18) exclude any entailment between them in either direction:

(17) Three pegs joined four boards.

(18) Four boards were joined by three pegs.

Surely there is no entailment between their alleged logical forms or between the sentences in (19) and (20), which transparently instantiate those forms:

(19) Three pegs, each perhaps with some of the other pegs, joined four boards.

(20) Four boards, each with at least some of the other boards, were joined by three pegs.

Suppose that each of three pegs by itself joins four boards and no other peg joins them. Then (19), but not (20), is true. Reflecting on such a situation, a speaker concludes that (19) does not entail (20) and no interpretation of these sentences would support such an entailment. But if the only logical forms for (17) and (18) are just those of (19) and (20) respectively, why is it obvious to speakers that (17) entails (18)? My answer is that in affirming an entailment between (17) and (18), a speaker seizes on their most salient interpretation. Disambiguated as a sum of plurals, the sentences do have logical forms that support the entailment, given that joins$(x, y) \leftrightarrow$ is-joined-by(y, x):[4]

(21) $[\exists x : 3(x) \wedge \forall z(z \in x \rightarrow Pz)][\exists y : 4(y) \wedge \forall z(z \in x \rightarrow Bz)]$
     joins(x, y)

(22) $[\exists y : 4(y) \wedge \forall z(z \in x \rightarrow Bz)][\exists x : 3(x) \wedge \forall z(z \in x \rightarrow Pz)]$
     is-joined-by(y, x)

Of course, sum-of-plurals interpretations are explicitly excluded in (19) and (20) by the distributive *each*, and so no entailment is felt there. Verkuyl and van der Does cannot discriminate speakers' judgments of the pair (17) and (18) from judgments about (19) and (20).

The exclusion of any entailment between (17) and (18) follows from the proposal that all the logical forms are unambiguously semidistributive and a denial of scope ambiguities. If the denial is now relinquished and we help ourselves to scope ambiguities, then sentences (17) and (18) do find logical forms that will bear out an entailment relation:

(23) Three pegs, each perhaps with some of the other pegs, joined four boards.

(24) Three pegs, each perhaps with some of the other pegs, is such that four boards (each perhaps with some of the other boards) are joined by it with perhaps the other pegs.

But if there are such scope ambiguities in (17) and (18), then they are also latent in (19) and (20). Why don't speakers readily affirm an entailment in the latter pair? With only semidistributive logical forms, an entailment exists within either pair only if one of the sentences is understood to have inverted the scope relations, as in (24). It is well-known that inverse scope, even in such simple examples as (25), is often not an especially salient or pragmatically neutral interpretation.[5]

(25) Some boy loves every girl.

Certainly there is more to the speaker's sense of entailments between (17) and (18) than his grasping a logical form with inverse scope for one of the sentences. If not, why is it so easy for a speaker to overlook the interpretations that fail to support the entailments, interpretations that should be more accessible since they do not involve inverse scope? Inverse scope is, of course, difficult in (19) and (20), and there speakers do neglect a possible entailment relation. In contrast, the entailment from (17) to (18) is unavoidable because their most salient logical forms, (21) and (22), represent interpretations, sums of plurals, distinct from any of the semidistributive interpretations.

To give their argument its due, we should consider how pragmatics can be expected to resolve ambiguities or alleviate vagueness. Verkuyl and van der Does suggest that an unambiguous (1) will work because a particular context of use can somehow convey truth conditions that are stronger than the weak conditions the sentence itself brings to interpretation. Hence, the appearance of a distributive interpretation arises when the semidistributive sentence is uttered in some appropriate context, and similarly for a sum-of-plurals interpretation. Shifting the burden to the pragmatics in the hope that it will come through is, of course, what anyone would do pursuing the strategy of assigning a sentence only its weakest interpretation.

Consider now the examples in (26) and (27):

(26) Cliff stood by a river or savings bank.

(27) Cliff stood by a bank.

Any intended or understood utterance of (27) eliminates an *ambiguity*. The sentence has two distinct logical forms, and eliminating ambiguity in a context of use amounts to a choice for the speaker or hearer between the two logical forms. Various considerations, pragmatics, will come to bear on that choice. Disambiguating (27), the speaker or hearer comes to believe that the utterance means the one thing and not the other. The hearer, of course, could be mistaken.

The N' in (26), *river or savings bank*, is vague in that it is true of both river banks and savings banks. Sentence (26) is analogous to the semidistributive interpretation that Verkuyl and van der Does take to be the unique meaning of the relevant sentences: weak enough to subsume all cases. Of course, most true utterances of (26) happen to be verified by something that is a river bank and not a savings bank or by something that is a savings bank and not a river bank. It is true that a speaker may utter (26) even when his grounds for the assertion warrant a more precise assertion, and in uttering (26), he may communicate something more precise to the hearer. The hearer may, for example, come to believe that it was a river bank when he hears of birds chirping in the background. None of this, however, amounts to eliminating the vagueness in the meaning of (26). Whatever the speaker or hearer has come to believe about the situation that has made (26) true, (26) does not express a proposition that, for example, entails the existence of water. In contrast, a judgment about the entailments of (27) is indeterminate until the utterance is disambiguated. If the speaker intends river banks, then he has expressed a proposition that entails the existence of water. One's grasp of the meaning expressed by an utterance is not to be confounded with the accrued beliefs about the situation that makes it true. Ambiguities are resolved in contexts of use, but vagueness in meaning is never eliminated. One just learns more about the particular situation at hand.

Verkuyl and van der Does claim that semantics gives only the semidistributive interpretation, which underinforms the language user, and pragmatics does the rest. My point is that pragmatics will not abide such an impoverished semantics. That three pegs joined four boards entails that four boards were joined by three pegs. On my view, there exist the logical forms to validate this inference. An appeal to pragmatics and to salience is necessary only to explain why the speaker is not distracted by the (semi)distributive interpretations of the sentences when he readily assents to the entailment. The task for pragmatics is the one familiar from example (27) above: disambiguation in context. For some reason, the sum-of-plurals interpretation is favored in (1), (17), and (18).

Crucially, the set of logical forms assigned to either (17) or (18) and the pragmatics of uttering one of these sentences, intending one of these logical forms, are not the same as the semantics and pragmatics for (19) or (20), sentences that make the semidistributive interpretation explicit.

(17) Three pegs joined four boards.

(18) Four boards were joined by three pegs.

(19) Three peg, each perhaps with some of the other pegs, joined four boards.

(20) Four boards, each with at least some of the other boards, were joined by three pegs.

Unlike (17) and (18), there is no relevant ambiguity in (19) and (20) (if we set aside the relative scope of the two quantifiers), no relevant disambiguation to be performed by the pragmatics, and no perceived entailment between the sentences. Now if one starts off with (17) having the same logical form as (19) and (18) having the same logical form as (20), how can pragmatics hope to restore a crucial distinction that has been effaced and recover the entailments between (17) and (18)?

Aside from the problem of distinguishing the explicit semidistributive interpretation from the implicit, what pragmatics would validate the inference from, say, (17) to (18)? Notice that the speaker's behavior, on Verkuyl and van der Does's view, turns out to be an error of comprehension; there is in fact no entailment between these sentences, according to their semantics. I guess the idea is that when uttering or hearing (17), one fixes on a prototypical situation, which happens to verify the sum-of-plurals interpetation and therefore (18) as well. One then assents to the inference, having neglected some of the relevant cases. In a similar vein, I can imagine someone saying or hearing (19), for example, and, when weighing the implications of what has just been said, forgetting to consider the degenerate case where three pegs, each by itself, join four boards.

This is not a very stable mental state. It is sure to be abandoned once the error is pointed out. But the speaker's judgment of an entailment between (17) and (18) is not so corrigible. It is hardly an error of comprehension. The problem with Verkuyl and van der Does's univocal semantics for (17) and (18) is that it just does not give the pragmatics anything to work with, anything that will sustain the speaker's judgments about entailment. These judgments reveal that the sentences are ambiguous among distinct propositions.[6]

The integrity of the sum of plurals interpretation is also evident in how one judges cross-reference to its participants. In (28a) there is a clear sense that the pronoun refers to three pianos, and along with this, one feels that the content of the definite description in (28b) reveals nothing that has not already been gleaned from the first sentence.

(28) a. Four boys lifted three pianos. They were Steinways.
     b. Four boys lifted three pianos. The three pianos were Steinways.

For Verkuyl and van der Does, (28) has just the logical forms it shares with (29).

(29) a. Four boys, each perhaps with some of the others, lifted three pianos. They were Steinways.
     b. Four boys, each perhaps with some of the others, lifted three pianos. The three pianos were Steinways.

Intuitions about cross-reference are however rather different in this case. In (29a) the pronoun refers to whatever pianos the four boys lifted, but one has no idea how many they are, at least not on a first encounter with the example. In (29b) the definite description can be understood in either of two ways. It can be taken to contain a new assertion that the pianos were in fact three in number. Interpreting it as a new assertion is the only way the definite description in (30) is understood, and it requires some focal stress on the numeral.

(30) Four boys, each perhaps with some of the others, lifted three pianos. The six pianos were Steinways.

Alternatively, if the intonation is more normal, fitting an anaphoric usage of the definite description, one senses that the definite description forces the first sentence to be disambiguated in favor of an interpretation that was not one's first guess, where *three pianos* had wide scope or was used referentially (see n. 5). Alerted to this alternative, one can, of course, return to (28a) and recognize that the pronoun may have been intended to refer to three pianos if the speaker intended *three pianos* to have wide scope in the first sentence.

Given Verkuyl and van der Does's view of *Four boys lifted three pianos*, we don't expect any differences to emerge to tell (28) and (29) apart. On my view, there is a logical form, representing the sum of plurals, available to (28) but not to (29), where it is explicitly excluded by the overt *each*. To refer to the pianos that verify the sum-of-plurals interpretation of (28) is to refer to three pianos.

To eliminate the sum-of-plurals interpretation, as Verkuyl and van der Does propose, we would have to assume that every context that admits a plural also admits semidistributivity. This is not true for a certain class that includes predicates of number, measure, or constitution.[7] For an example similar to those in (31) to (32), Lasersohn (1989) observes that the semidistributive interpretation is unacceptable.[8]

(31) a. The grains of rice weigh 25 mg.
     b. Some thirty grains of rice weigh 25 mg.

(32) a. The grains of rice fill five thimbles.
     b. Some thirty grains of rice fill five thimbles.

(33) Some customers yesterday amounted to 15 potential roof jobs and 23 extra-room installations.

Sentence (31a) can be understood to assert that each grain weighs 25 mg or that they all do. One rejects the meaning that each grain with perhaps some other grain weighs 25 mg. Why would anyone intend such an unstable and arbitrary measure? It would allow one to assert that the grains of rice weigh almost any amount between the 0.5 mg that the smallest grain weighs and the 25 mg that they weigh altogether. Note that semidistributivity can be restored, as Gillon (1990) and Schwarzschild (1991) point out, if one has reason to believe that the subgroups of rice weighing 25 mg correspond to particular events. Suppose that in each of a series of trials, one or more grains of rice is weighed, and, perhaps miraculously, the weight at each trial turns out to be 25 mg. The thirty grains of rice are all those tested during the trials. Of these grains, one could felicitously utter either (34) or (35), intending that each grain, perhaps with some of the others, weighed 25 mg in one of the trials.

(34) The grains of rice weighed 25 mg.

(35) The grains of rice, each perhaps with some of the others, weighed 25 mg.

But, these circumstances are rather different from an utterance of (31) as a simple measure of some rice sitting in a cup.

Where the sum-of-plurals, distributive, and semidistributive interpretations correspond to distinct logical forms, one comes to disambiguate (31) and (34), and one rejects out of hand that the speaker might have intended the semidistributive interpretation in a context where there is just some rice in a cup. This leaves the sum-of-plurals and distributive interpretations.[9] Of course, in (35) the speaker is quite explicit about his intentions, and the hearer is left to wonder whether anything cogent has been said. Verkuyl and van der Does cannot tell the two sentences apart if (34) is also unambiguous and semidistributive. In plucking out the only interpretation that Verkuyl and van der Does propose to represent all three interpretations, this context shows that all three are in fact distinct logical forms.[10]

Appendix II
Notation, Definitions, and Examples

1 Notation

1.1 Use of variables

$u, w, x, y, z, u', w', x',$
$y', z', \ldots$

$u_0, w_0, x_0, y_0, z_0, u_1,$
$w_1, x_1, y_1, z_1, \ldots$

$v_0, v_1, \ldots$ — first-order variables

$U, W, X, Y, Z, U', W',$
$X', Y', Z', \ldots$

$U_0, W_0, X_0, Y_0, Z_0, U_1,$
$W_1, X_1, Y_1, Z_1, \ldots$

$V_0, V_1, \ldots$ — second-order variables

$e, e', \ldots$

$e_0, e_1, \ldots$ — first-order variables over events

$E, E', \ldots$

$E_0, E_1, \ldots$ — second-order variables over events

$\mathfrak{C}, \mathfrak{C}_0, \mathfrak{C}_1, \ldots$ — second-order variables over events used only in the metalanguage as parameters for contexts of events

u, v — metavariables over first-order variables

U, V — metavariables over second-order variables

α, β, γ — metavariables over variables

i, j, k, l, m, n — variables over numbers, metavariables over numerals

$\mathbf{a}, \mathbf{b}, \mathbf{c}, \mathbf{d}, \ldots$ — nonlogical individual constants

A, B, C, D, ...	nonlogical predicates and relations
Q, Q', ...	
$Q_0, Q_1, \ldots$	quantifiers
Φ, Ψ, Γ	formulas
$\sigma, \sigma', \ldots$	
$\sigma_0, \sigma_1, \ldots$	assignment functions from variables to objects or events
$\Sigma, \Sigma', \ldots$	
$\Sigma_0, \Sigma_1, \ldots$	assignment relations between variables and objects or events
Θ	θ-roles
INFL(e_i, α), INFL$[e_i, \alpha]$	θ-roles assigned in subject position
OF(e_i, α), OF$[e_i, \alpha]$	θ-roles assigned in direct object position
TO(e_i, α), TO$[e_i, \alpha]$	θ-roles assigned in indirect object position
N, N', NP	nouns, N'-phrases, maximal Noun Phrases
V, V', VP	verbs, V'-phrases, maximal Verb Phrases
A, A', AP	adjectives, A'-phrases, maximal Adjective Phrases
P, P', PP	prepositions, P'-phrases, maximal Preposition Phrases
Det, DP	determiners, Determiner Phrases
Q, QP	quantifiers, Quantifier Phrases
S, S'	clauses, complement clauses
INFL, INFL', IP	inflections, INFL'-phrases, maximal Inflectional Phrases
COMP, COMP', CP	complementizers, COMP'-phrases, maximal Complementizer Phrases

1.2 Notational conventions

Expressions in the logical language, such as 'cluster(e)' in (30) (from chapter 1), appear in roman type.

(30) $\exists e(\text{cluster}(e) \wedge \forall x(\text{INFL}(e, x) \leftrightarrow \textit{the elms}(x)))$

When the details are irrelevant, I let expressions from the natural language stand for their own logical form. The use of italics, '*the elms*(x)' in (30), indicates such a borrowing from the natural language.

Quotation and quasi-quotation of variables are suppressed when it will not lead to confusion. Thus, '$\sigma(x) = \mathbf{a}$' appears rather than '$\sigma('x') = \mathbf{a}$' for 'σ assigns the object $\mathbf{a}$ to the variable 'x'', and '$\sigma(x_i) = \mathbf{a}$' rather than '$\sigma(\ulcorner x_i \urcorner) = \mathbf{a}$' for '$\sigma$ assigns the object $\mathbf{a}$ to the variable that is the result of writing 'x' followed by the subscripted numeral i'.

Predication is indicated by concatenation, as in 'Fx', 'Gxy', or by enclosing the arguments in parentheses, as in 'cluster(e)', 'INFL(e, x)'. Brackets are used, as in '$\Phi[v_1, \ldots, v_n]$', to list the variables free in an arbitrarily complex formula Φ rather than to mark argument positions. The latter convention is adapted to distinguish the interpretation of 'INFL$[e, x]$' from 'INFL(e, x)'. The first stands for a complex interpretation relating events and objects that is only spelled out in the semantic clauses. The second stands for the primitive thematic relation on which the definition of the first is based.

2 Definitions

The definitions and major rules for the syntax and semantics of plurality and quantification are collected below. The numbers occurring in an item, $i.j(k)[l.m(n), \ldots]$, indicate that it is introduced and discussed at length in chapter i, section j, example k, with pertinent discussion also found in the neighborhood of chapter l, section m, example n, etc. The same convention locates the discussion of the sample sentences and logical forms given below.

2.1 Mereology of events   5.3(97)

$x \mathbf{O} y$ x overlaps y

$x \leq y$ x is part of y

(1) a. $x \mathbf{O} x$

    b. $x \mathbf{O} y \leftrightarrow y \mathbf{O} x$

    c. $x \leq y \leftrightarrow \forall z (z \mathbf{O} x \rightarrow z \mathbf{O} y)$

    d. $x = y \leftrightarrow (x \leq y \wedge y \leq x)$

    e. $x \mathbf{O} y \leftrightarrow \exists z \, \forall u \, (u \mathbf{O} z \leftrightarrow (u \mathbf{O} x \wedge u \mathbf{O} y))$ (meet)

    f. $\forall x \, \forall y \, \exists z \, \forall u \, (u \mathbf{O} z \leftrightarrow (u \mathbf{O} x \vee u \mathbf{O} y))$ (join)

2.2 Syntax and rules of translation from LF to logical form

(2) The object language for which truth and satisfaction is defined below contains only the first-order variables, $e_0, e_1, \ldots, v_0, v_1, \ldots$ and the

second-order variables, $E_0, E_1, \ldots, V_0, V_1, \ldots$. The metalanguage contains second-order variables, $\mathfrak{C}_0, \mathfrak{C}_1, \ldots$, over events.

(3) Classification of NPs into first- and second-order quantifiers. Natural language NPs are classified as first-and second-order quantifiers. All definite and indefinite descriptions are second-order, e.g., *an elm, some elms, the elm, the elms, two elms, several elms*. The first-order quantifiers are exemplified by *every elm, most elms, exactly two elms, no elms, few elms* (3.1[2, 6.1.2, 7, 9.5, 10]).

(4) Types of event quantifiers (6.1). The core logical language includes three types of quantifiers over events: a second-order definite description '[$\hat{E}_i : \Phi$]', a second-order existential quantifier '$\exists E_i$', and a first-order restricted universal quantifier '[$\forall e_i : \text{VP}$]'. An extension of the language to include the cumulative interpretation of dependent quantifiers introduces an alternative second-order description, '[$?E_i : \Phi$]' (chapter 11). Except for '[$\hat{E}_i : \Phi$]', a clause contains no more than one event quantifier (6.1, 7.1.2, 7.2.3).

    a. '$\exists E_i$' takes the place of the first-order quantifier in standard Davidsonian logical forms (6.2, 5.4.2): $\exists E_i(\text{INFL}[e_i, \alpha] \text{ V}[e_i])$. An event variable e_i is bound by the proximate event quantifier, first- or second-order, with identical index (6.2).

    b. '[$\hat{E}_i : \Phi$]' is the basic device for cross-reference to the events described by an antecedent clause (see (11) below), and for picking out those events e in which a given individual is the only x such that $\Theta(e, x)$ (see (7) and (10)).

    c. The logical form of event-dependent interpretations uses '[$\forall e_i : \text{VP}$]' (1.3, 6.1).

(5) Semidistributive operator. The semidistributive operator *Co-* applies to θ-roles and takes as its restriction the restriction of the quantifier binding into the θ-role:

$$[\text{QN}'_j]_i (\ldots [\text{Co} : \text{N}'_j] - \Theta[e_k, t_i]\underline{\quad\quad}) \qquad\qquad 8.1(18)$$

(6) Quantifier raising.   6.1(6–11)[9.5]

$$[_{\Phi} \ldots \Theta[e_k, \text{NP}_i]\underline{\quad\quad}] \Rightarrow \text{NP}_i[_{\Phi} \ldots \Theta[e_k, t_i]\underline{\quad\quad}]$$

Quantifier raising derives LF from syntactic structures in which θ-roles (Chomsky 1981) are identified with Davidsonian relations to events, e.g., $[_{\text{IP}} \text{INFL}[e_k, \text{NP}_1][_{\text{VP}} \text{V}[e_k] \text{ P}_2[e_k, \text{NP}_2] \ldots \text{P}_n[e_k, \text{NP}_n]]]$. It applies obligatorily to first-order quantifiers and optionally to second-order quantifiers. If quantifier raising assigns the same scope to several quantifier phrases, a branching LF is derived:

$$[Q_1 \, N'_1]$$
$$\vdots \qquad \Phi \qquad\qquad\qquad\qquad\qquad\qquad 9.5(178)$$
$$[Q_n \, N'_n]$$

2.2.1 Rules of translation

Rules of translation apply to LF to derive logical forms, the structures interpreted by the semantics.

For NP first-order quantifiers,

(7) $[QN']_i \, [_\Phi \ldots \Theta[e_k, t_i] \text{——}] \Rightarrow [Qv_i : N'][\hat{E}_k : \Theta[e_k, v_i]][_\Phi \ldots \text{——}]$

$$7.1(16)$$

For NP second-order quantifiers,

(8) $\Theta[e_k, [\exists \, \Phi]] \Rightarrow [\exists V_i : \Phi] \, \Theta[e_k, V_i]$
(for NP left *in situ* at LF) $\qquad\qquad\qquad\qquad\qquad 7.2(34)$

(9) $[\exists \, \Phi]_i \, (\ldots \Theta[e_k, t_i] \text{——}) \Rightarrow [\exists V_i : \Phi](\ldots \Theta[e_k, V_i] \text{——}) \qquad 7.2(38)$

(10) $[\exists \, \Phi]_i \, (\ldots \Theta[e_k, t_i] \text{——}) \Rightarrow [\exists V_i : \Phi][\forall v_i : V_i v_i][\hat{E}_k : \Theta[e_k, v_i]]$
$\quad (\ldots \text{——}) \qquad\qquad\qquad\qquad\qquad\qquad\qquad 7.2(37)$

Rule (10) derives the distributive and semidistributive interpretations for second-order quantifiers. The rule is unnecessary if it is assumed that a tacit distributor, the first-order quantifier '$[\forall v_i : V_i v_i]$' (*each*), occurs at LF.

For branching structures,

(11) $[Q_1 N'_1]$
$$\vdots \qquad [_\Phi \text{——} \Theta_1[e_k, t_1] \ldots \Theta_n[e_k, t_n] \text{——}] \Rightarrow$$
$$[Q_n N'_n]$$

$[_\Psi [Q_1 N'_1][_\Phi \text{——} \Theta_1[e_k, t_1][\exists X_2 : \forall x(Xx \rightarrow N'_2(x))] \, \Theta_1[e_k, X_2] \ldots$
$\quad [\exists X_n : \forall x(Xx \rightarrow N'_n(x))] \, \Theta_n[e_k, X_n] \text{——}]_\Psi]$
$\wedge [\hat{E}_k : \Psi][Q_2 N'_2] \, \Theta_2[e_k, t_2] \wedge \ldots \wedge [\hat{E}_k : \Psi][Q_n N'_n] \, \Theta_n[e_k, t_n]$

$$9.2(16)$$

The quantifier-trace relations in the output of (11) are translated according to (7), (9), and (10).

2.3 Semantics

2.3.1 Abbreviations

(12) '$\sigma_k \approx_\alpha \sigma_l$' for '$\forall \beta(\alpha \neq \beta \rightarrow \sigma_k(\beta) = \sigma_l(\beta))$'.

The variable assignments σ_k and σ_l are identical except perhaps for the assignment to α.

(13) '$\Sigma_k \approx_\alpha \Sigma_l$' for '$\forall \beta(\alpha \neq \beta \rightarrow \forall x(\Sigma_k(\langle \beta, x\rangle) \leftrightarrow \Sigma_l(\langle \beta, x\rangle)))$'.

The variable assignments Σ_k and Σ_l are identical except perhaps for assignments to α (2.4.2).

(14) '$E_i \simeq E_j$' (read "E_i completely overlaps E_j") for

  '$\forall e(\exists e'(e\mathbf{O}e' \wedge E_i e') \leftrightarrow \exists e'(e\mathbf{O}e' \wedge E_j e'))$'   6.2(57)

The events E_i completely overlap the events E_j. That is, an event overlaps an event among the E_i if and only if it overlaps an event among the E_j.

(15) '$E_i \simeq \Sigma_k(\mathbb{C}_l)$' for

  '$\forall e(\exists e'(e\mathbf{O}e' \wedge E_i e') \leftrightarrow \exists e'(e\mathbf{O}e' \wedge \Sigma_k(\langle \mathbb{C}_l, e'\rangle)))$'   6.2(58)

The events E_i completely overlap the events assigned by Σ_k to $\mathbb{C}_l$.

Truth   6.2[5.4]

(16) A sentence Φ is true in a context of events C_0

  $\leftrightarrow \exists \Sigma$ (Σ are pairs assigning objects to variables

  $\wedge \forall e \forall i(C_0 e \leftrightarrow \Sigma(\langle \mathbb{C}_i, e\rangle)) \wedge \Sigma$ satisfy Φ)   6.2(47)

(17) A sentence Φ is true

  $\leftrightarrow \exists \Sigma$ (Σ are pairs assigning objects to variables

  $\wedge \forall e \forall i \Sigma(\langle \mathbb{C}_i, e\rangle) \wedge \Sigma$ satisfy Φ)   6.2(48)

Satisfaction

(18) Σ satisfy $\ulcorner V[e_i]\urcorner \leftrightarrow \exists e \Sigma(\langle \mathbb{C}_i, e\rangle) \wedge \forall e(\Sigma(\langle \mathbb{C}_i, e\rangle) \rightarrow Ve)$ 6.2(50)

(19) Σ satisfy $\ulcorner \Theta[e_i, V]\urcorner$

  $\leftrightarrow \exists E (E \simeq \Sigma(\mathbb{C}_i) \wedge [\forall z : \Sigma(\langle V, z\rangle)][\exists e : Ee] \Theta(e, z)$

  $\wedge [\forall e : Ee][\exists z : \Sigma(\langle V, z\rangle)] \Theta(e, z)$

  $\wedge [\forall e : Ee][\forall z : \Theta(e, z)] \Sigma(\langle V, z\rangle))$ 6.2.1(68)

(20) Σ satisfy $\ulcorner \Theta[e_i, v]\urcorner$

  $\leftrightarrow \exists E (E \simeq \Sigma(\mathbb{C}_i) \wedge [\forall z : \Sigma(\langle v, z\rangle)][\exists e : Ee] \Theta(e, z)$

  $\wedge [\forall e : Ee][\exists z : \Sigma(\langle v, z\rangle)] \Theta(e, z)$

  $\wedge [\forall e : Ee][\forall z : \Theta(e, z)] \Sigma(\langle v, z\rangle))$ 6.2.1(69)

(21) Σ satisfy $\ulcorner[Co : N']\text{-}\Theta[e_i, v]\urcorner$

$\quad \leftrightarrow [\exists X : \forall x(\Sigma(\langle v, x\rangle) \rightarrow Xx)$

$\qquad \land \forall x(Xx \rightarrow \exists\Sigma_0(\Sigma_0 \approx_v \Sigma \land \forall z(\Sigma_0(\langle v, z\rangle) \leftrightarrow z = x)$

$\qquad \land \Sigma_0 \text{ satisfy } N'))]$

$\quad \exists\Sigma_0(\Sigma_0 \approx_v \Sigma \land \forall x(\Sigma_0(\langle v, x\rangle) \leftrightarrow Xx) \land \Sigma_0 \text{ satisfy } \ulcorner\Theta[e_i, v]\urcorner)$

$\hfill 8(19)$

(22) Σ satisfy $\ulcorner \neg\Phi\urcorner \leftrightarrow \neg(\Sigma \text{ satisfy } \Phi)$

(23) Σ satisfy $\ulcorner\Phi \land \Psi\urcorner \leftrightarrow (\Sigma \text{ satisfy } \Phi \land \Sigma \text{ satisfy } \Phi)$

(24) Σ satisfy $\ulcorner[Qv_i : \Phi]\,\Psi\urcorner$

$\quad \leftrightarrow [Qx : \exists\Sigma_0(\forall y(\Sigma_0(\langle v_i, y\rangle) \leftrightarrow y = x) \land \Sigma_0 \approx_{v_i} \Sigma \land \Sigma_0 \text{ satisfy } \Phi)]$

$\quad \exists\Sigma_0(\forall y(\Sigma_0(\langle v_i, y\rangle) \leftrightarrow y = x) \land \Sigma_0 \approx_{v_i} \Sigma \land \Sigma_0 \text{ satisfy } \Psi)$

$\hfill 6.2(61)$

(25) Σ satisfy $\ulcorner[\exists V_i : \Phi]\,\Psi\urcorner$

$\quad \leftrightarrow [\exists X : \exists\Sigma_0(\forall x(\Sigma_0(\langle V_i, x\rangle) \leftrightarrow Xx) \land \Sigma_0 \approx_{V_i} \Sigma \land \Sigma_0 \text{ satisfy } \Phi)]$

$\quad \exists\Sigma_0(\forall x(\Sigma_0(\langle V_i, x\rangle) \leftrightarrow Xx) \land \Sigma_0 \approx_{V_i} \Sigma \land \Sigma_0 \text{ satisfy } \Psi)$

(26) Σ satisfy $\ulcorner[\exists E_i : \Phi]\,\Psi\urcorner$

$\quad \leftrightarrow [\exists E : \forall e(Ee \rightarrow \Sigma(\langle \mathfrak{C}_i, e\rangle)) \land \exists\Sigma_0(\forall e(\Sigma_0(\langle \mathfrak{C}_i, e\rangle) \leftrightarrow Ee)$

$\qquad \land \Sigma_0 \approx_{\mathfrak{C}_i} \Sigma \land \Sigma_0 \text{ satisfy } \Phi)]$

$\quad \exists\Sigma_0(\forall e(\Sigma_0(\langle \mathfrak{C}_i, e\rangle) \leftrightarrow Ee) \land \Sigma_0 \approx_{\mathfrak{C}_i} \Sigma \land \Sigma_0 \text{ satisfy } \Psi) \quad 6.2(56)$

(27) Σ satisfy $\ulcorner[\hat{E}_i : \Phi]\,\Psi\urcorner$

$\quad \leftrightarrow [\iota E : \text{render}(E, \Phi, \Sigma)]$

$\quad [\exists\Sigma_0 : \Sigma_0 \approx_{\mathfrak{C}_i} \Sigma \land E \simeq \Sigma_0(\mathfrak{C}_i)]\,\Sigma_0 \text{ satisfy } \Psi \quad 9.3(76)\,[7.1.1(22)]$

(28) $[\iota E : \Phi]\,\Psi \leftrightarrow_{df}$

$\quad [\exists E : \Phi \land \forall e(\exists E(Ee \land \Phi) \rightarrow \forall e'(e'\mathbf{O}e \rightarrow \exists e''(e'\mathbf{O}e'' \land Ee'')))]\,\Psi$

$\hfill 9.3(77)$

Render   9.3

(29) $\text{render}(E, \ulcorner V[e_i]\urcorner, \Sigma) \leftrightarrow \forall e(Ee \leftrightarrow (\Sigma \text{ satisfy } \ulcorner V[e_i]\urcorner \land \Sigma(\langle \mathfrak{C}_i, e\rangle)))$

$\hfill 9.3(83)$

(30) $\text{render}(E, \ulcorner\Theta[e_i, v]\urcorner, \Sigma)$

$\quad \leftrightarrow \forall e(Ee \leftrightarrow \exists E(Ee \land E \simeq \Sigma(\mathfrak{C}_i) \land \forall z(\Theta(e, z) \leftrightarrow \Sigma(\langle v, z\rangle))))$

$\hfill 9.3(78)$

(31) $\text{render}(E, \ulcorner\Theta[e_i, V]\urcorner, \Sigma)$

$\quad \leftrightarrow \forall e(Ee \leftrightarrow \exists E(Ee \land E \simeq \Sigma(\mathfrak{C}_i) \land \exists z\Theta(e, z)$

$\qquad \land \forall z(\Theta(e, z) \rightarrow \Sigma(\langle V, z\rangle))))$

$\hfill 9.3(79)$

(32) $\text{render}(E, \ulcorner \neg \Phi \urcorner, \Sigma)$
      $\leftrightarrow \forall e(Ee \leftrightarrow (\Sigma \text{ satisfy } \ulcorner \neg \Phi \urcorner \wedge \exists E(Ee \wedge \text{render}(E, \Phi, \Sigma))))$
                                                                        9.3(111)

(33) $\text{render}(E, \ulcorner \Phi \wedge \Psi \urcorner, \Sigma)$
      $\leftrightarrow \forall e(Ee \leftrightarrow [\exists E_0 : \text{render}(E_0, \Phi, \Sigma)]$
      $[\exists E_1 : \text{render}(E_1, \Psi, \Sigma)](E_0 e \wedge E_1 e))$ 9.3(82)

(34) $\text{render}(E, \ulcorner [Qv : \Phi] \Psi \urcorner, \Sigma)$
      $\leftrightarrow \Sigma \text{ satisfy } \ulcorner [Qv : \Phi] \Psi \urcorner$
      $\wedge \forall e(Ee$
      $\quad \leftrightarrow [\exists x : \exists \Sigma_0(\Sigma_0 \approx_v \Sigma \wedge \forall z(\Sigma_0(\langle v, z \rangle) \leftrightarrow z = x)$
      $\quad \wedge \Sigma_0 \text{ satisfy } \Phi)]$
      $\quad [\exists \Sigma_0 : \Sigma_0 \approx_v \Sigma \wedge \forall z(\Sigma_0(\langle v, z \rangle) \leftrightarrow z = x) \wedge \Sigma_0 \text{ satisfy } \Psi]$
      $\quad \exists E(Ee \wedge \text{render}(E, \Psi, \Sigma_0)))$ 9.3(81)

Chapter 10 replaces (34) with separate clauses for nonincreasing and increasing quantifiers:

(35) a. $\text{render}(E, \ulcorner [Q^{ni}v : \Phi] \Psi \urcorner, \Sigma)$
          $\leftrightarrow \Sigma \text{ satisfy } \ulcorner [Q^{ni}v : \Phi] \Psi \urcorner$
          $\wedge \forall e(Ee \leftrightarrow$
          $[\exists x : \exists \Sigma_0(\Sigma_0 \approx_v \Sigma \wedge \forall z(\Sigma_0(\langle v, z \rangle) \leftrightarrow z = x)$
          $\wedge \Sigma_0 \text{ satisfy } \Phi)]$
          $[\exists \Sigma_0 : \Sigma_0 \approx_v \Sigma \wedge \forall z(\Sigma_0(\langle v, z \rangle) \leftrightarrow z = x) \wedge \Sigma_0 \text{ satisfy } \Psi]$
          $\exists E(Ee \wedge \text{render}(E, \Psi, \Sigma_0)))$ 10.2.1(123)

      b. $\text{render}(E, \ulcorner [Q^i v : \Phi] \Psi \urcorner, \Sigma) \leftrightarrow$
          $[\exists X :$
          $[Q^i x : \exists \Sigma_0(\Sigma_0 \approx_v \Sigma \wedge \forall z(\Sigma_0(\langle v, z \rangle) \leftrightarrow z = x)$
          $\wedge \Sigma_0 \text{ satisfy } \Phi)] X x$
          $\wedge \forall x \exists \Sigma_0(Xx \to (\Sigma_0 \approx_v \Sigma \wedge \forall z(\Sigma_0(\langle v, z \rangle) \leftrightarrow z = x)$
          $\wedge \Sigma_0 \text{ satisfy } \Phi))]$
          $([\forall e : Ee][\exists x : Xx] \exists E_0$
          $[\exists \Sigma_0 : \Sigma_0 \approx_v \Sigma \wedge \forall z(\Sigma_0(\langle v, z \rangle) \leftrightarrow z = x) \wedge \Sigma_0 \text{ satisfy } \Psi]$
          $(\text{render}(E_0, \Psi, \Sigma_0) \wedge E_0 e)$
          $\wedge [\forall x : Xx] \exists E_0$
          $[\exists \Sigma_0 : \Sigma_0 \approx_v \Sigma \wedge \forall z(\Sigma_0(\langle v, z \rangle) \leftrightarrow z = x) \wedge \Sigma_0 \text{ satisfy } \Psi]$
          $(\text{render}(E_0, \Psi, \Sigma_0) \wedge \forall e(E_0 e \to Ee)$
          $\wedge \forall e \forall E_1$
          $[\forall \Sigma_1 : \Sigma_1 \approx_v \Sigma \wedge \forall z(\Sigma_1(\langle v, z \rangle) \leftrightarrow z = x) \wedge \Sigma_1 \text{ satisfy } \Psi]$
          $((\text{render}(E_1, \Psi, \Sigma_1) \wedge E_1 e \wedge Ee) \to E_0 e)))$ (10.2.1(125)

(36) $\text{render}(E, \ulcorner [\exists V : \Phi] \Psi \urcorner, \Sigma)$

$\quad \leftrightarrow [\exists X : \exists \Sigma_0 (\Sigma_0 \approx_V \Sigma \wedge \forall x (\Sigma_0 (\langle V, x \rangle) \leftrightarrow Xx) \wedge \Sigma_0 \text{ satisfy } \Phi)]$

$\quad [\exists \Sigma_0 : \Sigma_0 \approx_V \Sigma \wedge \forall x (\Sigma_0 (\langle V, x \rangle) \leftrightarrow Xx) \wedge \Sigma_0 \text{ satisfy } \Psi]$

$\qquad \text{render}(E, \Psi, \Sigma_0)$ 9.3(90)

(37) $\text{render}(E, \ulcorner [\exists E_i : \Phi] \Psi \urcorner, \Sigma)$

$\quad \leftrightarrow [\exists E' : \forall e (E'e \rightarrow \Sigma (\langle \mathfrak{C}_i, e \rangle))$

$\qquad \wedge \exists \Sigma_0 (\Sigma_0 \approx_{\mathfrak{C}_i} \Sigma \wedge \forall e (\Sigma_0 (\langle \mathfrak{C}_i, e \rangle) \leftrightarrow E'e) \wedge \Sigma_0 \text{ satisfy } \Phi)]$

$\quad [\exists \Sigma_0 : \Sigma_0 \approx_{\mathfrak{C}_i} \Sigma \wedge E' \simeq \Sigma_0 (\mathfrak{C}_i) \wedge \Sigma_0 \text{ satisfy } \Psi] \text{ render}(E, \Psi, \Sigma_0)$

9.3(84)

(38) $\text{render}(E, \ulcorner [\hat{E}_i : \Phi] \Psi \urcorner, \Sigma)$

$\quad \leftrightarrow \forall e (Ee \leftrightarrow [\imath E_0 : \text{render}(E_0, \Phi, \Sigma)]$

$\quad [\exists \Sigma_0 : \Sigma_0 \approx_{\mathfrak{C}_i} \Sigma \wedge E_0 \simeq \Sigma_0 (\mathfrak{C}_i)]$

$\qquad (\Sigma_0 \text{ satisfy } \Psi \wedge \exists E_1 (\text{render}(E_1, \Psi, \Sigma_0) \wedge E_1 e)))$ 9.3(85)

Schmender

(39) $\Sigma \text{ satisfy } \ulcorner [?E_i : \Phi] \Psi \urcorner$

$\quad \leftrightarrow [\exists E : \text{schmender}(E, \Phi, \Sigma)] [\exists \Sigma_0 : \Sigma_0 \approx_{\mathfrak{C}_i} \Sigma \wedge E \simeq \Sigma_0 (\mathfrak{C}_i)]$

$\quad \Sigma_0 \text{ satisfy } \Psi$ 11(105)

(40) $\text{schmender}(E, \ulcorner V[e_i] \urcorner, \Sigma)$

$\quad \leftrightarrow \forall e (Ee \leftrightarrow (\Sigma \text{ satisfy } \ulcorner V[e_i] \urcorner \wedge \Sigma (\langle \mathfrak{C}_i, e \rangle)))$ 11(106)

(41) $\text{schmender}(E, \ulcorner \Theta[e_i, v] \urcorner, \Sigma)$

$\quad \leftrightarrow \forall e (Ee \leftrightarrow \exists E (Ee \wedge E \simeq \Sigma (\mathfrak{C}_i) \wedge \forall z (\Theta(e, z) \leftrightarrow \Sigma (\langle v, z \rangle))))$

11(107)

(42) $\text{schmender}(E, \ulcorner \Theta[e_i, V] \urcorner, \Sigma)$

$\quad \leftrightarrow \forall e (Ee \leftrightarrow \exists E (Ee \wedge E \simeq \Sigma (\mathfrak{C}_i) \wedge \exists z \Theta(e, z) \wedge \forall z (\Theta(e, z)$

$\qquad \rightarrow \Sigma (\langle V, z \rangle))))$ 11(108)

(43) $\text{schmender}(E, \ulcorner \Phi \wedge \Psi \urcorner, \Sigma)$

$\quad \leftrightarrow \forall e (Ee$

$\qquad \leftrightarrow [\exists E_0 : \text{schmender}(E_0, \Phi, \Sigma)]$

$\qquad [\exists E_1 : \text{schmender}(E_1, \Psi, \Sigma)] (E_0 e \wedge E_1 e))$ 11(109)

(44) $\text{schmender}(E, \ulcorner [\exists V : \Phi] \Psi \urcorner, \Sigma)$

$\quad \leftrightarrow [\exists X : \exists \Sigma_0 (\Sigma_0 \approx_V \Sigma \wedge \forall x (\Sigma_0 (\langle V, x \rangle) \leftrightarrow Xx) \wedge \Sigma_0 \text{ satisfy } \Phi)]$

$\quad [\exists \Sigma_0 : \Sigma_0 \approx_V \Sigma \wedge \forall x (\Sigma_0 (\langle V, x \rangle) \leftrightarrow Xx)] \text{ schmender}(E, \Psi, \Sigma_0)$

11(110)

(45) $\text{schmender}(E, \ulcorner[Q^i v : \Phi] \, \Psi \urcorner, \Sigma) \leftrightarrow$

$[\exists X :$

$\quad [Q^i x : \exists \Sigma_0 (\Sigma_0 \approx_v \Sigma \wedge \forall z (\Sigma_0 (\langle v, z \rangle) \leftrightarrow z = x)$

$\quad\quad \wedge \Sigma_0 \text{ satisfy } \Phi)] X x$

$\quad \wedge \forall x \exists \Sigma_0 (X x \to (\Sigma_0 \approx_v \Sigma \wedge \forall z (\Sigma_0 (\langle v, z \rangle) \leftrightarrow z = x)$

$\quad\quad \wedge \Sigma_0 \text{ satisfy } \Phi))]$

$([\forall e : Ee][\exists x : Xx] \exists E_0$

$\quad [\exists \Sigma_0 : \Sigma_0 \approx_v \Sigma \wedge \forall z (\Sigma_0 (\langle v, z \rangle) \leftrightarrow z = x) \wedge \Sigma_0 \text{ satisfy } \Psi]$

$\quad (\text{schmender}(E_0, \Psi, \Sigma_0) \wedge E_0 e)$

$\wedge [\forall x : Xx] \exists E_0$

$\quad [\exists \Sigma_0 : \Sigma_0 \approx_v \Sigma \wedge \forall z (\Sigma_0 (\langle v, z \rangle) \leftrightarrow z = x) \wedge \Sigma_0 \text{ satisfy } \Psi]$

$\quad (\text{schmender}(E_0, \Psi, \Sigma_0) \wedge \forall e (E_0 e \to Ee)$

$\quad\quad \wedge \forall e \forall E_1$

$\quad\quad\quad [\forall \Sigma_1 : \Sigma_1 \approx_v \Sigma \wedge \forall z (\Sigma_1 (\langle v, z \rangle) \leftrightarrow z = x) \wedge \Sigma_1 \text{ satisfy } \Psi]$

$\quad\quad\quad ((\text{schmender}(E_1, \Psi, \Sigma_1) \wedge E_1 e \wedge Ee) \to E_0 e)))$ 11(111)

(46) $\text{schmender}(E, \ulcorner \exists E_i : \Phi] \, \Psi \urcorner, \Sigma)$

$\quad \leftrightarrow [\exists E' : \forall e (E' e \to \Sigma (\langle \mathfrak{C}_i, e \rangle))$

$\quad\quad \wedge \exists \Sigma_0 (\Sigma_0 \approx_{\mathfrak{C}_i} \Sigma \wedge \forall e (\Sigma_0 (\langle \mathfrak{C}_i, e \rangle) \leftrightarrow E' e) \wedge \Sigma_0 \text{ satisfy } \Phi)]$

$\quad [\exists \Sigma_0 : \Sigma_0 \approx_{\mathfrak{C}_i} \Sigma \wedge E' \simeq \Sigma_0 (\mathfrak{C}_i)] \, \text{schmender}(E, \Psi, \Sigma_0)$ 11(112)

(47) $\text{schmender}(E, \ulcorner[\hat{E}_i : \Phi] \, \Psi \urcorner, \Sigma)$

$\quad \leftrightarrow \forall e (Ee \leftrightarrow [\iota E : \text{schmender}(E, \Phi, \Sigma)]$

$\quad [\exists \Sigma_0 : \Sigma_0 \approx_{\mathfrak{C}_i} \Sigma \wedge E \simeq \Sigma_0 (\mathfrak{C}_i)] \, (\text{schmender}(E, \Psi, \Sigma_0) \wedge Ee))$

    11(113)

3   Examples

The following examples illustrate logical forms for the most basic types of interpretations. In each example, the first logical form is in the language of part 2 above. The examples end with a paraphrase. Where it is not cumbersome, a second logical form gives an equivalent of the first in a standard second-order logic augmented by restricted quantifiers, the second-order definite-description operator in (48), and the abbreviations in (49) through (52):

(48) $[\iota V : \Phi] \, \Psi \leftrightarrow_{\text{df}}$

$\quad [\exists Y : \Phi[V/Y] \wedge \forall y (\exists Z (Zy \wedge \Phi[V/Z]) \to Yy)] \, \Psi[V/Y]$

(Sharvy 1980)

(If Y is a variable that does not occur in Φ, $\Phi[V/Y]$ is the formula that substitutes Y for all occurrences of V free in Φ. Similarly for $\Phi[V/Z]$ and $\Psi(V/Y)$.)

(49) '$E_i \simeq E_j$' (read "E_i completely overlaps E_j") for

$\forall e(\exists e'(e\mathbf{O}e' \wedge E_i e') \leftrightarrow \exists e'(e\mathbf{O}e' \wedge E_j e'))$'

(50) '$V[E]$' for '$\forall e(Ee \rightarrow Ve)$'   (cf. (18))

(51) '$\Theta[E, V]$' for

$[\forall z : Vz][\exists e : Ee]\, \Theta(e, z) \wedge [\forall e : Ee][\exists z : Vz]\, \Theta(e, z)$

$\wedge [\forall e : Ee][\forall z : \Theta(e, z)]\, Vz$'   (cf. (19))

(52) '$\Theta[E, v]$' for

'$\exists e Ee \wedge [\forall e : Ee]\, \forall z(\Theta(e, z) \leftrightarrow z = v)$'   (cf. (20))

Sum of plurals   1.1, 1.2.1, 6.2, 7.2, 5.4.2

(53) a. Some students shared twenty-three pizzas.
   b. $\exists F_0([\exists V_0 : (> 1)(V_0) \wedge \exists F_1 \text{ student}[e_1, V_0]]\, \text{INFL}[e_0, V_0]$
       $\wedge \text{ share}[e_0] \wedge [\exists V_1 : 23(V_1) \wedge \exists E_1 \text{ pizza}[e_1, V_1]]\, \text{OF}[e_0, V_1])$
   c. $\exists E([\exists X : (> 1)(X) \wedge \forall x(Xx \rightarrow \text{student}(x))]$
       $[\exists E' : E \simeq E']\, \text{INFL}[E', X]$
       $\wedge \text{ share}[E]$
       $\wedge [\exists Y : 23(Y) \wedge \forall y(Yy \rightarrow \text{pizza}(y))][\exists E' : E \simeq E']\, \text{OF}[E', Y])$
   d. There are some events of sharing such that some students are
       sharers in events that completely overlap those events and
       in completely overlapping events twenty-three pizzas are shared.

Suppose that the communal sense of 'share' is intended, so students
swapping food at the fraternity table are sharing with each other but not
with the students in another fraternity. Sentence (53a) can report that
some students and 23 pizzas are distributed among several such fraternal
sharings. Thus the quantification over events is second-order. Suppose
further that the several fraternities share a common kitchen from which
they order pizza by the slice any number at a time. The sentence does not
require that any one pizza be consumed wholly within one fraternity, that
is, at just one of the tables. Its consumption may overlap several sharings.
Hence the interpretation of (53b) and the logical form (53c) refer to overlapping events (6.2).

   The text, like (53c), refrains from treating nouns as expressing relations
between objects and events, but there is every reason to think that they do,
as appears in (53b). See Higginbotham 1987 for some discussion.

Distributivity   1.2.2, 6.2, 7.1

(54) a. Every student ate a pizza.
   b. [every $v_0 : \exists E_1$ student$[e_1, v_0]$][$\hat{E}_0 :$ INFL$[e_0, v_0]$]
      $\exists E_0$(eat$[e_0] \wedge [\exists V_1 : 1(V_1) \wedge \exists F_1$ pizza$[e_1, V_1]]$ OF$[e_0, V_1]$)
   c. [every $x :$ student(x)][$\imath E : \forall e(Ee \leftrightarrow$ INFL$(e, x))$]
      $[\exists E' : \exists E''(E'' \simeq E \wedge \forall e(E'e \to E''e))]$
         $([\exists E'' : E'' \simeq E']$ eat$[E'']$
         $\wedge [\exists Y : 1(Y) \wedge \forall y(Yy \to$ pizza$(y))][\exists E'' : E'' \simeq E']$ OF$[E'', Y]$)
   d. Every student is such that whatever he did as an eater, if anything, is such that there are some events in which a pizza is eaten.

(55) a. Every student ate no pizza.
   b. [every $v_0 : \exists E_1$ student$[e_1, v_0]$][$\hat{E}_0 :$ INFL$[e_0, v_0]$]
      [no $v_1 : \exists E_1$ pizza$[e_1, v_1]$][$\hat{E}_0 :$ OF$[e_0, v_1]]\exists E_0$ eat$[e_0]$
   c. [every $x :$ student(x)][$\imath E : \forall e(Ee \leftrightarrow$ INFL$(e, x))$][no $y :$ pizza(y)]
      $[\imath E' : \exists E''(E'' \simeq E \wedge \forall e(E'e \leftrightarrow (E''e \wedge$ OF$(e, y))))]$
      $[\exists E : \exists E''(E'' \simeq E' \wedge \forall e(Ee \to E''e))]$ eat$[E]$
   d. Every student is such that whatever he did as an eater, if anything, is such that no pizza is such that whatever happened to it there, if anything, an eating.

(56) a. Some students (each) ate a pizza.
   b. $[\exists V_0 : (>1)(V_0) \wedge \exists E_1$ student$[e_1, V_0]][\forall v_0 : V_0 v_0]$
      $[\hat{E}_0 :$ INFL$[e_0, v_0]$]
      $\exists E_0$(eat$[e_0] \wedge [\exists V_1 : 1(V_1) \wedge \exists E_1$ pizza$[e_1, V_1]]$ OF$[e_0, V_1]$)
   c. $[\exists X : (>1)(X) \wedge \forall x(Xx \to$ student$(x))][\forall x : Xx]$
      $[\imath E : \forall e(Ee \leftrightarrow$ INFL$(e, x))$]
      $[\exists E' : \exists E''(E'' \simeq E \wedge \forall e(E'e \to E''e))]$
      (eat$[E']$
      $\wedge [\exists Y : 1(Y) \wedge \forall y(Yy \to$ pizza$(y))][\exists E'' : E'' \simeq E']$ OF$[E'', Y]$)

(57) a. Some students met at every reunion.
   b. $[\exists V_0 : (>1)(V_0) \wedge \exists E_1$ student$[e_1, V_0]]$
      [every $v_1 : \exists E_1$ reunion$[e_1, v_1]$]
      $[\hat{E}_0 :$ at$[e_0, v_1]]\exists E_0$(INFL$[e_0, V_0] \wedge$ meet$[e_0]$)
   c. $[\exists X : (>1)(X) \wedge \forall x(Xx \to$ student$(x))$][every $y :$ reunion(y)]
      $[\imath E : \forall e(Ee \leftrightarrow$ at$(e, y))][\exists E' : \exists E''(E'' \simeq E \wedge \forall e(E'e \to E''e))]$
      $([\exists E : E \simeq E']$ INFL$[E, X] \wedge$ meet$[E']$)

Semidistributivity   chap. 8

(58) a. Few composers collaborated.   8.1(14)

    b. [few $v_0 : \exists E_1$ composer$[e_1, v_0]$]
       $[\hat{E}_0 : [\text{Co} : \exists E_1$ composer$[e_1, v_0]]$-INFL$[e_0, v_0]]\exists E_0$ collaborate$[e_0]$

    c. [few $x :$ composer(x)]
       $[\iota E : \forall e(Ee \leftrightarrow \exists X \exists E(Ee \wedge Xx \wedge \forall x(Xx \rightarrow \text{composer}(x))$
       $\wedge \text{INFL}[E, X]))]$
       $[\exists E' : \exists E''(E'' \simeq E \wedge \forall e(E'e \rightarrow E''e))]$ collaborate$[E']$

    d. Few composers are such that whatever they and some other composers did as collaborators, if anything, is such that there is a collaboration.

Event dependence   1.3

(59) a. No more than ten students (ever) work on three problems.

                                               1.3(62)

    b. $[\forall e_0 : \text{work}[e_0] \wedge [\exists V_1 : 3(V_1) \wedge \exists E_1 \text{ problem}[e_1, V_1]] \text{ on}[e_0, V_1]]$
       $[(\leq 10) v_0 : \exists E_1 \text{ student}[e_1, v_0]][\hat{E}_0 : \text{INFL}[e_0, v_0]]\exists E_0 \text{ work}[e_0]$

    c. $[\forall E : \exists e(\text{work}(e) \wedge \forall e'(Ee' \leftrightarrow e' = e))$
       $\wedge [\exists Y : 3(Y) \wedge \forall y(Yy \rightarrow \text{problem}(y))][\exists E' : E \simeq E'] \text{ on}[E', Y]]$
       $[(\leq 10) x : \text{student}(x)]$
       $[\iota E' : \exists E''(E'' \simeq E \wedge \forall e(E'e \leftrightarrow (E''e \wedge \text{INFL}(e, x))))]$
       $[\exists E : \exists E''(E'' \simeq E' \wedge \forall e(Ee \rightarrow E''e))] \text{ work}[E]$

    d. Whenever there is a working on three problems, no more than ten students participate.

Cumulative quantification   chap. 9

(60) a. No more than two detectives solved no more than three crimes.

    b. $[_\Phi [(\leq 2) v_0 : \exists E_1 \text{ detective}[e_1, v_0]][\hat{E}_0 : \text{INFL}[e_0, v_0]]$
       $\exists E_0(\text{solve}[e_0] \wedge [\exists V_1 : \exists E_1 \text{ crime}[e_1, V_1]] \text{ OF}[e_0, V_1]) _\Phi]$
       $\wedge [\hat{E}_0 : \Phi][(\leq 3) v_1 : \exists E_1 \text{ crime}[e_1, v_1]][\hat{E}_0 : \text{OF}[e_0, v_1]]$
       $\exists E_0 \text{solve}[e_0]$

    c. No more than two detectives solved crimes, and *there* no more than three crimes were solved.

(61) a. No more than two detectives (each) solved two crimes, for no more than five agencies.

b. $[_\Phi [(\le 2)\, v_0 : \exists E_1\ \text{detective}[e_1, v_0]][\hat{E}_0 : \text{INFL}[e_0, v_0]]$
   $\exists E_0 (\text{solve}[e_0]$
   $\quad \wedge\ [\exists V_1 : 2(V_1) \wedge \exists E_1\ \text{crime}[e_1, V_1]]\ \text{OF}[e_0, V_1]$
   $\quad \wedge\ [\exists V_2 : \exists E_1\ \text{agency}[e_1, V_2]]\ \text{for}[e_0, V_2])\,_\Phi]$
   $\wedge\ [\hat{E}_0 : \Phi][(\le 5)\, v_2 : \exists E_1\ \text{agency}[e_1, v_2]][\hat{E}_0 : \text{for}[e_0, v_2]]$
   $\exists E_0 \text{solve}[e_0]$

c. No more than two detectives each solved two crimes for agencies, and whatever events there were of detectives each solving two crimes were solvings for no more than five agencies.

Notes

Chapter 1

1. The phrase and example (8) are from Boolos 1985b.

2. From Burge 1977.

3. The proposal goes back at least to Russell 1903/1938. It is developed more recently by Burge (1977), Carlson (1980, 1982), Higginbotham (1980, 1987), Cormack and Kempson (1981), Link (1983, 1987), Lønning (1987), and Scha (1981), among others. These authors variously identify plural objects with aggregates, groups, sets, or sums.

4. Definite descriptions of plural objects are discussed further in chapter 2, section 1.2.

5. See also Higginbotham and Schein 1989 and Schein 1986.

6. As emended by Castañeda (1967).

7. 'INFL' will be used throughout to stand for whatever θ-role is assigned to the subject. Similarly, 'OF' stands for the θ-role assigned to the direct object, and 'TO' the one assigned to an indirect object. Typically, θ-roles are taken to express notions like Agent, Theme, Goal, and Instrument, but see the discussion at the beginning of chapter 5.

8. (For my purposes, any primitive relation between events and other objects may serve as a θ-role. Thus, an acceptable alternative to (25) could be a logical form that has a verb doing duty as a θ-role: $\exists e(\text{Agent}(e, b) \ \& \ \text{stab}(e, c))$.)

9. See chapter 3, section 1; chapter 7; chapter 9, section 5; chapter 10 (especially n. 3); Higginbotham and Schein 1989; and Schein 1992 for further arguments supporting the classification of natural language quantifiers into first- and second-order.

10. So, if *the elms* refers to the plural object **a**, which is therefore available to be the subject of predication, the logical form for *The elms are clustered* will have to be as in (i):

(i) $\exists e(\text{cluster}(e) \wedge \text{INFL}(e, \mathbf{a}))$

11. See, for example, the arguments mustered in Parsons 1990.

12. One who rejects the earlier argument can meet Davidsonian arguments in the literature by adopting (i), where **a** and **b** are plural objects:

(i) '$V(e, \mathbf{a}, \mathbf{b})$' is true $\leftrightarrow$ Agent$(e, \mathbf{a}) \wedge V^*e \wedge$ Theme$(e, \mathbf{b})$

The formulation in (i) represents even less of a departure from the standard syntax.

13. Compare *Once, no more than three video games were played*, where a non-vacuous construal of *once* depends on the context.

14. Some speakers take exception to the clash in number agreement between the pronoun in (46a) and its superficial antecedent *a donkey*. I have no explanation for their behavior except to suggest that they rely on number agreement as a cue for disambiguating the pronoun. In (46c), there is no clash, and in (46b) content disambiguates despite it. I know of no semantic reason why the anaphoric possibilities of the pronoun and definite description should differ in this context. It suffices for our purpose that the pronoun in (46c) and the definite description in (46b) refer cumulatively to whatever donkeys farmers bought.

15. Compare interpretations of branching quantifiers:

(i) $[(\leq 2)x : Dx]$

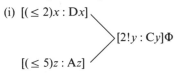

$[2!y : Cy]\Phi$

$[(\leq 5)z : Az]$

16. Verkuyl (1988), Lasersohn (1989) and van der Does (1992), who also cites Lønning (1991), observe that a plural definite or indefinite description, as in (i) and (ii), resists a semidistributive interpretation that includes the object quantifier within its scope.

(i) a. Forty men gathered in a public square.
    b. The forty men gathered in a public square.

(ii) a. Forty students collaborated on two problems.
     b. The forty students collaborated on two problems.

The forty are not divided among several public squares, and there are not, for example, four problems worked on in separate collaborations. The more general observation, found in Moltmann 1992, is that indefinite and definite descriptions resist any kind of distributivity. I have no particular account of this preference, which I do not think reflects the underlying semantics. There are contexts that bring out the distributive interpretations. It has been observed, for example, that the pragmatics of (iii) overcomes the preference:

(iii) Forty men ate a hamburger.

The preference in (i) and (ii) against semidistributivity can also be overcome, as Gillon (1990), Schwarzschild (1991), and Verkuyl and van der Does (1991) have noted. For (ii), the idea is to find a context that makes events of collaborating on two problems salient or makes it a significant property of an individual that he has collaborated on two problems with others. Suppose that there is a linguistics olympiad at which competing teams are each given two problems randomly chosen from a larger set. Each competing team constitutes a collaboration, and the rival teams together are obviously not a collaboration. It is a fair report of the olympiad to say (iv), intending to assert that there were forty students among the teams.

(iv) Forty students collaborated on two problems.

Participation in one of the teams is an event of collaborating on two problems.

For another example, suppose that a student director becomes eligible to join the directors guild only after collaborating on at least two productions with other students. Thus, having collaborated with others on two problems is an interesting property of individuals. Then (v) can report that forty students made the grade in some way or other, without implying that the forty students worked on the same two productions.

(v) Forty students collaborated on two productions.

Some further considerations suggest that the bias against (semi)distributivity is not a syntactic or semantic fact. First, the possibility of a bound variable within the object NP enhances the scope-dependent interpretation of the direct object:

(vi) a. Forty students collaborated on two productions that were good enough to get them admitted.
  b. Forty students collaborated on two productions that were good enough to get them a scholarship.

Second, the bias against (semi)distributivity seems to be confined to those cases, such as (i) to (iv), where a sum-of-plurals interpretation presents itself as the favored interpretation. If a quantifier in object position precludes this, as it does in (vii), then the (semi)distributive interpretation is once again made salient.

(vii) a. Forty students collaborated on fewer than two productions.
  b. Forty students worked on fewer than two productions.

The sentences in (vii) seem to be perfectly ambiguous. Either there were forty students whose work or collaboration amounted to fewer than two productions, or, (semi)distributively, forty students each worked or collaborated with others on fewer than two productions.

The syntax and semantics required for (vi) and (vii) will, it is true, assign to (i) through (iv) interpretations that they disfavor in the most neutral contexts. I see no way out from this if the semantics is to be generally adequate. To explain the bias, note that in the case of plural definite and indefinite descriptions, the (semi)distributive interpretations are obtained only through the intervention of a tacit distributive operator, '$[\forall x : Xx]$' in (viii).

(viii) a. $[\exists X : 40(X) \wedge \forall x(Xx \rightarrow Sx)][\forall x : Xx][\exists e : e \leq e']$
    $[\exists X : Xx \wedge \forall x(Xx \rightarrow Sx)] \forall z(\text{INFL}(e, z) \leftrightarrow Xx)\dots$
  b. $[\exists X : 40(X) \wedge \forall x(Xx \rightarrow Sx)][\forall x : Xx][\exists e : e \leq e']$
    $\forall z(\text{INFL}(e, z) \leftrightarrow z = x)\dots$

Perhaps, one prefers, ceteris paribus, to avoid the additional structure. This would at least distinguish plural definite and indefinite descriptions from the first-order quantifiers while allowing them to participate in (semi)distributive interpretations, as they do.

Moltmann (1992, 426, n. 7) acknowledges that the bias against scope interactions has exceptions, but only when "the predicates (VPs) describe well-established properties, i.e., with predicates that are lexicalized." She refers to a manuscript (1990), which I have not seen, for her full account of the phenomenon. However, guessing from the examples she cites, which are similar to (i) through (iv), I assume that the conditions under which a predicate describes a well-established property will pick out contexts such as those discussed above where there are salient events of collaborating on two problems or where it becomes an interesting property of individuals to have collaborated with others on two productions. She concludes from the restriction to well-established properties that the tacit distributive operator "may apply in the lexicon, though not in sentence meaning." There is here a descriptive claim that I think is mistaken because of the considerations mentioned above. A bound pronoun or a certain quantifier in object position is a sufficient cue for the (semi)distributive interpretation. Its felicity is in that case not restricted to special contexts. On Moltmann's account, it remains to be seen in what sense a VP will describe a well-established property whenever it contains a bound pronoun or a quantifier like *fewer than two productions*. Apart from the descriptive point, I have no objection to the suggestion that the restrictions on tacit distributive operators are more grammaticalized than in the pragmatic account I allude to above. Note, however, that Moltmann's lexicon must be a fairly syntactic place to form complex predicates incorporating arbitrary NPs appearing in object position. Plural descriptions engage in the usual scope interactions; only they do it elsewhere.

17. The event-dependent interpretation can be readily seen as a generic interpretation. As a point of fact, it is unclear to me whether that is the only interpretation or whether there is also a less nomic event-dependent interpretation. If it is generic and generics are quantificational, then replace the universal quantifier with the appropriate quantifier. It would serve my point just as well if, on the other hand, generics are derived by singular reference to a kind, as in Carlson 1977, so long as it is reference to a kind of event and the referring term is a bare VP.

Chapter 2

1. See Russell 1903/1938 and more recently Burge 1977; Carlson 1980, 1982; Cormack and Kempson 1981; Higginbotham 1980, 1987; Link 1983, 1987; Lønning 1987; Scha 1981; among others.

2. The sentence *Every one of the elms is tall* in (12) and (13) is but the shortest example that illustrates the relevant pattern. Sentences (i) through (iii) are some other examples:

(i)   Everything (that is (an elm)) among the elms is tall.

(ii) Every one of the many elms is tall.

(iii) The elms are each tall.

Other languages will have somewhat different ways to instantiate these inferences. Anna Szabolcsi (personal communication) offers (iv) as the Hungarian version of (12).

(iv) A   szilfák mindegyike magas ⊢ Minden szilfa magas
     The elms' every one is-tall   Every   elm   is-tall

Sentence (12) is valid if *the elms* refers to all the elms that there are. This may be obvious only in philosophers' jargon. Often 'the N'' is most naturally taken to be an incomplete description, although not always (compare *the real numbers*). If *the elms* is taken to refer to only some particular elms but *every elm* is nevertheless understood to quantify over all elms, then (12) will, of course, appear invalid.

Example (12) is a valid inference when the context identically restricts the definite description in the premise and the quantifier in the conclusion. Compare the following, where a (reduced) relative clause makes the restriction explicit.

(i) Every one of the elms in my backyard is tall $\vdash$ Every elm in my backyard is tall

(ii) Every one of the elms that there are is tall $\vdash$ Every elm that there is is tall

Here there is no disagreement between English and jargon. All of the discussion that follows in the text can be recast using such examples as (i) and (ii). With this understood, there is no harm if I rely on the jargon for the sake of brevity.

3. I will leave it to the reader to reproduce the argument for alternative analyses of definite descriptions.

4. One could choose to treat the definite description as an *objectual* quantifier rather than as a referring expression.

5. Compare, for example, set abstraction. The referring expression is not a description in the sense that $\{x : \text{elm}(x)\}$ is the set of all elms, which is not itself an elm. I could have taken *the elms* to be derived by abstraction.

6. We can set aside that a plural means at least two. All of the discussion can be recast using plural circumlocutions with the right meaning: *one or more elms* or *the one or more elms*. Or the logical forms for *elms* and *the elms* can elaborate that there are at least two. Analogues for all the inferences I discuss can also be found.

7. Here I follow Burge (1972), Sharvy (1980), Link (1983), and Lønning (1987), among others. Hoping that there is a unified analysis of singular and plural definite descriptions and mass definite descriptions, I intend the part-whole relation to serve in all of them. Should it turn out that there is no sensible relation for this purpose, it will not hinder the argument against the objectual view to treat the definite descriptions separately. All that is needed is for the language to contain some means of forming plural definite descriptions, if necessary, with a special operator:

(i) $\ulcorner(\iota_{\text{pl}}x)\Phi(x)\urcorner$ refers to $\mathbf{a} \leftrightarrow (y)(\Phi(y) \leftrightarrow y \subseteq \mathbf{a})$

Similarly, there would be a singular operator defined in the usual way:

(ii) $\ulcorner(\iota_{\text{sg}}x)\Phi(x)\urcorner$ refers to $\mathbf{a} \leftrightarrow (y)(\Phi(y) \leftrightarrow y = \mathbf{a})$

8. The biconditional description will not allow that the part-whole relation be spatiotemporal. Were this so, *the elms* would refer only when an elm's leaf is an elm. Burge (1977) further notes that spatiotemporal parts are not appropriate if *the water*, *the H_2O molecules*, and *the oxygen and hydrogen atoms* are to refer to three distinct objects. Consider the following contrasts:

(i) a. The water is wet. (true)
   b. The H_2O molecules are wet. (false)
   c. The oxygen and hydrogen atoms are wet. (false)

(Water $\neq H_2O$, and water $\neq O + H$.)

(ii) a. The oxygen and hydrogen atoms remain after the chemical bonds are broken. (true)
   b. The H_2O molecules remain after the chemical bonds are broken. (false)

($H_2O \neq O + H$.)

9. In this setting, compare '$x \leq y \leftrightarrow_{df} x = y \vee x \in y$', which defines a relation that is reflexive and antisymmetric but not transitive. Under this relation, the referent of *the elms* is the set **a** such that $(x)(\text{elms}(x) \leftrightarrow (x = \mathbf{a} \vee x \in \mathbf{a}))$. This set would include at least all *sets* of elms, and this set, which according to the description is itself elms, is a distinct object from the set of elms. Thus we would have two distinct plural objects falling under the concept 'elms(x)' and composed of the same singular objects. A transitive part-whole relation guarantees that *the elms* will refer to the set of elms. It is also consistent with a nominalistic domain, which allows only one object to be composed from some given individuals and thus excludes such distinctions as $\{\{a, b\}, c\}$ and $\{a, \{b, c\}\}$. A domain is nominalistic if, for a collection of individuals A, it is isomorphic to the power set minus the empty set, $\mathscr{P}(A) - \varnothing$. Individuals are identified with their singletons. (For discussion of these and related matters, see Goodman 1956, Eberle 1970, Burge 1977, and references cited therein.) Allowing a deviant reference for *the elms* will not save the objectual view, since my argument will concern the singular objects that compose it.

10. See "i-sum" formation in Link 1987. In a nominalistic domain of sets (n. 9), (41) is equivalent to 'elms$(x) \leftrightarrow \exists y (y \in x) \wedge (y)(y \in x \rightarrow \text{elm}(y))$'.

11. See Link 1987.

12. See the * operator in Scha 1981.

13. Object **a** is part of itself (reflexivity), and any singular object that is part of **a** (there is only **a**) is an elm. So **a** is elms.

14. See Eberle 1970.

15. Such as the following:

$\exists x \exists y \exists z (\text{elm}(x) \wedge \text{elm}(y) \wedge \text{elm}(z))$

$\vdash \exists u (x \leq u \wedge y \leq u \wedge z \leq u \wedge \text{elms}(u))$,

$\exists w \exists x \exists y \exists z (\text{elm}(w) \wedge \text{elm}(x) \wedge \text{elm}(y) \wedge \text{elm}(z))$

$\vdash \exists u (w \leq u \wedge x \leq u \wedge y \leq u \wedge z \leq u \wedge \text{elms}(u))$,

etc.

16. Again, without using the predicate 'elm(x)', one could assert the existence of an object that included them all: $\exists y \forall x (x \leq y)$. But this also includes nonelms; it is not the object the elms.

17. You can verify that the theory stands up to (i), the converse of (53), on the assumption that 'is-one-of(x, y)' is true of $\langle \mathbf{a}, \mathbf{b} \rangle \leftrightarrow \text{At}(\mathbf{a}) \wedge \mathbf{a} \leq \mathbf{b}$.

(i) Every elm is tall $\vdash$ Every one of the elms is tall

18. I introduce axioms, but the argument from speaker's competence shows, more exactly, that the theory must be extended so that comprehension principles are at least theorems. Whether the principles are basic or derived, the consequences for the objectual view will be the same.

19. Recall from n. 6 that we are ignoring that a plural means at least two. Were this taken into account, the statement of comprehension would be (i).

(i) $\exists x \exists y (N(x) \wedge N(y) \wedge x \neq y) \rightarrow \exists z \, z = (\iota x)(N + s(x))$

The argument is the same, *mutatis mutandis*.

20. The discussion of plural definite descriptions invited consideration of part-whole relations that are not transitive (see n. 9), in which case (61) is reduced no further. I leave it to the reader to show that (61) itself gives rise to Russell's paradox.

21. In discussions of set theory, comprehension principles are usually not conditionals, e.g., $\exists y \forall x(x \in y \leftrightarrow N(x))$. See Boolos 1975, 1984.

22. This section was much improved following discussions with Samuel Bayer, Jaap van der Does, and Peter Lasersohn. Samuel Bayer suggested the restricted version of mereological comprehension discussed below in (78).

23. The restriction to atomic x on the right side of the biconditional in (78) is necessary. Compare the comprehension principle in (i), where it is omitted, and consider substituting for '$N(x)$' the predicate 'object(x)', $\exists z(z = x)$, which gives (ii).

(i) $\exists x(N(x) \wedge At(x)) \rightarrow \exists y \forall x((At(x) \wedge x \leq y) \leftrightarrow N(x))$

(ii) $\exists x(\exists z(z = x) \wedge At(x)) \rightarrow \exists y \forall x((At(x) \wedge x \leq y) \leftrightarrow \exists z(z = x))$

Since there are atomic objects, (ii) gives way to (iii), which in turn leads to the contradictory result that *the objects* refers to an atomic object:

(iii) $\exists y \forall x((At(x) \wedge x \leq y) \leftrightarrow \exists z(z = x))$

(iv) $\forall x((At(x) \wedge x \leq \mathbf{a}) \leftrightarrow \exists z(z = x))$

(v) $(At(\mathbf{a}) \wedge \mathbf{a} \leq \mathbf{a}) \leftrightarrow \exists z(z = \mathbf{a})$

(vi) $At(\mathbf{a}) \leftrightarrow \exists z(z = \mathbf{a})$

(vii) $At(\mathbf{a})$

The comprehension principle as stated in (78) will only yield that $At(\mathbf{a}) \leftrightarrow (\exists z(z = \mathbf{a}) \wedge At(\mathbf{a}))$, that is, $At(\mathbf{a}) \leftrightarrow At(\mathbf{a})$.

24. See Boolos' (1984) discussion of such proposals and the references cited there.

25. Here variables range over individuals and classes.

26. It is open to the set theorist to extend his vocabulary with a hierarchy of classes so that 'the N_is' refers to objects on the $(i + 1)$th order. Thus, if we assume a zeroth order of atoms or individuals and classes of these to be the first order, then *the classes$_1$* would refer to the second-order object that included all the first-order objects. *The classes$_2$* would refer to a third-order object that included all the first- or second-order objects, and so on. Even so, and at a price that a mereologist with nominalist scruples cannot afford, there still remain plural terms beyond the reach of this extension, as in (i):

(i) The things that I believe there are fill up the infinite hierarchy.

So the claim would have to be that one does not refer to what one purports to refer to in (i). In this respect, it differs from treatments of the liar's paradox that appeal to an infinite hierarchy of truth predicates, where it is assumed that a speaker utters a sentence of form (ii) intending a truth predicate at whatever level fits the sentence referred to by the subject *that*.

(ii) That is true$_i$.

This implies no particular constraint on what can be thought. Even if the subject of (iii) refers to sentences scattered throughout the hierarchy, the analysis is just that each is true at its appropriate level, as in (iv).

(iii) Those are true.

(iv) [every x : those(x)] $\exists i$ true(i, x)

27. This follows closely the wording in Quine 1986, p. 68, and Boolos 1985b, p. 337.

28. This step is necessary. F is a simple predicate letter, but the substituends for '$N'(x)$' include complex formulas such as 'thing-that-is-not-a-member-of-itself(x)'.

29. Since *some things* implies that there is a thing, it translates '$\exists X(\exists xXx \wedge \ldots)$' rather than '$\exists X$'. Note that '$\exists X(\exists xXx \wedge \ldots)$' occurs in (95). Boolos (1984, 1985b) provides a rule to transform every formula '$\exists XF$' into a logically equivalent '$H \vee \exists X(\exists xXx \wedge F)$'. Such a rule is necessary to translate arbitrary sentences of second-order logic into the understood idiom, which uses *some things*. We, however, have no interest in translating arbitrary sentences of second-order logic into some natural-language equivalent. For us, it is enough to know that *some things* has the logical form '$\exists X(\exists xXx \wedge \ldots)$', with all that this entails for natural language sentences in which *some things* occurs.

30. Note that *of* is not meaningful. See Schein 1992 for an argument that this is correct. Alternatively, we might suppose that it is a higher-order predicate expressing a predication relation: x of $X \leftrightarrow_{\mathrm{df}} Xx$. To accept the inference in (101), the speaker, of course, would have to know the meaning of the extra item. For a discussion of higher-order predicates and the semantics of plurals, see Higginbotham and Schein 1989. Neither in this setting nor in the objectual theory, **of**(x, y) $\leftrightarrow$ At(x) $\wedge x \leq y$, is it obvious that a categorematic *of* is to be preferred in the analysis of *every one of the elms* or *every part of the book*: **That is one, and it is of the elms*, **That is a part, and it is of the book*. It seems that *part* is relational, and *of* is a dummy Case marker. Compare, *Every brother of Bill*.

31. Unless one is disabused of the naive interpretation as Boolos urges, it leads, as it led Quine (1986), to regard second-order logic, if not exactly as set theory, then as some kind of wolf in sheep's clothing. See Boolos 1975, 1984, for a discussion of Quine's position.

32. The paraphrase leaves out the definite description operator and the condition that something is denoted, which are not relevant for what follows.

33. The metalanguage is English with the addition of variables for cross-reference. As in Boolos 1984, 1985b, '$S(\langle V, x\rangle)$' is to be understood as 'the pair $\langle V, x\rangle$ is one of *them*$_S$.'

Since the object language is a fragment of English, I have omitted $\ulcorner[\exists V : N + s]\urcorner$, giving instead the semantics for 'some $N + s$', which, as it is equivalent to '$[\exists X : \exists xXx \wedge \ldots N \ldots]$', implies the existence of an N. The restriction to natural-language quantifiers allows me to depart from Boolos and use the English *some things* in the metalanguage. A clause for $\ulcorner\exists V\urcorner$, however, does use '$\exists X$', since it must allow that 'V' be assigned no objects. Consider, for example, '$\exists X\forall x(Xx \leftrightarrow x \neq x)$'. By comprehension, the existential quantification is true, but no objects are not identical to themselves. Boolos's formulation of the clause for $\ulcorner\exists V\urcorner$ is essentially (i):

(i) S satisfy $\ulcorner\exists VF\urcorner$

   $\leftrightarrow \exists X \exists T(\forall x(Xx \leftrightarrow T(\langle V, x\rangle))$
   $\land \forall u(u$ is a (first- or second-order) variable $\land u \neq V$
      $\rightarrow \forall x(T(\langle u, x\rangle) \leftrightarrow S(\langle u, x\rangle)))$
   $\land T$ satisfy $\ulcorner F\urcorner)$

Chapter 3

1. Further arguments for a second-order syntax are pursued in Higginbotham and Schein 1989 and Schein 1989, 1992.

2. See, e.g., Scha's (1981) * operator.

3. If the domain is a power set algebra $\mathscr{P}(A)\backslash\varnothing$ with which all nominalistic domains are isomorphic (Eberle 1970), '$x \leq y$' corresponds to '$x \subseteq y$' and 'At(x)' to 'x is a singleton set'. Recall that atomic individuals are identified with their singleton sets in such a domain. See chapter 2 and references cited there for discussion.

4. Compare, e.g., Scha's (1981) treatment of quantifiers. In a set-theoretic setting, (11) amounts to the condition that

$$|\bigcup\{x : \mathrm{elms}(x) \land \mathrm{clustered}(x)\}| = \mathrm{few}.$$

5. This includes the lexical semantics of the distributive operator D in (6). Note that the operator binds an unsorted variable.

6. I ignore the inverse scope interpretation that assigns widest scope to *exactly ten amendments*, assuming that it will not be a distraction.

7. The logical form of semidistributivity is not at issue, so the shorter logical forms interpreted according to (11) are shown.

8. Axiom (45) is a Davidsonian analysis for a predicate denoting plural objects. See the introduction to chapter 5 for a comparison of this approach to mine.

Chapter 4

1. The formulation "NPs related to plural objects" is intentionally vague. Separation is also essential for the truth conditions of semidistributivity. I consider the semidistributive NP *few video games* in (i) to be "related to plural objects" via '$[\exists X : Xx \ldots]$'.

(i) a. Few video games taught every quarterback two new plays.
    b. [few x : Gx][every y : Qy][$\exists Z$: 2(Z)...Pz...][$\exists X$: $Xx \land \ldots Gx \ldots$]
        $\exists e$ teach(X, y, Z, e)

Since it is not within the scope of *every quarterback*, the interpretation turns out to be a case of essential separation. Later remarks will explain how this is so. The argument for essential separation is, however, developed around such simpler examples as (1).

2. See, e.g., Scha 1981, Link 1983.

3. There is the further question of whether the tacit *each* is in construction with the NP or applies to the VP. These syntactic subtleties do not bear on the issue.

4. So the argument applies as well to logical forms without a place for events: '$V(X, y, Z)$'.

5. *Exactly two passwords* may be understood distributively or semidistributively. The contexts in (23) verify neither interpretation. In (21), the nonincreasing quantifier is replaced by an indefinite description, *two offers*, which also has no effect on the suitability of the description. The placement of the existential event quantifier is also immaterial.

The contexts in (23) also verify semidistributive interpretations of sentences (20) to (22) (see n. 1):

(22) Three automatic tellers gave (the) two new members (each) exactly two passwords.

(i) a. $[\exists X : 3(X) \wedge \forall x(Xx \rightarrow Ax)][\forall x : Xx]$
$\exists e([\exists X : Xx \wedge \forall x(Xx \rightarrow Ax)]\forall x(\text{INFL}(e, x) \leftrightarrow Xx)$
$\wedge \; [\iota Y : 2(Y) \wedge \forall y(Yy \rightarrow My)][\forall y : Yy][\exists e' : e' \leq e]$
$(\text{give}(e') \wedge \forall z(\text{TO}(e', z) \leftrightarrow z = y)$
$\wedge \; [2!z : Pz][\exists e'' : e'' \leq e']\forall x(\text{OF}(e'', x) \leftrightarrow z = x)))$

   b. Three automatic tellers are among the givers in events of (the) two new members each being given exactly two passwords.

The semidistributive interpretation allows the three automatic tellers to be distributed among possibly several events of the kind described by the VP. It happens that a single event in (23) in which all three participated makes the interpretation true. Crucially, the event fits the description in (24), which is a part of (i) above as well. Polyadic logical form best approximates the semidistributive interpretation as (ii) or (iii). (Again, it is immaterial whether *exactly two new passwords* is construed distributively or semidistributively.)

(ii) $[\exists X : 3(X) \wedge \forall x(Xx \rightarrow Ax)][\forall x : Xx][\iota Y : 2(Y) \wedge \forall y(Yy \rightarrow My)]$
$[\forall y : Yy][2!z : Pz]\exists e[\exists X : Xx \wedge \forall x(Xx \rightarrow Ax)] \, \text{give}(X, y, z, e)$

(iii) $[\exists X : 3(X) \wedge \forall x(Xx \rightarrow Ax)][\forall x : Xx][\iota Y : 2(Y) \wedge \forall y(Yy \rightarrow My)]$
$[\forall y : Yy][2!z : Pz]\exists e[\exists X : Xx \wedge \forall x(Xx \rightarrow Ax)][\exists Z : Zz \wedge \forall z(Zz \rightarrow Pz)]$
$\text{give}(X, y, Z, e)$

The event in (23), however, will not verify (iv) or (v) for any value of 'x' and any way of construing the predicate that is adequate for distributivity (see pp. 60–61):

(iv) $[\iota Y : 2(Y) \wedge \forall y(Yy \rightarrow My)][\forall y : Yy][2!z : Pz]$
$\exists e[\exists X : Xx \wedge \forall x(Xx \rightarrow Ax)] \, \text{give}(X, y, z, e)$

(v) $[\iota Y : 2(Y) \wedge \forall y(Yy \rightarrow My)][\forall y : Yy][2!z : Pz]$
$\exists e[\exists X : Xx \wedge \forall x(Xx \rightarrow Ax)][\exists Z : Zz \wedge \forall z(Zz \rightarrow Pz)] \, \text{give}(X, y, Z, e)$

The event-dependent interpretations of sentences (20) to (22) are also true in (23), unless we add to the contexts an event that falsifies the universal quantifier over events. I did not make this addition in the text, assuming that this interpretation will not be a distraction. Each figure in (vi) shows an event in which (the) two individuals each are related to exactly two other individuals, but have just one INFLer.

(vi)   (20)   (21)   (22)

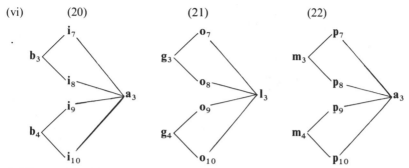

6. The semidistributive interpretations discussed in nn. 1, 5 are also false, as well as all other acceptable interpretations for the sentences, except the event-dependent interpretations, which are vacuously true unless we add to the contexts falsifying events, such as those in (vi) in n. 5.

7. The variant with the indefinite description *two passwords* replaces the last conjunct in (35b) with (i).

(i) $[\exists Z : 2(Z) \wedge \forall z(Zz \rightarrow Pz)]\forall z(OF(e', z) \leftrightarrow Zz)$

I also allow a variant in which the quantifier *exactly two passwords* is interpreted semidistributively, in which case the last conjunct is replaced with (ii).

(ii) $[2!z : Pz][\exists e'' : e'' \leq e'][\exists Z : Zz \wedge \forall z(Zz \rightarrow Pz)]\forall z(OF(e'', z) \leftrightarrow Zz)$

None of these variants affect the argument.

8. If we ignore the event-dependent interpretations discussed in n. 5.

9. The expression *Automatic tellers give new members passwords* has a usage according to which a group of automatic tellers is considered, through some notion of collective action, to have given a new member passwords even though some of the tellers do not appear to do anything. I chose a mechanical agent in order to favor an interpretation in which the predicate has precise conditions, but for any given notion of collective agency that may intrude, we can always fix the context represented by a diagram like (23) so that indeed automatic teller a_1 does not participate in a collective action toward new member m_2 and automatic tellers a_2 and a_3 are not part of any collective action involving new member m_1, or more simply, fix it so that the three automatic tellers are not a collective agent in any action. Although collective agency will excuse some tellers from ejecting passwords, I assume that it is not in general true that if some automatic teller has given out a password, then any *arbitrary* group of tellers containing that teller can be said to have given passwords. Although that teller's action may count for some group of tellers A, it does not count for arbitrary supersets of A. Any given collective interpretation has some condition C defining which collections are collective agents. Maybe the tellers all have to work for the same bank to be considered a collective agent. Simply flesh out circumstances so that $\{a_1, a_2, a_3\}$ does not meet C for any notion of collective action one can think of. This will falsify the interpretations of sentence (22) that ascribe collective agency. Then at that point in the argument of the text where I assert that $\{a_1, a_2, a_3\}$ did not give passwords to m_1, they did not do so as a collective agent or as a mechanical agent.

Tellers $\mathbf{a}_2$ and $\mathbf{a}_3$ simply had nothing to do with new member $\mathbf{m}_1$. Similar remarks apply to the relation of $\{\mathbf{a}_1, \mathbf{a}_2, \mathbf{a}_3\}$ to $\mathbf{m}_2$.

I set up these contexts to anticipate and discourage the more obvious collective-agent interpretations of *Automatic tellers give new members passwords*. Recall that the tellers may be transmitting passwords for any number of Christmas clubs at any number of different banks. None of the tellers are dedicated to any of the banks or Christmas clubs. They function indiscriminately, like telephones. A new member who enters the location can use any of the automatic tellers to obtain one password at a time from any Christmas club. We can specify that in fact the two new members are enrolling in different clubs at different banks, and so the automatic tellers are not working with each other. Sentence (22) is just a report of the automatic tellers that the two new members used. If you are inclined to think of all the automatic tellers at the one location as some collective genius, let us say that the location has many more than three automatic tellers. It would then be anomalous to single out three of the automatic tellers. What is it about them that puts them in a noteworthy relation to the two new members? Elaborating the context as necessary, we can be sure that the atomic predicate of (22) does not express a true relation that holds of the group of three automatic tellers and either of the individual new members.

10. The semidistributive interpretation in (i) is similarly false (see nn. 1, 5).

(i) $[\exists X : 3(X) \wedge \forall x(Xx \to \mathrm{ATM}(x))][\forall x : Xx]$
   $[\iota Y : 2(Y) \wedge \forall y(Yy \to \mathrm{member}(y))][\forall y : Yy][2!z : \mathrm{password}(z)]$
   $[\exists Z : Zz \wedge \forall z(Zz \to Pz)][\exists X : Xx \wedge \forall x(Xx \to \mathrm{ATM}(x))]\,\mathrm{give}(X, y, Z, e)$

Formula (i) is true only if for *each* of two new members, each of three automatic tellers was among some tellers that gave him, the *individual* new member, two passwords. But automatic teller $\mathbf{a}_1$ belongs to no group of tellers that gave passwords to $\mathbf{m}_2$, and neither $\mathbf{a}_2$ or $\mathbf{a}_3$ are among the givers of passwords to $\mathbf{m}_2$.

11. A more general discussion of n-ary quantifiers is provided in chapter 12, section 2. Readers unfamiliar with the notion may be better off returning to this section after consulting that chapter.

12. The distributivity of (*the*) *two new members* is incorporated into the definition of the binary quantifier. Hence the distributive operator '$[\forall y : Yy]$' does not appear in (46).

13. We need not consider undivided reference for the binary quantifier, as in (i).

(i) $\ulcorner[\exists X : \Phi[X]] \times [\iota Y : \Psi[Y]]\Gamma[X, y]\urcorner$ is true only if
   $[\exists A : \ulcorner\Phi[X]\urcorner$ is true of $A][\iota M : \ulcorner\Psi[Y]\urcorner$ is true of $M][\forall m : Mm]$
   $\ulcorner\Gamma[X, y]\urcorner$ is true of $\langle A, m \rangle$

Interpreting the binary quantifier in (47) to have undivided reference to sets of automatic tellers results in an interpretation, equivalent to those in the preceding section, which is false in (23).

14. Perhaps it could be disputed that *a pink slip of paper* binds a variable over individual objects. If not, exhaustivity would not be relativized to slips of paper, and the logical form would be false in (36). It could be claimed, parallel to my proposal that all descriptions, singular or plural, are second-order and differ in the cardinality predicates they contain, that *a pink slip of paper* binds a variable over

plural objects. The argument goes through, ceteris paribus, with a change of example. Under the scope assignment shown, (i) has the same truth conditions as (35) with respect to all the contexts considered.

(i) a. Three automatic tellers gave two new members (each) two passwords on each of one or two pink slips of paper.

b. $\exists e([\exists X : 3(X) \wedge \forall x(Xx \rightarrow Ax)]\forall x(\text{INFL}(e, x) \leftrightarrow Xx)$
$\wedge\ [\iota Y : 2(Y) \wedge \forall y(Yy \rightarrow My)][\forall y : Yy][\exists e' : e' \leq e]$
$(\text{give}(e') \wedge \forall z(\text{TO}(e', z) \leftrightarrow z = y)$
$\wedge\ [\exists W : 1 \leq W \leq 2 \wedge \forall w(Ww \rightarrow Sw)][\forall w : Ww][\exists e'' : e'' \leq e']$
$\forall z(\text{on}(e'', z) \leftrightarrow z = w)$
$\wedge\ [\exists Z : 2(Z) \wedge \forall z(Zz \rightarrow Pz)](\forall z(\text{OF}(e'', z) \leftrightarrow Zz))))$

In particular, every member's two passwords must appear on the same slip of paper. The quantifier enforcing the condition *each of one or two pink slips* undeniably binds a variable over individual objects, and so exhaustivity is again relativized to pairs of members and slips of paper.

One might wish to relativize exhaustivity to only one of the variables over individual objects. There being no principled choice between them, one of the interpretations of the atomic predicate would relativize exhaustivity to the variable bound by *a pink slip of paper*. But this is fine-grained enough to make logical form (57) true in (36). This strategy will in any case fail. Sentence (ii) differs from (35) in assigning narrowest scope to the plural *one or more pink slips of paper*.

(ii) Three automatic tellers gave two new members each two passwords each on one or more pink slips of paper.

The individual variables are bound by *two new members each* and *two passwords each*. It is true in (iii), but (iii) falsifies the logical form that locates the event quantifier outside the scope of the binary quantifier and relativizes exhaustivity to either or both of the variables over individual objects.

(iii)

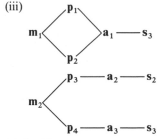

15. In this extension to the simple branching discussed in chapter 12, the branches are themselves allowed to contain sequences of linearly ordered quantifiers. For discussion, see Hintikka 1974, Fauconnier 1975, Barwise 1979, and McCawley 1981. The application to natural language is extremely limited at best.

16. This argument is retraced in Schein 1986, section 6.4.

Chapter 5

1. See, e.g., Fillmore 1968, Gruber 1965 and Jackendoff 1972.

2. To entertain the idea that thematic relations such as Agent or Theme might not

exist is not to imagine that θ-roles then end up as defined or derived from more primitive polyadic relations. It is rather to suppose that the primitives, the θ-roles, are more numerous than the thematic relations usually invoked.

Suppose that Venusians, organisms of lower intelligence, have a vocabulary of just three verbs: *eat*, *enjoy*, and *surround*. They accept inferences and treat plurals in such a way that Davidson, Parsons, and I would conclude that the logical form of these verbs is decomposed. Notice that we would say of our own language that the subject of *eat* is an Agent, that of *enjoy* an Experiencer, and that of *surround* a Theme. But to the Venusian, with only these three verbs, each subject is sui generis. Moreover, let us assume that the Venusian language also lacks any of the grammatical phenomena that appeal to thematic relations for explanation: no middle formation, no unaccusativity, no affectedness condition, etc. Venusians also don't make excuses. So there are not Davidson's reasons to think that the Venusian grasps a notion of Agency. In the circumstances, it seems fair to say that the Venusian, in using the verb *eat*, nevertheless grasps three primitive concepts, which we can best characterize as 'eater(x, e)', 'eat(e)', and 'eaten(e, y)'. The evidence for this is the Davidsonian pattern of inference and the behavior of plurals. It would be out of place, however, to attribute to the Venusian a knowledge of concepts like Agent(e, x) or Theme(e, y). There are no grounds to suppose that the Venusian grasps anything like what we mean by them. These concepts are quite beyond this simple organism. I assume that there is no epistemological problem here, nor do we need to attribute to the Venusian prior knowledge of a polyadic predicate 'eat(e, x, y)' in order to derive the subject θ-role as 'eater$(e, x) \leftrightarrow_{df} \exists y$ eater(e, x, y)'. The Venusian does not derive his θ-roles. The verb *eat* just is a collection of the three primitive concepts.

Now suppose that Venusians evolve so that their vocabulary now includes three more verbs: *drink*, *admire*, and *abut*. It could be that they grasp verbs in just the same way that the earlier Venusians did. That is, the new verbs, which are primitives, also come with new θ-roles, also primitive: 'drinker(e, x)', 'drink(e)', 'drunk(e, y)'. It would be odd to imagine that the Venusians will now face an epistemological problem *unless* they actually know more, namely, that the subject of *eat* and *drink* have Agency in common, which the other arguments to other verbs do not. Maybe they know this, maybe they don't. As the Venusian language comes to resemble our own, the reasons to attribute to them a notion of Agency get better.

To completely eliminate 'drinker(e, x)' and 'eater(e, x)' as primitives, it is not enough that they both entail that x is an Agent of e. It must be that this is all they mean. If you have misgivings that a univocal semantics will not be found to underwrite all cases that the grammar would classify as Themes, for example, I would point out that the Davidsonian logical form does not depend on the successful outcome of that project. It would not harm my claim if prepositions and abstract elements 'INFL', 'OF', etc., had meanings as numerous and diverse as the lexical items they occur with. There are imaginable circumstances where decomposition is justified but higher-order notions like Agency and Theme are not. Of course, the existence of thematic relations is congenial to the claim that there are θ-roles, and a stronger theory would construct a finite list of thematic relations (among which are prepositions, e.g., 'in(e, x)', 'against(e, x)'), all with interpretations that are invariant across verbs. Parsons, whose discussion draws together thematic relations and θ-roles, is careful to note that the logical-form proposal does not require it (1990, 99–104).

3. Similarly, (i) and (ii) cannot be true in virtue of some rocks that rained down or some unionists that gathered.

(i) A rock rained down.

(ii) A unionist gathered.

4. See G. Carlson 1984, Krifka 1992a, Parsons 1990.

5. Davidson in fact proposes the logical form in (i), where only the prepositional phrases correspond to independent conjuncts:

(i) $\exists e(\text{butter}(e, j, t) \wedge \text{in}(e, b) \wedge \text{with}(e, k) \wedge \text{at}(e, m))$

See below for discussion.

6. On the plausible interpretation, the prepositional phrases are all adverbial modifiers. Real-world knowledge excludes construing the prepositional phrases as reduced relative clauses: countries are not in parks, and parks are not in cabins.

7. See, e.g., Dowty 1989.

8. Recall the example from chapter 1, where separation is first introduced, that separates out the subject θ-role:

(i) Three video games taught every football player a new play.

9. J. Bennett (1988) gives a full treatment of the metaphysics of events.

10. This should hardly be surprising in the face of such wayward uses of the copula as *Mary's praising of John was her disapproving of Peter.*

11. Some examples depend on the assumption that θ-roles or modifiers are not relativized to the verb. If a sphere rotates and simultaneously heats up, then the rotating is putatively identical to the heating up. If the identity were true, then the truth of (i) should entail (ii), which is, however, false.

(i) a. The sphere heated slowly.
     b. $\exists e(\text{heat}(e) \wedge \text{Theme}(e, s) \wedge \text{slow}(e))$

(ii) a. The sphere rotated slowly.
     b. $\exists e(\text{rotate}(e) \wedge \text{Theme}(e, s) \wedge \text{slow}(e))$

The conclusion that the heating must not be the rotating does not go through if the logical form for the attributive adverb *slowly* is relativized, *slowly for heating*, as in (iii) and (iv) (the same event may be slow for heating but fast for rotating).

(iii) a. The sphere heated slowly.
     b. $\exists e(\text{heat}(e) \wedge \text{Theme}(e, s) \wedge \text{slow}(e, \text{`heat}(e)\text{'}))$

(iv) a. The sphere rotated slowly.
     b. $\exists e(\text{rotate}(e) \wedge \text{Theme}(e, s) \wedge \text{slow}(e, \text{`rotate}(e)\text{'}))$

A similar demonstration that flipping a light-switch cannot be the same as alerting a burglar relies on the assumption that there are thematic relations with invariant content. Only under that assumption does the identity of the two events and the logical forms in (v) and (vi) imply that John flipped the burglar:

(v)   a. John flipped the light-switch.
      b. $\exists e(\text{flip}(e) \wedge \text{Agent}(e, \text{j})\text{Theme}(e, \text{l}))$
(vi) a. John alerted the burglar.
      b. $\exists e(\text{alert}(e) \wedge \text{Agent}(e, \text{j}) \wedge \text{Theme}(e, \text{b}))$
(vii) a. John flipped the burglar.
      b. $\exists e(\text{flip}(e) \wedge \text{Agent}(e, \text{j}) \wedge \text{Theme}(e, \text{b}))$

Hence thematic relations do vary in content. Note that Higginbotham's example and the example based on symmetric predicates lead to the finer-grained ontology without auxiliary assumptions.

12. Assumption (96) is modeled on Cartwright's (1975) Covering Principle for scattered objects. I deviate from his formulation in not stipulating that exactly one thing occupies A, since I do not intend to prejudice the question of whether distinct events can occupy the same spatiotemporal region. It may turn out, as in n. 11, that the sphere's rotating is not the same event as its heating up. If so, we would expect that for each fraction of a degree it heats up, there is an event of it heating up to that degree and there is a coincident but distinct event of it rotating some amount.

Cartwright's Covering Principle, which takes regions as sets of points, is carefully formulated so that, for example, two regions that disagree at only a finite number of points are not occupied by distinct objects. To avoid entering into a discussion of topology, I have not been as careful in (96).

13. Presumably, there are spatiotemporal subregions of a pizza-eating event that are not pizza eatings. I assume that this is so not because these regions are not events but rather because these events are not pizza eatings. That is, (i) is false:

(i) $\forall e \forall e'((e' \leq e \wedge \text{pizza-eating}(e)) \rightarrow \text{pizza-eating}(e'))$

Similarly, there will be event concepts of, for example, eating two pizzas that are not closed under fusion, although the underlying domain of events is.

14. Eberle 1970 is an encyclopedic study of mereologies.

15. See Parsons 1990, 203–206, for further discussion of states in arithmetic.

16. Of course, for any given combination, different buildings are also obtained by rearranging the same atoms. There is no sense in which the atoms of an individual event can be rearranged, but this lapse in the analogy is not relevant, as will become clear shortly. The example below of quantifying over bunches of leaves is more like events in this respect. Although the leaves of a bunch can be rearranged, we do not thereby obtain a new bunch.

17. More or less, because of cases such as two buildings that share a connecting corridor. The atomic rooms forming the corridor belong to both buildings. Note that the requirement that no atom occupy more than one location is still observed. Hence, this property is the one defining reifications.

18. Explicitly adding "in a session" to (114), as in (i), will not eliminate the unwanted proper parts, since these too were all in some session or another.

(i) a. Twenty-five hogs fit into stalls in a session.
    b. Whenever there is a fitting of hogs into stalls in a session . . .

19. There is an alternative way to reconcile the event-dependent and sum-of-plurals interpretations. Suppose that contexts of events are not in general closed under recombination of parts, especially those that are actual. Suppose, however, that speakers and hearers assume, unless there is reference to a specific context, that the unmarked context contains all possible events that could be constructed from what is actually going on in the relevant region of the world. Then the inference in (119) will be judged valid, since no one has in mind a particular context when considering it. The problem is then the event-dependent interpretation. Since it too is being considered in isolation from any particular context, why isn't there at least a tendency to think that (117) entails that the same 20 truckers worked every truck? Perhaps the event quantifier in event-dependent interpretations has more structure than the simple translation as a universal quantifier would suggest. Suppose the quantifier were a count or sortal determiner, like *every* rather than *all* (compare *every cup* versus **every water*, *all cups* versus *all water*). Note that the denotation of 'load-up-one-or-more-trucks(e)' is nonsortal, like the denotation of 'water(x)'. So, to accommodate the sortal determiner, speakers assume a sortalizing, or reifying, context of events.

Chapter 6

1. A definition of truth will also fend off a worry about circularity: that the idiom that paraphrases away cumulative quantifiers will turn out on analysis to rely on some form of cumulative quantification.

2. Note that the second conjunct cannot be treated simply as sentential anaphora. The predicate does not allow sentential subjects:

(i) *That no more than two detectives found solutions (to crimes) was to no
     more than five crimes.

3. See, e.g., Chomsky 1976; Jackendoff 1972; Kroch 1979; Lakoff 1971, 1972; May 1977, 1985; McCawley 1970, 1972.

4. The representations and discussion slight questions of adjunction site, cyclicity, or the family of constraints that have come to characterize LF. See May 1985 and Longobardi 1991 for a survey.

5. See the discussion of LF and LF′ in May 1985.

6. That the preposed, bare VP is interpreted only as a universal quantifier might be explained by an analogy to bare NPs, which are also obligatorily generic when preposed, as in *Bears, John shot.*

7. Consider, *The FBI considers him loyal to no one.* QR adjoins to a category that includes 'loyal(e)'.

8. May (1985) and Chomsky (1986) rely on adjunctions to VP and IP. Chomsky's argument for VP adjunction, based on May 1985, is, however, also an argument for PP adjunction, with slightly different examples.

9. Higginbotham and Schein (1989) stipulate that all and only the traces exposed by QR are translated as singular variables, from which it follows that a first-order quantifier, which must bind a singular variable, must undergo QR. Note that this stipulation will have the effect that QR applied to a second-order quantifier will

force it to have a (semi)distributive interpretation. It becomes necessary for the distributive operator to intervene in order to bind the exposed trace now required to be singular.

Fodor and Sag (1982) observe that indefinites, no matter how deeply embedded, may be interpreted as if they had widest scope. But this interpretation does not force a plural indefinite to be (semi)distributed. It should if the indefinite plural was quantifier-raised a long distance and exposed traces are obligatorily singular. Following Ludlow and Neale 1991, I am skeptical of Fodor and Sag's alternative to QR, which then leaves me doubting the stipulation in Higginbotham and Schein 1989. (See chapter 9, n. 35, for further discussion of wide-scope indefinites.)

The stipulation played a role in an account of the contrast between (i) and (ii):

(i)   The Apostles are twelve (in number).

(ii)   *Some Apostles are twelve (in number).

The thought was that predicates of measure or constitution, such as 'twelve(X)', were genuine instances of higher-order predicates, unlike so-called collective predicates, e.g., *gather*, which reduce to first-order predication. If all quantifiers undergo QR at LF, QR would then expose a trace in (ii). As stipulated, the exposed trace would be a first-order variable, obstructing the intended interpretation. On this account, definite descriptions had at least the option of being interpreted as terms rather than quantifiers, so that in (i) it is interpreted *in situ*: 'twelve$((\iota X)(\Phi))$'. Abandoning the stipulation gives up this account of the contrast between (i) and (ii). The generalization that contrasts higher-order and collective predicates is, however, suspect, as Taub (1989) has shown. (My thanks to Elena Herburger for pointing out that the stipulation is inconsistent with the view I take of wide-scope indefinites).

10. For discussions of the issues raised by such examples as (27) through (29), see Barwise 1981, J. Bennett 1988, Croft 1984, Davies 1991, Higginbotham 1983, McConnell-Ginet 1982, Neale 1988, Parsons 1990, Taylor 1985, Vermazen 1985, and Vlach 1983.

11. It remains unexplained, however, why these are impossible to grasp, in contrast to (i), where at least to my ear, one can imagine a vacuous interpretation:

(i)   *A*: Once, nothing arrived.

        B: What do you mean? Almost always nothing arrives.

12. If the verb can occur outside the scope of the decreasing quantifier, it must be supplemented by an account of why the interpretation goes undetected when it is contradictory. The filtering out of some contradictions occurs elsewhere, and more than analytical contradictions are filtered out. Why is it impossible to hear the pronouns as *whatever senators voted for JFK* in (i) and *whatever donkeys the farmers bought* in (ii)?

(i)   No senator voted for JFK, and they supported no democratic bill.

(ii)   No farmers bought donkeys. They came with no guarantees.

Note that it is not that the plural pronouns entail existence:

(iii)   Few senators voted for JFK, and they supported no democratic bill.

(iv)   Few farmers bought donkeys. They came with no guarantees.

In (iii) and (iv) the pronouns can be heard that way, but they leave open the possibility that in fact no senators voted for JFK and no farmers bought donkeys. The speaker is warranted in his second assertion if he knows that whatever senators voted for JFK, if any, would not support a democratic bill. Similarly for the donkeys. Of course, in (i) and (ii) the speaker knows that there are no relevant senators or donkeys. It violates Gricean maxims to speak of a possible reference known to be foreclosed. All this goes into excluding the interpretation and an account of the reported behavior, but it need not affect the semantics of descriptive anaphora.

13. Note that we must also assume that the verb is interpreted in its d-structure position. Thus it will be reconstructed to that position at LF if it has been moved at s-structure to the COMP position, as often assumed in analyses of verb-second phenomena.

14. I make the simplifying assumption that all NPs are quantificational, and hence that there are no singular or plural terms. Names are definite descriptions, as in Burge 1973, with the provisos noted in Higginbotham 1988. See Higginbotham and Schein 1989 for some evidence that plural definite descriptions are second-order terms rather than second-order quantifiers.

15. Interestingly, the resulting typology coincides with the distinction in Karttunen 1976, Heim 1982, and Kamp 1981 between NPs that introduce discourse referents and those that are purely quantificational.

Nothing crucial hangs on this treatment of the singular descriptions. One could insist on singular reference, '$[\iota x : \Phi]$' and '$[\exists x : \Phi]$', and translate them like other objectual quantifiers, with the odd result that QR would be obligatory for *the elm* and *some elm* but not for their plurals. The second-order treatment adopted in the text leaves unexplained why (i) and (ii) contrast:

(i)   The children each ate a pizza.

(ii)   *The child each ate a pizza.

It is not clear, however, that reclassifying *the child* as an objectual quantifier promises to answer the question, What would then distinguish the quantifiers in (ii) and (iv) from *few children* in (iii), which is presumably an objectual quantifier binding a singular variable?

(iii)   Few children each ate a pizza.

(iv)   *No (more than one) child each ate a pizza.

16. There is an interpretation of modal operators where the implicit quantification over possible worlds is restricted by an accessibility relation to the world introduced by a superior operator. See Hazen 1976 for a discussion comparing modal languages and explicitly quantificational ones.

17. Note that the description is of whatever solvings there are, if any, as in (i), and not of *the* solvings, as in (ii):

(i) $[\exists E : \forall e(Ee \leftrightarrow \ldots \text{solve}(e) \ldots)]$

(ii) $[\exists E : \exists e Ee \wedge \forall e(Ee \leftrightarrow \ldots \text{solve}(e) \ldots)]$

18. '$\Sigma_0 \approx_{\mathfrak{C}_i} \Sigma$' abbreviates

'$\forall\alpha(\alpha$ is a (first- or second-order) variable

$\quad\to(\alpha\neq\mathbb{C}_i\to\forall x(\Sigma_0(\langle\alpha,x\rangle)\leftrightarrow\Sigma(\langle\alpha,x\rangle))))$'.

which says that Σ and Σ_0 are identical except perhaps for their assignments to $\mathbb{C}_i$.

19. One could just as well stipulate singular reference in the clause for $\ulcorner\Theta[e_i,v]\urcorner$:

Σ satisfy $\ulcorner\Theta[e_i,v]\urcorner$

$\leftrightarrow\exists e\Sigma(\langle\mathbb{C}_i,e\rangle)\wedge[\forall z:\Sigma(\langle v,z\rangle)][\forall e:\Sigma(\langle\mathbb{C}_i,e\rangle)]\forall x(\Theta(e,x)\leftrightarrow z=x)$

20. '$\Sigma_0\approx_{\mathbb{C}_i}\Sigma$' abbreviates

'$\forall\alpha(\alpha$ is a (first- or second-order) variable

$\quad\to(\alpha\neq\mathbb{C}_i\to\forall x(\Sigma_0(\langle\alpha,x\rangle)\leftrightarrow\Sigma(\langle\alpha,x\rangle))))$'.

21. I assume a standard (atomless) mereology of events, where *overlaps* ($x\mathbf{O}y$) and *is a part of* ($x\leq y$) are related as follows:

(i) $x\mathbf{O}x$

(ii) $x\mathbf{O}y\leftrightarrow y\mathbf{O}x$

(iii) $x\leq y\leftrightarrow\forall z(z\mathbf{O}x\to z\mathbf{O}y)$

(iv) $x=y\leftrightarrow(x\leq y\wedge y\leq x)$

(v) $x\mathbf{O}y\leftrightarrow\exists z\forall u(u\mathbf{O}z\leftrightarrow(u\mathbf{O}x\wedge u\mathbf{O}y))$ (meet)

(vi) $\forall x\forall y\exists z\forall u(u\mathbf{O}z\leftrightarrow(u\mathbf{O}x\vee u\mathbf{O}y))$ (join)

22. Consider asserting (32) with the intention that there is one large collaboration embracing the 20 composers and 7 shows or asserting any of (62) and (64) through (66) intending it to describe one large supper among 17 turtles. We then have the logical forms in (34), (i), and (ii):

(34) $[\exists E_i:1(E)]([\exists X:20(X)\wedge\forall x(Xx\to Cx)\,\mathrm{INFL}[e_i,X]\wedge\mathrm{collaborate}[e_i]$
$\qquad\wedge[\exists Y:7(Y)\wedge\forall y(Yy\to Sy)]\,\mathrm{on}[e_i,Y])$

(i) $[\exists E_i:1(E)]([\exists X:17(X)\wedge\forall x(Xx\to Tx)]\,\mathrm{INFL}[e_i,X]\wedge\mathrm{share}[e_i]$
$\qquad\wedge[\exists Y:23(Y)\wedge\forall y(Yy\to Py)]\,\mathrm{on}[e_i,Y])$

(ii) $[\exists E_i:1(E)]([\exists X:17(X)\wedge\forall x(Xx\to Tx)]\,\mathrm{INFL}[e_i,X]\wedge\mathrm{eat}[e_i]$
$\qquad\wedge\mathrm{Adverbial}[e_i]\wedge[\exists Y:23(Y)\wedge\forall y(Yy\to Py)]\,\mathrm{on}[e_i,Y])$

The singular event quantifier requires that there is one collaboration and that 20 composers and 7 shows participate in it. Similarly, the singular event quantifier requires that there is a sharing or an eating that satisfies the adverbial condition and has 17 turtles and 23 pizzas participating. Notice that the modified θ-roles in (68) and (69) do not directly state that any of these participants need bear the θ-role to the one large event. Bearing the θ-role to a part of that event could suffice. I do not, however, expect this to derail the interpretation. The truth conditions would go awry if it were possible to bear a θ-role to a proper part of the large event and not bear it to the larger event itself. But such a situation will not arise. Given the weakness of θ-roles (see the beginning of chapter 5), I expect that if $\Theta(e,x)$ and $e\leq e'$, then $\Theta(e',x)$. Thus a pizza is eaten in that event in which it alone is eaten but also in that event that includes the eating of the other pizzas as well. The mereological condition modifying the θ-roles appears then to be harmless in this context, with no ill effect on the truth conditions of a sum-of-plurals interpretation asserting the existence of a singular event.

23. This is not to say, however, four events for four turtles. For any one, there is the event where he alone eats his four quarters, but there are also events where he alone eats a slice. As far as I can tell, there is no need for more structure in the denotation of *there*, such as a requirement that it partition the event space.

24. The events E that make the second conjunct true must minimally include for every event that overlaps any of the turtles' individual actions (the events assigned to $\mathfrak{C}_i$), some overlapping event e such that

(i) $[\exists y : \text{pizza}(y)]\forall z(\text{OF}(e, z) \leftrightarrow z = y)$.

It could be that only events meeting condition (i) are among the events E, but it would also make (72) true to choose events E that, for example, also included the events individuated by the turtles' actions. As in n. 23, events E are allowed to overlap each other, provided they completely overlap the events originally assigned to $\mathfrak{C}_i$.

25. Note that this move makes definition (47) of *truth in a context of events* superfluous. Since the restriction to C_0 is explicit, definition (48) of truth *simpliciter* is sufficient.

Chapter 7

1. This definition of the operator is provisional until chapter 9 on cumulative quantification.

2. Of course, *two pies* might also be understood to mean two and no more than two pies, or exactly two pies, in which case it would have a distinct logical form: '$[2!x : Px]$'. We certainly would not want this sense to encroach on the indefinite description.

3. The semidistributive interpretation is derived when translation applies to a θ-role modified by the semidistributive operator:

(i) $[\exists V : \Phi]_i (\ldots \text{Co-}\Theta[e, t_i]\underline{\quad\quad})$
$\Rightarrow [\exists V : \Phi]([\forall v : Vv][\hat{E} : \text{Co-}\Theta[e, v]](\ldots\underline{\quad\quad})$

4. To anticipate the discussion in chapter 9, n. 35, the (semi)distributive interpretations of definite and indefinite descriptions obey the same conditions as first-order quantifiers. The nondistributive interpretation does not (see Fodor and Sag 1982, Farkas 1981). Thus (i) allows a wide-scope interpretation of *three crimes*, but it does not allow *three crimes* to be distributed so that each is related to its own two victims.

(i) Every detective identified two victims that three crimes had ruined.

The movement of the second-order quantifier is apparently exempt from conditions on movement, but, not surprisingly, the first-order operator '$[\forall v : Vv]$' respects them (see (ii)).

(ii) Every detective identified two victims that {every/each} crime had ruined.

This suggests, contrary to the simpleminded translation rule in (37), that the distributive operator is already present at LF, where it undergoes QR subject to the usual conditions.

5. There is an irrelevant interpretation of (69) that might cause some confusion and unfortunately comes out true in (72). Although the structure clearly discour-

ages such a construal, it is perhaps possible to understand the antecedent of *each* to be *four video games* rather than *exactly three quarterbacks*. So understood, the sentence would assert that there is an event of four video games' each teaching a new play and exactly three quarterbacks were taught there. Such an event is the one comprising the actions of video games g_2, g_3, and g_4 and, say, video game g_1's teaching quarterback q_1. In this event, each of the four video games teaches one new play, and they teach to a total of three quarterbacks. Similarly, it would be true to say of the relevant context that a hundred and two video games, each teaching a new play, taught three quarterbacks, leaving vague the distribution between quarterbacks and new plays. I assume, however, that these interpretations, if they exist, are easily set aside in favor of those that respect the surface structure and let *exactly three quarterbacks* serve as the antecedent to *each*.

Chapter 8

1. This contrasts with the view, for example, that applies a semidistributive operator only to a VP.

2. I hold that it can bind the plural pronoun in (2) as well, although the context provided is not fine-grained enough to distinguish the bound interpretation from the one paraphrased in (i), where the pronoun *they* is understood as a (first-order) variable bound to *exactly a dozen bakers*:

(i) Exactly a dozen bakers$_i$ helped some other bakers eat the pies that they$_i$
   (= he$_i$) and some other bakers baked.

A distinguishing context is obtained if we imagine that there was, say, one baker who belonged to two teams, one of which ate its products and the other of which did not. According to the interpretation in (i), this baker should not be counted among the dozen. He did not help eat the pies that he helped bake. The pies that he baked with the strong-willed team, he did not eat. On the bound interpretation, he is among the dozen, since he does belong to a team where the pies were eaten by the bakers. The two interpretations correspond to whether the pronoun is construed as in (ii) or as in (iii):

(ii) Exactly a dozen bakers ate the pies that the bakers baked.

(iii) Exactly a dozen bakers ate the pies that bakers baked.

This ambiguity also surfaces in (6), which, in addition to the salient bound interpretation, can be understood as in (iv):

(iv) Few composers agreed that composers should collaborate.

3. This proposal appears in Schein 1986 and Higginbotham and Schein 1989, from which I depart.

4. Sentences (i) and (ii) are, of course, not synonymous, but I let the burden of distinguishing them fall on the event concepts 'author(e)' and 'coauthor(e)'.

(i) The writers authored these books.

(ii) The writers coauthored these books.

5. Ludlow (1987) reduces the descriptive content of E-type pronouns to just the θ-role of its antecedent rather than the entire scope of the antecedent. My pro-

posal extends the analysis to pronouns in other contexts. This invites the suggestion that anaphoric dependence is always interpreted this way. The only bound variable is 'e':

(i) Every boy loves his mother.

(ii) [every $x : Bx$][$\hat{E} : INFL_i[e, x]$]$\exists e$(love[e] & $(\ldots (\iota x)(INFL_i[e, x])\ldots))$

6. Along with other questions about reference in intentional contexts, we do not take up the question of why (20) lacks (23)'s de dicto reading.

7. The placement of θ-roles and the verb is not relevant for what follows.

8. Note that a similar problem arises for all those (e.g., L. Carlson [1980], Heim, Lasnik, and May [1991], Langendoen [1978]) who would assign the reciprocal in (i) an interpretation equivalent to (ii):

(i) The composers collaborated with each other on no more than three operas.

(ii) The composers each collaborated with some of the others on no more than three operas.

9. This locality condition is no help with the interpretation of the reciprocal in n. 8.

10. Several authors have noted the effect of focus on quantification (see, e.g., Rooth 1985, Krifka 1992c, Partee 1991 and references cited therein). If (i) bears the focus indicated by small capitals, it acquires an interpretation equivalent to (ii).

(i) Most ships pass through the lock at NIGHT. (Rooth 1985)

(ii) [most $x :$ ship(x) & x passes through the lock] x passes through the lock at night

The focused constituent becomes, as it were, the main predicate, while the unfocused remnant joins the restriction to the quantifier. As Herburger (1993) observes, focusing a constituent internal to the quantified NP has an effect suggesting extraposition in logical form. She provides contexts for (iii) that demand the interpretation (iv).

(iii) a. Few INCOMPETENT cooks applied.
     b. Few cooks that were INCOMPETENT applied.

(iv) [few $x :$ cook(x) & applied(x)] incompetent(x)

Recalling similar observations in Guéron (1980), Herburger points out that a focused phrase internal to a quantified NP extraposes to become the logical main predicate only if the quantified NP is weak in the sense of Milsark (1977). To avoid this effect of focus, I have taken care to construct the argument around relative clauses internal to strong NPs, as in (37). See Herburger (1993) for further discussion.

11. In a theory that permits coarse-grained identities, where dancings can be singings, 'coincide(e, e')' means complete overlap. In a finer-grained ontology, it means that the events are coextensive in space and time.

Chapter 9

1. A quantifier Q is *increasing* according to this classification just in case (i) is true for all Φ and Ψ:

(i) $[Qv : \Phi] \Psi \leftrightarrow [\exists X : [Qv : \Phi] Xv][\forall v : Xv] \Psi$

Most, *every*, and *all* are thus increasing, along with definite descriptions, existentials, and cardinals. The nonincreasing quantifiers include decreasing quantifiers, like *no, few, no more than n*, and nonmonotonic quantifiers, like *exactly n*.

2. See, however, van der Does 1992 for an interesting alternative. He defines a class of predicate operators that allow him to derive Scha's (1981) cumulative quantification within a syntax where the quantifiers are linearly ordered. For expository reasons, my arguments below against earlier treatments of the semantics are cast in terms of branching syntax, but they apply as well to semantically equivalent alternatives.

3. As I first mentioned at the beginning of chapter 6, the idea that the scope of the later quantifiers includes only their θ-roles will have to be qualified (see section 5.1 below) in light of such long-distance cases as (i):

(i) No more than two detectives found solutions to no more than five crimes.

4. Recall that the θ-role bound by a first-order quantifier is taken up into a second-order description of events. I have assumed that the associated event concept is always available to be the scope of the operator. In effect, the scope of the cumulative quantifiers will always include at least a θ-role and an event concept.

5. But see section 5.1.

6. Cumulative asymmetry is thus an argument against *n*-ary quantification, which treats the branching quantifiers symmetrically, as we see below. Compare the standard interpretations of branching quantifiers:

(i)

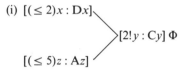

$[(\leq 2)x : Dx]$

$[2!y : Cy] \Phi$

$[(\leq 5)z : Az]$

7. See, e.g., Heim 1990, Ludlow 1987, and Neale 1990.

8. See Scha's compound numericals.

9. I say "more or less" because *every* and *most* are increasing (see n. 1 above) but since they tend to be distributive and respect the conditions on movement, I have assumed that they are first-order. See chapter 10, n. 3, for further discussion.

10. It would similarly fail to allow a quantifier over groups of agencies to include *exactly two crimes* within its scope. The example needs to be changed somewhat. Sentence (i) is true in (iii). Exactly three detectives each solved exactly two crimes for agencies, and exactly three agencies were involved.

(i) Exactly three detectives (each) solved exactly two crimes for exactly three agencies.

(ii) $[2!x : Dx][\hat{E} : \text{INFL}[e, x]][2!y : Cy][\hat{E} : \text{OF}[e, y]]$
    $\exists E(\text{solve}[e] \wedge [\exists Z : \forall z(Zz \rightarrow Az)] \text{ for}[e, Z])$
    $\wedge [3!z : Az][\exists Z : Zz \wedge \forall z(Zz \rightarrow Az)][2!y : Cy][\hat{E} : \text{OF}[e, y]]$
    $\exists E([\exists X : \forall x(Xx \rightarrow Dx)] \text{ INFL}[e, X] \wedge \text{solve}[e] \wedge \text{for}[e, Z])$

(iii)

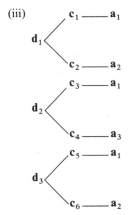

Formula (ii), however, is false, since only a_2 is a group on its own related to exactly two crimes. By itself, a_1 is related to three crimes, and a_3 to one crime. The groups of more than one agency are all related to three or more crimes.

11. Or consider (i), which defines a fine if pathological n-ary quantifier that requires the extension of Φ to include a Cartesian product of Q_1 many N_1's and only some N_2's.

(i) $\ulcorner [Q_1 : N_1]$

$\hspace{4cm} \Phi \urcorner$ is true $\leftrightarrow$

$[Q_2 : N_2]$

$\exists X[Q_1 x : N_1]\, Xx \wedge \exists Y[Q_2 y : N_2]\, Yy \wedge \forall x \forall y (\Phi(x,y) \rightarrow (Xx \wedge Yy))$
$\wedge\, \exists Z(\forall z(Zz \rightarrow Yz) \wedge \forall x \forall z((Xx \wedge Zz) \rightarrow \Phi(x,z)))$

See chapter 12 for the typology of n-ary quantifiers.

12. This point is not contested when the antecedent is a decreasing quantifier, as it is in (60). Increasing antecedents are another matter, as discussed in chapter 10 and the references cited there. Contrary to Evans's (1977) view that the would-be descriptive content fixes the reference of the pronoun but the pronoun itself is not a definite description restricted by it, Davies (1981) shows that the descriptive content of the pronoun enters into scope relations with other operators. See also Neale 1990 for a discussion of this point and for discussion on the exact relationship between descriptive content and the pronoun.

13. Note that the description left by abstracting 'Y' does not describe a unique Y. If some of the farmers each bought many donkeys, then there will be distinct Y of which it is true to say that the farmers bought them. So, unique reference must be imposed by the operator, which a comprehensive account of definite descriptions—singular, plural, and mass—would doubtless show (see, e.g., Sharvy 1980). The description '$[\iota V : \Phi]$' ought to be of the least Y that includes all the things that Φ. That is,

(i) $[\iota V : \Phi]\, \Psi \leftrightarrow_{\mathrm{df}} [\exists Y : \Phi[V/Y] \wedge \forall y(\exists Z(Zy \wedge \Phi[V/Z]) \rightarrow Yy)]\, \Psi[V/Y]$.

(For Y a variable that does not occur in Φ, $\Phi[V/Y]$ is the formula that substitutes Y for all occurrences of V free in Φ. Similarly for $\Phi[V/Z]$ and $\Psi[V/Y]$.)

14. Had $\mathbf{f}_1$ fed another pair of donkeys one bag of oats, this pair of donkeys and bag of oats would be included in the cumulative reference of the unbound anaphors. Farmer $\mathbf{f}_1$'s action would just be another event of the relevant type. In the circumstances, he would have given donkeys more than one bag of oats just among the relevant events.

15. The algorithm behind the attempts to find a suitable description generalizes upon those that have been proposed for standard cases of descriptive anaphora. In Neale's (1990) discussion, the restriction and scope of the antecedent is copied. Thus the content of a pronoun referring to the farmers in (i) is *the farmers who each gave two donkeys each two bags of oats*, as in (iii).

(i)   Few farmers gave two donkeys each two bags of oats, and they all belonged to the Central Park mule train.

(ii) $[\text{few } x : Fx]_i[\hat{E} : \text{INFL}[e, x]]\exists E[\exists Y : 2(Y) \wedge \forall y(Yy \to Dy)][\forall y : Yy]$
       $[\hat{E} : \text{TO}[e, y]](\text{give}[e] \wedge [\exists Z : 2(Z) \wedge \forall z(Zz \to Bz)] \text{OF}[e, Z]),$ and they$_i$ ...

(iii) $[\iota X : [\forall x : Xx] Fx \wedge [\forall x : Xx][\hat{E} : \text{INFL}[e, x]]$
       $\exists E[\exists Y : 2(Y) \wedge \forall y(Yy \to Dy)][\forall y : Yy][\hat{E} : \text{TO}[e, y]]$
       $(\text{give } [e] \wedge [\exists Z : 2(Z) \wedge \forall z(Zz \to Bz)] \text{OF}[e, Z])]$

For cumulative reference to the donkeys or to the bags of oats, it is again necessary that the pronoun contain the restriction and scope of the antecedent, but the quantifiers superior to the antecedent also have their effect on the content of the pronoun. The attempt is to characterize this effect by adding to the descriptive content a descriptive anaphor and an appropriate θ-role for each of the superior quantifiers. The pronoun referring to the donkeys in (i) contains the scope Φ_1 of *two donkeys* because it should not include in its reference donkeys given only one bag of oats. Of course, the farmers should be mentioned, since the pronoun does not refer to donkeys given oats only by nonfarmers. A rough schema for cumulative reference is shown in (iv), and (v) through (viii) fix the content of a pronoun referring to the donkeys.

(iv) $[Q_0 x : N_0'](_{\Phi_0} \Delta [Q_1 y : N_1'](_{\Phi_1}\Gamma[Q_2 z : N_2'] \Phi_2))$
       a. they$_0$ = $[\iota X : \ldots N_0' \ldots \wedge \Phi_0]$
       b. they$_1$ = $[\iota Y : \ldots N_1' \ldots \wedge \text{they}_0 \Delta \wedge [\forall y : Yy] \Phi_1]$
       c. they$_2$ = $[\iota Z : \ldots N_2' \ldots \wedge \text{they}_0 \Delta \wedge \text{they}_1 \Gamma \wedge [\forall z : Zz] \Phi_2]$

(v)   the donkeys that *the farmers* gave two bags of oats each
       $\Rightarrow$ the donkeys that the farmers who each gave two donkeys each two bags of oats gave two bags of oats each

(vi) $[\text{few } x : Fx](_{\Phi_0} [\hat{E} : \text{INFL}[e, x]]\exists E[\exists Y : 2(Y) \wedge \forall y(Yy \to Dy)]$
       $[\forall y : Yy](_{\Phi_1} [\hat{E} : \text{TO}[e, y]][\exists Z : 2(Z) \wedge \forall z(Zz \to Bz)] \text{OF}[e, Z]))$

(vii) $[\iota Y : [\forall y : Yy] Dy$
       $\wedge \exists E([\iota X : [\forall x : Xx] Fx \wedge [\forall x : Xx] \Phi_0] \text{INFL}[e, X] \wedge [\forall y : Yy] \Phi_1)]$

(viii) $[\iota Y : [\forall y : Yy] Dy$
       $\wedge \exists E([\iota X : [\forall x : Xx] Fx$
       $\wedge [\forall x : Xx][\hat{E} : \text{INFL}[e, x]]\exists E[\exists Y : 2(Y) \wedge \forall y(Yy \to Dy)]$
       $[\forall y : Yy][\hat{E} : \text{TO}[e, y]]$
       $[\exists Z : 2(Z) \wedge \forall z(Zz \to Bz)] \text{OF}[e, Z]] \text{INFL}[e, X]$
       $\wedge [\forall y : Yy][\hat{E} : \text{TO}[e, y]][\exists Z : 2(Z) \wedge \forall z(Zz \to Bz)] \text{OF}[e, Z])]$

16. No.

17. On this question, see Taylor 1976, 1985, and Barwise and Perry 1983.

18. According to the definition in the text, reference is definite only up to complete overlap. That is, the description will apply equally to distinct E and E' that completely overlap. The definition could be strengthened to describe a unique E, as in (i):

(i) $[\iota E : \Phi] \Psi \leftrightarrow_{df} [\exists E : \Phi \wedge \forall E'(\Phi[e/e'] \rightarrow \forall e(E'e \rightarrow Ee))] \Psi$

The unique E is simply the union of all events that are Φ, and they themselves are Φ.

19. Definition (76) replaces (22) from chapter 7, section 1.1:

(22) Σ satisfy $\ulcorner[\hat{E}_i : \Phi]\Psi\urcorner$
$$\leftrightarrow [\exists E : \forall e(Ee \leftrightarrow \exists E'\exists\Sigma_0(E' \simeq \Sigma(\mathbb{C}_i) \wedge \forall e(\Sigma_0(\langle\mathbb{C}_i, e\rangle) \rightarrow E'e)$$
$$\wedge \; \Sigma_0 \approx_{\mathbb{C}_i} \Sigma \wedge \Sigma_0(\langle\mathbb{C}_i, e\rangle) \wedge \Sigma_0 \text{ satisfy } \Phi))]$$
$$\exists\Sigma_0(E \simeq \Sigma_0(\mathbb{C}_i) \wedge \Sigma_0 \approx_{\mathbb{C}_i} \Sigma \wedge \Sigma_0 \text{ satisfy } \Psi)$$

Given the interaction with first-order quantifiers, the discussion in chapter 7, section 1.1, found that the operator had to be mereological, quantifying over the events that overlap Σ's assignment to $\mathbb{C}_i$. This mereological aspect has to turn up somewhere in the interpretation of '$[\hat{E}_i : \Phi]$'. The definition of *rendering* in the text locates it in the clauses for the θ-roles. An alternative, which, like (22), makes the operator mereological, would replace (22) with (ii) rather than with (76):

(ii) Σ satisfy $\ulcorner[\hat{E}_i : \Phi]\Psi\urcorner$
$$\leftrightarrow [\exists E : \forall e(Ee \leftrightarrow \exists E\exists\Sigma_0(Ee \wedge E \simeq \Sigma(\mathbb{C}_i) \wedge \forall e(\Sigma_0(\langle\mathbb{C}_i, e\rangle) \leftrightarrow Ee)$$
$$\wedge \; \Sigma_0 \approx_{\mathbb{C}_i} \Sigma \wedge \text{render}(E, \Phi, \Sigma_0)))]$$
$$[\exists\Sigma_0 : E \simeq \Sigma_0(\mathbb{C}_i) \wedge \Sigma_0 \approx_{\mathbb{C}_i} \Sigma] \Sigma_0 \text{ satisfy } \Psi$$

The clauses for rendering θ-roles would then not need to mention overlapping events:

(iii) $\text{render}(E, \ulcorner\Theta[e_i, v]\urcorner, \Sigma)$
$$\leftrightarrow \forall e(Ee \leftrightarrow (\Sigma(\langle\mathbb{C}_i, e\rangle) \wedge \forall z(\Theta(e, z) \leftrightarrow \Sigma(\langle v, z\rangle))))$$

(iv) $\text{render}(E, \ulcorner\Theta[e_i, V]\urcorner, \Sigma)$
$$\leftrightarrow \forall e(Ee \leftrightarrow (\Sigma(\langle\mathbb{C}_i, e\rangle) \wedge \exists z\Theta(e, z) \wedge \forall z(\Theta(e, z) \rightarrow \Sigma(\langle V, z\rangle))))$$

I am unaware of any grounds that chooses between the alternatives.

20. Negation in the scope of a cumulative quantifier presents a special problem, discussed in the next section. Rendering a negated formula is defined there.

21. See n. 13 for the meaning of the second-order definite description assumed here.

In sentences where the antecedent is more deeply embedded, the θ-role that enters the descriptive content of the pronoun is elliptical for an expression reconstructed along the lines mentioned on p. 113 and discussed more fully in section 5.1.1 below. The truth conditions of (i) are the same as those of (86):

(i) a. Exactly two farmers each fed two donkeys one bag of oats. The oats weighed two pounds, and the donkeys ate for twenty minutes.

   b. Exactly two farmers each fed two donkeys one bag of oats$_i$. They$_i$ weighed two lbs., and they ate for twenty minutes.

The content of the anaphor referring to oats ought to be something like the oats that a farmer fed one bag of to two donkeys. Copying just the θ-role bound by the antecedent and the descriptive content of the antecedent yields the elliptical (ii.b), with free variable Z. Formula (ii.c) is the reconstructed description.

(ii) a. $(_\Phi\,[2!x:Fx][\hat{E}:\text{INFL}[e,x]]$
$\exists E(\text{feed}[e] \wedge [\exists Y:2(Y) \wedge \forall y(Yy \to Dy)]\,\text{TO}[e,Y]$
$\wedge\,[\exists Z:1(Z) \wedge \forall z(Zz \to Bz)$
$\wedge\,[\exists W:\exists wWw \wedge \forall w(Ww \to Ow)]\,\text{of}[Z,W]]\,\text{OF}[e,Z]))$

b. $[\hat{E}:\Phi]([\imath W:\forall w(Ww \to Ow) \wedge \text{of}[Z,W]]$ weighed two lbs., and ...)

c. $[\hat{E}:\Phi]([\imath W:\forall w(Ww \to Ow)$
$\wedge\,\exists E(\text{feed}[e] \wedge [\exists Z:\forall z(Zz \to Bz)] \wedge \text{of}[Z,W]]$
$\text{OF}[e,Z])]$ weighed two lbs., and ...)

22. Compare the following two sentences:

(i)   Few senators voted for JFK, and they were all junior.

(ii) *No senators voted for JFK, and they were all junior.

23. Perhaps the determiner that appears in the translation of unbound anaphora is identical not to *whichever* but to a certain kind of demonstrative whose use is thwarted if the speaker knows that the referent does not exist but whose sense does not entail that the referent exists.

24. If such a schema is admitted, it must be allowed to bind only predicate positions that denote singular objects (no plural objects). Chapter 4 shows that extending n-ary quantifiers to plural predication will generate many unacceptable interpretations, for example, (45) through (47) above, in addition to missing the target cases of separation. Even if one observes the restriction to singular objects, the attempt to give a uniform semantics for branching that treats increasing and nonincreasing quantifiers alike leads to further unacceptable interpretations (see chapter 12, especially section 3).

25. The choice of predicate seems to matter. Compare (131) and (133). Remko Scha (personal communication) finds the quantification in (133) over pairs of individual detective and agency strikingly inaccessible, and I tend to agree. The accessibility of this reading will turn on how easily the relation can be thought of as an action between the pair involved. Compare (i) and (ii):

(i)   What did Philby do to the Soviets? He sold them nothing.

(ii) ?What did Spade do for the agency? He solved no crimes for it.

Selling somebody nothing is something one can do to somebody. Solving no crimes is not so easily thought of as something done for someone, unless, for example, one has in mind that one has done something for one agency by solving no crimes for another agency, a competitor.

26. See n. 27 below.

27. Note that contextual restrictions to a particular domain of events must appear in the logical form, as '$C[e]$' in (136), for the reasons discussed in chapter 6, section 2.3. The interpretation of '$[\hat{E}:\text{INFL}[e,x]]$' immediately introduces events that overlap the given domain. If a logical form without the explicit restriction were evaluated simply with respect to the intended domain of events, the overlapping events made available would undermine the intended effect of the restriction. One

could not infer that an official's sale of two defense documents is a sale to one superpower. Some completely overlapping events reconstitute the four events in (134) into two events where indeed each official sells two defense documents. Without the explicit restriction, (136) would come out true.

28. Such cases are discussed extensively in chapter 11.

29. I offer here no analysis of so-called specific indefinites. I am content with Fodor and Sag's (1982) observation that indefinites may be freely interpreted as if they had wide scope, no matter how deeply embedded. Thus there must be some structure where *two officials* includes within its scope *two superpowers*, but the latter is understood to have wide scope. See Farkas 1981, Ludlow and Neale 1991, and Enç 1991 for further discussion.

30. The events depicted in the bottom half of (155) falsify (154) and relatd interpretations where any of the shown scope relations are interpreted semidistributively. The top half of (155) falsifies (153) and its related interpretations. My discussion is focused on (153), which is the interpretation of (151) speakers are most likely to confound with May's reading. The top half of (155) is sufficient to distinguish these two.

May is vague about whether strong or weak branching is intended. He must surely admit the latter. If not, then the paraphrase cited in (153) is adequate for the intended interpretation, without branching.

31. See the references cited in chapter 6, n. 10.

32. See sec. 5.1.1 for further discussion of cumulative quantification into an opaque context.

Logical form (164) follows example (159) rather than example (161), introducing the relational 'events x of y'. The alternative in (i), which introduces something like the adverb in (161), is not pursued for a technical reason.

(i) $[\exists X : 2(X) \wedge \forall x(Xx \rightarrow Ox)][\forall x : Xx][\hat{E} : \text{INFL}[e, x]][\exists E : N[e] \wedge C[e]]$
$[\text{no } z : Dz][\hat{E} : \text{OF}[e, z]](\text{sell}[e] \wedge [\exists Y : \forall y(Yy \rightarrow Sy)] \text{to}[e, Y])$
$\wedge [\hat{E} : \Phi][\exists Y : 2(Y) \wedge \forall y(Yy \rightarrow Sy)] \text{to}[e, Y])$

As I have defined *rendering*, the term referring to the events that render the antecedent clause still denotes no events. Even if the context does contain a relevant event of selling no documents, such an event is among the rendering events only if it is a selling of some documents. Formula (i) then expresses a contradictory interpretation, which is filtered out, as observed in the previous section. The relational 'some event e of e' ' (*a selling of no documents*) as it appears in the logical form is immune to this problem. Note that the evaluation of what renders the antecedent clause does not contain a step evaluating what renders '[no z : Dz] Ψ'.

33. My examples have all involved actions, but nothing in these remarks should be taken to suggest that May's readings or the idiom of negative events is restricted to them. As earlier, May's reading of (i) is the only one true in (ii): line 1 connects star 2 to no dots, and line 2 connects star 1 to no dots.

(i) Two lines connect no dots to two stars.

(ii) l_1: d_1 —— s_1

l_2: d_2 —— s_2

l_3, l_4: s_3 —— d_3 —— s_4

May's reading is accessible only if one imagines that a state of connecting no dots is interesting.

A logical form that resembles (164) does leave me with the following commitment. Suppose that we have accounted for the idiom in which *is an event of selling no defense documents* and *is a state of connecting no dots* are sortal predicates of events. These negative events, such as they are, must be fine-grained, in the following sense. If x is the said agent in an event of selling no defense documents, we do not want it to imply that x sold no defense documents ever. We want instead that it imply that there is some y such that x never sold y defense documents. Thus there will be many distinct events that are nonvacuously described as events of selling no defense documents. Fine-grained, negative events are necessary if (164) is to recover the dependence of *no more than one defense document* on the choice of the individual superpower. Similarly, states of connecting no dots must also be fine-grained.

34. See Ross 1972, Larson 1988, and Lombard 1985, among others.

35. Fodor and Sag (1982) observe that an embedded indefinite NP may also be independent even within the scope of a distributive quantifier. An interpretation of (i) entails that the detectives are related to the same three crimes (compare the definite *these three crimes* in (iii)):

(i)   Every detective identified two victims that three crimes had ruined.

(ii) $[\exists Z : 3(Z) \wedge \forall z(Zz \rightarrow Cz)][\forall x : Dx][\hat{E} : \text{INFL}[e, x]]$
      $\exists E(\text{identify}[e] \wedge [\exists Y : 2(Y) \wedge \forall y(Yy \rightarrow Vy)$
      $\wedge \exists E'(\text{INFL}[e', Z] \wedge \text{ruin}[e'] \wedge \text{OF}[e', Y])] \text{OF}[e, Y])$

(iii) Every detective identified two victims that these three crimes had ruined.

They conclude that indefinites are sometimes referential, which is what gives the appearance of violating conditions on movement. Interpreting *three crimes* as referential would entail (ii) without assigning (i) a logical form as such. Ludlow and Neale (1991) are properly skeptical about the notion of referentiality appealed to, and Farkas (1981) points out that not all indefinites appearing to violate conditions on movement can be said to be referential. *A crime* in (iv) can be understood as outside the scope of *every victim* but dependent on *every detective*: each detective selects a crime and then identifies every victim that it has ruined.

(iv) Every detective identified every victim that a crime had ruined.

(v) $[\forall x : Dx][\hat{E} : \text{INFL}[e, x]][\exists Z : 1(Z) \wedge \forall z(Zz \rightarrow Cz)]$
      $[\forall y : Vy \wedge [\hat{E} : \text{OF}[e', y]]\exists E'(\text{INFL}[e', Z] \wedge \text{ruin}[e'])][\hat{E} : \text{OF}[e, y]]$
      $\exists E \text{ identify}[e]$

Fodor and Sag would not consider the indefinite in an intermediate scope position to be referential. To elaborate Farkas's conclusion to fit my observations in the text, (ii) and (v) seem to show that second-order quantifiers are exempt from the conditions on movement. Compare (175) in the text to (v), and note that the first-order quantifier '$[\forall z : Zz]$' distributing *three crimes* in (175) does violate the conditions on movement, with the result that the interpretation is unacceptable.

With all this duly noted, it remains that *two detectives* and *three crimes* have logical forms in which they are independent without long-distance movement, as (174) attests. In contrast, independence between the first-order quantifiers in (170), *no more than two detectives* and *no more than three crimes*, would require it, and the interpretation is therefore unacceptable. That (ii) and (v) show movement of second-order quantifiers to be completely free only reinforces the syntactic distinction between second-order and first-order quantifiers. Their divergent behavior with respect to the conditions on movement argues against the view that would unify independence among quantifiers under a branching representation:

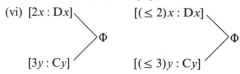

(vi) $[2x : Dx]$ $\searrow$ Φ $\qquad$ $[(\le 2)x : Dx]$ $\searrow$ Φ

$[3y : Cy]$ $\qquad\qquad$ $[(\le 3)y : Cy]$

36. Robert May (1985) has shown how QR need not fully disambiguate semantic scope relations. By deriving an intermediate structure subject to the conditions on movement, distinct interpretations that diverge in logical form only later are seen to fall under the same constraints.

Note that for us too the structures derived by QR are intermediate in that they are not the interpreted logical form. For concreteness, however, I have held QR to be fully disambiguating. Thus the rules of translation that subsequently apply derive a unique logical form. I intend my departure from May (1985) to be simplifying rather than contrary.

May points out a constraint that, in my terms, is stated as follows: in the prefix to any clause, either all the quantifiers are linearly ordered or no quantifier includes within its scope any other. Thus the following, which mix the patterns in (177) and (178), are all excluded:

(i)
$\ldots [Q_1 N'_k] \ldots [Q_2 N'_n]$ $\bigg\langle$ $\begin{array}{c} [Q_i N'_i] \\ \\ [Q_j N'_j] \end{array}$ $\bigg\rangle$ Φ

(ii) $[Q_i N'_i]$ $\begin{array}{c} \\ \vdots \\ \\ [Q_j N'_j] \end{array}$ $\searrow$ $[Q_1 N'_k] \ldots [Q_2 N'_k] \; \Phi$

(iii) $\ldots [Q_i N'_i] \ldots [Q_{i+m} N'_{i+m}] \ldots$
$\qquad\qquad\qquad\qquad\qquad\qquad \searrow \Phi$
$\ldots [Q_j N'_j] \ldots [Q_{j+n} N'_{j+n}] \ldots$

Partial orderings that appear to be counterexamples are shown to involve quantifiers that do not belong to the same prefix. Thus, *No more than two boys each gave exactly two girls exactly two roses*, which appears to be an instance of (i), has the following structure:

(iv)

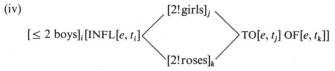

$[\le 2 \text{ boys}]_i [\text{INFL}[e, t_i]$ $\bigg\langle$ $\begin{array}{c} [2! \text{girls}]_j \\ \\ [2! \text{roses}]_k \end{array}$ $\bigg\rangle$ $\text{TO}[e, t_j] \text{ OF}[e, t_k]]$

May's constraint has the consequence that cumulative quantifiers cannot include within their scope any quantifier that c-commands them at s-structure.

37. This logical form, which simplifies a number of details, is surely incorrect. It assumes that the infinitival of complement of *try* is an indefinite description of events and that *try* expresses an extensional relation to the events described. Officially, I have been assuming that θ-roles are fronted to a clause-initial position, that is, pied-piped. Formula (189) should be (i), or (ii) if pied-piping is clause-bound. Pied-piping would apply as well to (186) in the text.

(i) ..., that $[(\le 5)y : Ay][\hat{E}' : \text{for}[e', y]]$
$\exists E(\text{try}[e] \wedge [\exists E' : \text{INFL}[e', \text{PRO}_i] \wedge \text{work}[e']] \text{OF}[E, E'])$

(ii) ..., that $[(\le 5)y : Ay]$
$\exists E(\text{try}[e] \wedge [\exists E' : [\hat{E} : \text{for}[e', y]](\text{INFL}[e', \text{PRO}_i] \wedge \text{work}[e'])] \text{OF}[E, E'])$

38. See Larson and Ludlow (1993) for a recent discussion of intentional contexts.

39. The argument assumes that *de re* belief does not tacitly introduce another argument position: believe(x, y, S'). If it did, we could have (i):

(i) No more than two prosecutors believed of some suspects that few witnesses could give them alibis, and *there* some things were believed of no more than five suspects.

Of course, the cumulative quantification is not truly long-distance in this case, since both quantifiers bind argument positions in the matrix predicate.

40. Note that nothing has been said about the relation between the adjunct and the antecedent clause. It is not obvious, for example, that the reference of *that* in (207) is to an event rather than to a fact or proposition. If it is to an event, then we must make sense of negative events, an event of no more than two victims' dying.

The adjunct expresses a causal relation, and thus shares all the problems of this class of predicates, including apparent intentionality. Thus, although John's swimming the Channel was his going to Calais, (i) and (ii) may differ in truth value:

(i) John went to Calais because of Marie's invitation.

(ii) John swam the Channel because of Marie's invitation.

For a recent discussion of causal relations and related issues, see Bennett 1988 and references cited there.

41. For discussion, see Oehrle 1976, Stowell 1981, and Larson 1988, among others.

Chapter 10

1. I assume a logical form where *two crimes* is dependent on *few detectives*. The possibility of assigning wide scope to *two crimes*, as in (i), is irrelevant.

(i) $[\exists Y : 2(Y) \wedge \forall y(Yy \rightarrow Cy)][\text{few } x : Dx] \text{solve}(x, Y) \ldots$

2. See Davies 1981, pp. 176 ff., for a survey of the conditions under which reference is nonmaximal.

3. The shorter discourses in (i) and (ii) also contrast, presumably because of the implicit pronoun *others besides them*, which must be maximal when the antecedent is nonincreasing:

(i)   Two men came to the office today. Perhaps there were even others.

(ii) *Few men came to the office today. Perhaps there were even others.

Here and throughout the text, the contrast between (5) and (6) and between (i) and (ii) is described as an opposition between increasing and nonincreasing quantifiers. Dorit Ben-Shalom (personal communciation) observes, however, that not all increasing quantifiers allow anaphoric pronouns to refer nonmaximally. Thus, (iv) through (vi) contrast with (5) and (iii).

(5)   Two men came to the office today. They tried to sell encyclopedias. Perhaps there were even others who did the same.

(iii) Many men came to the office today. The tried to sell encyclopedias. Perhaps there were even others who did the same.

(iv) ?Most (of the) men came to the office today. They tried to sell encyclopedias. Perhaps there were even others who did the same.

(v)   ?More than two men came to the office today. They tried to sell encyclopedias. Perhaps there were even others who did the same.

(vi) ?At least two men came to the office today. They tried to sell encyclopedias. Perhaps there were even others who did the same.

I should rather characterize the opposition in terms of NPs that are classified as second-order quantifiers, '$[\exists X : 2(X)\ldots]$' and '$[\exists X : many(X)\ldots]$', versus those that are treated as first-order quantifiers, '$[most\ x : N']$', '$[(> 2)x : N']$', and '$[(\geq 2)x : N']$', where only the second-order quantifiers allow nonmaximal reference. Unlike *many*, which can simply mean numerous, *most* has only a proportional interpretation. So it is no surprise that it cannot occur as a cardinality predicate inside a second-order quantifier, *'$[\exists X : most(X)\ldots]$'. There is, however, no good semantic reason for *at least two* or *more than two* not to do so: '$[\exists X : (\geq 2)(X)\ldots]$' and '$[\exists X : (> 2)(X)\ldots]$'. Nevertheless, there appears to be evidence for the distinction between bare and modified numerals. Liu (1990) notes that they differ in their scope-assignment properties, and Anna Szabolcsi (personal communication) has remarked that they also differ in their syntactic distribution in Hungarian, where *at least two* and *more than two* pattern more like other first-order quantifiers. For further discussion, see Beghelli 1993 and Ben-Shalom 1993.

Perhaps all numeral phrases are ambiguous between first- and second-order quantifiers, in that bare and modified numerals occur both as quantifiers and as cardinality predicates. (Compare Milsark 1977 and see Herburger 1993 for a recent discussion.) In (v) and (vi), pragmatic considerations may favor construing the numeral as a quantifier. Note that if, for example, the speaker knows that two men came, (vi) risks violating Gricean conditions on felicity. To use (v) or (vi), the speaker must in some sense lack more precise information. If he is formulating a general proposition about how many men came to the office, such ignorance is quite natural. Perhaps he saw two come and can therefore conclude that at least two came but nothing more precise. However, in such a circumstance he could not utter (vi), intending the subject as an indefinite description. If he saw two and means to say what they did, (vi) represents him as knowing too little about their number. Using an indefinite description, the speaker draws attention to some men who are not to be thought of as all the men that came, whose number he knows only to be at least two, in short, to some group of men of unknown number containing at least two men. My prediction is that if one is careful to construct such a context, then (v) and (vi) become possible, which does not seem far off the mark.

4. The collective *panned together* preempts the suggestion that the second conjunct be read as 'and then for every student, *some of the movies that he was shown* were panned together in *The New Yorker*'.

5. As in Heim 1982 and Kamp 1981. But the logical forms in (24) and (25) below depart from Heim's and Kamp's representations. In particular, the logical forms in (24) and (25) assume that the pronoun is a descriptive anaphor in both cases and look for a minimal contrast to characterize increasing and nonincreasing antecedents. In their representations, the contrast takes on a more radical form: pronouns as discourse referents are distinguished from pronouns as descriptive anaphors. There is then a restriction on the quantifiers that can participate in discourse reference.

6. See Evans 1977, 1980; Kadmon 1990; and Neale 1990 for further discussion.

7. Kadmon cites the pairs in (i) and (ii).

(i)   a.   John has a cat. Its name is Felix.
      b.   John has a cat whose name is Felix.

(ii) a.   A cat walked in. It sat down.
      b.   A cat who walked in sat down.

While (i) sustains the claim, (ii) is a less compelling example. The NP *a cat who walked in* suggests that there are other cats who walked in. The appropriate comparison is (iii), where the impression of a contrast in reference is diminished.

(iii) a.   A cat walked in. It sat down.
      b.   A cat walked in and sat down.

8. This is Sommers's (1982) view, although he locates the ambiguity in the pronoun's determiner. The pronoun is always a descriptive anaphor when it is not within the scope of its antecedent, and by itself it is ambiguous between a definite and an indefinite description.
    Sommers (1982, 70 f.) offers the following minimal pair:

(i)   Some Hondurans are very rich; they keep mistresses; they have yachts.

(ii) Some Hondurans are very rich; *they* can afford Perrier at 79 cents a bottle, I can't!

Not all very rich Hondurans need keep mistresses, but they can all afford Perrier.

9. See, e.g., Evans 1977, 1980; Davies 1981, chapter 7; Neale 1990; and Kadmon 1990. Neale (pp. 241 ff.) is the most explicit about endorsing this view and calls attention to Evans's (1980, p. 223, n. 7) lapse from it.
    Kadmon shares with the other authors the view that the pronoun is a descriptive anaphor and that its nonmaximal reference is to be attributed solely to the pragmatics of incomplete definite descriptions. Conforming to the earlier approach, she in effect assumes, however, that indefinites do fall within the scope of a discourse-level existential quantifier, which distinguishes them formally from

other quantifiers. Thus (4) is equivalent to (i). Note that the pronoun, despite being dependent on the existential quantifier '∃*C*', refers maximally to all the sheep that John owns.

(i) $\exists C([\exists X : (\geq 2)(X) \wedge \forall x(Xx \leftrightarrow (Sx \wedge Cx))][_\Phi$ John owns $X]$,
and $[\iota X : \forall x(Xx \leftrightarrow Cx) \wedge \forall x(Xx \leftrightarrow (Sx \wedge \Phi))]$ Harry vaccinated X)

Kadmon differs in another respect, which logical form (i) is not faithful to. A felicitous pronoun token is *not* necessarily a definite description that can be completed in the given context. Instead, a pronoun is used felicitously if it occurs in a discourse that allows one eventually to grasp a maximal referent. Thus the first two tokens of *they* (*them*) in (ii) are felicitous in that discourse, because their referent is all the colleagues that I have to show this document to who are in a meeting.

(ii) I have to show this document to three colleagues. They are in a meeting, and I am waiting for them. I have to show it to at least two other colleagues, but THEY have already left, and I'll have to catch them tomorrow. (Kadmon 1990, 289).

Note that the completed description cannot gloss the first token without trivializing the sentence in which it occurs:

(iii) *The colleagues I have to show this document to who are in a meeting are in a meeting.

Kadmon's model respects the fact that the hearer is revising how best to complete the descriptions encountered as the discourse unfolds. The hearer need not reach a final state where the pronouns correspond to completed definite descriptions and make sense *in situ*.

10. Davies's provides an ingenious example to illustrate how far-flung the relevant factors can be: "Suppose that *A*, on the basis of his general beliefs about crime and about the alphabetical distribution of victims, comes to believe that Smith has been murdered, and on the basis of his general beliefs about genetics comes to believe that the culprit is tall and blond. Suppose that *A* decides to make a pronouncement and says

Smith's murderer is tall and blond.

Suppose that, in reality, a tall, blond man did go to Smith's house intending to kill Smith and indeed did put a bullet through Smith, but that Smith was already dead from a heart attack. Then *B*, knowing these facts, might reply (intuitively correctly)

You are almost right. He was tall and blond but he didn't really murder Smith.

In this case, *A*'s evidence, such as it was, cannot be said to provide a causal route to the man who put a bullet through Smith" (1981, 181).

11. Note that an utterance of (35), with the definite description overt, can indeed be construed coherently if one is careful to dissociate in some way the content of the definite description from the preceding sentence, as (i) makes explicit:

(i) In all, few men came to the office today. The few I have in mind sold encyclopedias. Perhaps there were even others.

This observation might suggest, but to no avail, a certain formal constraint on the descriptive content that a speaker or hearer grasps in order to use a pronoun felicitously. The constraint would require the content of a pronoun to be *identical* to the understood content and scope of its antecedent. Let C stand for what the speaker provides upon demand to complete the descriptive content of a pronoun. Then a discourse containing the pronoun is felicitous only if C is also understood to be part of the descriptive content of the antecedent of the pronoun. If the pronoun is referentially dependent, as in (ii), a felicitous discourse may be understood as in (iii) but not as in (iv).

(ii) $[Q : \Phi]_i \Psi \ldots \text{They}_i \ldots$

(iii) $[Q : \Phi \,\&\, C] \Psi \ldots [\iota V : \Phi \,\&\, C \,\&\, \Psi] \ldots$

(iv) $*[Q : \Phi] \Psi \ldots [\iota V : \Phi \,\&\, C \,\&\, \Psi] \ldots$

The constraint will, for example, keep the pronoun in (6) from being cashed out as in (i), where, crucially, the relative clause *that I have in mind* restricts the definite description and not the quantifier *few men*. Under the constraint, nonmaximal reference in (5) and (6) is possible only if the speaker is prepared to supply upon demand a C so that (v) and (vi) are true:

(v)   [Two : men & C] came to the office today. [The : men & C that came to the office today] tried to sell encyclopedias. Perhaps, there were even others who did the same.

(vi)   [Few : men & C] came to the office today. [The : men & C that came to the office today] tried to sell encyclopedias. Perhaps, there were even others who did the same.

For (v) to be coherent, the others that did the same must be men who came to the office today to sell encyclopedias other than those who are also C. But again, such an understanding also makes (vi) coherent and again fails to distinguish increasing and nonincreasing antecedents.

12. For discussion of the analogy between tense and pronouns, see Burge 1974 and Partee 1973, 1984b.

13. On demonstrative uses of the past tense, see Burge 1974 and Partee 1973.

14. Hinrichs (1981) and Partee (1984b) exploit this feature of the tense system in a theory addressed to sequence of tense and its interaction with aspect.

15. Neale (1990, 244) points out that events should be quantified over rather than times, as suggested in Evans's informal remarks. Neale (1990) and Heim (1990) both discuss a class of examples due to Jan van Eijck and Hans Kamp that challenge proposals to relativize definite descriptions to events or situations:

(i) If a man resembles another man, he hates him.

Because the predicate is symmetric, they claim that the description 'the man that resembles another man in e' will not have a unique referent. Ludlow (1987) answers the objection, at least for proposals based on Davidsonian events. A symmetric predicate is one that validates (ii) but not (iii):

(ii) $\exists e \, V(x, y, e) \leftrightarrow \exists e \, V(y, x, e)$

(iii) $*V(x, y, e) \leftrightarrow V(y, x, e)$

Thus, x's resembling y is not the same event as y's resembling x, although the one exists if and only if the other does too. Compare x's buying from y and y's selling to x.

16. The astute reader will observe that the dilemma is more extensive. It also undermines the expected conditions for definite descriptions. Thus the possible logical forms shown should make (i) and (ii) indistinguishable:

(i) a. Once, the man arrived.
　　b. $[\exists e : \text{Past}(e)][\iota x : Mx \wedge R(x, e)] \text{ arrive}(x, e)$

(ii) a. Once, a man arrived.
　　b. $[\exists e : \text{Past}(e)][\exists x : Mx \wedge R(x, e)] \text{ arrive}(x, e)$

17. In the context Heim (1982) provides for (47), she has broken three glasses, two of them cheap and of no interest to her. The third, however, was expensive, and its breaking upset her. Then, of course, she utters (47), prepared to identify the glass whose breaking upset her as the unique referent of the pronoun.

18. Also consider the discourses under a propositional attitude. In the given context, any sentence in (i) and (ii) is felicitous, in contrast to (iii):

(i) a. Look, all I know is that there was a wine glass broken last night that was very expensive.
　　b. Look, all I know is that a wine glass that was very expensive was broken last night.

(ii) a. Look, all I know is that there was a wine glass broken last night, and it was very expensive.
　　b. Look, all I know is that a wine glass was broken last night, and it was very expensive.

(iii) *Look, all I know is that the wine glass that was broken last night was very expensive.

19. Also the variants on Geach's strategy in (i) and (ii) (from Evans 1980):

(i) John bought a sheep that was not the only one he bought, and Harry vaccinated it.

(ii) John bought some sheep that were not the only ones he bought, and Harry vaccinated them.

20. Goldsmith and Woisetschlaeger (1982) discuss the "phenomenal" nature of the progressive.

21. Another sort of California semantics. I will draw freely on our intuitions about how a scene might be filmed. Cinematic convention is not arbitrary. It constitutes a practical study of how we associate images to narrative, and it would not work if it broke too many rules.

22. Obviously, the parameters for audition and other modalities are something else.

23. No analysis of *there* insertion is intended. The term 'be(e')' can be omitted if the copula is a dummy verb.

24. I leave it open whether observable versus nonobservable coincides with stage-level versus individual-level predicates.

25. Note that what is considered an observed event is context-dependent. The speaker's epistemic condition may provide a rationale for relating an event or situation to the speaker's observations (see the discussion of the progressive above). Suppose a detective is searching Leif's apartment for evidence and utters Kadmon's (64) and things like it as he discovers relevant items: "Aha, he has a scuffed shoe." Kadmon's example is not quite felicitous, since being in the kitchen, where the search has now taken him, is presumably part of the background. The moment when the detective discovers that Leif has a chair should not be followed by a declaration that it is in the kitchen. Better if he then realizes that the chair is in front of the safe:

(i) Leif has a chair. It is in front of the safe.

26. Recall that an NP denotes all those things bearing a given θ-role to an event. Given that *Leif has a chair* is true if he has more than one, there must proper parts of the situation that correspond to having a chair. An alternative is presented by a logical form similar to those suggested by Lombard (1985). We might gloss (i) as *Leif's state of possession relates to there being a chair*.

(i) $\exists e(\text{INFL}(e, l) \wedge \exists e'(\text{R}(e, e') \wedge [\exists y : \text{chair}(y)] \text{OF}(e', y))$

Suppose that the meaning of the verb has it that Leif is never in more than one state of possession, but that state (event) may be related by 'R' to events with different possessions. Then an implication of uniqueness is recovered if only the first quantifier over events, '$\exists e$', has discourse scope. The definite description then refers to the chair that Leif's state of possession relates to:

$[\iota y : \text{chair}(y) \wedge \text{INFL}(e, l) \wedge \exists e'(\text{R}(e, e') \text{OF}(e', y))]$.

This type of logical form, which introduces a new event quantifier with each θ-role, will not rescue uniqueness for intransitives as in (70).

27. Partee (1984) cites Kamp 1979, 1980, and Bach 1980, 1981, for treating events as primitives rather than as times.

28. Note that *doing the same thing* cannot require a strict identity with the antecedent predicates. Doing the same thing is coming to the office today and trying to sell encyclopedias, but it must omit $\Pi(e^p, e)$ if the discourse is not to be contradictory.

29. Biconditionals can replace the conditionals if 'V_i' and 'V_j' are restricted to predicates denoting observable events and the theory of perspectives has it that if an observable event occurs, there is some perspective on it. This certainly comports with my understanding of the notion.

30. Perspective is the only means to mute the felicity conditions of an absolute definite description. Thus, simpler contrasts such as the one in (i) and (ii) follow immediately from the absence of a predicate of events in the definite description (if the predicate is '$\text{man}(x, e)$', then this contrast will just be another instance that falls under the constraint on perspective):

(i) The man came to the office today.

(ii) A man came to the office today.

This accounts for the problem raised in n. 16.

31. The discourse in (102) has *only* a contradictory reading. I assume that the semantics of *unique* will require that the uniquely held property be held uniquely

from all perspectives. Note that the constraint on perspective keeps any definite description from introducing perspective as in (i).

(i) $\exists \Pi \exists e^P([\exists x : \exists e(N(x,e) \wedge \Pi(e^P,e))]\exists e \; F(x,e).$

$[\iota x : \exists e(N(x,e) \wedge \Pi(e^P,e)) \wedge \exists e \; F(x,e)]\exists e \; G(x,e).)$

The constraint is not sufficient, however, for (102). The problem is that nothing prevents the dependency shown in (ii), even though the definite description is not itself anaphoric.

(ii) $\exists \Pi \exists e^P([\exists x : \exists e(N(x,e) \wedge \Pi(e^P,e))]\exists e \; F(x,e).$

$[\iota x : \exists e(N(x,e) \wedge \Pi(e^P,e)) \wedge \exists e \; F(x,e)]\exists e \; G(x,e).)$

32. Alternatively, one could elaborate the content of the pronoun referring to the donkeys. The text follows the treatment given in chapter 9, section 3, where the cross-reference to events is restricted by the antecedent clause and the pronominal content is minimal.

33. Except for the special contexts discussed in n. 25.

34. The judgment is not so clear in (116). There is some inclination to understand it to mean exactly two, so that roommates who have more than two chairs are indeed irrelevant. Note that if a roommate has, say, three chairs, a, b and c, the events relevant to (116) are his having a and b, his having a and c, and his having b and c, and so 'Φ' in '$[\hat{E}:\Phi]$' is not a sortal if it denotes all of these. Suppose, however, that the quantifier selects a sortal complement (more like 'all the areas that F' rather than 'all the area that F'), and that the hearers accommodate this by assuming that an individual event corresponds to a roommate's largest event of having chairs. Then only those roommates are relevant that have exactly two chairs. In contrast, the description of events in (115) is sortal without any special accommodation if no part of a roommate's having chair a is part of his having chair b. Notice that such minimal events will in fact cover all of a roommate's having chairs, which accounts for the judgments reported. On this view, the difference between (115) and (116) has less to do with any semantic difference between *a chair* and *two chairs* than with the nature of the cross-reference to events. This view finds some support in the following. Consider the roommates who each have many pairs of chairs, each pair next to a different lamp:

(i) Once, no one is certain when, few roommates had two chairs next to a lamp; they were in the kitchen all together.

The pronoun readily refers to all the chairs among these pairs, even though a given roommate may have more than two chairs. In the context, the events denoted are a sortal: no part of a roommate's having chairs a and b next to lamp l is a part of his having chairs c and d next to lamp m. Examples like (i) suggest that the difference noted between (115) and (116) is not a formal one.

35. In my logical forms, which modalize the quantification over events and move θ-roles to a clause-initial position, the syntactic characterization in terms of linking does not apply. So I fall back on the semantic characterization.

36. An alternative to an antecedent presentational clause would give a complex analysis to the transitive predicate along the lines of (i).

(i) Every boy did something to two girls, which was to give them none of his toys.

This cannot be a simple causative, that every boy caused two girls to have none of his toys, relating each boy's action to some caused events. As in the text, this would defeat exact description of the number of girls involved if a boy caused several events of two girls having none of his toys. The higher predicate must itself supply θ-roles to all the relevant arguments, as in (i). And if it is anything like *do*, its object is not a particular event but something like a kind of activity. This is more than I wish to deal with here. For discussion of *do* and the related use of *by* in *John alerted the burglar by flipping the light switch*, see J. Bennett 1988, Parsons 1990, Thomson 1977, Vendler 1984.

Chapter 11

1. I have been assuming that cross-reference between conjuncts is by an unbound anaphor whenever the event variable is not free in one of the conjuncts. Thus the logical forms ought to be those in (i).

(i) a. $\exists E([\exists X : 3(X) \wedge \forall x(Xx \to Cx)] \text{INFL}[\text{that}_i, X]$
$\wedge (_i [\exists Y : 2(Y) \wedge \forall y(Yy \to Vy)][\hat{E} : \text{in}[e, Y]]$
$(\text{ride}[e] \wedge [\exists W : 1(W) \wedge \forall w(Ww \to Zw)] \text{to}[e, W]))) $
b. $\exists E([\exists X : 3(X) \wedge \forall x(Xx \to Cx)] \text{INFL}[\text{that}_i, X]$
$\wedge (_i [\exists Y : 2(Y) \wedge \forall y(Yy \to Vy)][\hat{E} : \text{in}[e, Y]]$
$[(\leq 1)w : Zw][\hat{E} : \text{to}[e, w]] \text{ride}[e]))$

They remain true in situation (22). The first trip by the three children coincides exactly with whatever the two vans did jointly or severally on the way to one zoo.

2. Alternatively, one could allow a logical form like (28). Observe, however, that clefting the verb does not seem to allow the jointly or severally interpretation. Sentence (28) cannot be true if only one boy arrives. So, for whatever reason, the structure does not yield the unwanted interpretation.

3. The example has the form of the cases that demonstrate essential separation (see chapter 4).

4. See, e.g., Belnap 1969, 1982; Belnap and Steel 1976; Engdahl 1986; Groenendijk and Stokhof 1984; Hamblin 1973; Higginbotham 1991; Higginbotham and May 1981; Karttunen 1977; Lahiri 1991; Scha 1983.

5. This formulation is deliberately vague. The list of pairs corresponds to a true, complete answer to the question. On some accounts, the list is not directly represented in the reference of the question. See the partition theories of Belnap (1982), Belnap and Steel (1976), Higginbotham (1991), Higginbotham and May (1981), and Groenendijk and Stokhof (1984).

6. Engdahl's example is not quite right, since presumably an average grade does depend on each grade in the sample. Replace *depend on* with *is completely determined by*.

7. I do not accept a singular, count head:

(i) *John made a pile out of what paper {each student/the students} turned in.

Thus there appears to be a difference between referring expressions and indirect questions. This is not surprising if the referring expressions *embed* the question within an ordinary relative clause:

(ii) $[\exists X : \forall x (Xx$

$\quad \leftrightarrow (\text{paper}(x) \wedge R(x, \{_{\text{question}} \text{ what papers each student turned in}\})))]$

(iii) $[\exists X : 1(X) \wedge \forall x (Xx$

$\quad \leftrightarrow (\text{paper}(x) \wedge R(x, \{_{\text{question}} \text{ what papers each student turned in}\})))]$

8. Engdahl (1986, 167 f.) refines this to quantifying over functions in intension. Higginbotham (1991) advocates a substitutional interpretation of the *wh* when it quantifies over nonarguments.

9. One may wonder why a pair list is tied to quantifying over questions. Since there is also quantifying over functions, why can't one specify the function by a list? Suppose, as in Higginbotham 1991, that so-called functional answers reply to a substitutional *wh*-quantifier rather than an objectual quantifier over functions. Then an answer must take the form of something that can replace the *wh*-phrase. Obviously, a list does not have the appropriate form.

10. Question (i) asks a question about each Englishman, and the answers to these many questions appear in the pair list.

(i) Who does every Englishman admire?

(ii) What function f is such that every Englishman-x admires $f(x)$?

It is plausible, in this case, to view the family of questions as instead a single question about a certain function, as in (ii), the extension of which the pair-list answer then specifies. Groenendijk and Stokhof (1984) point out that this correspondence to a single question about functions does not extend to all cases that pose a family of questions. In particular, indefinite NPs offer a choice of questions to be answered. Thus, the relevant interpretation of (iii) invites the respondent to choose some two Englishmen and to answer for each of them the question about whom he admires.

(iii) Who do two Englishmen admire?

There are various ways to comply with the question and give a complete answer. It would, for example be enough to answer that Moore admires Russell and Russell admires Moore, and excessive to say anything more. However, none of the pair lists sufficient for (i) correspond to a complete answer to either of the questions in (iv).

(iv) a. What function f is such that two Englishmen each-x admire $f(x)$?
     b. What functions f are such that two Englishmen each-x admire $f(x)$?

Since there are more than two Englishmen, the presupposition of a unique function deprives (iv.a) of any answer. As for (iv.b), an answer sufficient for (iii) complies only partially with what is asked for. In an answer that mentions only Russell and Moore, the respondent fails to indicate what are the other functions that map two Englishmen into their admirees. Thus (iii)'s family of questions cannot be identified with any single question about functions.

Even where they are plausible, as in (i), it is doubtful that pair lists answer a question about functions.

It is often noted that contexts will vary as to how complete an answer is expected. To the question *Who does Moore admire?* it is sometimes enough of an answer to say he admires the Queen Mother, although he also admires others. This observation extends to pair-list answers, so that in replying to (i), it may be enough, when one gets to Moore on the list, to mention only the Queen Mother. But partiality cannot be extended to the other dimension in a pair-list answer. If Moore is in the relevant domain, one cannot answer the question and neglect to mention him. This is not surprising if pair-list answers go with quantifying into questions: '[every Englishman][who] Φ'. To neglect Moore is to ignore one of the questions that has been put forward. Quantifying over functions or functions-in-intension cannot account for this constraint on pair-list answers. Suppose that there is an objectual quantifier over such functions, and we may even allow that its domain is restricted to total functions:

(v)   What total function f is such that every-Englishman-x admires $f(x)$?

(vi) Russell admires the author of *Waverly*.

To a question that quantifies objectually, as in (vii), any partial answer is good that relieves some ignorance. The answer in (viii) informs us that it is some royal prig that Moore admires, perhaps among others.

(vii)   Who does Moore admire?

(viii) Some royal prig.

Why then isn't (vi) a good partial answer to (i), conveying the information that some total function that assigns to Russell the author of *Waverly* is a function f? To use the substitutional interpretation of '[wh- F]' (see Higginbotham 1991), an answer to (ix) is true just in case substituting it for F yields a truth:

(ix) [wh- F] every Englishman admires F?

This does have the desirable result that the answer in (x) implies that *every* Englishman admires his mother and the answer in (xi), that *every* Englishman admires some royal prig or another.

(x)   His mother.

(xi) Some royal prig or another.

But the substitutional interpretation does not support a pair-list answer, since it cannot be substituted for F. Thus the constraint on a pair-list answer, that something must be said about every Englishman, which follows from quantifying into a question, has no account if the quantifying is over functions.

A further complication attends this view of pair-list answers. Suppose that Russell and Moore are the only Englishmen. A felicitous pair-list answer to (i) would be that Moore admires the Queen Mother and Russell admires no one at all. (The issue is not one of rejecting a presupposition. Consider instead *Who if anyone does every Englishman admire.*) If the pair-list specifies a function f, what, then, is f(Russell)? The function f cannot simply be a partial function that does not specify a value for Russell if we are to distinguish this answer from one that fails to be informative about him. It would have to be that an answer is a function f from individuals to generalized quantifiers such that $f(x)(\lambda y(x \text{ admires } y))$. As above, it must be stipulated that f is a total function. It also becomes a more difficult question how to relate the reference of *what everyone bought* to an *f* whose range consists of generalized quantifiers.

There is also syntactic evidence to suggest that a pair-list answer is tied to quantifying into a question rather than to a question about functions. Quantifying into a question requires a movement of a quantifier to a position that includes the question within its scope. Movement is subject to constraints, and these should therefore be reflected in the distribution of pair-list answers if indeed pair-list answers are tied to quantifying in. Constraints on movement should not affect the distribution of functional answers. Thus, the syntax of certain questions will exclude pair-list answers but admit functional answers, which is unexpected if the pair lists simply spell out the extensions of functional answers. In this connection, consider pairs of quantifiers, such as those in (xii) and (xiii), that have been observed to resist inverse scope (for general discussions of the problem, see, e.g., Kroch 1979; May 1977, 1985; Liu 1990; Beghelli 1993; and Ben-Shalom 1993).

(xii)   No one recommended every book to Ludi.

(xiii) Only Russell recommended every book to Ludi.

Although *every book* freely inverts in other contexts, *no one* and *only Russell* obstruct its movement to wide-scope position. This opacity also makes it more difficult for *every book* to quantify into the question in (xvii), which thereby excludes the pair-list answer in (xix). In contrast, (xvii) allows the functional answer in (xviii), which does not require wide scope to be assigned to *every book*.

(xiv)   *Q*:   Which student did Russell recommend every book to?

(xv)   *A*:   He recommended every book to the student that would most appreciate it.

(xvi)   *A*:   He recommended *Principia Mathematica* to Ludi and *Principia Ethica* to David.

(xvii) *Q*:   Which student did {no one/only Russell} recommend every book to?

(xviii) *A*:   {No one/only Russell} recommended every book to the student least able to understand it.

(xix)   *A*:   *{No one/only Russell} recommended *Principia Mathematica* to David, and {no one/only Russell} recommended *Principia Ethica* to Ludi.

The noted contrast also extends to the cases of long-distance quantifying-in reported in May 1985. I find the possibility of the pair-list answer in (xxii) marginal, but it is far better than the pair-list answer (xxv) to question (xxiii), where the matrix quantifiers *only you* or *no one* keeps *everyone* from quantifying into the question.

(xx)   *Q*:   Which friend of yours do you think everyone invited?

(xxi)   *A*:   Everyone invited the friend I introduced him to.

(xxii) *A*:   ?Hilary invited Robin, and Sandy invited Terry.

(xxiii) *Q*:   Which friend of yours {do only you/does no one} think everyone invited?

(xxiv) *A*:   {Only I think/No one thinks} that everyone invited the friend I introduced him to.

(xxv)   *A*: *{Only I think/No one thinks} that Hilary invited Robin, and {only I
             think/no one thinks} that Sandy invited Terry.

(Note that this case is a counterexample to the proposal in Chierchia 1993, according to which *everyone* acquires the same scope as the *wh*-phrase via absorption, with the *wh*-trace in the embedded complementizer position.)

   The left-branch condition is another constraint that distinguishes quantifying
into a question from a question about functions. Question (xxvi) is awkward
because of a slight violation of subjacency. It nevertheless elicits the functional
answer (xxvii) but not the pair-list answer (xxviii). To quantify into the question,
every character would need to be extracted from the NP, which violates the left-
branch condition.

(xxvi)   *Q*: What subject do you want every character's opinion about?

(xxvii) *A*: I want every character's opinion about his whole life.

(xxviii) *A*: *I want Sonia's opinion about love and Boris's opinion about death.

Note that the acceptability of the pair-list answer (xxxi) to question (xxix) suggests
the movement at LF of the entire NP *every character's lines* in order not to violate
the left-branch condition. This option is presumably unavailable to the quantified
NP in (xxvi), which contains the *wh*-trace *'[every character's opinion about t_i]
what subject$_i$'.

(xxix)   *Q*: What page did you write every character's lines on?

(xxx)   *A*: On the page beginning with his name.

(xxxi)   *A*: I wrote Sonia's lines on the first page and Boris's lines on the second.

There is thus some syntactic evidence against reducing the family-of-questions
interpretation to a question about functions.

   For the purposes of our discussion, the proposal in Chierchia 1993 should be
counted among those that quantify into questions. Chierchia uses functions only
to claim, in effect, that quantifying into questions is quantifying into questions
about functions. So the family of questions (xxxii) that appears to ask for a list of
professors turns out to be a family of questions each of which asks for a student's
professor-function, like (xxxiii).

(xxxii) Which professor does every student like?

(xxxiii) Which function f (from students to professors) is such that every
         student-x likes $f(x)$?

The proposal does not treat (xxxii) as a question about a function, the extension
of which a pair-list answer lists.

11. Some steps are missing from this argument. Note that the reference of *what
everyone bought* is determined by the range of the *unique* function that assigns to
each person everything he bought. Of course, many functions f meet the description 'everyone-x bought $f(x)$' and answer the question, *What did everyone buy?*
Presumably, in the analysis of the referring expression, one should refer to the
maximal f such that everyone-x bought $f(x)$. This analysis should, in principle, be
available to (52). Thus if no student reads his teachers' recommendations and
none reads his parents' recommendations, then the maximal f will assign to each

student at least his teachers' and his parents' recommended reading. The range of such a maximal f will still not coincide with the reference of the expression in (52).

12. I assume that names and conjunctions of names, e.g., *Mary, Sue, and Alice*, can be assimilated to definite descriptions.

13. There is some disagreement in the literature about the status of indefinite NPs quantifying into questions. Belnap (1982), Engdahl (1986), Higginbotham (1991), and Scha (1983) cite examples similar to (54). Groenendijk and Stokhof (1984) and May (1985) formulate conditions that would exclude them.

14. Note *some two, some few* but also **some many, *some most*.

15. To my ear, such an interpretation is even a distant possibility where the embedded quantifier is decreasing, as in (53).

16. The difficulties of quantifying over negative events could be avoided altogether in this case if the structure of cumulative quantification were assumed to be different, along the lines of (i).

(i) What students the dons recommended few books to were no more than two students.

17. I do not think the possibility for collective agency is what excuses customers from buying appliances. Suppose that invoices ordering appliances may come in prepaid or not. A contrast similar to the one discussed in the text distinguishes the following examples, where there is no question of collective agency:

(i) The clerk put in one consignment {what/the} appliances the invoices prepaid for.

(ii) The clerk put in one pneumatic tube {what/the} invoices {∅/that} prepaid for the appliances.

It seems that *what invoices prepaid for the appliances* in (ii) denotes some invoices only if the appliances were prepaid for. Since some invoices prepay and others do not, the clerk in (i) put the appliance in the consignment if and only if one of the invoices prepaid for it.

In light of the earlier contrast between singular and plural *wh*-questions, I must assume that the relative clause is parasitic on a singular question if the c-command effect is to hold. Why this is so is unexplained.

18. Note the form of (102): $[?E : \Phi][5!z : Az][E' : \text{for}[e', z]]$ solve$[e']$. The solving events ('E''') of the separated clause are not those of the antecedent event quantifier '$[?E : \Phi]$'. The separated θ-role has been extracted from a complex description, 'events(e) that are of detectives' solving(e') no more than two crimes *for agencies*.' Reconstruction, as in chapter 9, section 3.1.1, is required to properly relate the separated clause to the antecedent event quantifier.

19. Invoked nowhere, this clause is defined arbitrarily.

Chapter 12

1. From Barwise 1979.

2. As Sher (1990) points out, since any connected pair corresponds to a Cartesian product of two singleton sets, this interpretation is equivalent to the simpler,

Fewer than three dots are connected to stars, and fewer than three stars are connected to dots.

3. See Keenan (1987) for a discussion of Lindstrom's (1966) typology of *n*-ary quantifiers. The discussion of *n*-ary quantifiers in Keenan (1987) and in Sher (1990) is especially helpful.

4. See Barwise 1979, L. Carlson 1980, Higginbotham and May 1981, Keenan 1987, May 1989, Scha 1981, and Sher 1990, among others.

5. Rather, it in fact says that exactly two detectives solved a crime, and exactly three crimes were solved by a detective. Plural predication, however, is not at issue. In paraphrasing the logical forms, I will simply assume that *n*-ary quantification has accommodated it.

6. Sher (1990) notes that maximality will apply in (i), entailing that no other detectives solved other crimes.

(i) Two detectives solved three crimes.

She suggests that this is a benign consequence, since one is always talking about maximal sets. If so, it is difficult to see what to make of the contrast between (i) and (ii) (see chapter 10):

(ii)   Two men came to the office today with two encyclopedias. They tried to sell them to the staff. Perhaps there were others who did the same.

(iii)   *Exactly two men came to the office today with exactly two encyclopedias. They tried to sell them to the staff. Perhaps there were others who did the same.

For Scha (1981), the contrast presents no particular problem, since he admits (iv) alongside the interpretation of (i) as a cumulative quantifier.

(iv) $[\exists x : 2(x) \wedge \forall y(y \in x \rightarrow Dx)][\exists z : 3(z) \wedge \forall y(y \in z \rightarrow Cz)]$ solve(x, z)

Logical form (iv) presumably underlies (ii). I have been worried by the claim that all independent quantifiers have one look and one meaning, that of branching quantifiers interpreted according to one schema. If that schema is (40), then the contrast between (ii) and (iii) counts against the claim. There must be an alternative representation available to increasing quantifiers, which represents them as existential.

7. From Barwise 1979.

8. We should want the translation of *pairwise completely* inside Φ and beginning line (Ψ) to be the same if it is to be univocal inside and outside Φ. If, for example, there were plural objects and the second-order definitions were recast with first-order variables referring to plural objects, then 'pairwise completely $(\alpha, \beta, \alpha$ is connected to $\beta)$' could be uniformly translated as 'every one of α is connected to every one of β', which would fit both 'pairwise completely $(X, Y, X$ is connected to $Y)$' from (51) and 'pairwise completely $(x, y, x$ is connected to $y)$' from (57). See the univocal adverbs in section 1.

9. The last Cartesian product in (63) falsifies the generic interpretation in which the VP restricts a quantifier over events: *Whenever dots are connected to stars pairwise completely, few stars and few dots are connected.*

10. See Westerståhl 1987, proposition 2.4, p. 275.

11. To defend (68) unemended, one might reject the analysis of 'between n and m' and like quantifiers and suggest instead that (ii) underlies (i):

(i) [between n and m : A] B

(ii) for some k between n and m, [exactly k : A] B

The claim is that no quantifier imposes distinct upper and lower bounds, and thus (68) is adequate. Appearances to the contrary in (i), sentences (iii) and (iv) are the result of an underlying structure that quantifies over nonmonotonic quantifiers imposing an identical upper and lower bound k, as in (ii) and (v).

(iii) Many but not most dots are connected.

(iv) No more than half but at least several dots are connected.

(v) For some k that is many dots but not most dots, exactly k dots are connected.

Appendix I

1. They concede that cumulative quantification is independent.

2. See, e.g., Reinhart 1979 and the discussion in Chierchia and McConnell-Ginet 1990, pp. 116 ff.

3. Chierchia and McConnell-Ginet (1990) cite similar arguments against eliminating scope ambiguity.

4. Plural reference and the decomposition of the predicate are not at issue.

5. But Gruber (1967) points out such cases as (i), where inverse scope is the only interpretation.

(i) An oak grew out of every acorn.

An inverse scope relation is difficult just in case the quantifier that ends up with narrow scope is dependent on the raised quantifier. Thus example (25) in the text contrasts with (ii):

(25) Some boy loves every girl.

(ii) Every boy loves some girl.

While inverse scope in (25) and in (17) through (18) is relatively difficult, inverse scope in (ii), or a so-called referential use of the indefinite *some girl*, is never hindered. See Fodor and Sag 1982.

6. Van der Does (1992, 40) also concludes that the sum-of-plurals interpretation must be distinct from the semidistributive interpretation. His argument is the following. Sentence (ii) cannot be inferred from (i), even though Miles and Chet are trumpet players.

(i) Miles made music, and Chet made music.

(ii) Some trumpet players made music together.

The semidistributive interpretation of (ii), however, validates the inference. Therefore, (ii) must have a distinct, sum-of-plurals interpretation, which makes the inference invalid as perceived. The flaw in the argument is the premise that the semidistributive interpretation, paraphrased in (iii), validates the inference.

(iii) Some trumpet players, each perhaps with others, made music together.

Semidistributivity allows players denoted by the subject to be distributed among possibly distinct groups of trumpet players that made music together. Sentence (i) does not guarantee these conditions, since both Miles and Chet may have been solo trumpeters. The semidistributive (iii) does not follow from (i). Any interpretation of (ii) will invalidate the inference.

The semidistributive interpretation will, however, license an inference from (iv) to (v), but this is as it should be, as Schwarzschild (1991) has emphasized:

(iv) Miles and Wynton made music together, and Chet and Dizzy made music together.

(v) Four trumpet players made music together.

Van der Does's argument would have to be that there is also a sense in which the inference from (iv) to (v) is invalid corresponding to when (v) is understood as a sum of plurals. Granted that there is an invalid inference to be represented here, it is still not an argument for a distinct sum-of-plurals interpretation. The ambiguity of (v) can be attributed to the anaphoric possibilities raised by *together*. Staying with the assumption that the quantification is unambiguously semidistributive, we could have (vi), paraphrasing the interpretation that validates the inference, and (vii), paraphrasing the interpretation that invalidates it.

(vi) Four trumpet players, each perhaps with some others$_i$, made music with all of them$_i$.

(vii) Four trumpet players$_i$, each perhaps with some others, made music with all of them$_i$.

Even helping oneself to distinct logical forms for the sum-of-plurals interpretations would not help represent the invalid inference if one is using my logical forms for it (see chapter 6, section 1.2). The semantics for the sum-of-plurals interpretations on its own does not invalidate the inference. To the extent that there is a reading on which the inference is invalid, we would have to assume either that there are alternative antecedents for *together*, as in (vi) and (vii), or that the (second-order) existential event quantifier '$[\exists E : \Phi]$' that prefixes the logical form for the sum of plurals may contain a tacit cardinal restriction, '$[\exists E : 1(E) \wedge \Phi]$'. This would have the effect of stipulating that there was one event at which four trumpet players made music together. Either possibility sounds plausible.

7. This is not a reliable description of the relevant class of predicates. Taub (1989), appealing to Aktionsarten, provides the most interesting characterization.

8. Dowty (1987) discusses the contrast in (i):

(i) The trees are dense in the middle of the forest.

(ii) *The trees are all dense in the middle of the forest.

For such examples, Verkuyl and van der Does need only acknowledge that their account of plurals does not subsume reference to kinds, which the context in (i) seems to require. Note that the following are all excluded:

(iii) *The five hundred trees are dense in the middle of the forest.

(iv) *(Some) (five hundred) trees are dense in the middle of the forest.

Interestingly, these contexts distinguish different ways of referring to kinds:

(v)   Accidents were frequent in Los Angeles.

(vi)   *The accidents were frequent in Los Angeles.

(vii)   *Houses are dense in the middle of Los Angeles.

(viii) The houses are dense in the middle of Los Angeles.

9. The remaining two interpretations, the distributive and the sum-of-plurals, must be distinct, since neither entails the other.

10. The logic of this argument, showing that the sum-of-plurals and distributive interpretations are distinct from the semidistributive interpretation by providing a context that admits the former but excludes the latter, is plain in van der Does's (1992) rejection of Verkuyl and van der Does 1991. But here he takes the extreme position that (i) *never* has the semidistributive interpretation that the earlier paper claims to be its only one.

(i) Four boys lifted three pianos.

So, of course, the remaining distributive and sum-of-plurals interpretations are on their own. The facts seem to be that various pragmatic factors govern the accessibility of the semidistributive interpretation, as I remarked in the text and in chap. 1, n. 16. Given Verkuyl and van der Does' expectations from pragmatics, it is odd that some constraints on the semidistributive interpretation should prompt van der Does to abandon it.

References

Bach, Emmon. 1980. "Tenses and Aspects as Functions on Verb-Phrases." In Christian Rohrer, ed., *Time, Tense and Quantifiers*, Linguistiche Arbeiten 83, Tübingen: Niemeyer Verlag, pp. 19–37.

Bach, Emmon. 1981. "On Time, Tense, and Aspect: An Essay in English Metaphysics." In Peter Cole, ed., *Radical Pragmatics*, pp. 63–81. New York: Academic Press.

Barwise, Jon. 1979. "On Branching Quantifiers in English." *Journal of Philosophical Logic* 8:47–80.

Barwise, Jon. 1981. "Scenes and Other Situations." *Journal of Philosophy* 78: 369–397.

Barwise, Jon, and John Perry. 1983. *Situations and Attitudes*. Cambridge: MIT Press.

Bäuerle, Rainer, Urs Egli, and Arnim von Stechow, eds. 1979. *Semantics from Different Points of View*, Berlin: Springer-Verlag.

Bäuerle, Rainer, Christoph Schwarze, and Arnim von Stechow, eds. 1983. *Meaning, Use and Interpretation of Language*. Berlin: Walter de Gruyter.

Beghelli, Filippo. 1993. "A Minimalist Approach to Quantifier Scope." To appear in Amy Schafer, ed., *Proceedings of the North Eastern Linguistic Society* 23, Graduate Linguistics Students Association. U. Mass., Amherst.

Belnap, Nuel. 1969. "Questions: Their Presuppositions and How They Can Fail to Arise." In Karel Lambert, ed., *The Logical Way of Doing Things*, pp. 23–38. New Haven: Yale University Press.

Belnap, Nuel. 1982. "Questions and Answers in Montague Grammar." In S. Peters and E. Saarinen, eds., *Processes, Beliefs, and Questions*, pp. 165–198. Dordrecht: D. Reidel.

Belnap, Nuel, and T. Steel. 1976. *The Logic of Questions and Answers*. New Haven: Yale University Press.

Bennett, Jonathan. 1988. *Events and Their Names*. Indianapolis: Hackett Publishing Co.

Bennett, Michael. 1972. "Accommodating the Plural in Montague's Fragment of English." In Rodman 1972, pp. 25–65.

Bennett, Michael. 1979. *Questions in Montague Grammar*. Indiana University Linguistics Club.

Ben-Shalom, Dorit. 1993. "Object Wide Scope and Semantic Trees." To appear in Utpal Lahiri, ed., *Proceedings of the Third Semantics and Linguistic Theory Conference* (SALT III). University of California, Irvine.

Boolos, George. 1975. "On Second-Order Logic." *Journal of Philosophy* 72, no. 16: 509–527.

Boolos, George. 1984. "To Be Is to Be a Value of a Variable (or to Be Some Values of Some Variables)." *Journal of Philosophy* 81, no. 8: 430–449.

Boolos, George. 1985a. "Nominalist Platonism." *Philosophical Review* 94, no. 3: 327–344.

Boolos, George. 1985b. "Reading the *Begriffsschrift*." *Mind* 94, no. 375: 331–344.

Burge, Tyler. 1972. "Truth and Mass Terms." *Journal of Philosophy* 69, no. 10: 263–282.

Burge, Tyler. 1973. "Reference and Proper Names." *Journal of Philosophy* 70: 425–439. Reprinted in Davidson and Harman 1975, pp. 200–209.

Burge, Tyler. 1974. "Demonstrative Constructions, Reference, and Truth." *Journal of Philosophy* 71, no. 7: 205–223.

Burge, Tyler. 1977. "A Theory of Aggregates." *Noûs* 11: 97–117.

Carlson, Greg N. 1977. "Reference to Kinds in English." Ph.D. diss., U. Mass., Amherst.

Carlson, Greg. N. 1984. "Thematic Roles and Their Role in Semantic Interpretation." *Linguistics* 22: 259–279.

Carlson, Lauri. 1980. "Plural Quantification." Ms., MIT.

Carlson, Lauri. 1982. "Plural Quantifiers and Informational Independence." *Acta Philosophica Fennica* 35: 163–174.

Cartwright, Richard. 1975. "Scattered Objects." In Keith Lehrer, ed., *Analysis and Metaphysics*. Dordrecht: D. Reidel. Reprinted in Richard Cartwright, *Philosophical Essays* (Cambridge: MIT Press, 1987), pp. 171–186.

Castañeda, Hector-Neri. 1967. Comments. In Rescher 1967.

Chierchia, Gennaro. 1993. "Questions with Quantifiers." *Natural Language Semantics* 1, no. 2: 181–234.

Chierchia, Gennaro, and Sally McConnell-Ginet. 1990. *Meaning and Grammar: An Introduction to Semantics*. Cambridge: MIT Press.

Chomsky, Noam. 1976. "Conditions on Rules of Grammar." In Noam Chomsky, *Essays on Form and Interpretation*. New York: North-Holland.

Chomsky, Noam. 1981. *Lectures on Government and Binding*. Dordrecht: Foris.

Chomsky, Noam. 1986. *Barriers*. Cambridge: MIT Press.

Clark, Robin, and Keenan, Edward. 1987. "The Absorption Operator and Universal Grammar." *Linguistic Review* 5: 113–136.

Cormack, Annabel, and Ruth Kempson. 1981. "Ambiguity and Quantification." *Linguistics and Philosophy* 4: 259–309.

Croft, William. 1984. "Issues in the Logical Form of Adverbs and Adjectives." Ms., Stanford University and SRI International.

Davidson, Donald. 1967. "The Logical Form of Action Sentences." In Rescher 1967. Reprinted in Davidson 1980, pp. 105–122.

Davidson, Donald. 1980. *Essays on Actions and Events*. Oxford: Oxford University Press.

Davidson, Donald, and Gilbert Harman, eds. 1975. *The Logic of Grammar*. Encino, Calif.: Dickenson Publishing Co.

Davies, Martin. 1981. *Meaning, Quantification, Necessity: Themes in Philosophical Logic*. London: Routledge and Kegan Paul.

Davies, Martin. 1982. "Individuation and the Semantics of Demonstratives." *Journal of Philosophical Logic* 11:287–310.

Davies, Martin. 1989. "Two Examiners Marked Six Scripts: Interpretations of Numerically Quantified Sentences." *Linguistics and Philosophy* 12:293–323.

Davies, Martin. 1991. "Acts and Scenes." In Neil Cooper and Pascal Engel, eds., *New Inquiries into Meaning and Truth*, pp. 41–82. New York: St. Martin's Press.

Donnellan, Keith. 1978. "Speaker Reference, Descriptions, and Anaphora." In P. Cole, ed., *Pragmatics*, pp. 47–68. Syntax and Semantics, vol. 9. New York: Academic Press.

Dowty, David. 1987. "A Note on Collective Predicates, Distributive Predicates, and *All*." In F. Marshall, ed., *Proceedings of the Third Eastern States Conference on Linguistics (ESCOL 86)*, pp. 97–115. Ohio State University.

Dowty, David. 1989. "On the Semantic Content of the Notion 'Thematic Role'." In Gennaro Chierchia, Barbara Partee, and Ray Turner, eds., *Properties, Types, and Meaning*, vol. 2, pp. 69–130. Dordrecht: Kluwer.

Eberle, Rolf A. 1970. *Nominalistic Systems*. Dordrecht: Reidel.

Enç, Mürvet. 1991. "The Semantics of Specificity." *Linguistic Inquiry* 22, no. 1: 1–25.

Engdahl, Elisabet. 1986. *Constituent Questions: The Syntax and Semantics of Questions with Special Reference to Swedish*. Dordrecht: D. Reidel.

Evans, Gareth. 1977. "Pronouns, Quantifiers, and Relative Clauses (I)." *Canadian Journal of Philosophy* 7, no. 3: 467–536. Reprinted in Evans 1985, pp. 76–152.

Evans, Gareth. 1980. "Pronouns." *Linguistic Inquiry* 11, no. 2: 337–362. Reprinted in Evans 1985, pp. 214–248.

Evans, Gareth. 1981. "Semantic Theory and Tacit Knowledge." In S. Holtzman and C. Leich, eds., *Wittgenstein: To Follow a Rule*. London: Routledge and Kegan Paul. Reprinted in Evans 1985, pp. 322–342.

Evans, Gareth. 1985. *Collected Papers*. Oxford: Oxford University Press.

Evans, Gareth, and John McDowell, eds. 1976. *Truth and Meaning*. Oxford: Oxford University Press.

Farkas, Donka. 1981. "Quantifier Scope and Syntactic Islands." In Roberta Hendrick, Carrie Masek, and Mary Francis Miller, eds., *Papers from the 17th Regional Meeting of the Chicago Linguistic Society*, pp. 59–67. University of Chicago.

Fauconnier, Gilles. 1975. "Do Quantifiers Branch?" *Linguistic Inquiry* 6:555–567.

Fillmore, Charles. 1968. "The Case for Case." In E. Bach and R. Harms, eds., *Universals in Linguistic Theory*. New York: Holt, Rinehart and Winston.

Fodor, Janet Dean, and Ivan Sag. 1982. "Referential and Quantificational Indefinites." *Linguistics and Philosophy* 5, no. 3: 355–398.

Gärdenfors, Peter, ed. 1987. *Generalized Quantifiers: Linguistic and Logical Approaches*. Dordrecht: D. Reidel.

Gillon, Brendan. 1990. "Plural Noun Phrases and Their Readings: A Reply to Lasersohn." *Linguistics and Philosophy* 13:477–485.

Goldsmith, John, and Erich Woisetschlaeger. 1982. "The Logic of the English Progressive." *Linguistic Inquiry* 13, no. 1: 79–89.

Goodman, Nelson. 1956. "A World of Individuals." In The Problem of Universals: A Symposium. Notre Dame: University of Notre Dame Press. Reprinted in C. Landesman, ed., *The Problem of Universals* (New York: Basic Books, 1971).

Groenendijk, Jeroen, T. Janssen, and M. Stokhof, eds. 1981. *Formal Methods in the Study of Language*. Amsterdam: Mathematical Centre Tracts, nos. 135, 136.

Groenendijk, Jeroen, T. Janssen, and M. Stokhof, eds. 1984. *Truth, Interpretation, and Information*. Dordrecht: Foris Publications.

Groenendijk, Jeroen, and M. Stokhof. 1984. "Studies on the Semantics of Questions and the Pragmatics of Answers." Unpublished doctoral diss., University of Amsterdam.

Gruber, Jeffrey. 1965. "Studies in Lexical Relations." Ph.D. diss., MIT. Distributed by the Indiana University Linguistics Club.

Guéron, Jacqueline. 1980. "On the Syntax and Semantics of PP Extraposition." *Linguistic Inquiry* 11, no. 4: 637–678.

Hamblin, C. L. 1973. "Questions in Montague English." Foundations of Language, vol. 10. Reprinted in B. Partee, ed., *Montague Grammar* (New York: Academic Press, 1976) pp. 247–259.

Hazen, Allen. 1976. "Expressive Completeness in Modal Language." *Journal of Philosophical Logic* 5:25–46.

Heim, Irene. 1982. "The Semantics of Definite and Indefinite Noun Phrases." Ph.D. diss., U. Mass., Amherst.

Heim, Irene. 1990. "E-Type Pronouns and Donkey Anaphora." *Linguistics and Philosophy* 13, no. 2: 137–177.

Heim, Irene, Howard Lasnik, and Robert May. 1991. "Reciprocity and Plurality." *Linguistic Inquiry* 22, no. 1: 63–101.

Herburger, Elena. 1993. "Focus and the LF of NP Quantification." To appear in Utpal Lahiri, ed., *Proceedings of the Third Semantics and Linguistic Theory Conference* (SALT III). University of California, Irvine.

Higginbotham, James. 1980. "Reciprocal Interpretation." *Journal of Linguistic Research* 1, no. 2: 97–117.

Higginbotham, James. 1983. "The Logic of Perceptual Reports: An Extensional Alternative to Situation Semantics." *Journal of Philosophy* 80:100–127.

Higginbotham, James. 1985. "On Semantics." *Linguistic Inquiry* 16:547–594.

Higginbotham, James. 1987. "Indefiniteness and Predication." In Reuland and ter Meulen 1987, pp. 43–70.

Higginbotham, James. 1988. "Contexts, Models, and Meanings: A Note on the Data of Semantics." In Ruth M. Kempson, ed., *Mental Representations: The Interface between Language and Reality*, pp. 29–48. Cambridge: Cambridge University Press.

Higginbotham, James. 1990. "Frege, Concepts, and the Design of Language." In Villanueva 1990, pp. 153–171.

Higginbotham, James. 1991. "Interrogatives, I." In Lisa Cheng and Hamida Demirdash, eds., *More Papers on Wh-Movement*, pp. 47–76. MIT Working Papers in Linguistics, no. 15.

Higginbotham, James, and Robert May. 1981. "Questions, Quantifiers, and Crossing." *Linguistic Review* 1:47–79.

Higginbotham, James, and Barry Schein. 1989. "Plurals." In Juli Carter and Rose-Marie Déchaine, eds., *Proceedings of the North Eastern Linguistics Society* 19:161–175. Graduate Linguistics Students Association, U. Mass., Amherst.

Hinrichs, Erhard. 1981. "Temporale Anaphora im Englischen." Unpublished Zulassungarbeit, University of Tübingen.

Hintikka, Jaakko. 1974. "Quantifiers vs. Quantification Theory." *Linguistic Inquiry* 5:153–177.

Jackendoff, Ray. 1972. *Semantic Interpretation in Generative Grammar*. Cambridge: MIT Press.

Kadmon, Nirit. 1990. "Uniqueness." *Linguistics and Philosophy* 13, no. 3: 273–324.

Kamp, Hans. 1979. "Events, Instants, and Temporal Reference." In Bäuerle, Egli, and von Stechow 1979, pp. 376–417.

Kamp, Hans. 1980. "Some Remarks on the Logic of Change, Part I." In Christian Rohrer, ed., *Time, Tense, and Quantifiers*, pp. 135–179. Tübingen: Max Niemeyer Verlag.

Kamp, Hans. 1981. "A Theory of Truth and Semantic Representation." In Groenendijk, Janssen, and Stokhof 1984.

Karttunen, Lauri. 1976. "Discourse Referents." In James D. McCawley, ed., *Notes from the Linguistic Underground*, Syntax and Semantics, vol. 7, pp. 363–385. New York: Academic Press.

Karttunen, Lauri. 1977. "The Syntax and Semantics of Questions." *Linguistics and Philosophy* 1, no. 1: 3–44.

Keenan, Edward. 1987. "Unreducible *n*-ary Quantifiers in Natural Language." In Gärdenfors 1987.

Kenny, Anthony. 1963. *Action, Emotion, and Will*. New York: Humanities Press.

Krifka, Manfred. 1992a. "Thematic Relations as Links between Nominal Reference and Temporal Constitution." In Ivan A. Sag and Anna Szabolcsi, eds., *Lexical Matters*, CSLI Lecture Notes, no. 24, pp. 29–53. Center for the Study of Language and Information, Stanford University.

Krifka, Manfred. 1992b. "Definite NPs Aren't Quantifiers." *Linguistic Inquiry* 23, no. 1: 156–163.

Krifka, Manfred. 1992c. "A Framework for Focus-Sensitive Quantification." In Chris Barker and David Dowty, eds., *Proceedings of the Second Conference on Semantics and Linguistic Theory* (SALT II), pp. 215–236. Ohio State University, Columbus.

Kroch, Anthony S. 1979. *The Semantics of Scope in English*. New York: Garland Publishing.

Kuno, Susumu, and Jane Robinson. 1972. "Multiple *Wh* Questions." *Linguistic Inquiry* 3: 465–487.

Lahiri, Utpal. 1991. "Embedded Interrogatives and Predicates That Embed Them." Ph.D. diss., MIT.

Lakoff, George. 1971. "On Generative Semantics." In Danny D. Steinberg and Leon A. Jakobovits, eds., *Semantics: An Interdisciplinary Reader in Philosophy, Linguistics and Psychology*, pp. 232–296. Cambridge: Cambridge University Press.

Lakoff, George. 1972. "Linguistics and Natural Logic." In Donald Davidson and Gilbert Harman, eds., *Semantics of Natural Language*, pp. 545–665. Dordrecht: D. Reidel.

Langendoen, D. T. 1978. "The Logic of Reciprocity." *Linguistic Inquiry* 9: 177–197.

Larson, Richard K. 1988. "On the Double Object Construction." *Linguistic Inquiry* 19, no. 3: 335–391.

Larson, Richard K., and Peter Ludlow. 1993. "Interpreted Logical Forms." To appear in *Synthese* 95, no. 3.

Lasersohn, Peter. 1989. "On the Readings of Plural Noun Phrases." *Linguistic Inquiry* 20, no. 1: 130–134.

LePore, Ernest, and Brian McLaughlin, eds. 1985. *Actions and Events: Perspectives on the Philosophy of Donald Davidson*. Oxford: Basil Blackwell.

Lindstrom, P. 1966. "First-Order Predicate Logic with Generalized Quantifiers." *Theoria* 32: 186–195.

Link, Godehard. 1983. "The Logical Analysis of Plurals and Mass Terms: A Lattice-Theoretical Approach." In Bäuerle, Schwarze and von Stechow 1983, pp. 302–323.

Link, Godehard. 1987. "Generalized Quantifiers and Plurals." In Gärdenfors 1987, pp. 151–180.

Liu, Feng-hsi. 1990. "Scope Dependency in English and Chinese." Ph.D. diss., UCLA.

Lombard, Lawrence B. 1985. "How Not to Flip the Prowler: Transitive Verbs of Action and the Identity of Actions." In LePore and McLaughlin 1985, pp. 268–281.

Longobardi, Giuseppe. 1991. "In Defense of the Correspondence Hypothesis: Island Effects and Parasitic Constructions in LF." In J. Huang and R. May, eds., *Linguistic Structure and Logical Structure*, pp. 149–196. Dordrecht: D. Reidel.

Lønning, Tore. 1987. "Collective Readings of Definite and Indefinite Noun Phrases." In Gärdenfors 1987, pp. 203–235.

Lønning, Tore. 1991. "Among Readings: Some Comments on 'Among Collections'." In Jaap van der Does, ed., *Quantification and Anaphora*, vol. 2, pp. 37–51. DYANA deliverable 2.2.b, Edinburgh.

Ludlow, Peter. 1987. "Conditionals, Events, and Unbound Pronouns." Ms., SUNY, Stony Brook. Revised 1991.

Ludlow, Peter, and Stephen Neale. 1991. "Indefinite Descriptions: In Defense of Russell." *Linguistics and Philosophy* 14, no. 2: 171–202.

McCawley, James D. 1970. "Semantic Representation." In Paul Garvin, ed., *Cognition: A Multiple View*, pp. 227–247. New York: Spartan.

McCawley, James D. 1972. "A Program for Logic." In Donald Davidson and Gilbert Harman, eds., *Semantics of Natural Language*, pp. 157–212. Dordrecht: D. Reidel.

McCawley, James D. 1981. *Everything That Linguists Have Always Wanted to Know about Logic but Were Ashamed to Ask*. Chicago: University of Chicago Press.

McConnell-Ginet, Sally. 1982. "Adverbs and Logical Form: A Linguistically Realistic Theory." *Language* 58: 144–184.

May, Robert. 1977. "The Grammar of Quantification." Ph.D. diss., MIT. Distributed by Indiana University Linguistics Club.

May, Robert. 1985. *Logical Form: Its Structure and Derivation*. Cambridge: MIT Press.

May, Robert. 1989. "Interpreting Logical Form." *Linguistics and Philosophy* 12, no. 4: 387–435.

Milsark, Gary. 1977. "Toward an Explanation of Certain Peculiarities of the Existential Construction in English." *Linguistic Analysis* 3, no. 1: 1–29.

Moltmann, Friederike. 1990. "On the Part Relation in Semantics." Ms., MIT.

Moltmann, Friederike. 1992. "Reciprocals and *Same/Different*: Towards a Semantic Analysis." *Linguistics and Philosophy* 14, no. 5: 411–462.

Montague, Richard. 1974a. "Pragmatics." In Richmond H. Thomason, ed., *Formal Philosophy: Selected Papers of Richard Montague*, pp. 95–119. New Haven: Yale University Press.

Montague, Richard. 1974b. "Pragmatics in Intensional Logic." In Richmond H. Thomason, ed., *Formal Philosophy: Selected Papers of Richard Montague*, pp. 119–148. New Haven: Yale University Press.

Neale, Stephen. 1988. "Events and 'Logical Form'." *Linguistics and Philosophy* 11:303–321.

Neale, Stephen. 1990. *Descriptions.* Cambridge: MIT Press.

Oehrle, Richard. 1976. "The Grammatical Status of the English Dative Alternation." Ph.D. diss., MIT.

Parsons, Terence. 1990. *Events in the Semantics of English: A Study in Subatomic Semantics.* Cambridge: MIT Press.

Partee, Barbara. 1973. "Some Structural Analogies between Tenses and Pronouns in English." *Journal of Philosophy* 70, no. 18: 601–609.

Partee, Barbara. 1984a. "Compositionality." In Fred Landman and Fred Veltman, eds., *Varieties of Formal Semantics.* Dordrecht: Foris.

Partee, Barbara. 1984b. "Nominal and Temporal Anaphora." *Linguistics and Philosophy* 7:243–286.

Partee, Barbara. 1991. "Topic, Focus, and Quantification." In Steven Moore and Adam Zachary Wyner, eds., *Proceedings of the First Semantics and Linguistic Theory Conference* (SALT I), pp. 159–187. Cornell University, Working Papers in Linguistics, no. 10.

Quine, W. V. 1986. *Philosophy of Logic.* 2nd ed. Cambridge: Harvard University Press. 1st ed., 1970.

Reichenbach, Hans. 1947. *Elements of Symbolic Logic.* London: Collier-Macmillan. Excerpts reprinted in Davidson and Harman 1975.

Reinhart, Tanya. 1979. "Syntactic Domains for Syntactic Rules." In F. Guenthner and S. J. Schmidt, eds., *Formal Semantics and Pragmatics for Natural Language.* Dordrecht: D. Reidel.

Rescher, Nicholas. 1962. "Plurality Quantification." *Journal of Symbolic Logic* 38, no. 3: 373–374.

Rescher, Nicholas, ed. 1967. *The Logic of Decision and Action.* Pittsburgh: University of Pittsburgh Press.

Reuland, Eric, and ter Meulen, Alice, eds. 1987. *The Representation of (In)definiteness.* Cambridge: MIT Press.

Rodman, R., ed. 1972. "Montague Grammar." MS., UCLA.

Rooth, Mats. 1985. "Association with Focus." Ph.D. diss., U. Mass., Amherst.

Ross, John Robert. 1972. "Act." In Donald Davidson and Gilbert Harman, eds., *Semantics of Natural Language,* pp. 70–126. Dordrecht: D. Reidel.

Russell, Bertrand. 1938. *The Principles of Mathematics.* 2nd ed. New York: W. W. Norton. 1st ed., 1903.

Scha, Remko. 1981. "Distributive, Collective, and Cumulative Quantification." In Groenendijk, Janssen, and Stokhof 1981. Reprinted in Groenendijk, Janssen, and Stokhof 1984, pp. 131–158.

Scha, Remko. 1983. "Logical Foundations for Question Answering." Unpublished doctoral diss., University of Gröningen.

Schein, Barry. 1986. "Event Logic and the Interpretation of Plurals." Unpublished doctoral diss., MIT.

Schein, Barry. 1989. "Plurality and Conjunction." Ms., UC Irvine and MIT.

Schein, Barry. 1992. "Conjunction Reduction Redux." Ms., USC.

Schwarzschild, Roger. 1991. "On the Meaning of Definite Plural Noun Phrases." Ph.D. diss., U. Mass., Amherst.

Sharvy, Richard. 1980. "A More General Theory of Definite Descriptions." *Philosophical Review* 89, no. 4: 607–624.

Sher, Gila. 1990. "Ways of Branching Quantifiers." *Linguistics and Philosophy* 13, no. 4: 393–422. Reprinted (with minor revisions) in Gila Sher, *The Bounds of Logic: A Generalized Viewpoint* (Cambridge: MIT Press, 1991), chapter 5, pp. 105–129.

Sloan, Kelly. 1991. "Wh-Quantifier Ambiguity." In Lisa Cheng and Hamida Demirdash, eds., *More Papers on Wh-Movement*, pp. 219–237. MIT Working Papers in Linguistics, no. 15.

Sommers, Fred. 1982. *The Logic of Natural Language*. Oxford: Oxford University Press.

Stowell, Timothy A. 1981. "Origins of Phrase Structure." Ph.D. diss., MIT.

Taub, Alison. 1989. "Collective Predicates, Aktionsarten, and *All*." In Emmon Bach, Angelika Kratzer, and Barbara Partee, eds., *Papers on Quantification*. Department of Linguistics, U. Mass., Amherst.

Taylor, Barry. 1976. "States of Affairs." In Evans and McDowell 1976.

Taylor, Barry. 1980. "Truth-Theory for Indexical Languages." In Mark Platts, ed., *Reference, Truth, and Reality*, pp. 182–198. London: Routledge and Kegan Paul.

Taylor, Barry. 1985. *Modes of Occurrence*. Oxford: Basil Blackwell.

Thomson, Judith Jarvis. 1977. *Acts and Other Events*. Ithaca: Cornell University Press.

Van Benthem, Johann. 1986. "Polyadic Quantifiers." *Linguistics and Philosophy* 12:437–464.

Van der Does, Jaap. 1992. "Applied Quantifier Logics: Collectives, Naked Infinitives." Ph.D. diss., University of Amsterdam.

Vendler, Zeno. 1984. "Agency and Causation." In Peter A. French, Theodore E. Uehling, Jr., and Howard K. Wettstein, eds., *Causation and Causal Theories*, Midwest Studies in Philosophy, vol. 9, pp. 371–384. Minneapolis: University of Minnesota Press.

Verkuyl, Henk. 1988. "Aspectual Asymmetry and Quantification." In Veronika Ehrich and Heinz Vater, eds., *Temporalsemantik: Beitrage zur Linguistik der Zeitreferenz*, pp. 220–259. Tübingen: Max Niemeyer Verlag.

Verkuyl, Henk, and Jaap van der Does. 1991. "The Semantics of Plural Noun Phrases." ITLI Prepublication Series for Logic, Semantics and Philosophy of Language. University of Amsterdam.

Vermazen, Bruce. 1985. "Negative Acts." In Bruce Vermazen and Merrill B. Hintikka, eds., *Essays on Davidson: Action and Events*, pp. 93–104. Oxford: Oxford University Press.

Villanueva, E., ed. 1990. *Information, Semantics, and Epistemology*. Oxford: Basil Blackwell.

Vlach, Frank. 1983. "On Situation Semantics for Perception." *Synthese* 54:129–152.

Westerståhl, Dag. 1987. "Branching Generalized Quantifiers and Natural Language." In Gärdenfors 1987, pp. 269–298.

Wiggins, David. 1980. "'Most' and 'All': Some Comments on a Familiar Programme, and on the Logical Form of Quantified Sentences." In Mark Platts, ed., *Reference, Truth, and Reality: Essays on the Philosophy of Language*, pp. 318–346. London: Routledge & Kegan Paul.

Subject Index

Author Index